TUNISIAN CROCHET

A Stitch Dictionary with 501 Stitches to Explore

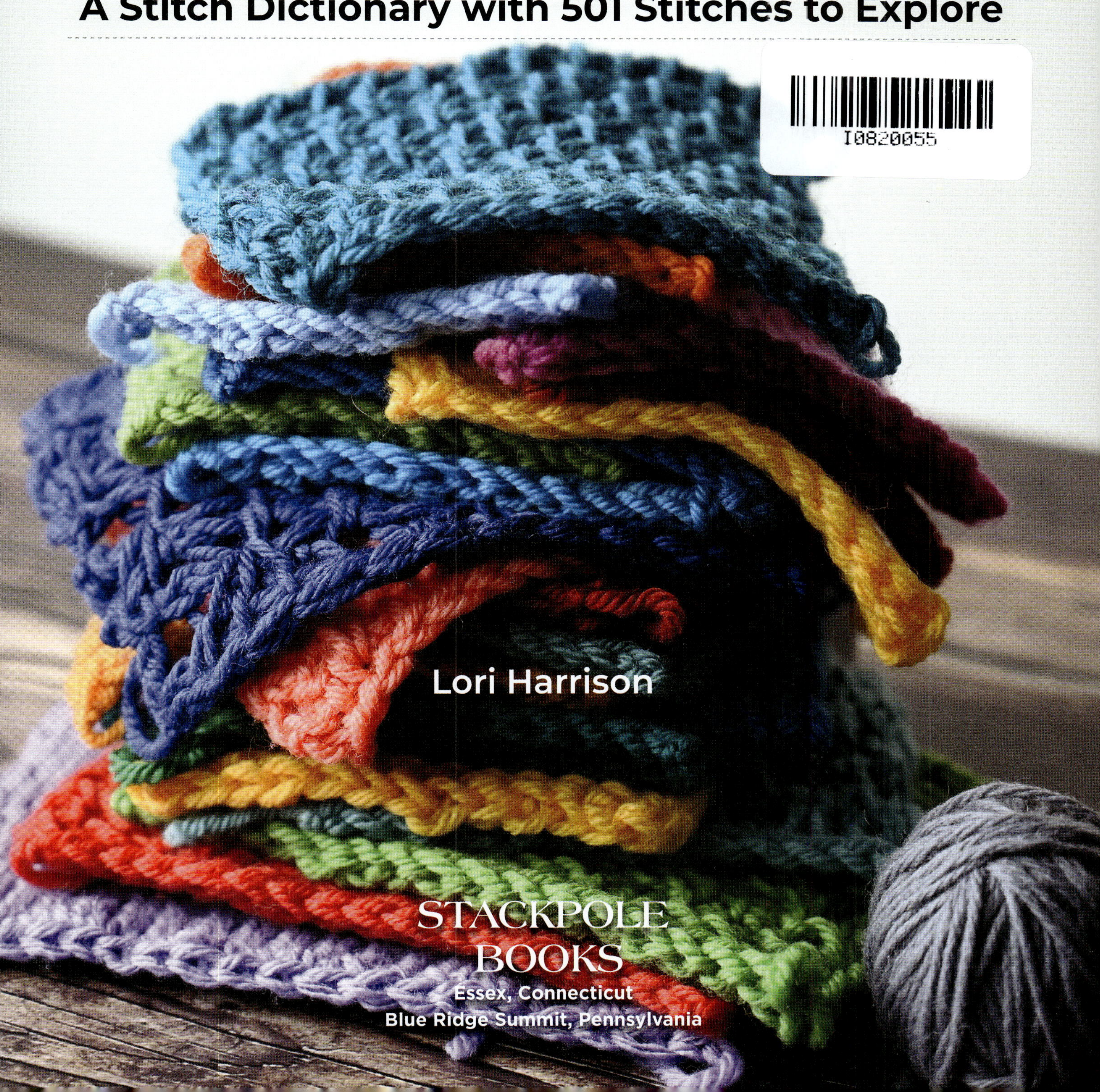

Lori Harrison

STACKPOLE BOOKS
Essex, Connecticut
Blue Ridge Summit, Pennsylvania

STACKPOLE BOOKS
An imprint of The Globe Pequot Publishing Group, Inc.
64 South Main Street
Essex, CT 06426
www.globepequot.com

Distributed by NATIONAL BOOK NETWORK
800-462-6420

British Library Cataloguing in Publication Information available

Library of Congress Cataloging-in-Publication Data available

ISBN 978-0-8117-7654-7 (paper : alk. paper)
ISBN 978-0-8117-7655-4 (electronic)

™ The paper used in this publication meets the minimum requirements of American National Standard for Information Sciences—Permanence of Paper for Printed Library Materials, ANSI/NISO Z39.48-1992.

First Edition

This book is dedicated to all the makers out there who love exploring Tunisian crochet as much as I do.

CONTENTS

INTRODUCTION

My first book, *Exploring Tunisian Crochet*, was the book I had wanted when I was first starting to learn the craft. This stitch dictionary is the book I have been longing for ever since. This volume starts with the basic stitches and their many variations before exploring everything else that Tunisian crochet has to offer: cables, lace, colorwork, and fabulous textures. While expansive, this book is far from comprehensive. Tunisian crochet has limitless ways to combine stitches and colors. My goal with this book is to inspire further exploration.

Lori

Tunisian Crochet Terminology and Notation

Tunisian Crochet Rows

There are three types of rows in Tunisian crochet: the foundation row, the standard row, and the bind-off row. A Tunisian crochet project starts with a foundation row, in which the number of stitches is established for the first row of the project. Standard rows are the main part of the pattern and can be any combination of Tunisian crochet stitches. The final row of any pattern is the bind-off row, which closes the last standard row of stitches.

Tunisian crochet has as many standard rows as desired.

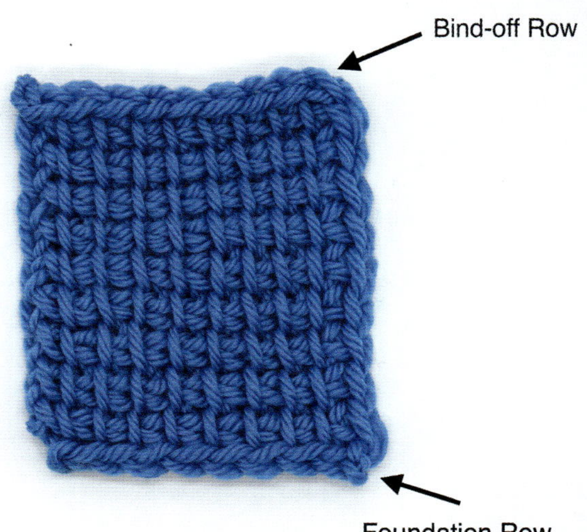

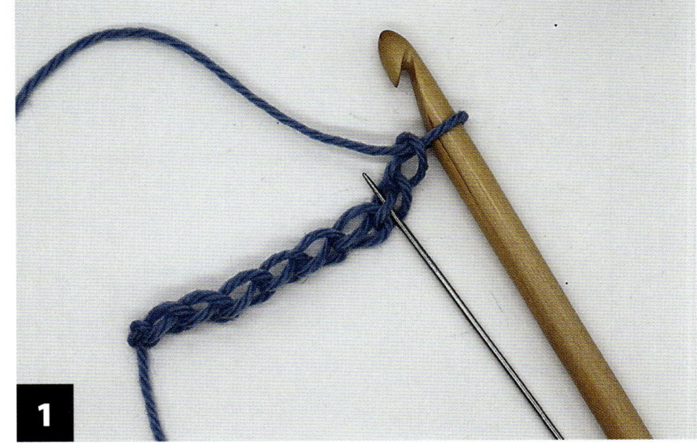

Foundation Row

The first row in Tunisian crochet is always the foundation row. The most common way to start a Tunisian crochet foundation row is with a row of chain stitches.

1. Chain any number of stitches.

2. Skip the first chain from the hook. Photo 1 shows where the first loop will be picked up.

3. Insert the hook under the back bump of the second chain from the hook. Yarn over and pull loop through the chain and leave loop on hook (photo 2).

4. Continue picking up a loop in the back bump of each remaining chain (photo 3). The number of loops on the hook will be the same as the number of starting chains.

5. After all the required loops are on the hook, work a standard return pass.

6. Do not turn the fabric. Chain 1.

7. Yarn over and pull through 2 loops (photo 4).

8. Repeat *yarn over and pull through 2 loops* until all stitches have been closed and there is only 1 loop left on the hook (photo 5). The loop remaining on the hook is now the first loop on your hook for the first row.

Standard Row

A standard Tunisian crochet row consists of two parts: a forward pass and a return pass.

Forward Pass (FP): The first part of a row in Tunisian crochet is the forward pass. Rows in Tunisian crochet start with one loop on the hook, and the first set of vertical bars of the row is skipped. The first stitch of the row is always worked into the second set of vertical bars (unless otherwise stated).

Return Pass (RP): The second part of a row in Tunisian crochet is the return pass. This closes all the stitches from the forward pass. The return pass for all stitches and stitch patterns in this stitch dictionary is a standard return pass (unless otherwise stated).

Standard Return Pass (Std RP): Chain 1, yarn over and pull through 2 loops. Repeat [yarn over and pull through 2 loops] until 1 loop remains on hook.

If the return pass is not a standard return pass, the following return pass notation will be used.

Return Pass Notation

RP-2: Yarn over and pull through 2 loops. RP-2 is a standard return pass stitch that closes 1 stitch.

RP-3: Yarn over and pull through 3 loops. RP-3 closes 2 stitches together.

RP-4: Yarn over and pull through 4 loops. RP-4 closes 3 stitches together.

When closing more than one stitch together in the return pass, treat all stitches closed together as a single stitch in the next forward pass.

A standard return pass in this notation would be:

Std RP Ch 1, RP-2 until 1 loop rem on hook.

Bind-off Row

After the last standard row of the pattern has been completed, a bind-off row is required so that the fabric doesn't look unfinished. The two most common bind-off stitches are the slip stitch bind-off (slstBO) and the single crochet bind-off (SC BO).

Slip Stitch Bind-off (slstBO)

The slip stitch bind-off with Tunisian simple stitch (Tss) is the most common bind-off.

1. Insert the hook for stitch indicated (shown for Tss).

2. Yarn over and pull the loop through the stitch.

3. Slip stitch through the loop on hook so that 1 loop remains on the hook.

4. Repeat steps 1–3 until all stitches have been worked.

Single Crochet Bind-off (SC BO)

A single crochet bind-off gives a stretchier edge compared to the slip stitch bind-off.

1. Insert the hook for the stitch indicated (shown for Tss) and pull up a loop.

2. Yarn over.

3. Pull through both loops on hook.

Working Row

While most stitches are worked into the current row, some stitches are worked into rows that have been already worked.

Current row

Prior row refers to one row below the current row.

Prior row

Rows below the prior row are referred to by the number of rows below the current row. For example, if the instructions say to work 2 rows below the current row, that is the same as the row below the prior row.

Anatomy of a Tunisian Crochet Stitch

A Tunisian crochet stitch consists of five bars: two vertical bars and three horizontal bars.

1. Front Vertical Bar
The front vertical bar is in the front of the stitch and to the left of the back vertical bar.

2. Back Vertical Bar
The back vertical bar is behind and to the right of the front vertical bar.

3. Top Horizontal Bar
The top horizontal bar is to the front of the three horizontal bars.

4. Back Horizontal Bar
The back horizontal bar is the back bump of the return pass. It is directly over the vertical bars.

5. Bottom Horizontal Bar
The bottom horizontal bar is below and behind the top and back horizontal bars.

Stitch Space (st sp)

The stitch space is the space between two sets of vertical bars. When this book refers to "the next stitch space," this is the space before the next set of vertical bars. When this book refers to "the second stitch space," this is the space after the next set of vertical bars.

The next stitch space

The second stitch space

Yarn over

Yarn Over (yo)

When a yarn over is needed, wrap the yarn around hook from back to front.

Working stitches into a yarn over

Tks (Tunisian knit stitch) in yo
Insert hook from front to back in the open space created by the yarn over.

Tss in yo
Insert hook behind next front vertical bar.

Double yarn over

Double Yarn Over (yo 2)

A double yarn over is two yarn overs in a row. On the return pass, work each yarn over as a separate stitch.

Working stitches into a double yarn over

Tks in double yo
Insert hook from front to back in the open space created by the double yarn over.

Tss in first yo
Insert hook behind next front vertical bar of the first yo. The front vertical bar will be wrapped along the return pass chain.

Tss in second yo
Insert hook behind next front vertical bar of the second yarn.

Yarn under

Yarn Under (yu)

When a yarn under is needed, wrap the yarn around hook from front to back.

How to Use This Stitch Dictionary

Each entry starts with the stitch number and a name with the abbreviation if there is a commonly accepted name for the stitch. It states how many stitches and rows are required for the stitch pattern. This number does not include the first loop on the hook at the beginning of the forward pass or the edge stitch at the end of the forward pass. Instructions for the foundation and bind-off rows are not included.

Whenever possible, a chart is included for the stitch patterns. A stitch repeat in the written instructions may differ from the chart for ease of reading. However, both text and chart are accurate.

If you are unfamiliar with any of the techniques in this stitch dictionary, I encourage you to consult my previous book, *Exploring Tunisian Crochet*, for detailed tutorials to guide you through the techniques.

This stitch dictionary frequently uses abbreviations for conciseness and ease of reading. Refer to the "Stitches and Abbreviation Index" at the end of the book beginning on page 273 to look up the abbreviations and to find the instructions for unfamiliar stitches.

Written Instructions Notations

Multiple stitches: Tss 4 is shorthand for "work a Tss stitch in the next 4 stitches."

Brackets [ ] indicate a group of stitches to be repeated. For example, [Tss, Tks] 2 times is the same as Tss, Tks, Tss, Tks. If brackets are not used to indicate a group of stitches to repeat, repeat only the stitch just prior to the "rep" instruction.

Asterisks * are used to indicate a longer group of stitches to be repeated. For example, Row 8: Tss, Tks, *Tss, [Tks, Tss] 2 times, Tps 3; rep from * 15 times. In this example, the instructions between the first asterisk and the semicolon are repeated 15 times while the two stitches before the * are worked only once.

Parentheses ( ) indicate that multiple stitches are to be worked into the next stitch. For example, (Tss, Tks) means work a Tss in the next stitch and then also work a Tks into the same stitch.

Repeat until: When the pattern states "rep until 2 st rem," that means the repeated portion of the forward pass should be continued until there are two sets of vertical bars left in the forward pass: the edge stitch and the last set of vertical bars before the edge stitch.

How to Read a Tunisian Crochet Chart

A Tunisian crochet chart is read from the bottom up. Each Tunisian crochet row has two lines: one for the forward pass, one for the return pass. The forward pass is read from right to left. The return pass is read from left to right.

Each stitch has a symbol associated with it. The "Stitch Key" explains the symbols. The foundation row is omitted. The first loop on the hook of the forward pass is shown in the first box of the forward pass row. The blue box highlights the repeated section. The boxed section can be repeated as many times as desired.

The full instructions for the sample chart are as follows:

Row 1 FP: [Tss, Tks] rep, Tss, Te.

Row 1 RP: Ch 1, [yo and pull through 2 loops] rep until 1 loop on hook.

Row 2 FP: [Tks, Tss] rep, Tks, Te.

Row 2 RP: Ch 1, [yo and pull through 2 loops] rep until 1 loop on hook.

In this book, the written instructions are only for the stitch pattern. The return pass is included only when it is not a standard return pass. The written instructions for the sample chart are:

Worked over a multiple of 2 + 1 sts.

Row 1: [Tss, Tks] rep until 1 st rem, Tss.

Row 2: [Tks, Tss] rep until 1 st rem, Tks.

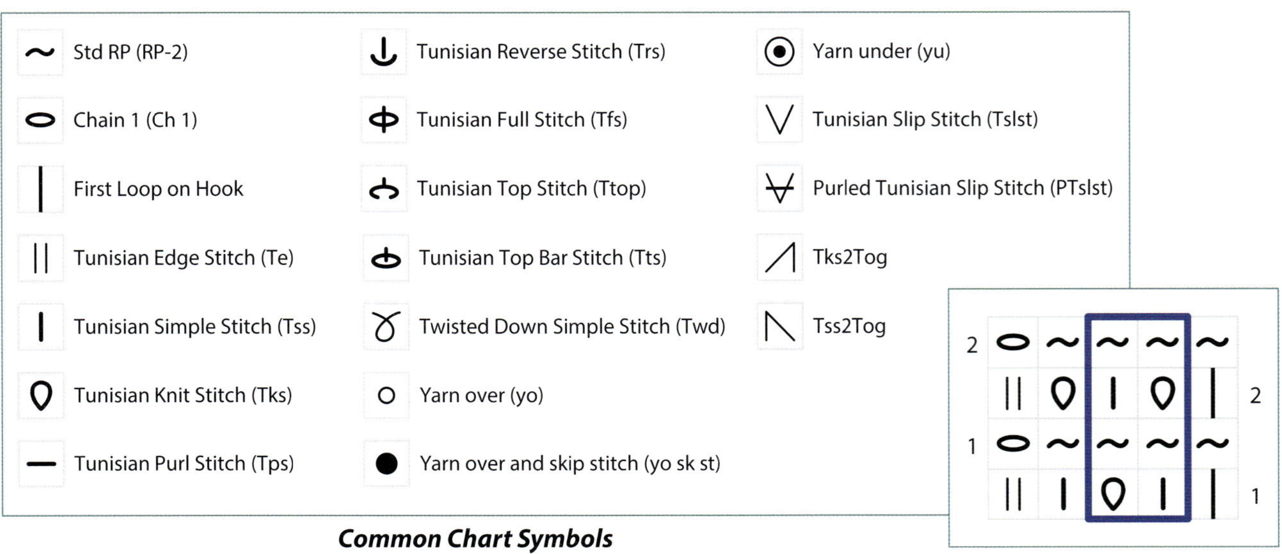

Common Chart Symbols

Sample Chart

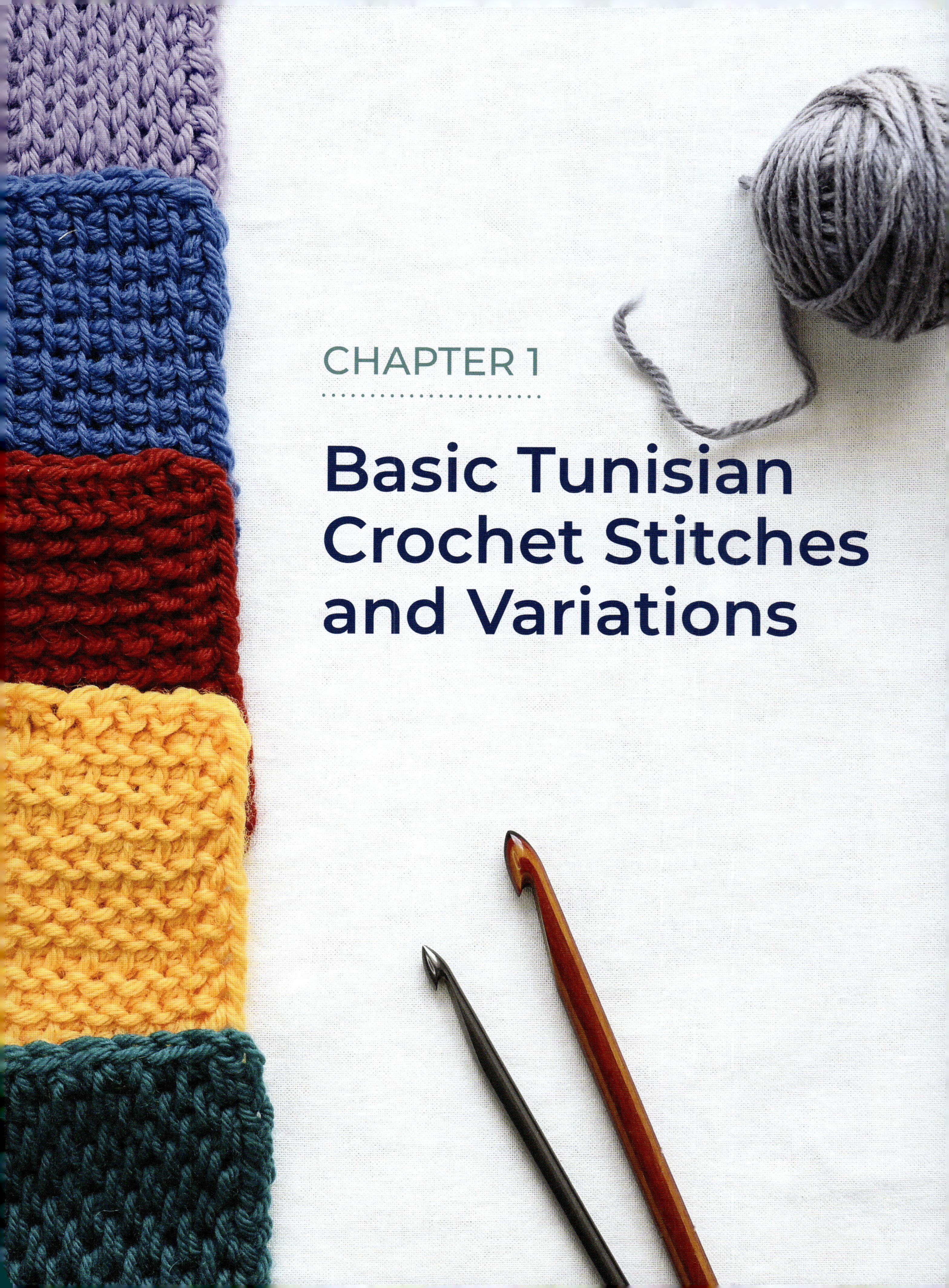

CHAPTER 1

Basic Tunisian Crochet Stitches and Variations

Tunisian Simple Stitch and Variations

1 TUNISIAN SIMPLE STITCH (Tss)

Worked over any number of stitches.

Insert hook behind front vertical bar from right to left*. Yarn over and pull up a loop. Leave loop on hook.

**Left-handed makers: Insert hook from left to right.*

Reverse

Tss hook location

2 EXTENDED TUNISIAN SIMPLE STITCH (ExTss)

Worked over any number of stitches.

Insert hook behind front vertical bar from right to left* (photo 1). Yarn over and pull up a loop (photo 2). Chain 1 (photo 3). Leave loop on hook.

**Left-handed makers: Insert hook from left to right.*

Reverse

1

2

3

3 TUNISIAN EDGE STITCH (Te)

Worked into the last stitch of the forward pass.

The Tunisian Edge Stitch is worked into the last set of vertical bars in the forward pass. Insert hook behind the outer two vertical bars. Yarn over and pull up a loop. Leave loop on hook.

Te hook location

4 TUNISIAN EXTENDED EDGE STITCH (ExTe)

Worked into the last stitch of the forward pass.

The Tunisian Extended Edge Stitch is worked into the last set of the vertical bars in the forward pass. Insert hook behind the outer two vertical bars (photo 1). Yarn over and pull up a loop (photo 2). Chain 1 (photo 3). Leave loop on hook.

5 MODIFIED TUNISIAN SIMPLE STITCH (Tmss)

Worked over any number of stitches.

Insert hook behind front vertical bar from right to left* and top horizontal bar. Yarn over and pull up a loop. Leave loop on hook.

**Left-handed makers: Insert hook from left to right.*

Reverse

Tmss hook location

6 TWISTED UP TUNISIAN SIMPLE STITCH (Twup)

Worked over any number of stitches.

Insert hook behind front vertical bar from left to right (photo 1), and then rotate hook counterclockwise* (photos 2–4). Yarn over and pull up a loop. Leave loop on hook.

Note: The resulting stitch will appear to slant toward the previous stitch.

**Left-handed makers: Insert hook from right to left and then rotate hook clockwise.*

Reverse

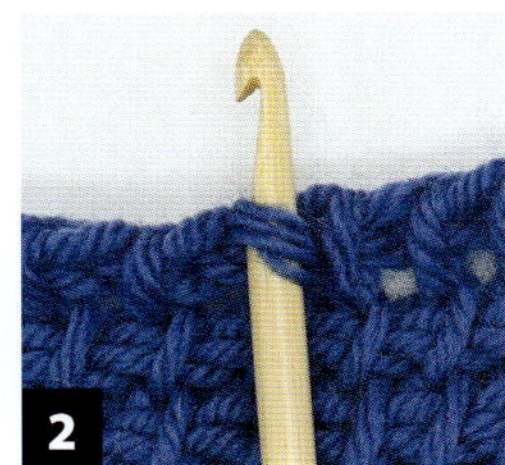

7 TWISTED DOWN TUNISIAN SIMPLE STITCH (Twd)

Worked over any number of stitches.

Insert hook behind front vertical bar from left to right (photo 1), and then rotate hook clockwise* (photos 2–3). Yarn over and pull up a loop. Leave loop on hook.

Note: The resulting stitch will resemble a Tss with a twist at the top.

**Left-handed makers: Insert hook from right to left and then rotate hook counterclockwise.*

Reverse

1

2

3

8 TUNISIAN BACK BAR SIMPLE STITCH (Tbss)

Worked over any number of stitches.

Insert hook behind back vertical bar from right to left*. Yarn over and pull up a loop. Leave loop on hook.

**Left-handed makers: Insert hook from left to right.*

Reverse

Tbss hook location

9 TUNISIAN DOUBLE CROCHET (Tdc)

Worked over any number of stitches.

Yarn over (photo 1) and insert hook behind front vertical bar from right to left*. Yarn over and pull up a loop (photo 2). Yarn over and pull through 2 loops (photo 3). Leave loop on hook.

**Left-handed makers: Insert hook from left to right.*

Reverse

1

2

3

10 TUNISIAN TREBLE CROCHET (Ttc)

Worked over any number of stitches.

Yarn over twice (photo 1) and insert hook behind front vertical bar from right to left*. Yarn over and pull up a loop (photo 2). Yarn over and pull through 2 loops twice (photos 3 and 4). Leave loop on hook.

**Left-handed makers: Insert hook from left to right.*

Reverse

1

2

3

4

11 TUNISIAN SIMPLE STITCH WITH BOTTOM HORIZONTAL BAR (TssBth)

Worked over any number of stitches.

Insert hook behind front vertical bar from right to left* and bottom horizontal bar. Yarn over and pull up a loop. Leave loop on hook.

**Left-handed makers: Insert hook from left to right.*

Reverse

TssBth hook location

12 TUNISIAN SIMPLE STITCH WITH BACK HORIZONTAL BAR (TssBkH)

Worked over any number of stitches.

Insert hook behind front vertical bar from right to left* and back horizontal bar. Yarn over and pull up a loop. Leave loop on hook.

**Left-handed makers: Insert hook from left to right.*

Reverse

TssBkH hook location

13 TWISTED TUNISIAN BACK BAR SIMPLE STITCH (TwTbss)

Worked over any number of stitches.

Move front vertical bar to the right* of the back vertical bar (photo 1) and insert hook behind back vertical bar from right to left* (photo 2). Yarn over and pull up a loop. Leave loop on hook.

**Left-handed makers: Move front vertical bar to the left of the back vertical bar; insert hook from left to right.*

Reverse

1

2

Tunisian Knit Stitch and Variations

14 TUNISIAN KNIT STITCH (Tks)

Worked over any number of stitches.

Insert hook between vertical bars from front to back. Yarn over and pull up a loop. Leave loop on hook.

Reverse

Tks hook location

15 EXTENDED TUNISIAN KNIT STITCH (ExTks)

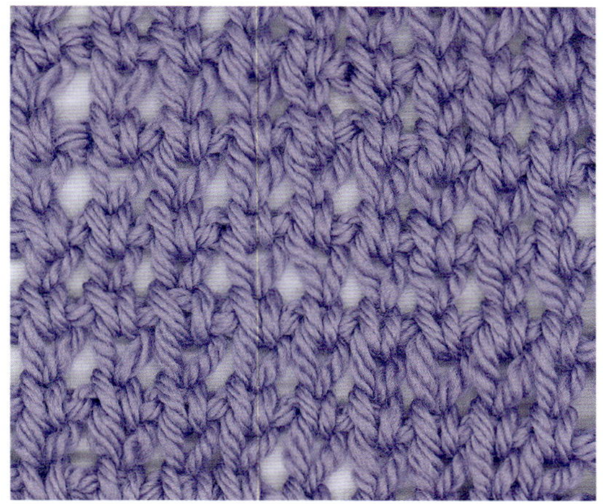

Worked over any number of stitches.

Insert hook between vertical bars from front to back. Yarn over and pull up a loop (photo 1). Chain 1 (photo 2). Leave loop on hook.

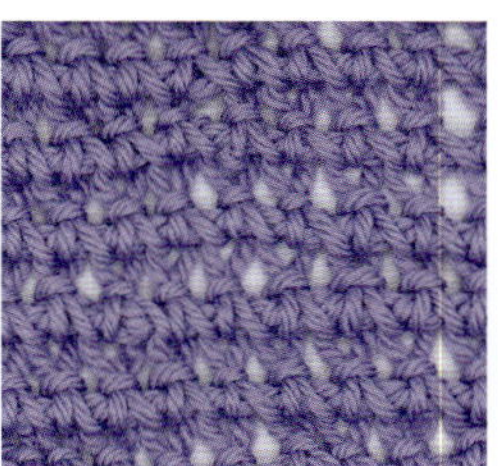

Reverse

16 MODIFIED TUNISIAN KNIT STITCH (Tmks)

Worked over any number of stitches.

Insert hook between vertical bars and under top and back horizontal bars from front to back. Yarn over and pull up a loop. Leave loop on hook.

Reverse

Tmks hook location

17 TWISTED TUNISIAN KNIT STITCH (TwTks)

Worked over any number of stitches.

Move front vertical bar to the right of back vertical bar* and insert hook between vertical bars from front to back. Yarn over and pull up a loop. Leave loop on hook.

**Left-handed makers: Move front vertical bar to the left of the back vertical bar.*

Reverse

TwTks hook location

18 TWISTED BACK BAR TUNISIAN KNIT STITCH (TwbTks)

Worked over any number of stitches.

Move back vertical bar to the left of front vertical bar* (photo 1) and insert hook between vertical bars from front to back (photo 2). Yarn over and pull up a loop. Leave loop on hook.

**Left-handed makers: Move back vertical bar to the right of the front vertical bar.*

Reverse

19 REVERSE TUNISIAN KNIT STITCH (RTks)

Worked over any number of stitches.

Move yarn to front of fabric and insert hook between vertical bars from back to front. Yarn over and pull up a loop. Leave loop on hook.

Reverse

RTks hook location

20 PURLED TUNISIAN KNIT STITCH (PTks)

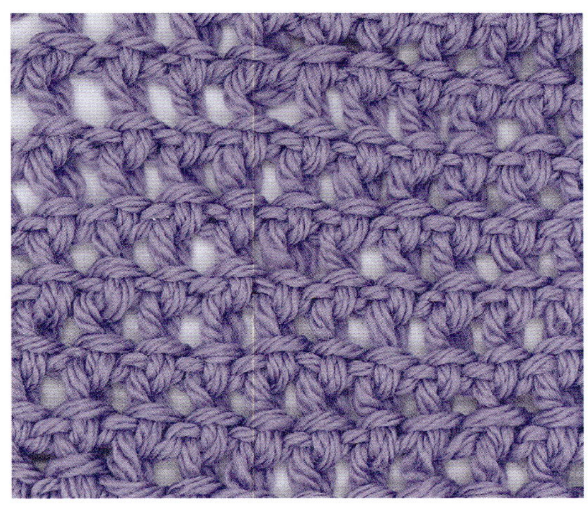

Worked over any number of stitches.

Move yarn to front of fabric and insert hook between vertical bars from front to back. Yarn over and pull up a loop. Leave loop on hook.

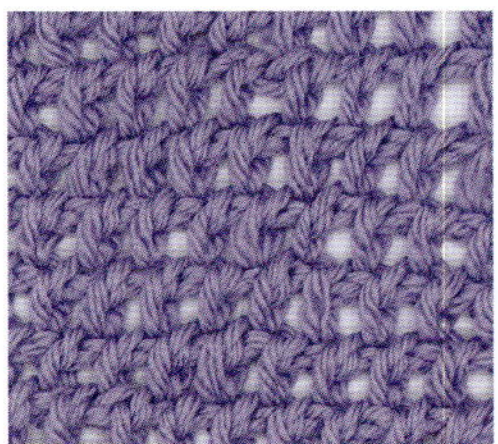

Reverse

PTks hook location

21 TUNISIAN KNIT DOUBLE CROCHET (Tkdc)

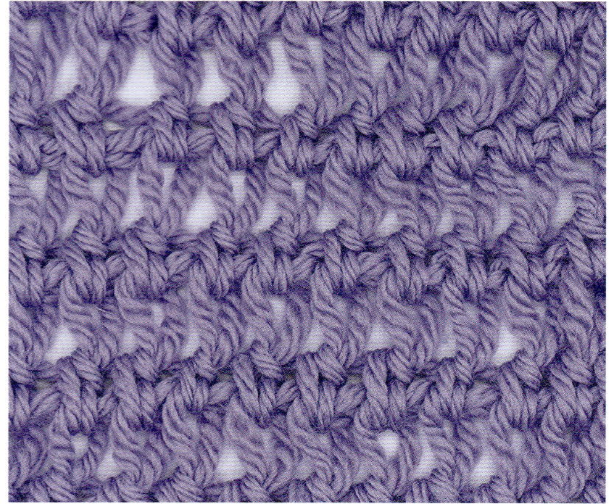

Worked over any number of stitches.

Yarn over and insert hook between vertical bars from front to back. Yarn over and pull up a loop (photo 1). Yarn over and pull through 2 loops (photo 2). Leave loop on hook.

Reverse

22 TUNISIAN KNIT TREBLE CROCHET (Tktc)

Worked over any number of stitches.

Yarn over twice and insert hook between vertical bars from front to back. Yarn over and pull up a loop (photo 1). Yarn over and pull through 2 loops twice (photo 2). Leave loop on hook.

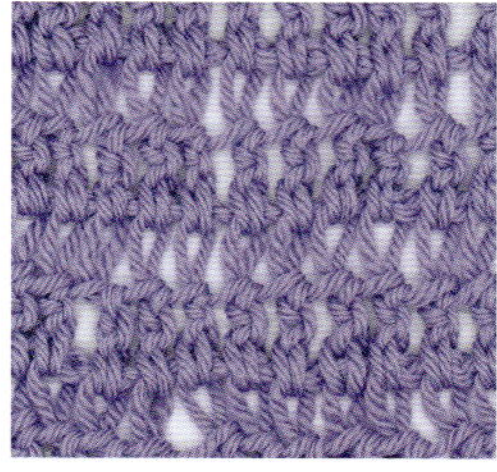

Reverse

23 PURLED MODIFIED TUNISIAN KNIT STITCH (PTmks)

Worked over any number of stitches.

Move yarn to front of fabric and insert hook between vertical bars and under top and back horizontal bars from front to back. Yarn over and pull up a loop. Leave loop on hook.

Reverse

PTmks hook location

24 PURLED TWISTED TUNISIAN KNIT STITCH (PTwTks)

Worked over any number of stitches.

Move yarn to front of fabric and insert hook as for TwTks. Yarn over and pull up a loop. Leave loop on hook.

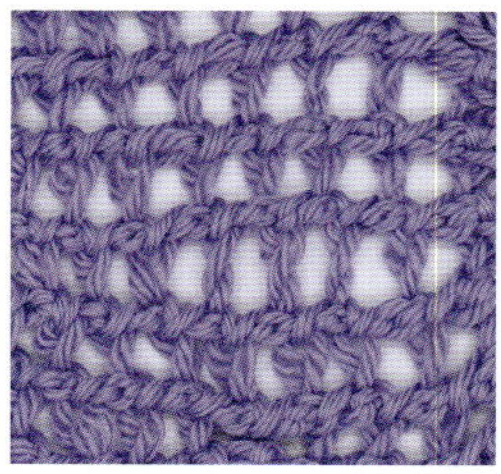

Reverse

PTwTks hook location

Tunisian Reverse Stitch and Variations

25 TUNISIAN REVERSE STITCH (Trs)

Worked over any number of stitches.

With hook on reverse side of fabric, insert hook behind back vertical bar from right to left* (photo 1). Yarn over and pull up a loop. Leave loop on hook.

**Left-handed makers: Insert hook from left to right.*

Reverse

Trs hook location

Trs hook location (reverse side)

26 EXTENDED TUNISIAN REVERSE STITCH (ExTrs)

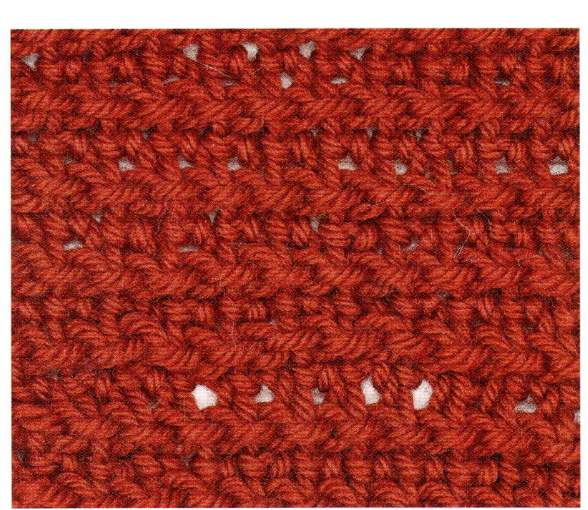

Worked over any number of stitches.

With hook on reverse side of fabric, insert hook behind back vertical bar from right to left*. Yarn over and pull up a loop (photo 1). Chain 1 (photo 2). Leave loop on hook.

**Left-handed makers: Insert hook from left to right.*

Reverse

1

2

27 MODIFIED TUNISIAN REVERSE STITCH (Tmrs)

Worked over any number of stitches.

With hook on reverse side of fabric, insert hook behind back vertical bar and bottom horizontal bar from right to left*. Yarn over and pull up a loop. Leave loop on hook.

**Left-handed makers: Insert hook from left to right.*

Reverse

Tmrs hook location (reverse side)

28 TWISTED UP TUNISIAN REVERSE STITCH (TwupTrs)

Worked over any number of stitches.

With hook on reverse side of fabric, insert hook behind back vertical bar from left to right and rotate hook counterclockwise*. Yarn over and pull up a loop. Leave loop on hook.

**Left-handed makers: Insert hook from right to left and rotate hook clockwise.*

Reverse

TwupTrs hook location (reverse side)

29 TWISTED DOWN TUNISIAN REVERSE STITCH (TwdTrs)

Worked over any number of stitches.

With hook on reverse side of fabric, insert hook behind back vertical bar from left to right and rotate hook clockwise*. Yarn over and pull up a loop. Leave loop on hook.

**Left-handed makers: Insert hook from right to left and rotate hook counterclockwise.*

Reverse

TwdTrs hook location (reverse side)

30 TUNISIAN REVERSE FRONT BAR STITCH (Tfrs)

Worked over any number of stitches.

With hook on reverse side of fabric, insert hook behind front vertical bar from right to left*. Yarn over and pull up a loop. Leave loop on hook.

**Left-handed makers: Insert hook from left to right.*

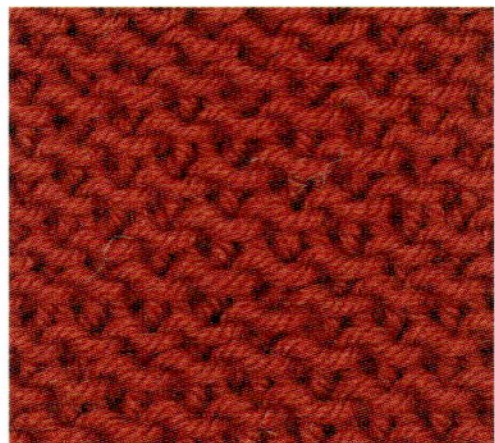

Reverse

Tfrs hook location (reverse side)

31 PURLED TUNISIAN REVERSE STITCH (PTrs)

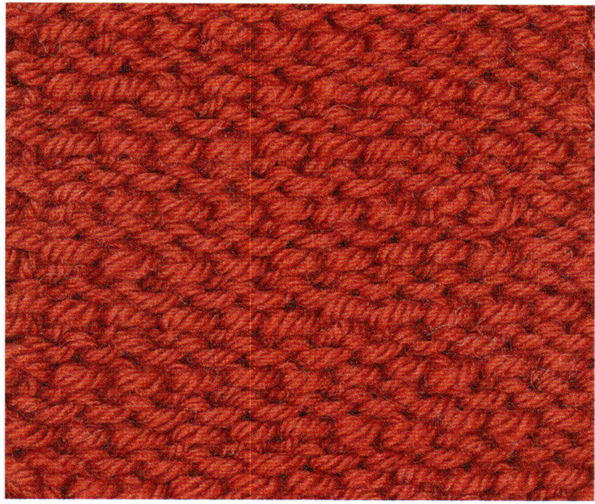

Worked over any number of stitches.

Move yarn to front of fabric. With hook on reverse side of fabric, insert hook behind back vertical bar from right to left*. Yarn over and pull up a loop. Leave loop on hook.

**Left-handed makers: Insert hook from left to right.*

Reverse

Reverse PTrs hook location

32 TUNISIAN REVERSE DOUBLE CROCHET (Trdc)

Worked over any number of stitches.

From back side of fabric, yarn over and insert hook behind back vertical bar from right to left*. Yarn over and pull up a loop (photo 1). Yarn over and pull through 2 loops (photo 2). Leave loop on hook.

**Left-handed makers: Insert hook from left to right.*

Reverse

1

2

33 TUNISIAN REVERSE TREBLE CROCHET (Trtc)

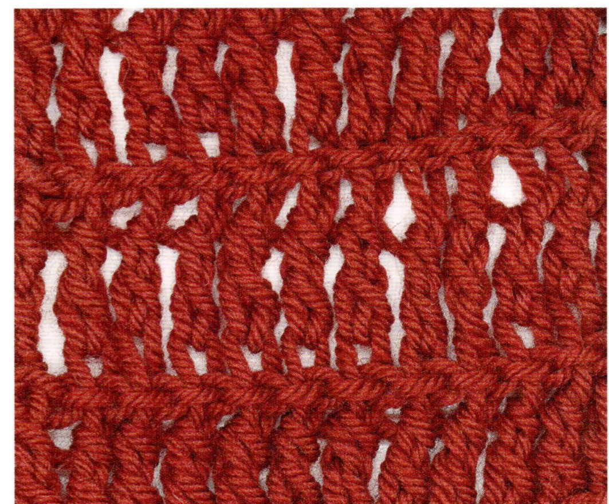

Worked over any number of stitches.

From back side of fabric, yarn over twice and insert hook behind back vertical bar from right to left*. Yarn over and pull up a loop (photo 1). Yarn over and pull through 2 loops twice (photo 2). Leave loop on hook.

**Left-handed makers: Insert hook from left to right.*

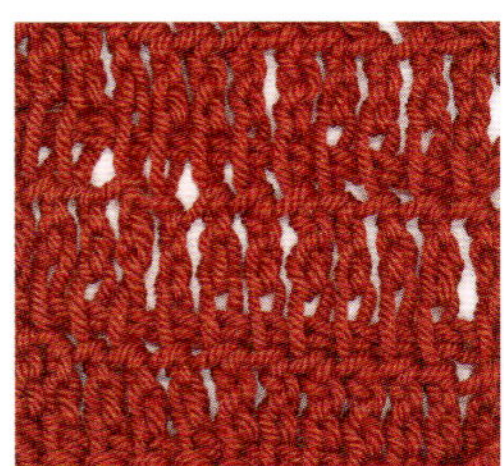

Reverse

Tunisian Purl Stitch and Variations

34 TUNISIAN PURL STITCH (Tps)

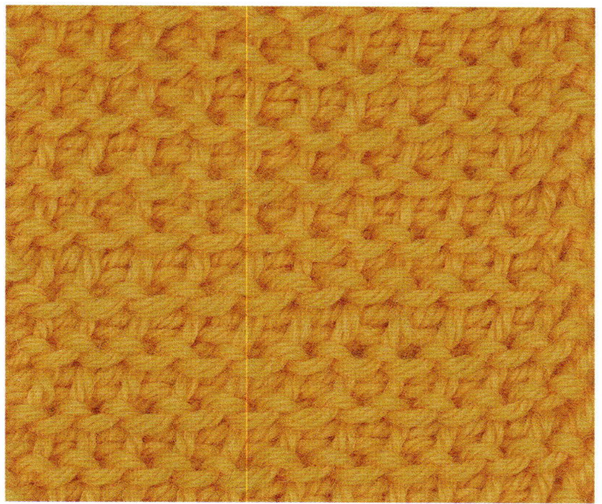

Worked over any number of stitches.

Move yarn to front of fabric and insert hook behind front vertical bar from right to left*. Yarn over and pull up a loop. Leave loop on hook.

**Left-handed makers: Insert hook from left to right.*

Reverse

Tps hook location

35 EXTENDED TUNISIAN PURL STITCH (ExTps)

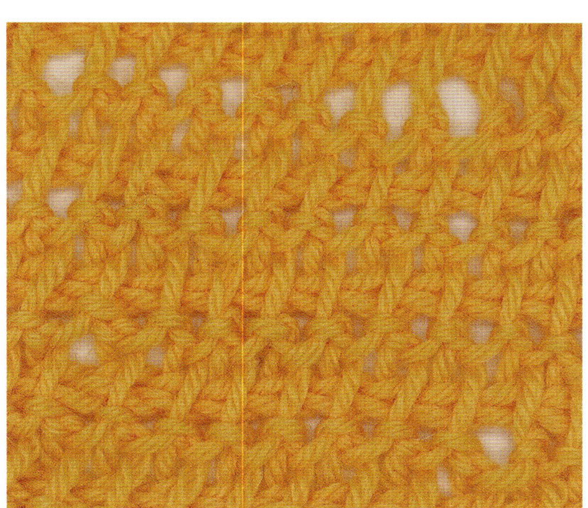

Worked over any number of stitches.

Move yarn to front of fabric and insert hook behind front vertical bar from right to left*. Yarn over and pull up a loop (photo 1). Chain 1 (photo 2). Leave loop on hook.

**Left-handed makers: Insert hook from left to right.*

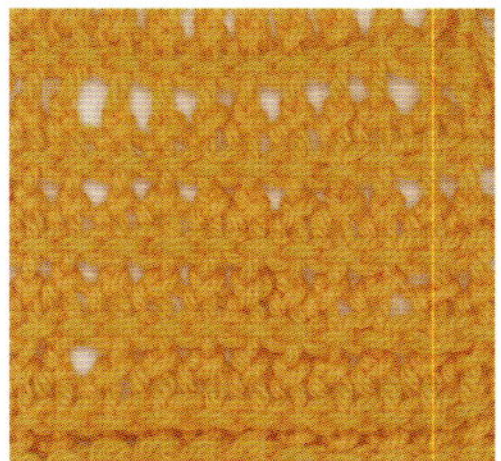

Reverse

1

2

36 MODIFIED TUNISIAN PURL STITCH (Tmps)

Worked over any number of stitches.

Move yarn to front of fabric and insert hook behind front vertical bar from right to left* and behind top horizontal bar. Yarn over and pull up a loop. Leave loop on hook.

**Left-handed makers: Insert hook from left to right.*

Reverse

Tmps hook location

37 TUNISIAN PURL STITCH WITH YARN UNDER (Tpsu)

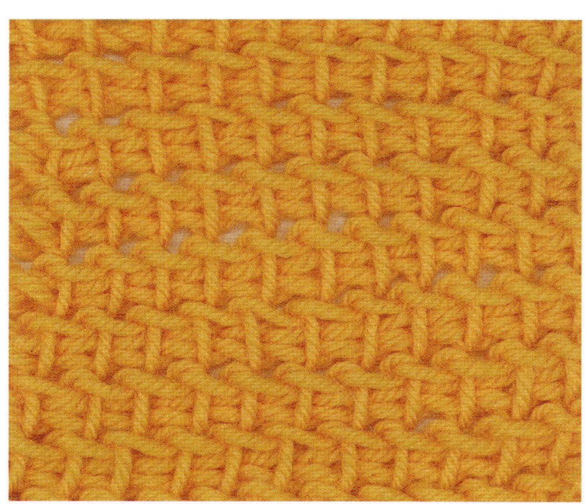

Worked over any number of stitches.

Move yarn to front of fabric and insert hook behind front vertical bar from right to left*. Yarn under (note the difference in how the yarn is wrapped compared to a regular Tps) and pull up a loop. Leave loop on hook.

**Left-handed makers: Insert hook from left to right.*

Reverse

Tpsu hook location

38 TWISTED TUNISIAN PURL STITCH (TwTps)

Worked over any number of stitches.

Move yarn to front of fabric. Insert hook behind front vertical bar from left to right and rotate hook clockwise*. Yarn over and pull up a loop. Leave loop on hook.

**Left-handed makers: Insert hook from right to left and rotate hook counterclockwise.*

Reverse

TwTps hook location

39 TWISTED UP TUNISIAN PURL STITCH (TwupTps)

Worked over any number of stitches.

Move yarn to front of fabric. Insert hook behind front vertical bar from left to right and rotate hook counterclockwise*. Yarn over and pull up a loop. Leave loop on hook.

**Left-handed makers: Insert hook from right to left and rotate hook clockwise.*

Reverse

TwupTps hook location

40 BACK BAR TUNISIAN PURL STITCH (Tbps)

Worked over any number of stitches.

Move yarn to front of fabric and insert hook behind back vertical bar from right to left*. Yarn over and pull up a loop. Leave loop on hook.

**Left-handed makers: Insert hook from left to right.*

Reverse

Tbps hook location

41 BACK BAR TUNISIAN PURL STITCH WITH YARN UNDER (Tbpsu)

Worked over any number of stitches.

Move yarn to front of fabric and insert hook behind back vertical bar from right to left*. Yarn under and pull up a loop. Leave loop on hook.

**Left-handed makers: Insert hook from left to right.*

Reverse

Tbpsu hook location

42 TUNISIAN PURL DOUBLE CROCHET (Tpdc)

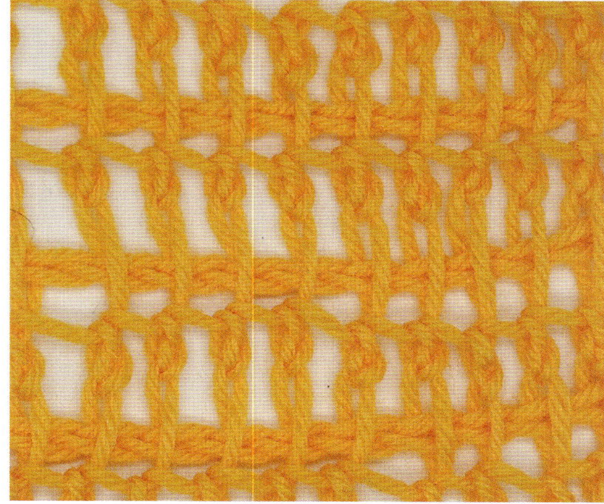

Worked over any number of stitches.

Move yarn to front of fabric. Yarn under and insert hook behind front vertical bar from right to left*. Yarn over and pull up a loop (photo 1). Yarn over and pull through 2 loops (photo 2). Leave loop on hook.

**Left-handed makers: Insert hook from left to right.*

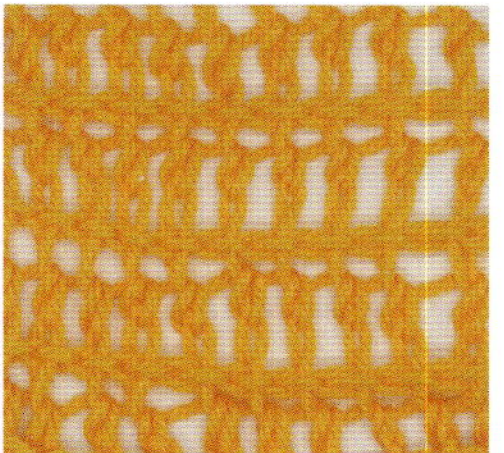

Reverse

1

2

43 TUNISIAN PURL TREBLE CROCHET (Tptc)

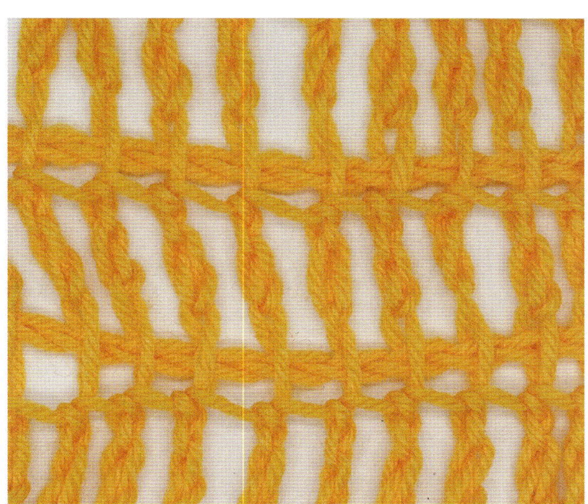

Worked over any number of stitches.

Move yarn to front of fabric. Yarn under twice and insert hook behind front vertical bar from right to left*. Yarn over and pull up a loop (photo 1). Yarn over and pull through 2 loops twice (photo 2). Leave loop on hook.

**Left-handed makers: Insert hook from left to right.*

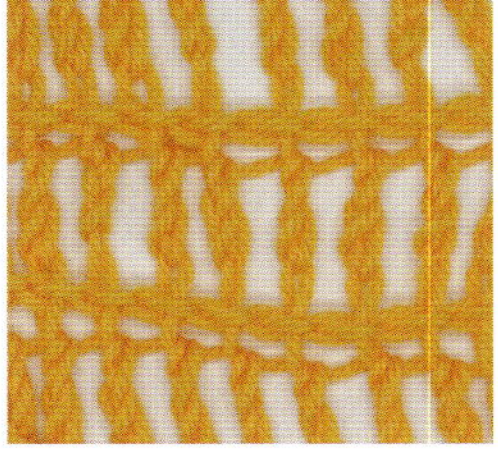

Reverse

1

2

Tunisian Full Stitch and Variations

These stitches are all worked in the stitch space or in the horizontal bars. When using these stitches, it is important to note that if a stitch is worked in all available stitch spaces or horizontal bars, then the stitch count will increase by 1 for each row. To avoid this, alternate skipping either the first or the last stitch space or horizontal bars of each row.

44 TUNISIAN FULL STITCH (Tfs)

Worked over any number of stitches.

Insert hook in next stitch space (under all three horizontal bars) from front to back. Yarn over and pull up a loop. Leave loop on hook.

Reverse

Tfs hook location

45 EXTENDED TUNISIAN FULL STITCH (ExTfs)

Worked over any number of stitches.

Insert hook in next stitch space from front to back. Yarn over and pull up a loop (photo 1). Chain 1 (photo 2). Leave loop on hook.

Reverse

46 MODIFIED TUNISIAN FULL STITCH (Tmfs)

Worked over any number of stitches.

Insert hook under next top and back horizontal bars from front to back. Yarn over and pull up a loop. Leave loop on hook.

Reverse

Tmfs hook location

47 TUNISIAN FULL DOUBLE CROCHET (Tfdc)

Worked over any number of stitches.

Yarn over and insert hook in next stitch space from front to back. Yarn over and pull up a loop (photo 1). Yarn over and pull through 2 loops (photo 2). Leave loop on hook.

Reverse

48 TUNISIAN FULL TREBLE CROCHET (Tftc)

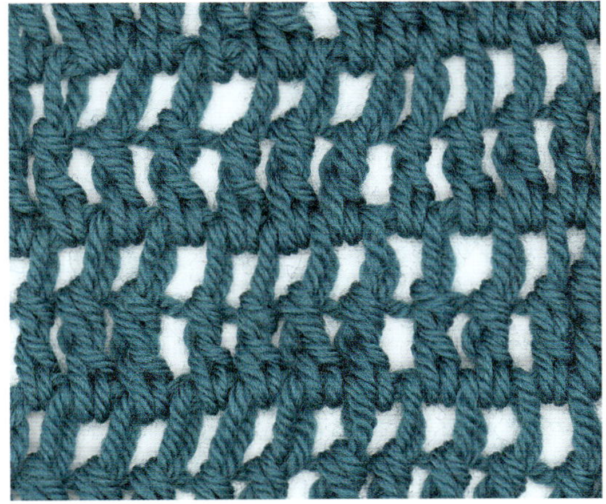

Worked over any number of stitches.

Yarn over twice and insert hook in next stitch space from front to back. Yarn over and pull up a loop (photo 1). Yarn over and pull through 2 loops twice (photo 2). Leave loop on hook.

Reverse

49 REVERSE TUNISIAN FULL STITCH (RTfs)

Worked over any number of stitches.

Insert hook in next stitch space from back to front. Yarn over and pull up a loop. Leave loop on hook.

Reverse

RTfs hook location

50 PURLED TUNISIAN FULL STITCH (PTfs)

Worked over any number of stitches.

Move yarn to front of fabric. Insert hook in next stitch space from front to back. Yarn over and pull up a loop. Leave loop on hook.

Reverse

PTfs hook location

51 TUNISIAN TOP STITCH (Ttop)

Worked over any number of stitches.

Insert hook under next back horizontal bar from front to back. Yarn over and pull up a loop. Leave loop on hook.

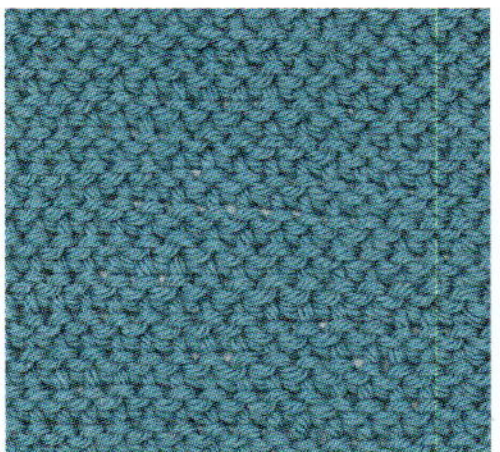

Reverse

Ttop hook location

52 PURLED TUNISIAN TOP STITCH (PTtop)

Worked over any number of stitches.

Move yarn to front of fabric. Insert hook under next back horizontal bar from front to back. Yarn over and pull up a loop. Leave loop on hook.

Reverse

PTtop hook location

53 REVERSE TUNISIAN TOP STITCH (RTtop)

Worked over any number of stitches.

Move yarn to front of fabric. Insert hook under next back horizontal bar from back to front. Yarn over and pull up a loop. Leave loop on hook.

Reverse

RTtop hook location

54 TUNISIAN TOP BAR STITCH (Tts)

Worked over any number of stitches.

Insert hook under next top horizontal bar from front to back. Yarn over and pull up a loop. Leave loop on hook.

Reverse

Tts hook location

55 PURLED TUNISIAN TOP BAR STITCH (PTts)

Worked over any number of stitches.

Bring yarn to front of fabric. Insert hook under next top horizontal bar from front to back. Yarn over and pull up a loop. Leave loop on hook.

Reverse

PTts hook location

56 REVERSE TUNISIAN TOP BAR STITCH (RTts)

Worked over any number of stitches.

Move yarn to front of fabric. Insert hook under next top horizontal bar from back to front. Yarn over and pull up a loop. Leave loop on hook.

Reverse

RTts hook location

57 TUNISIAN BOTTOM BAR STITCH (Tbs)

Worked over any number of stitches.

Insert hook under next bottom horizontal bar from front to back. Yarn over and pull up a loop. Leave loop on hook.

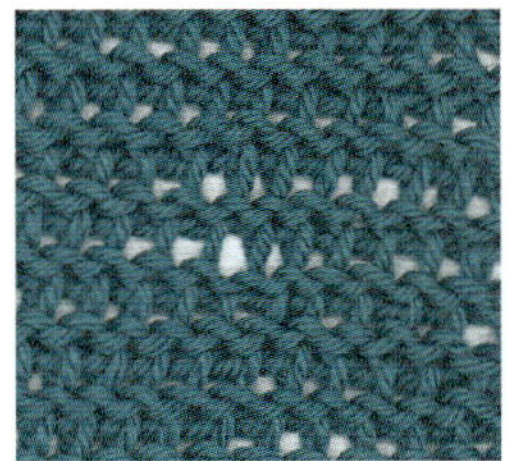

Reverse

Tbs hook location

58 PURLED TUNISIAN BOTTOM BAR STITCH (PTbs)

Worked over any number of stitches.

Bring yarn to front of fabric. Insert hook under next bottom horizontal bar from front to back. Yarn over and pull up a loop. Leave loop on hook.

Reverse

PTbs hook location

59 REVERSE TUNISIAN BOTTOM BAR STITCH (RTbs)

Worked over any number of stitches.

Move yarn to front of fabric. Insert hook under next bottom horizontal bar from back to front. Yarn over and pull up a loop. Leave loop on hook.

Reverse

RTbs hook location

Other Basic Stitches and Variations

60 FRONT POST TUNISIAN STITCH (Fptc)

Worked over any number of stitches.

Insert hook behind both vertical bars from right to left*.
Yarn over and pull up a loop. Leave loop on hook.

**Left-handed makers: Insert hook from left to right.*

Reverse

Fptc hook location

61 EXTENDED FRONT POST TUNISIAN STITCH (ExFptc)

Worked over any number of stitches.

Insert hook behind both vertical bars from right to left*. Yarn over and pull up a loop (photo 1). Chain 1 (photo 2). Leave loop on hook.

**Left-handed makers: Insert hook from left to right.*

Reverse

62 FRONT POST DOUBLE CROCHET (FptcDc)

Worked over any number of stitches.

Yarn over and insert hook behind both vertical bars from right to left*. Yarn over and pull up a loop (photo 1). Yarn over and pull through 2 loops (photo 2). Leave loop on hook.

**Left-handed makers: Insert hook from left to right.*

Reverse

1

2

63 FRONT POST TREBLE CROCHET (FptcTc)

Worked over any number of stitches.

Yarn over twice and insert hook behind both vertical bars from right to left*. Yarn over and pull up a loop (photo 1). Yarn over and pull through 2 loops twice (photo 2). Leave loop on hook.

**Left-handed makers: Insert hook from left to right.*

Reverse

1

2

64 PURLED FRONT POST TUNISIAN STITCH (PFptc)

Worked over any number of stitches.

Move yarn to front of fabric. Insert hook behind both vertical bars from right to left*. Yarn over and pull up a loop. Leave loop on hook.

**Left-handed makers: Insert hook from left to right.*

Reverse

PFptc hook location

65 EXTENDED PURLED FRONT POST TUNISIAN STITCH (ExPFptc)

Worked over any number of stitches.

Move yarn to front of fabric. Insert hook behind both vertical bars from right to left*. Yarn over and pull up a loop (photo 1). Chain 1 (photo 2). Leave loop on hook.

**Left-handed makers: Insert hook from left to right.*

Reverse

1

2

66 BACK POST TUNISIAN STITCH (Bptc)

Worked over any number of stitches.

With hook on reverse side of fabric, insert hook behind both vertical bars from right to left*. Yarn over and pull up a loop. Leave loop on hook.

**Left-handed makers: Insert hook from left to right.*

Reverse

Bptc hook location

67 EXTENDED BACK POST TUNISIAN STITCH (ExBptc)

Worked over any number of stitches.

With hook on reverse side of fabric, insert hook behind both vertical bars from right to left*. Yarn over and pull up a loop (photo 1). Chain 1 (photo 2). Leave loop on hook.

**Left-handed makers: Insert hook from left to right.*

Reverse

1

2

68 BACK POST DOUBLE CROCHET (BptcDc)

Worked over any number of stitches.

With hook on reverse side of fabric, yarn over and insert hook behind both vertical bars from right to left*. Yarn over and pull up a loop (photo 1). Yarn over and pull through 2 loops (photo 2). Leave loop on hook.

**Left-handed makers: Insert hook from left to right.*

Reverse

1

2

69 BACK POST TREBLE CROCHET (BptcTc)

Worked over any number of stitches.

With hook on reverse side of fabric, yarn over twice and insert hook behind both vertical bars from right to left*. Yarn over and pull up a loop (photo 1). Yarn over and pull through 2 loops twice (photo 2). Leave loop on hook.

**Left-handed makers: Insert hook from left to right.*

Reverse

1

2

70 PURLED BACK POST TUNISIAN STITCH (PBptc)

Worked over any number of stitches.

Move yarn to front of fabric. With hook on reverse side of fabric, insert hook behind both vertical bars from right to left* (photo 1). Yarn over and pull up a loop (photo 2). Leave loop on hook.

**Left-handed makers: Insert hook from left to right.*

Reverse

1

2

71 TUNISIAN SLIP STITCH (Tslst)

Worked over any number of stitches.

Insert hook behind next front vertical bar from right to left*. Leave loop on hook.

Note: Tslst shown alternating with Tss, as the stitch must be used with other stitches.

**Left-handed makers: Insert hook from left to right.*

Reverse

Tslst hook location

72 TUNISIAN PURLED SLIP STITCH (PTslst)

Worked over any number of stitches.

Move yarn to front of fabric. Insert hook behind next front vertical bar from right to left*. Leave loop on hook.

Note: PTslst shown alternating with Tss, as the stitch must be used with other stitches.

**Left-handed makers: Insert hook from left to right.*

Reverse

PTslst hook location

Increases and Decreases

73 TUNISIAN SIMPLE STITCH DECREASES

Tunisian Simple Stitch Two Together (Tss2Tog): Insert hook behind next 2 front vertical bars from right to left* (photo 1). Yarn over and pull up a loop (photo 2). Leave loop on hook.

**Left-handed makers: Insert hook from left to right.*

Tss3Tog: Insert hook behind next 3 front vertical bars.

Tss4Tog: Insert hook behind next 4 front vertical bars.

ExTss2Tog: Tss2Tog, ch 1.

Reverse

74 TUNISIAN KNIT STITCH DECREASES

Tunisian Knit Stitch Two Together (Tks2Tog): Insert hook behind next set of front vertical bars from right to left* and between the second set of vertical bars from front to back (photo 1). Yarn over and pull up a loop (photo 2). Leave loop on hook.

**Left-handed makers: Insert hook from left to right.*

Tks3Tog: Insert hook behind next 2 front vertical bars and between the 3rd set of vertical bars.

ExTks2Tog: Tks2Tog, ch 1.

Reverse

1

2

75 TUNISIAN REVERSE STITCH DECREASES

Tunisian Reverse Stitch Two Together (Trs2Tog): From the back side of the fabric, insert hook behind next 2 back vertical bars from right to left* (photo 1). Yarn over and pull up a loop (photo 2). Leave loop on hook.

**Left-handed makers: Insert hook from left to right.*

Trs3Tog: From back side of fabric, insert hook behind next 3 back vertical bars.

ExTrs2Tog: Trs2Tog, ch 1.

Reverse

1

2

76 TUNISIAN PURL STITCH DECREASES

Tunisian Purl Stitch Two Together (Tps2Tog): Move yarn to front of fabric and insert hook behind next 2 front vertical bars from right to left* (photo 1). Yarn over and pull up a loop (photo 2). Leave loop on hook.

**Left-handed makers: Insert hook from left to right.*

Tps3Tog: Move yarn to front of fabric and insert hook behind next 3 front vertical bars.

ExTps2Tog: Tps2Tog, ch 1.

Reverse

1

2

77 TWO STITCHES IN ONE STITCH INCREASE

It is possible to work multiple stitches into a single stitch and this can be done for just about any combination of stitches. For a (Tss, Tmss) increase, first work a Tss (photo 1) and then a Tmss (photo 2) into the same stitch. *Note:* The order of the stitches is important, as (Tss, Tmss) is different from (Tmss, Tss).

1

2

78 THREE STITCHES IN ONE STITCH INCREASE

Any number of stitches can be worked into the same stitch as long as they are not the same stitch in a row. For (Tss, Tks, Tss) increase, work a Tss stitch (photo 1), then work a Tks stitch (photo 2), and then work a second Tss stitch (photo 3).

79 K-YO-K INCREASE

Yarn overs can also be created between stitches to allow for multiple increases. For a k-yo-k increase, work a Tks stitch (photo 1), yo (photo 2), and then work a second Tks stitch (photo 3).

CHAPTER 2

Stitch Patterns

Vertical Stripes

80 TSS & TKS VERTICAL STRIPE

Worked over a multiple of 2 stitches.

Row 1: [Tss, Tks] rep.

Repeat Row 1.

Reverse

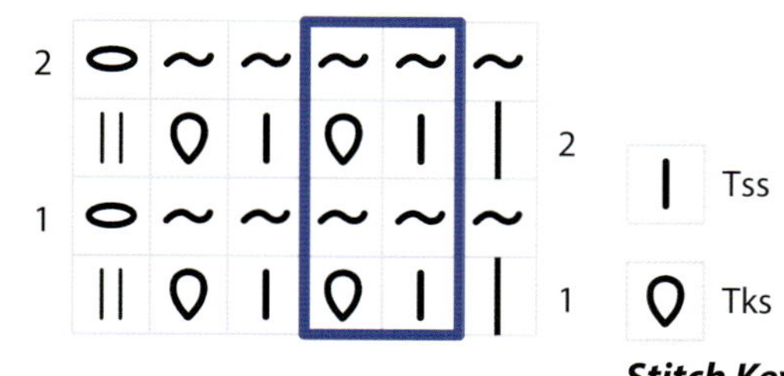

Stitch Key

81 TSS & TRS VERTICAL STRIPE

Worked over a multiple of 2 stitches.

Row 1: [Tss, Trs] rep.

Repeat Row 1.

Reverse

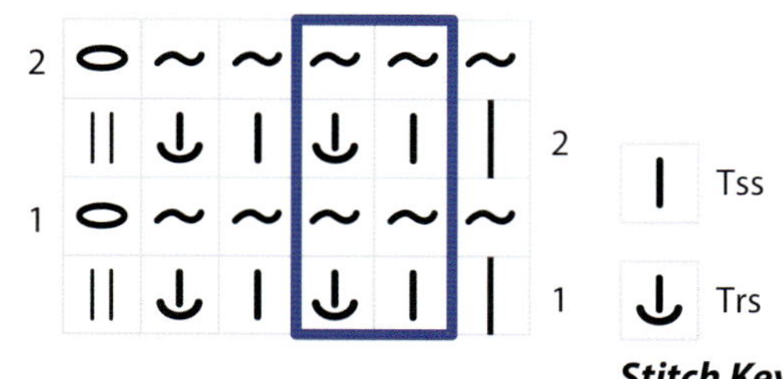

Stitch Key

82 TSS & TPS VERTICAL STRIPE

Worked over a multiple of 2 stitches.

Row 1: [Tss, Tps] rep.

Repeat Row 1.

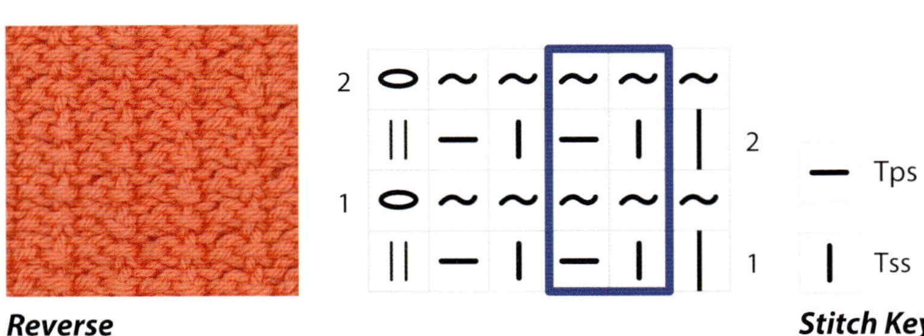

Reverse

Stitch Key

83 TKS & TPS VERTICAL STRIPE

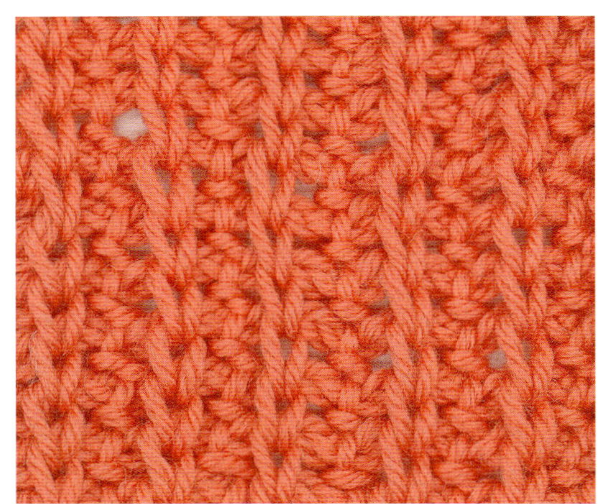

Worked over a multiple of 2 stitches.

Row 1: [Tks, Tps] rep.

Repeat Row 1.

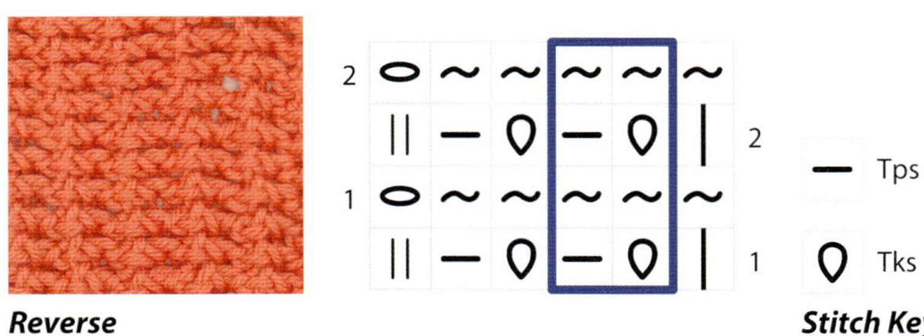

Reverse

Stitch Key

84 TKS & TRS VERTICAL STRIPE

Worked over a multiple of 2 stitches.

Row 1: [Tks, Trs] rep.

Repeat Row 1.

Reverse

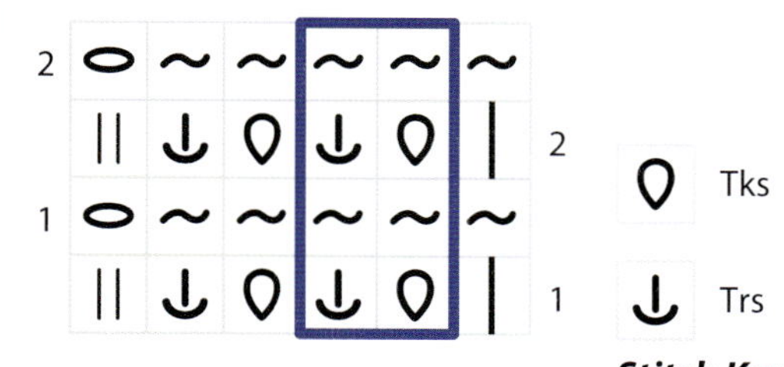

Tks

Trs

Stitch Key

85 TRS & TPS VERTICAL STRIPE

Worked over a multiple of 2 stitches.

Row 1: [Trs, Tps] rep.

Repeat Row 1.

Reverse

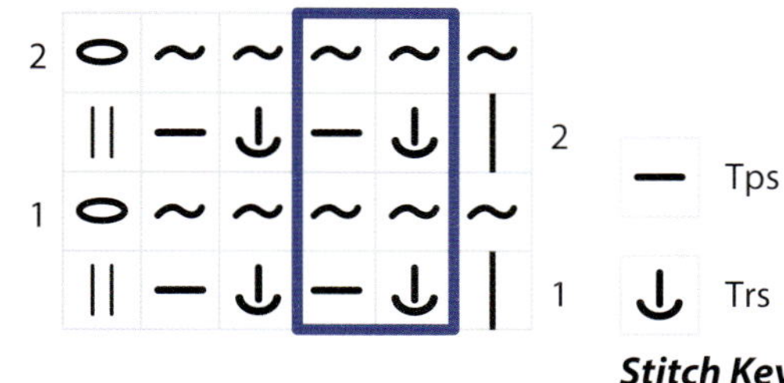

Tps

Trs

Stitch Key

86 TSS & TWD VERTICAL STRIPE

Worked over a multiple of 2 stitches.

Row 1: [Tss, Twd] rep.

Repeat Row 1.

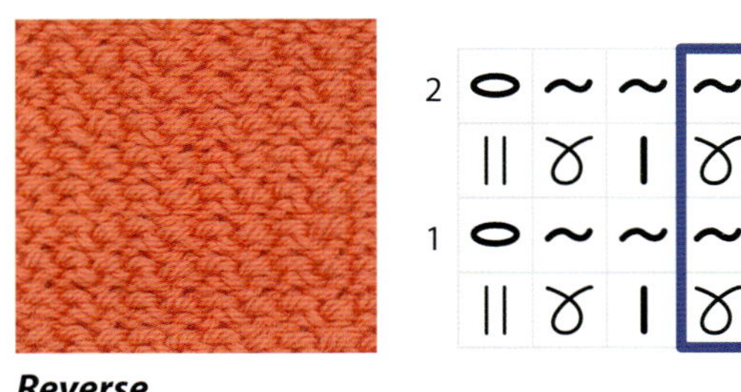

Reverse

Twd

Tss

Stitch Key

87 TKS & TWD VERTICAL STRIPE

Worked over a multiple of 2 stitches.

Row 1: [Tks, Twd] rep.

Repeat Row 1.

Reverse

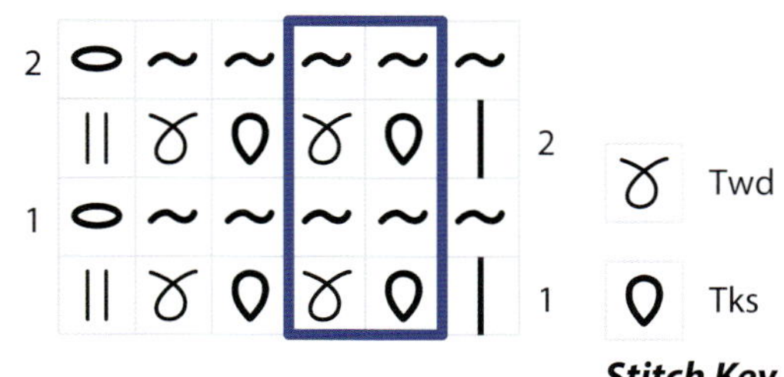

Twd

Tks

Stitch Key

88 TSS & TWUP VERTICAL STRIPE

Worked over a multiple of 2 stitches.

Row 1: [Tss, Twup] rep.

Repeat Row 1.

Reverse

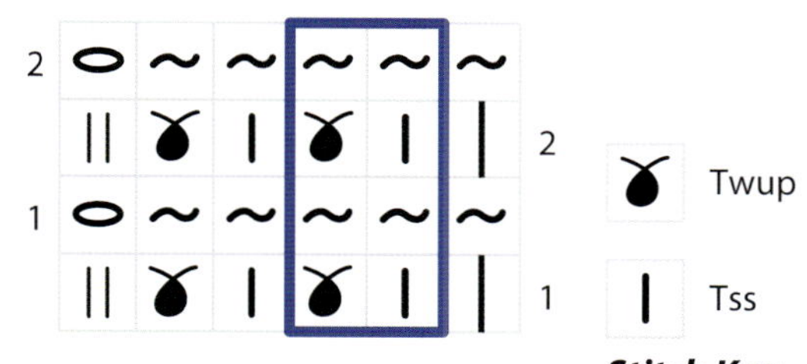

Stitch Key

89 TRS & PTRS VERTICAL STRIPE

Worked over a multiple of 2 stitches.

Row 1: [Trs, Ptrs] rep.

Repeat Row 1.

Reverse

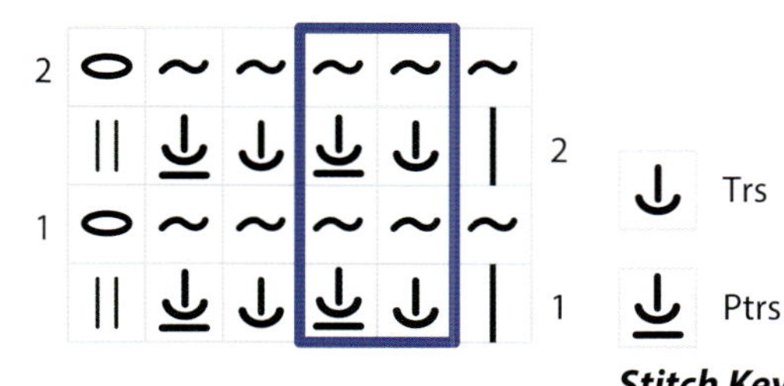

Stitch Key

90 TSS & TBSS VERTICAL STRIPE

Worked over a multiple of 2 stitches.

Row 1: [Tss, Tbss] rep.

Repeat Row 1.

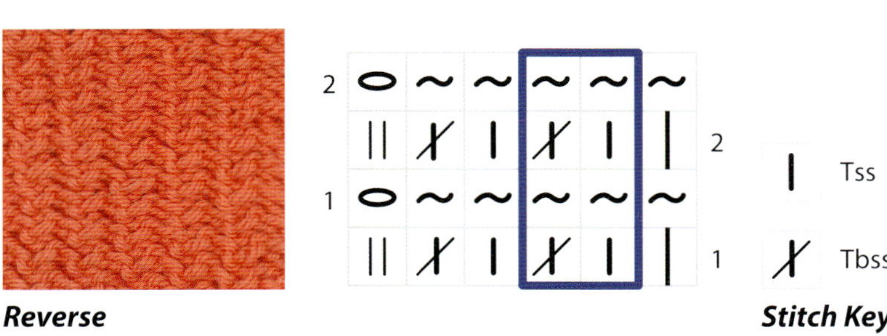

Reverse

Tss

Tbss

Stitch Key

91 TKS & TBSS VERTICAL STRIPE

Worked over a multiple of 2 stitches.

Row 1: [Tks, Tbss] rep.

Repeat Row 1.

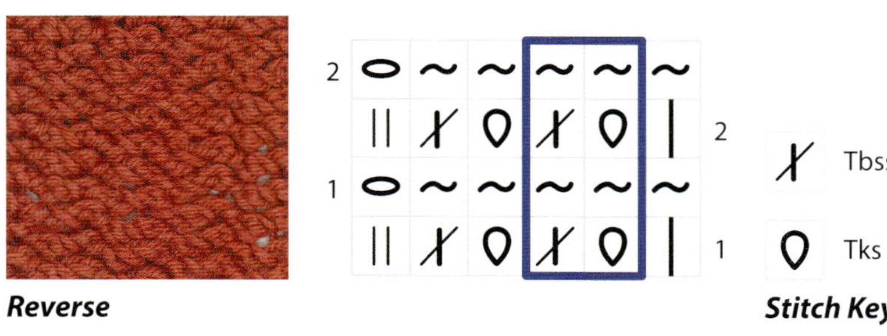

Reverse

Tbss

Tks

Stitch Key

92 TRS & TBSS VERTICAL STRIPE

Worked over a multiple of 2 stitches.

Row 1: [Trs, Tbss] rep.

Repeat Row 1.

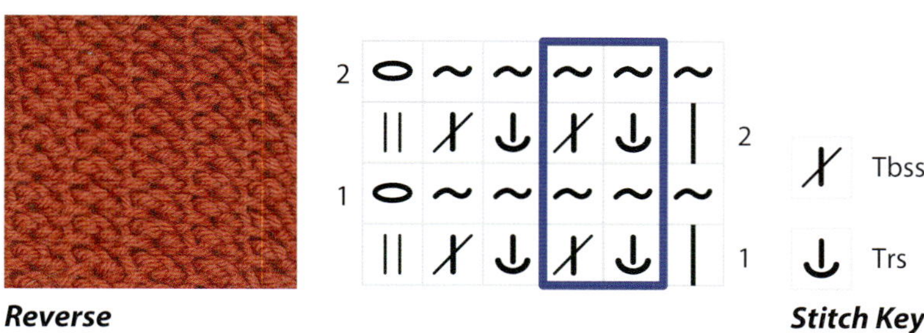

Reverse

Stitch Key

93 TPS & TBSS VERTICAL STRIPE

Worked over a multiple of 2 stitches.

Row 1: [Tps, Tbss] rep.

Repeat Row 1.

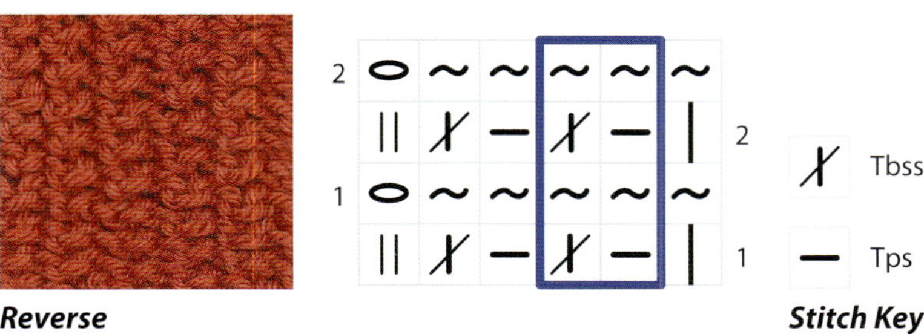

Reverse

Stitch Key

94 TSS & TFRS VERTICAL STRIPE

Worked over a multiple of 2 stitches.

Row 1: [Tss, Tfrs] rep.

Repeat Row 1.

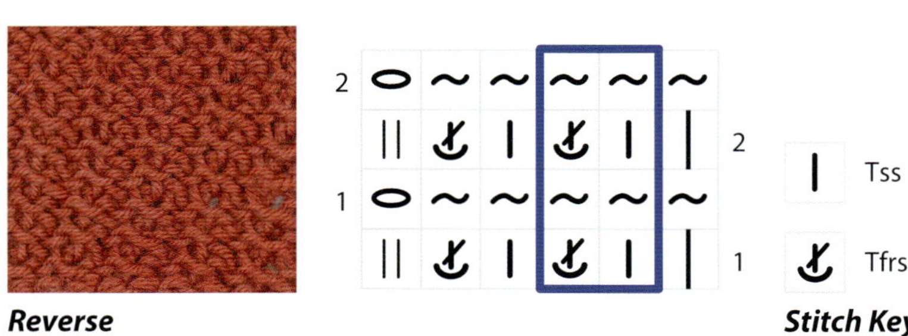

Reverse

Stitch Key

95 TKS & TFRS VERTICAL STRIPE

Worked over a multiple of 2 stitches.

Row 1: [Tks, Tfrs] rep.

Repeat Row 1.

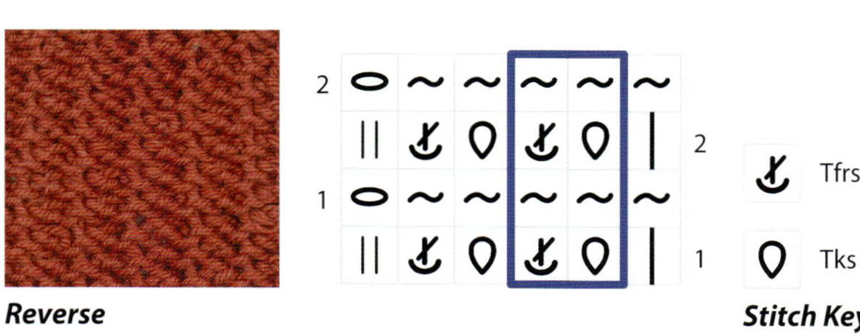

Reverse

Stitch Key

96 TPS & TFRS VERTICAL STRIPE

Worked over a multiple of 2 stitches.

Row 1: [Tps, Tfrs] rep.

Repeat Row 1.

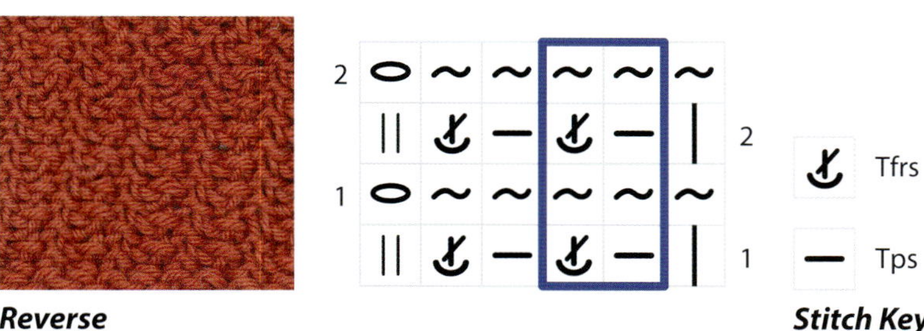

Reverse

Stitch Key

97 TRS & TWD VERTICAL STRIPE

Worked over a multiple of 2 stitches.

Row 1: [Trs, Twd] rep.

Repeat Row 1.

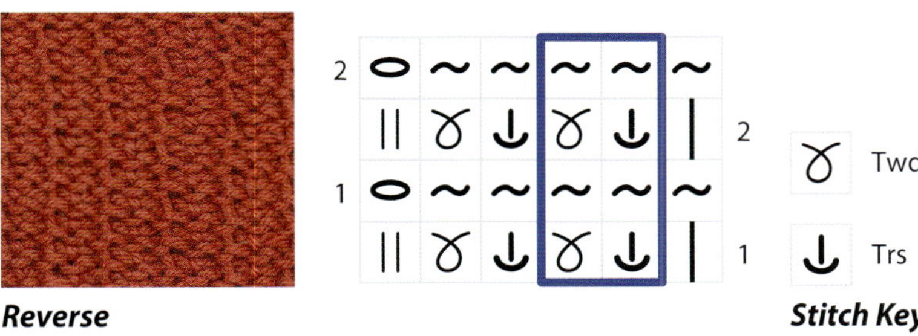

Reverse

Stitch Key

98 TPS & TWD VERTICAL STRIPE

Worked over a multiple of 2 stitches.

Row 1: [Tps, Twd] rep.

Repeat Row 1.

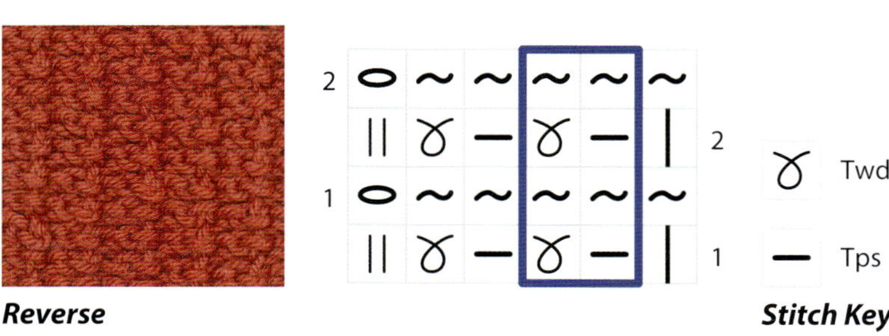

Reverse

ɤ Twd

— Tps

Stitch Key

99 TKS & TTOP VERTICAL STRIPE

Worked over a multiple of 2 stitches.

Row 1: [Tks, Ttop] rep.

Repeat Row 1.

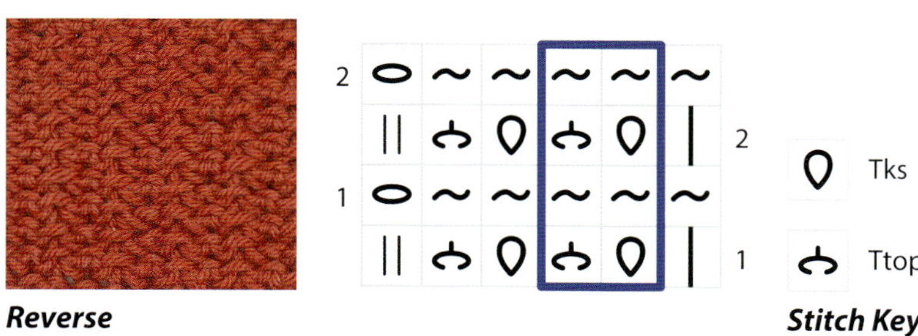

Reverse

Tks

Ttop

Stitch Key

100 TSS & PTRS VERTICAL STRIPE

Worked over a multiple of 2 stitches.

Row 1: [Tss, Ptrs] rep.

Repeat Row 1.

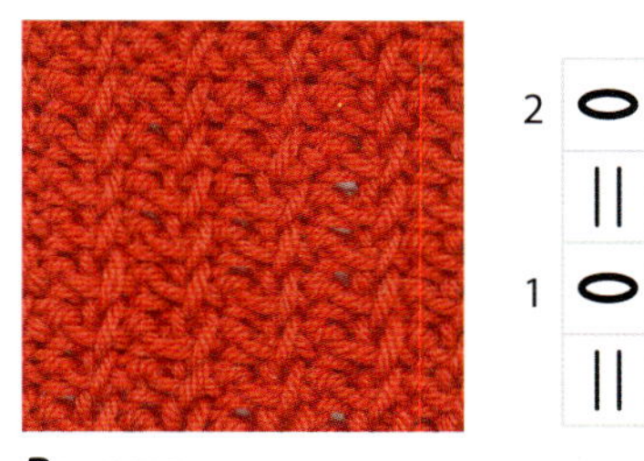

Reverse

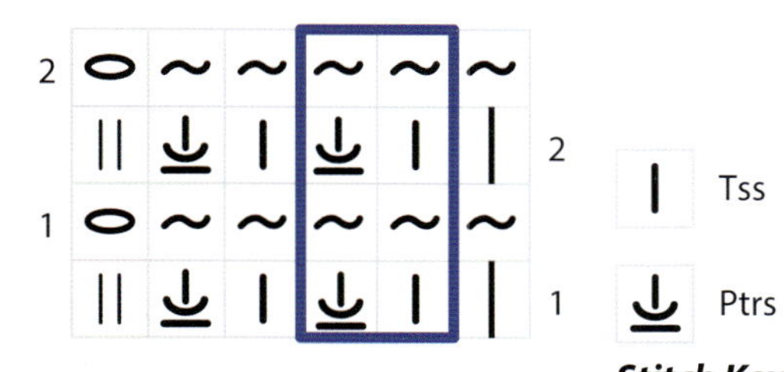

Stitch Key

Symbol	Stitch
|	Tss
⊥	Ptrs

101 TSS & TKS WIDE VERTICAL STRIPE

Worked over a multiple of 4 stitches.

Row 1: [Tss 2, Tks 2] rep.

Repeat Row 1.

Reverse

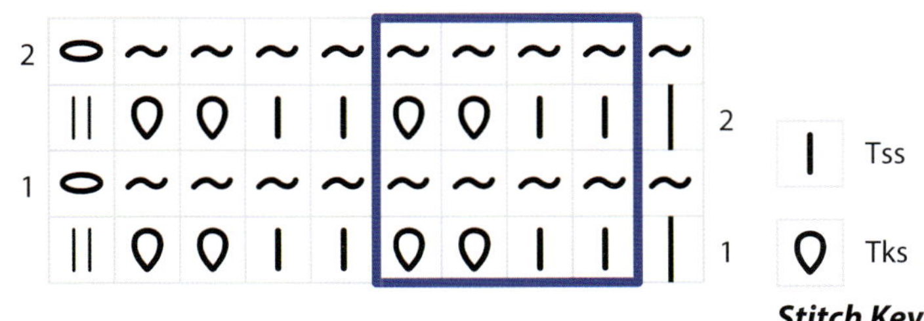

Stitch Key

Symbol	Stitch
|	Tss
O	Tks

102 TSS & TRS WIDE VERTICAL STRIPE

Worked over a multiple of 4 stitches.

Row 1: [Tss 2, Trs 2] rep.

Repeat Row 1.

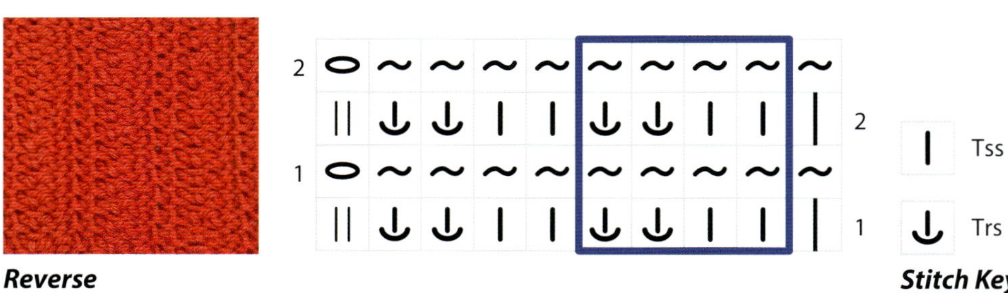

Reverse

Stitch Key

103 TSS & TPS WIDE VERTICAL STRIPE

Worked over a multiple of 4 stitches.

Row 1: [Tss 2, Tps 2] rep.

Repeat Row 1.

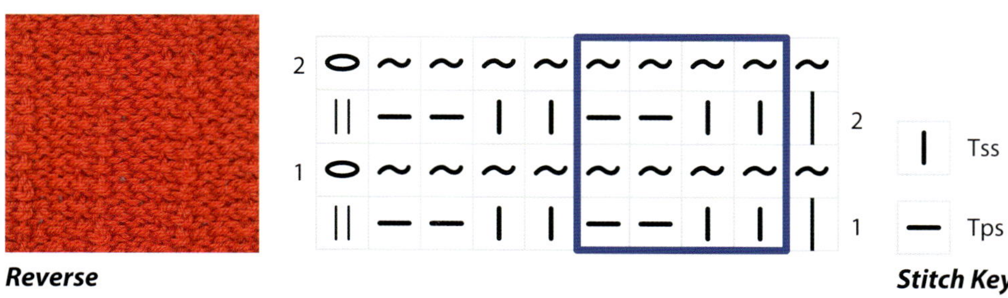

Reverse

Stitch Key

104 TRS & TPS WIDE VERTICAL STRIPE

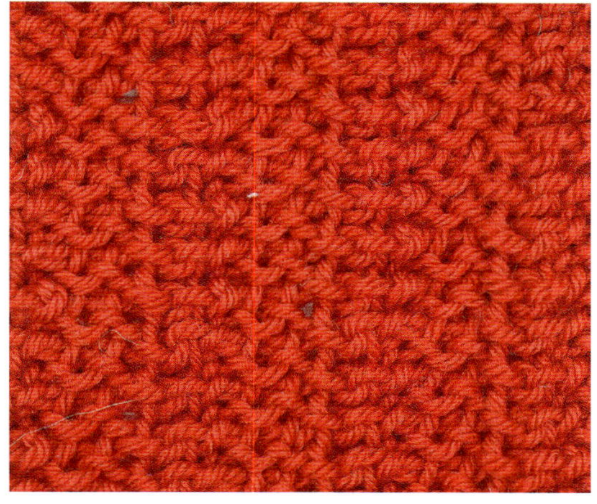

Worked over a multiple of 4 stitches.

Row 1: [Trs 2, Tps 2] rep.

Repeat Row 1.

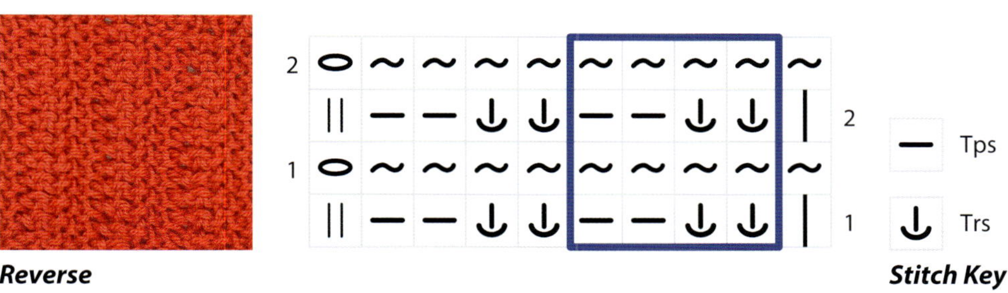

Reverse

Stitch Key

105 TKS & TRS WIDE VERTICAL STRIPE

Worked over a multiple of 4 stitches.

Row 1: [Tks 2, Trs 2] rep.

Repeat Row 1.

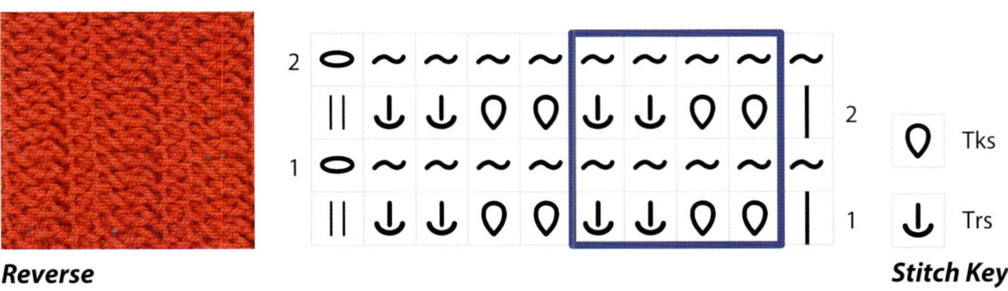

Reverse

Stitch Key

106 TPS & TWTKS WIDE VERTICAL STRIPE

Worked over a multiple of 4 stitches.

Row 1: [Tps 2, TwTks 2] rep.

Repeat Row 1.

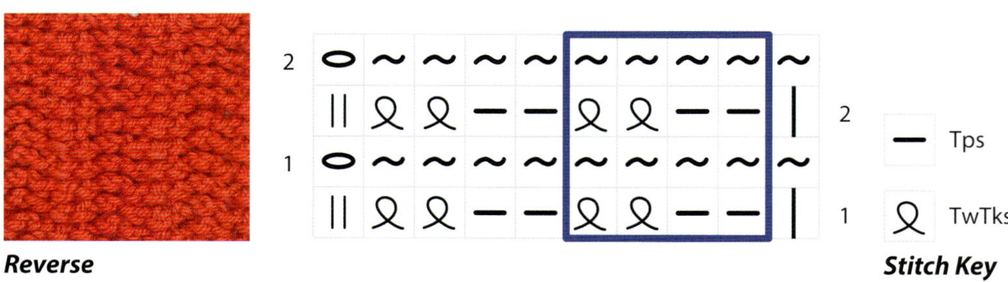

Reverse

Stitch Key

107 TPS & TX WIDE VERTICAL STRIPE

Worked over a multiple of 4 stitches.

Row 1: [Tps 2, Tx] rep.

Repeat Row 1.

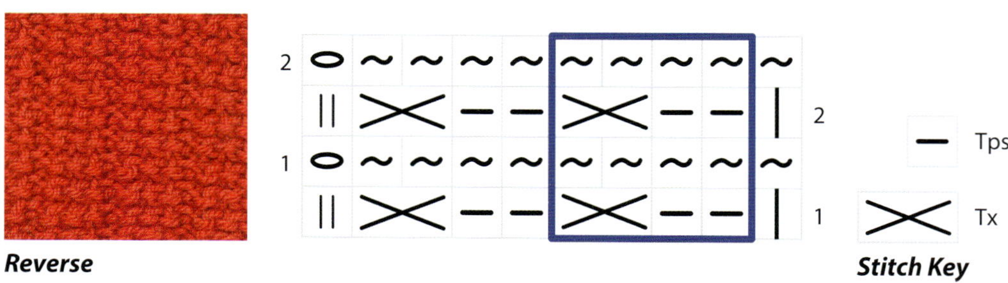

Reverse

Stitch Key

108 TPS & TSS THICK VERTICAL STRIPE

Worked over a multiple of 4 stitches.

Row 1: [Tps 3, Tss] rep.

Repeat Row 1.

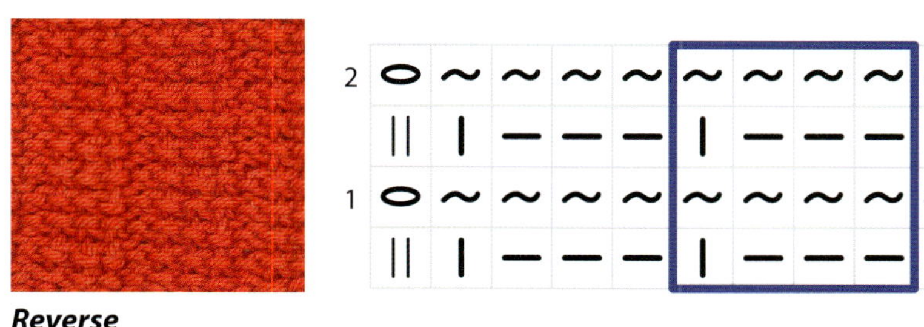

Reverse

— Tps

| Tss

Stitch Key

109 TSS & TPS THICK VERTICAL STRIPE

Worked over a multiple of 4 stitches.

Row 1: [Tss 3, Tps] rep.

Repeat Row 1.

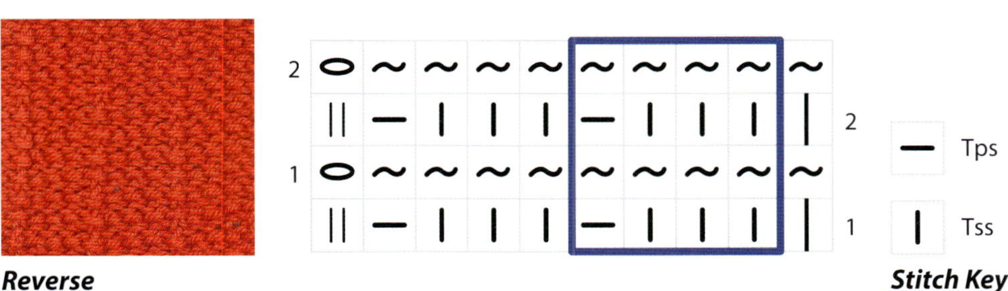

Reverse

— Tps

| Tss

Stitch Key

110 TKS & TPS THICK VERTICAL STRIPE

Worked over a multiple of 4 stitches.

Row 1: [Tks 3, Tps] rep.

Repeat Row 1.

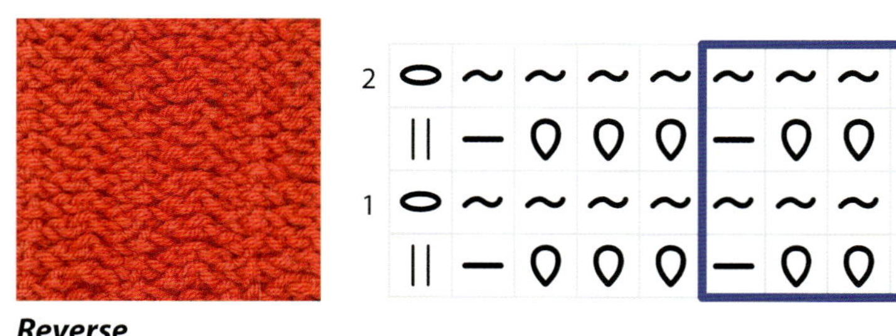

Reverse

— Tps

Tks

Stitch Key

111 TKS & TPS WIDE VERTICAL STRIPE

Worked over a multiple of 4 stitches.

Row 1: [Tks 2, Tps 2] rep.

Repeat Row 1.

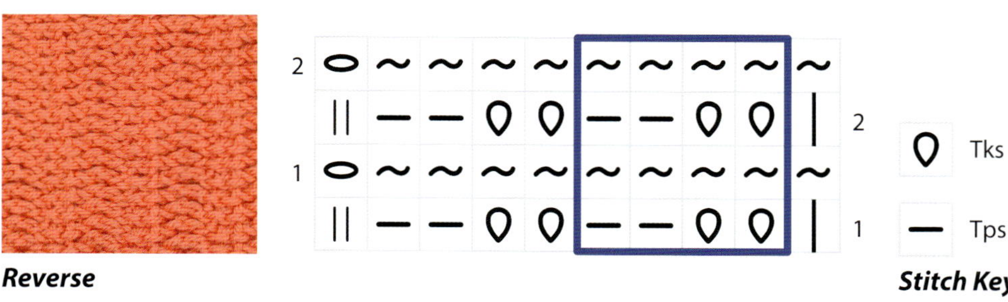

Reverse

Tks

— Tps

Stitch Key

112

Worked over a multiple of 5 stitches.

Row 1: [Tks, Tss, Tps, Tss, Tks] rep.

Repeat Row 1.

Reverse

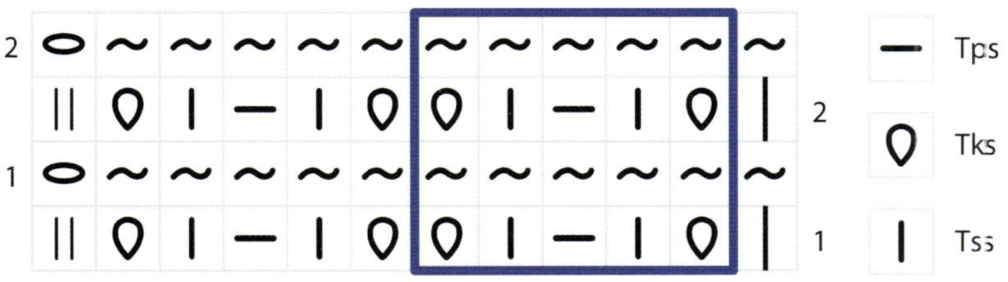

Stitch Key

— Tps

Tks

| Tss

Horizontal Stripes

113 TSS & TKS HORIZONTAL STRIPE

Worked over any number of stitches and 2 rows.

Row 1: Tss rep.

Row 2: Tks rep.

Repeat Rows 1 and 2.

Reverse

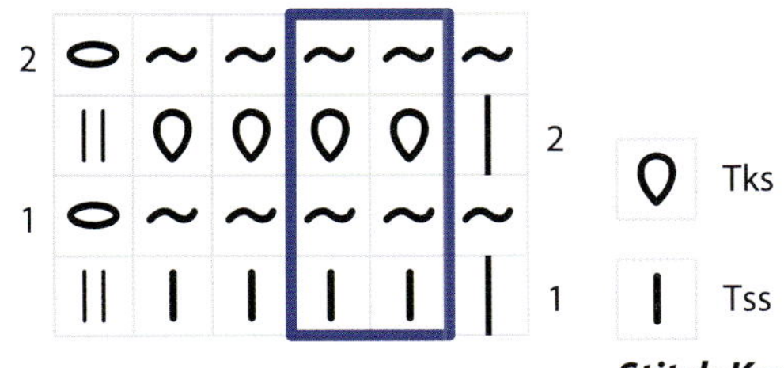

Stitch Key

Tks

| Tss

114 TSS & TRS HORIZONTAL STRIPE

Worked over any number of stitches and 2 rows.

Row 1: Tss rep.

Row 2: Trs rep.

Repeat Rows 1 and 2.

Reverse

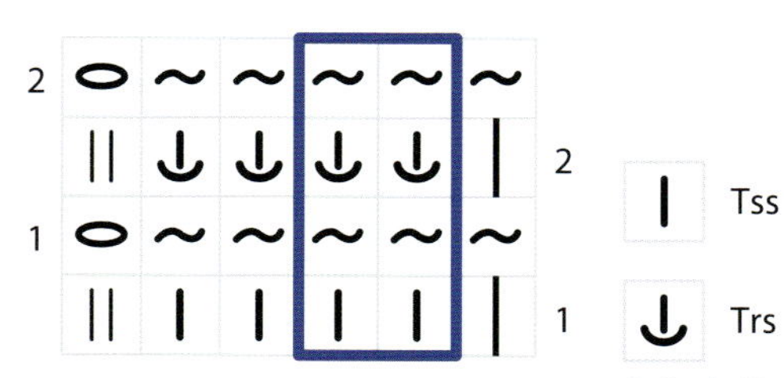

Symbol	Stitch
|	Tss
⫰	Trs

Stitch Key

115 TSS & TPS HORIZONTAL STRIPE

Worked over any number of stitches and 2 rows.

Row 1: Tss rep.

Row 2: Tps rep.

Repeat Rows 1 and 2.

Reverse

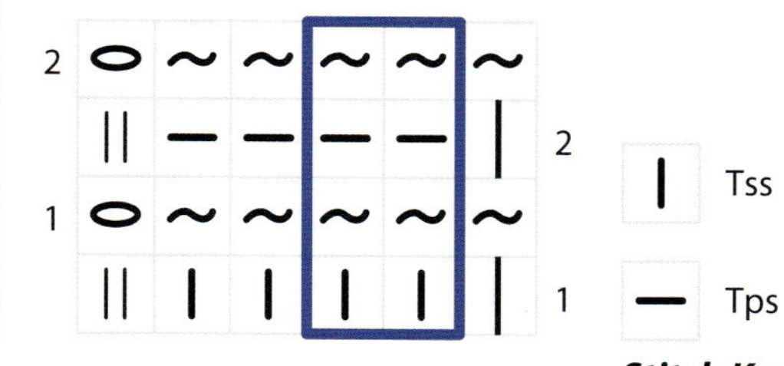

Symbol	Stitch
|	Tss
—	Tps

Stitch Key

116 TSS & PTRS HORIZONTAL STRIPE

Worked over any number of stitches and 2 rows.
Row 1: Tss rep.
Row 2: Ptrs rep.
Repeat Rows 1 and 2.

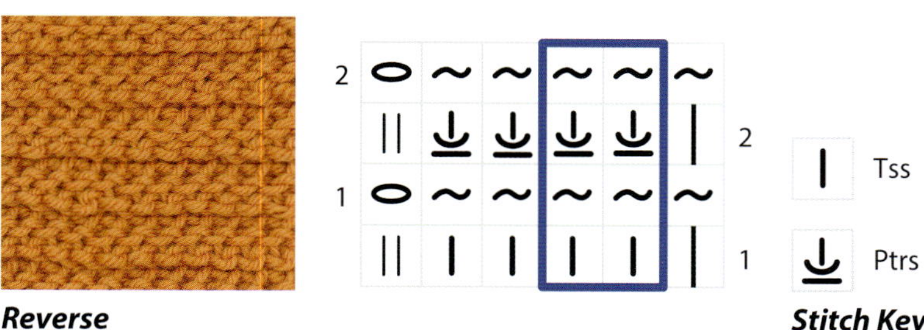

Reverse

Stitch Key

117 TKS & TRS HORIZONTAL STRIPE

Worked over any number of stitches and 2 rows.
Row 1: Tks rep.
Row 2: Trs rep.
Repeat Rows 1 and 2.

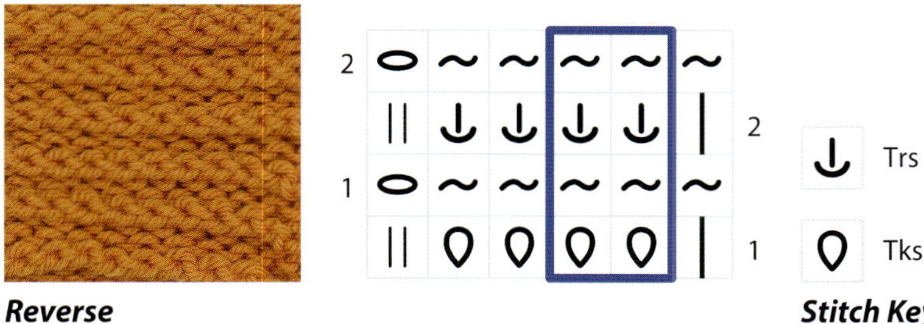

Reverse

Stitch Key

118 TKS & TPS HORIZONTAL STRIPE

Worked over any number of stitches and 2 rows.

Row 1: Tks rep.

Row 2: Tps rep.

Repeat Rows 1 and 2.

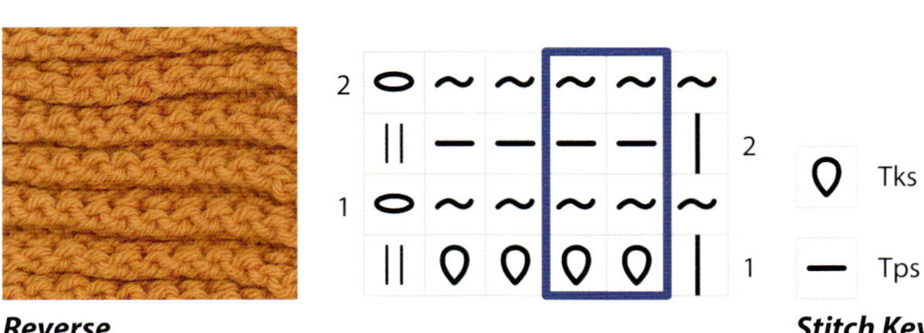

Reverse

Stitch Key

119 TKS & PTRS HORIZONTAL STRIPE

Worked over any number of stitches and 2 rows.

Row 1: Tks rep.

Row 2: Ptrs rep.

Repeat Rows 1 and 2.

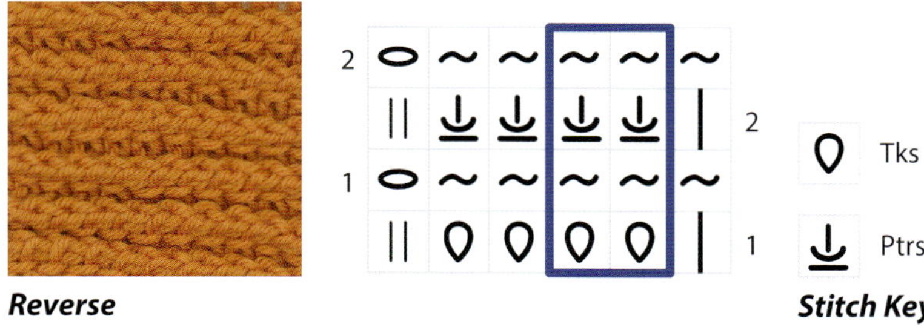

Reverse

Stitch Key

120 TKS & RTKS HORIZONTAL STRIPE

Worked over any number of stitches and 2 rows.

Row 1: Tks rep.

Row 2: RTks rep.

Repeat Rows 1 and 2.

Reverse

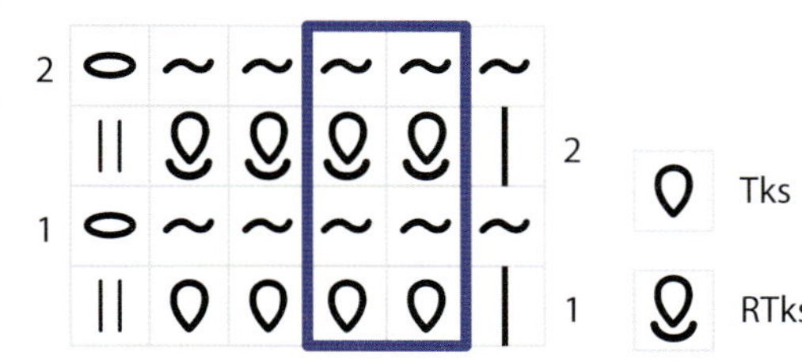

Tks

RTks

Stitch Key

121 TPS & TRS HORIZONTAL STRIPE

Worked over any number of stitches and 2 rows.

Row 1: Tps rep.

Row 2: Trs rep.

Repeat Rows 1 and 2.

Reverse

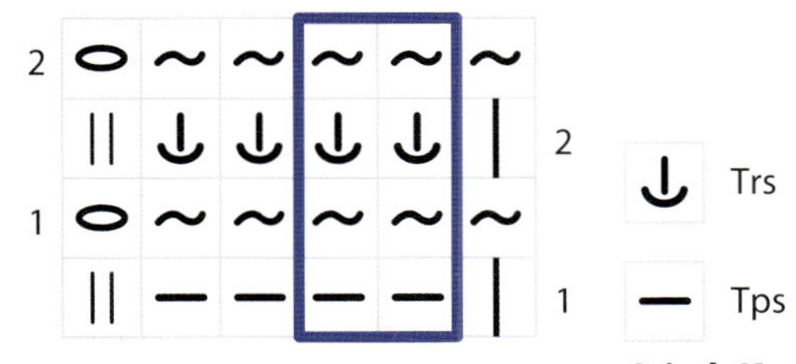

Trs

Tps

Stitch Key

122 TPS & PTRS HORIZONTAL STRIPE

Worked over any number of stitches and 2 rows.

Row 1: Tps rep.

Row 2: Ptrs rep.

Repeat Rows 1 and 2.

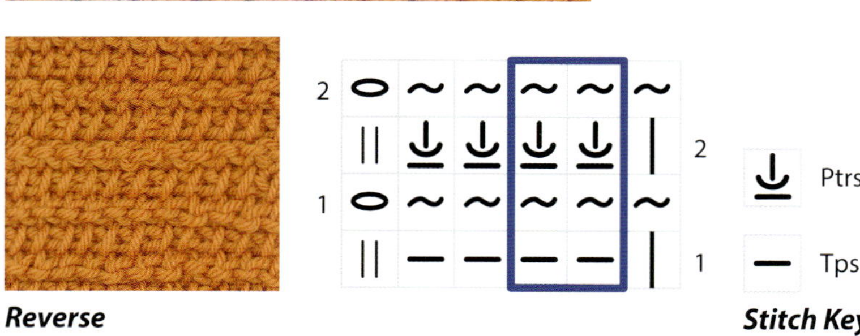

Reverse

Stitch Key

123 TSS, TPS, & TRS HORIZONTAL STRIPE

Worked over any number of stitches and 3 rows.

Row 1: Tss rep.

Row 2: Tps rep.

Row 3: Trs rep.

Repeat Rows 1–3.

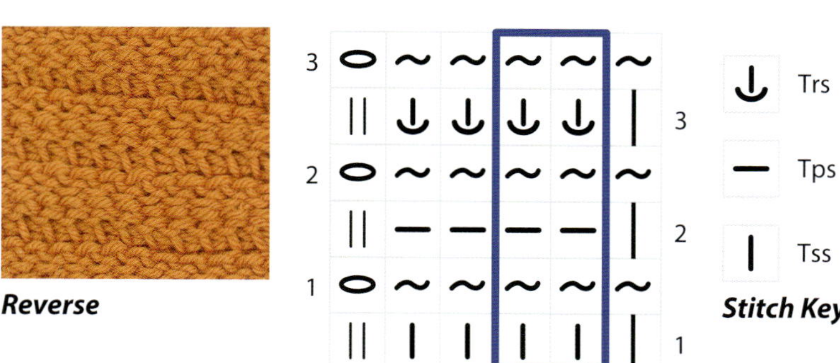

Reverse

Stitch Key

124 TSS, TPS, & PTRS HORIZONTAL STRIPE

Worked over any number of stitches and 3 rows.

Row 1: Tss rep.

Row 2: Tps rep.

Row 3: Ptrs rep.

Repeat Rows 1–3.

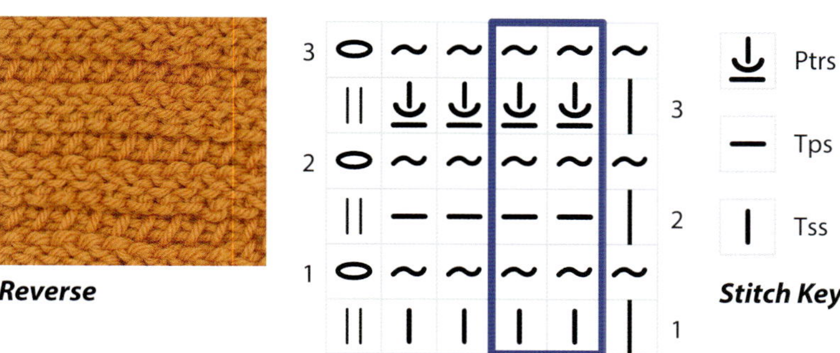

Reverse

Stitch Key

125 TSS & TWD HORIZONTAL STRIPE

Worked over any number of stitches and 2 rows.

Row 1: Tss rep.

Row 2: Twd rep.

Repeat Rows 1 and 2.

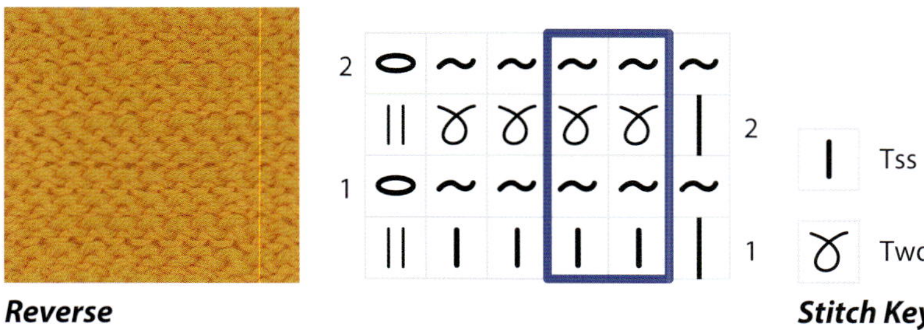

Reverse

Stitch Key

126 TKS & TWD HORIZONTAL STRIPE

Worked over any number of stitches and 2 rows.

Row 1: Tks rep.

Row 2: Twd rep.

Repeat Rows 1 and 2.

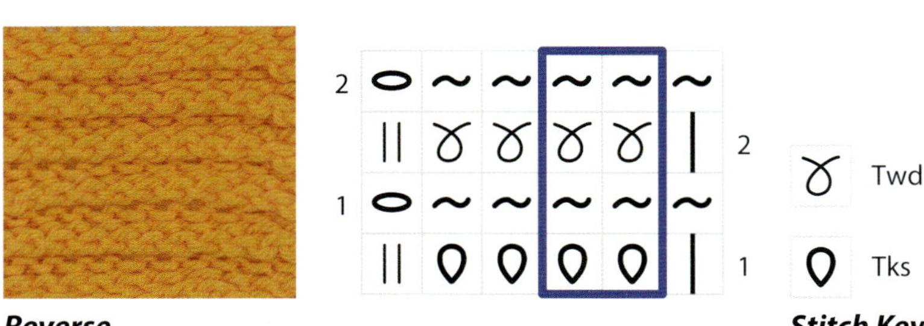

Reverse

Stitch Key

127 TPS & TWD HORIZONTAL STRIPE

Worked over any number of stitches and 2 rows.

Row 1: Tps rep.

Row 2: Twd rep.

Repeat Rows 1 and 2.

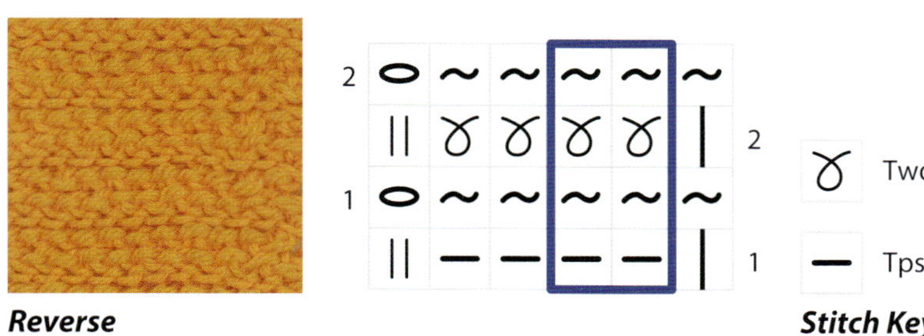

Reverse

Stitch Key

128 TRS & TWD HORIZONTAL STRIPE

Worked over any number of stitches and 2 rows.
Row 1: Trs rep.
Row 2: Twd rep.
Repeat Rows 1 and 2.

Reverse

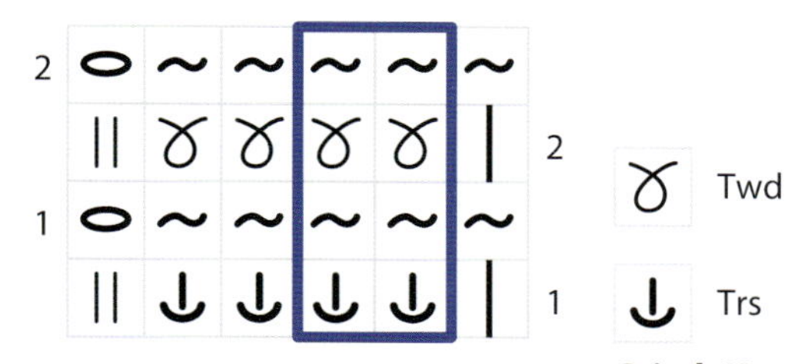

Stitch Key

Twd

Trs

129 FPTC & BPTC HORIZONTAL STRIPE

Worked over any number of stitches and 2 rows.
Row 1: Fptc rep.
Row 2: Bptc rep.
Repeat Rows 1 and 2.

Reverse

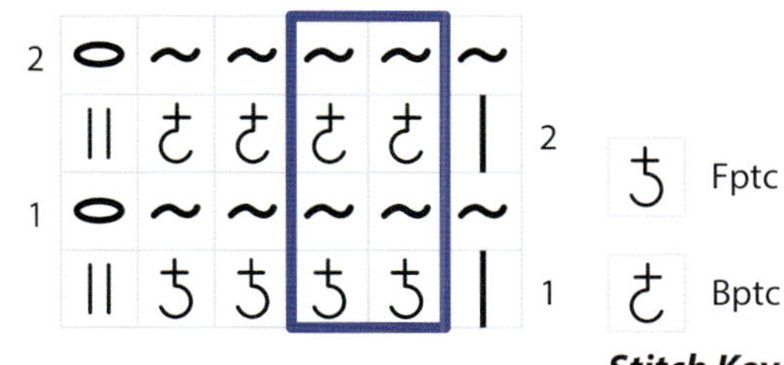

Stitch Key

Fptc

Bptc

130 PFPTC & TMSS HORIZONTAL STRIPE

Worked over any number of stitches and 2 rows.

Row 1: PFptc rep.

Row 2: Tmss rep.

Repeat Rows 1 and 2.

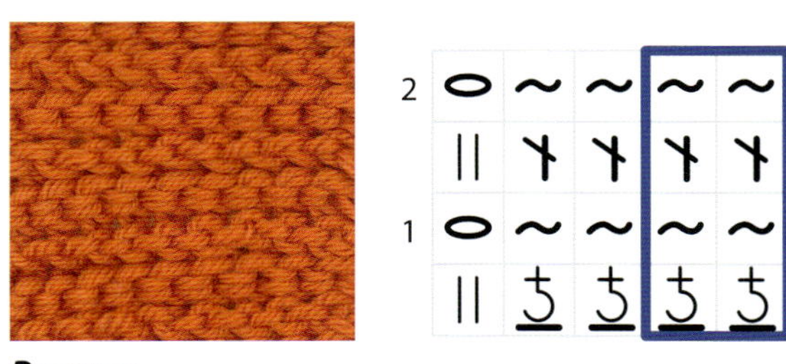

Reverse

PFptc

Tmss

Stitch Key

131 PFPTC & TKS HORIZONTAL STRIPE

Worked over any number of stitches and 2 rows.

Row 1: PFptc rep.

Row 2: Tks rep.

Repeat Rows 1 and 2.

Reverse

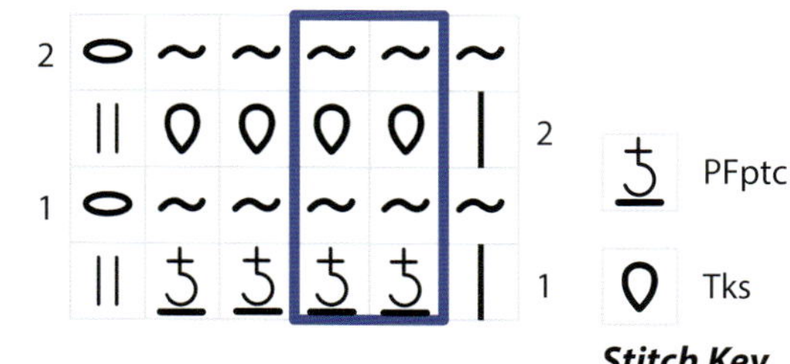

PFptc

Tks

Stitch Key

132 TSS & TBSS HORIZONTAL STRIPE

Worked over any number of stitches and 2 rows.

Row 1: Tss rep.

Row 2: Tbss rep.

Repeat Rows 1 and 2.

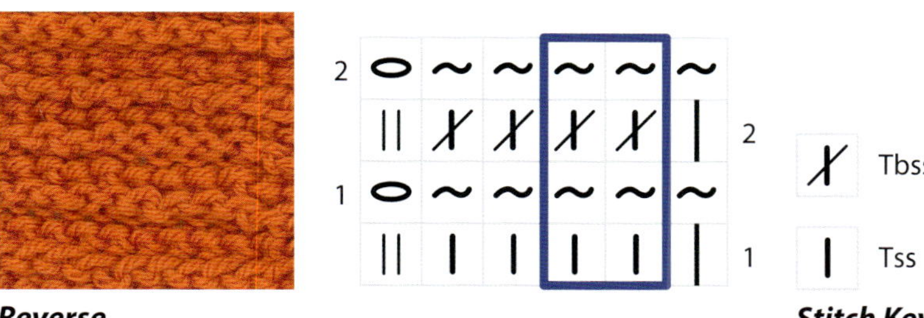

Reverse

Stitch Key

133 TKS & TBSS HORIZONTAL STRIPE

Worked over any number of stitches and 2 rows.

Row 1: Tks rep.

Row 2: Tbss rep.

Repeat Rows 1 and 2.

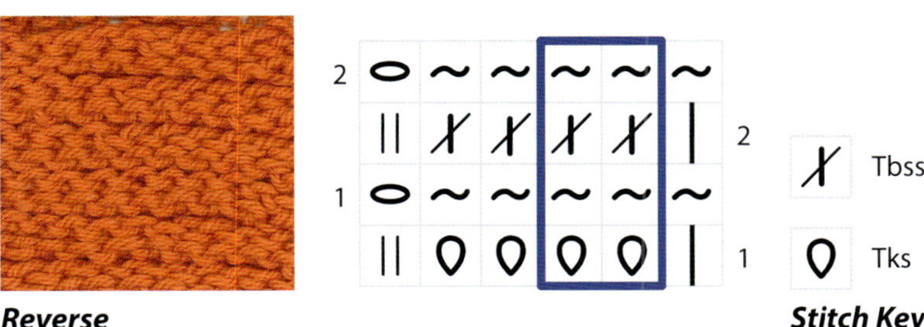

Reverse

Stitch Key

134 TRS & TBSS HORIZONTAL STRIPE

Worked over any number of stitches and 2 rows.

Row 1: Trs rep.

Row 2: Tbss rep.

Repeat Rows 1 and 2.

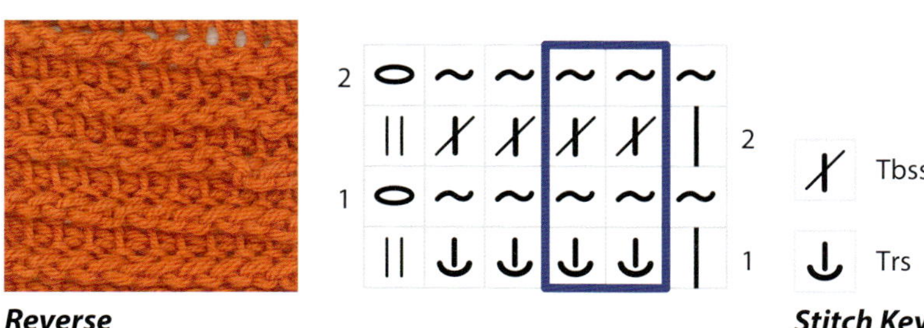

Reverse

Stitch Key

135 TPS & TBSS HORIZONTAL STRIPE

Worked over any number of stitches and 2 rows.

Row 1: Tps rep.

Row 2: Tbss rep.

Repeat Rows 1 and 2.

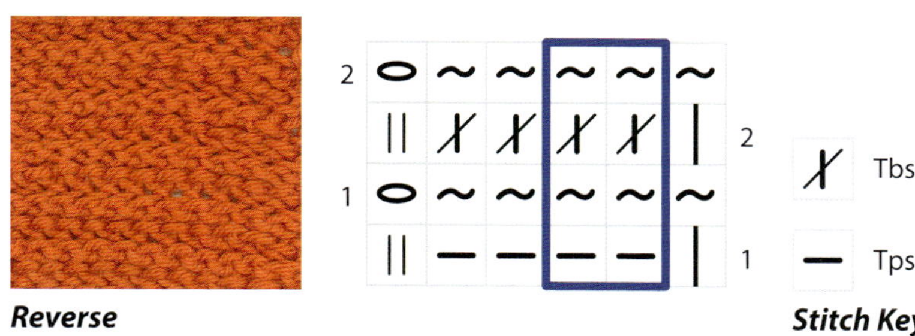

Reverse

Stitch Key

136 TWD & TBSS HORIZONTAL STRIPE

Worked over any number of stitches and 2 rows.

Row 1: Twd rep.

Row 2: Tbss rep.

Repeat Rows 1 and 2.

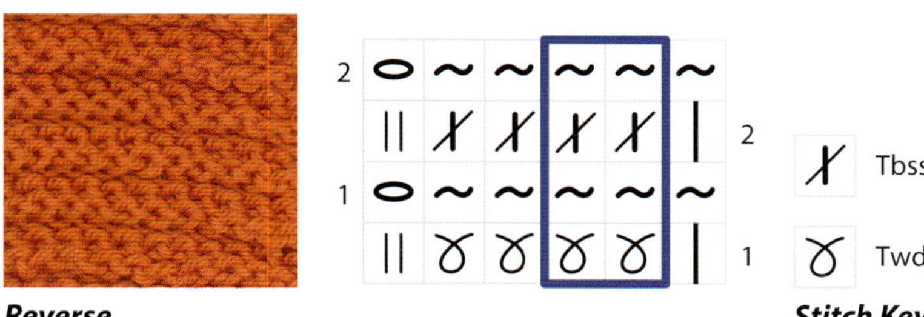

Reverse

Stitch Key

137 TMSS & PTKS HORIZONTAL STRIPE

Worked over any number of stitches and 2 rows.

Row 1: Tmss rep.

Row 2: Ptks rep.

Repeat Rows 1 and 2.

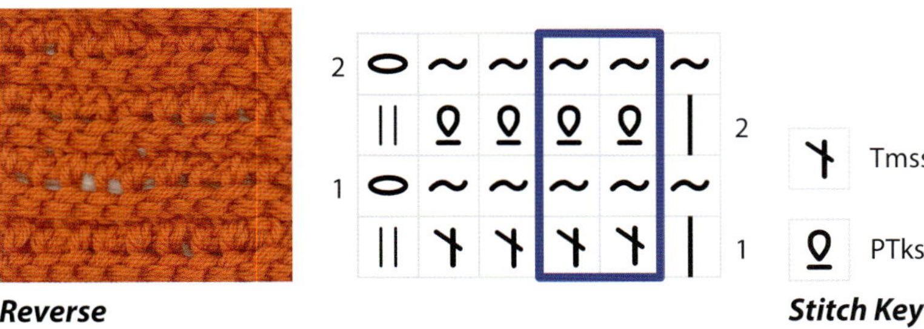

Reverse

Stitch Key

138 TMSS & TMRS HORIZONTAL STRIPE

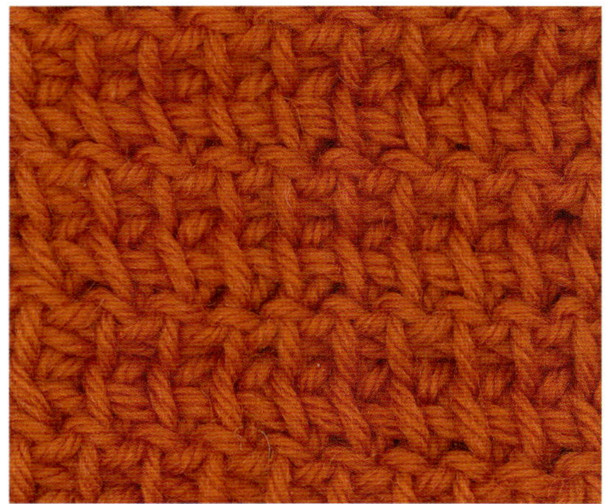

Worked over any number of stitches and 2 rows.

Row 1: Tmss rep.

Row 2: Tmrs rep.

Repeat Rows 1 and 2.

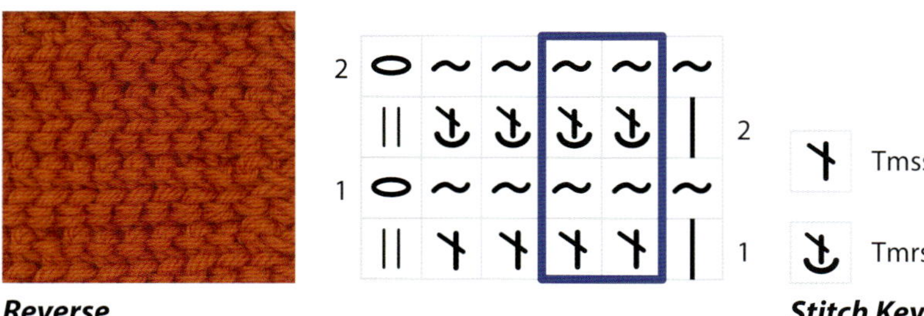

Reverse

Stitch Key

139 TWTKS & TPS HORIZONTAL STRIPE

Worked over any number of stitches and 2 rows.

Row 1: TwTks rep.

Row 2: Tps rep.

Repeat Rows 1 and 2.

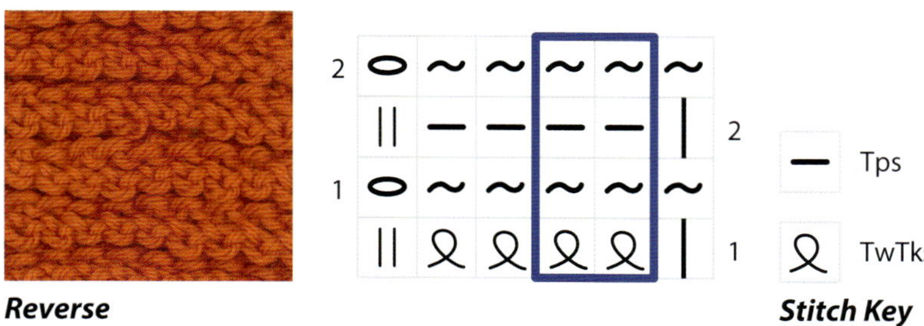

Reverse

Stitch Key

140 TSSBTH & TPS HORIZONTAL STRIPE

Worked over any number of stitches and 2 rows.

Row 1: TssBtH rep.

Row 2: Tps rep.

Repeat Rows 1 and 2.

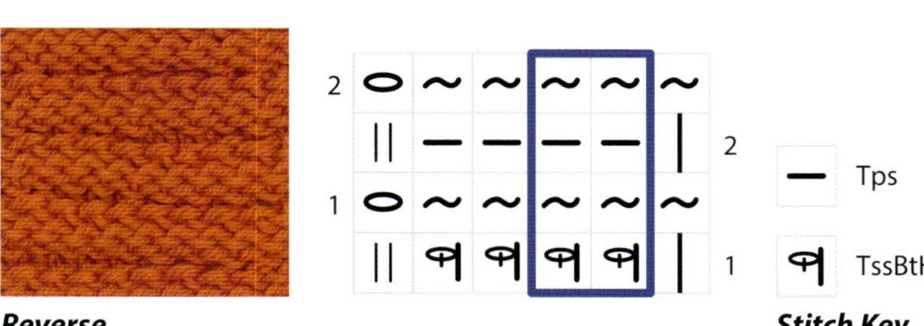

Reverse

Stitch Key

141 TSS & TDC HORIZONTAL STRIPE

Worked over any number of stitches and 2 rows.

Row 1: Tss rep.

Row 2: Tdc rep.

Repeat Rows 1 and 2.

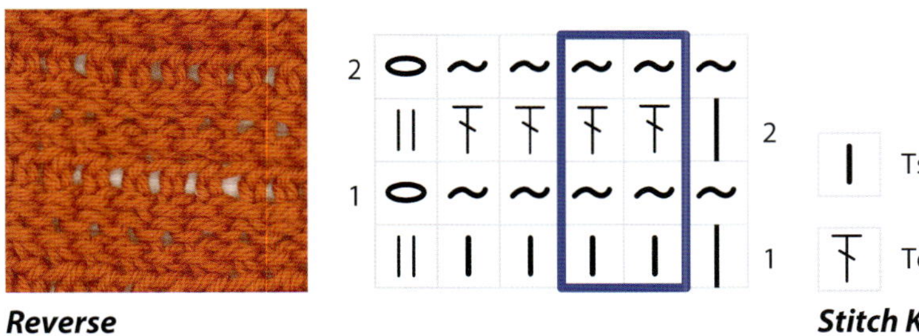

Reverse

Stitch Key

Honeycomb Stitches

142 TSS & TKS HONEYCOMB

Worked over a multiple of 2 stitches and 2 rows.

Row 1: [Tss, Tks] rep.

Row 2: [Tks, Tss] rep.

Repeat Rows 1 and 2.

Reverse

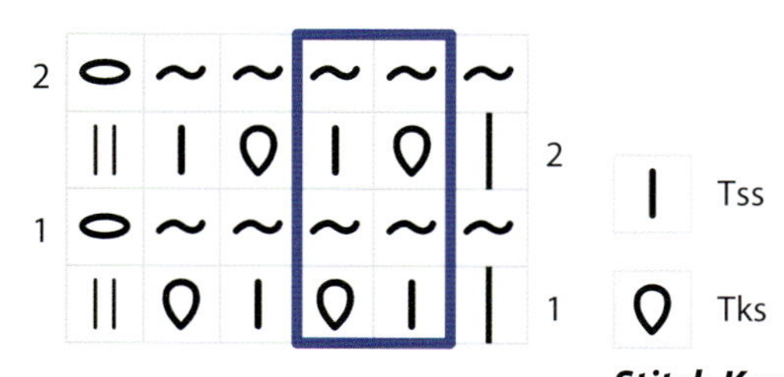

Stitch Key

143 TSS & TRS HONEYCOMB

Worked over a multiple of 2 stitches and 2 rows.

Row 1: [Tss, Trs] rep.

Row 2: [Trs, Tss] rep.

Repeat Rows 1 and 2.

Reverse

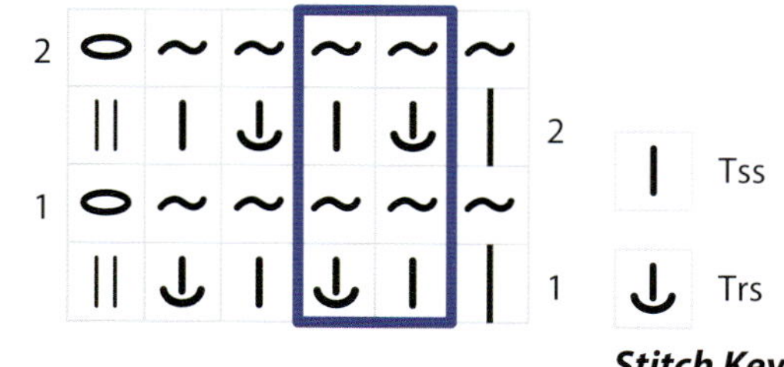

Stitch Key

144 TSS & TPS HONEYCOMB

Worked over a multiple of 2 stitches and 2 rows.

Row 1: [Tss, Tps] rep.

Row 2: [Tps, Tss] rep.

Repeat Rows 1 and 2.

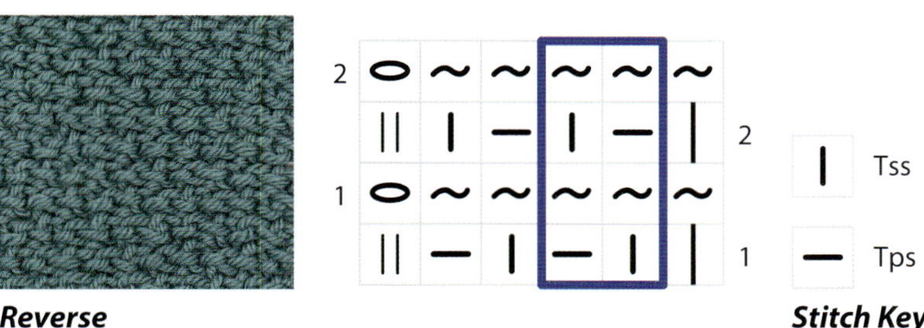

Reverse

Stitch Key

145 TSS & TWD HONEYCOMB

Worked over a multiple of 2 stitches and 2 rows.

Row 1: [Tss, Twd] rep.

Row 2: [Twd, Tss] rep.

Repeat Rows 1 and 2.

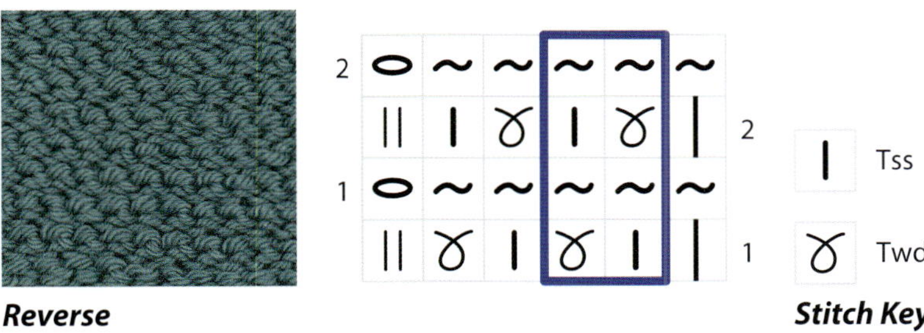

Reverse

Stitch Key

146 TSS & TWTKS HONEYCOMB

Worked over a multiple of 2 stitches and 2 rows.

Row 1: [Tss, TwTks] rep.

Row 2: [TwTks, Tss] rep.

Repeat Rows 1 and 2.

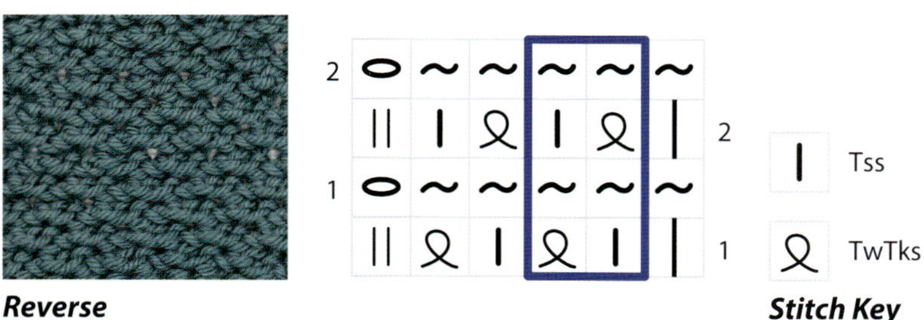

Reverse

Stitch Key

147 TSS & TPSU HONEYCOMB

Worked over a multiple of 2 stitches and 2 rows.

Row 1: [Tss, Tpsu] rep.

Row 2: [Tpsu, Tss] rep.

Repeat Rows 1 and 2.

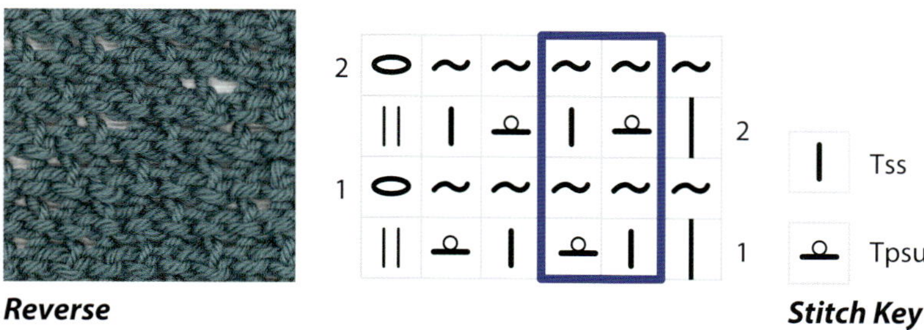

Reverse

Stitch Key

148 TKS & TRS HONEYCOMB

Worked over a multiple of 2 stitches and 2 rows.

Row 1: [Tks, Trs] rep.

Row 2: [Trs, Tks] rep.

Repeat Rows 1 and 2.

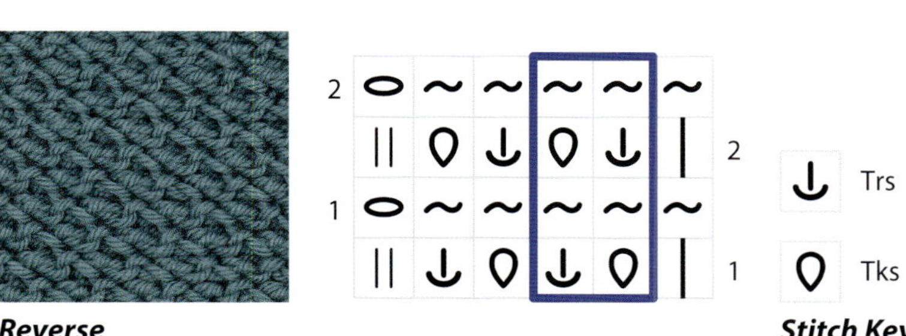

Reverse

Stitch Key

149 TKS & TPS HONEYCOMB

Worked over a multiple of 2 stitches and 2 rows.

Row 1: [Tks, Tps] rep.

Row 2: [Tps, Tks] rep.

Repeat Rows 1 and 2.

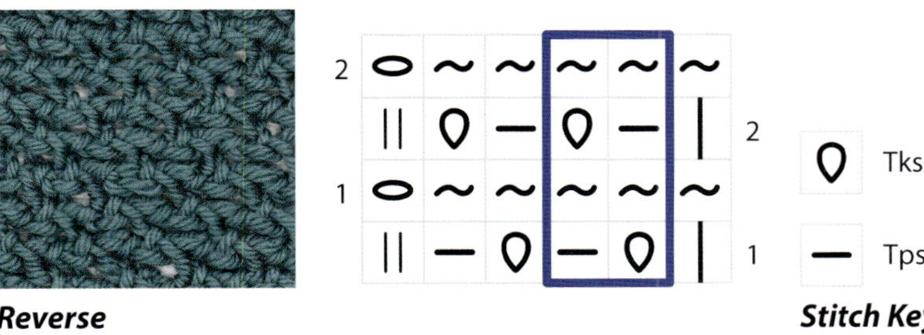

Reverse

Stitch Key

150 TKS & TWD HONEYCOMB

Worked over a multiple of 2 stitches and 2 rows.

Row 1: [Tks, Twd] rep.

Row 2: [Twd, Tks] rep.

Repeat Rows 1 and 2.

Reverse

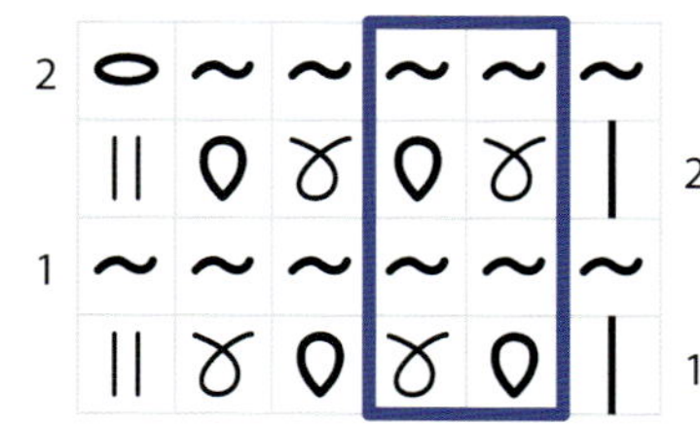

Tks

Twd

Stitch Key

151 TKS & PTKS HONEYCOMB

Worked over a multiple of 2 stitches and 2 rows.

Row 1: [Tks, PTks] rep.

Row 2: [PTks, Tks] rep.

Repeat Rows 1 and 2.

Reverse

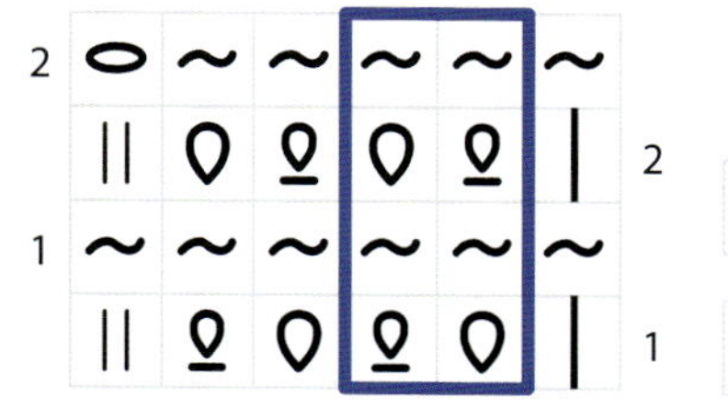

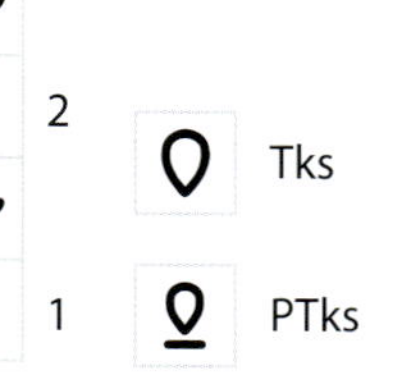

Stitch Key

152 TRS & TPS HONEYCOMB

Worked over a multiple of 2 stitches and 2 rows.

Row 1: [Trs, Tps] rep.

Row 2: [Tps, Trs] rep.

Repeat Rows 1 and 2.

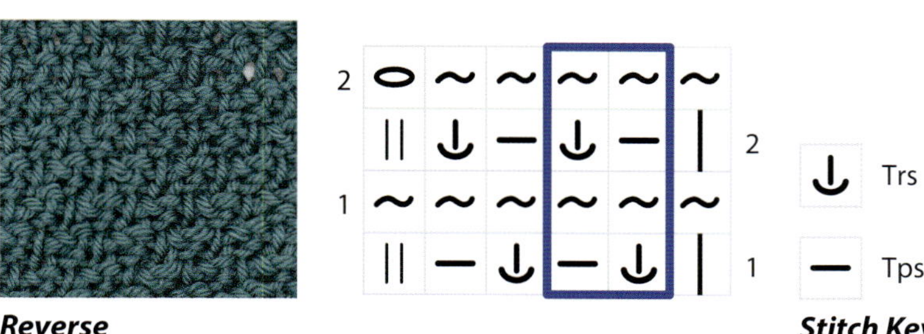

Reverse

Stitch Key

153 TRS & TWD HONEYCOMB

Worked over a multiple of 2 stitches and 2 rows.

Row 1: [Trs, Twd] rep.

Row 2: [Twd, Trs] rep.

Repeat Rows 1 and 2.

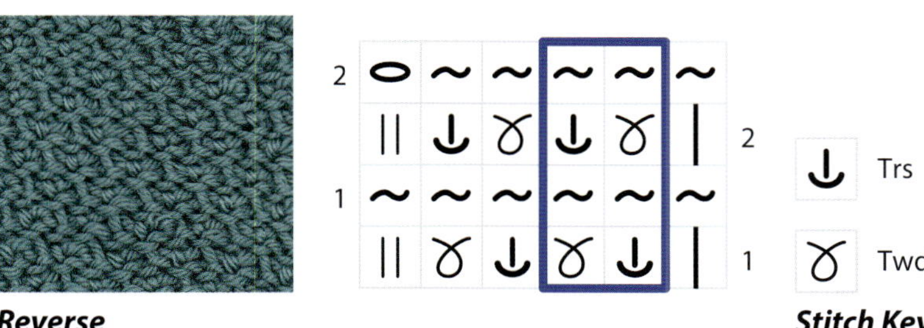

Reverse

Stitch Key

154 TPS & TWD HONEYCOMB

Worked over a multiple of 2 stitches and 2 rows.

Row 1: [Tps, Twd] rep.

Row 2: [Twd, Tps] rep.

Repeat Rows 1 and 2.

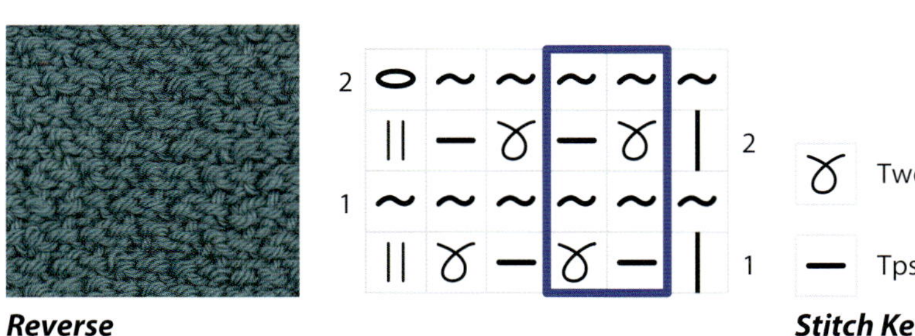

Reverse

Stitch Key

155 TPS & PTKS HONEYCOMB

Worked over a multiple of 2 stitches and 2 rows.

Row 1: [Tps, PTks] rep.

Row 2: [PTks, Tps] rep.

Repeat Rows 1 and 2.

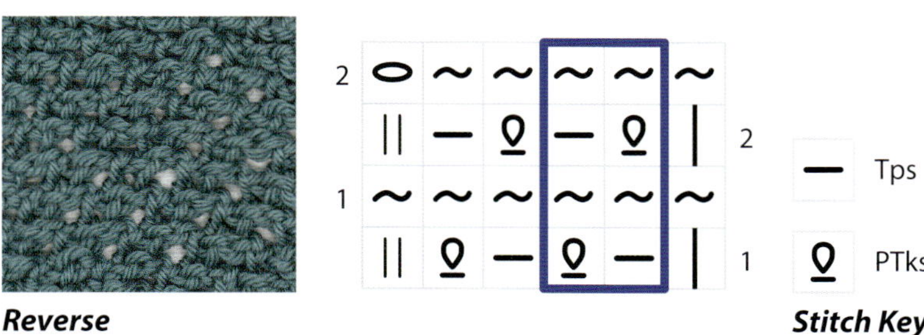

Reverse

Stitch Key

156 FPTC & BPTC HONEYCOMB

Worked over a multiple of 2 stitches and 2 rows.
Row 1: [Fptc, Bptc] rep.
Row 2: [Bptc, Fptc] rep.
Repeat Rows 1 and 2.

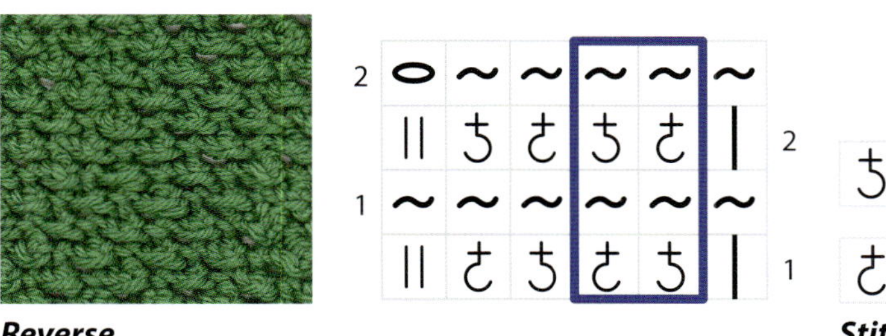

Reverse

Fptc

Bptc

Stitch Key

157 EXFPTC & EXBPTC HONEYCOMB

Worked over a multiple of 2 stitches and 2 rows.
Row 1: [ExFptc, ExBptc] rep.
Row 2: [ExBptc, ExFptc] rep.
Repeat Rows 1 and 2.

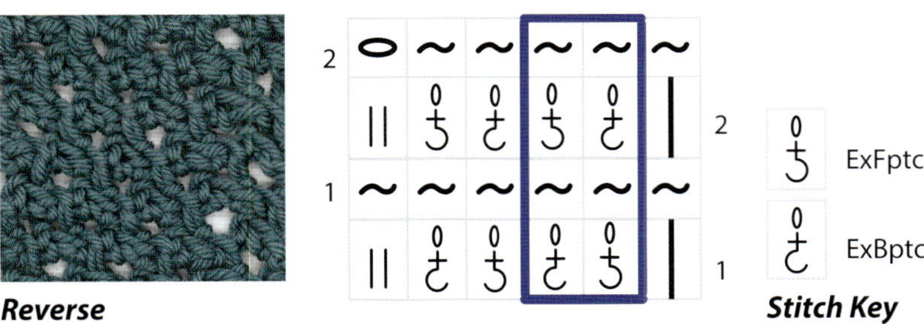

Reverse

ExFptc

ExBptc

Stitch Key

158 FPTCDC & BPTCDC HONEYCOMB

Worked over a multiple of 2 stitches and 2 rows.

Row 1: [FptcDc, BptcDc] rep.

Row 2: [BptcDc, FptcDc] rep.

Repeat Rows 1 and 2.

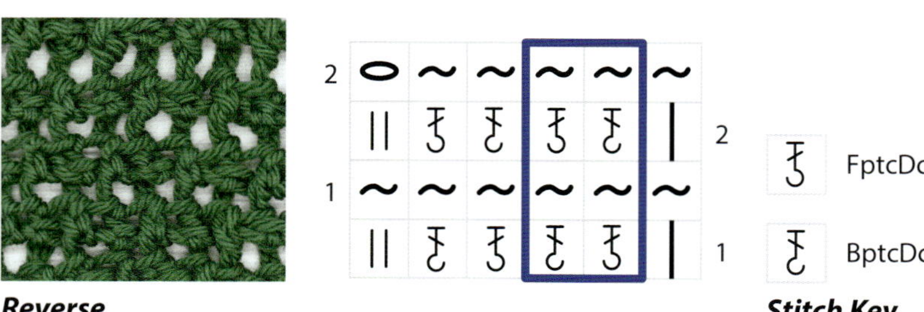

Reverse

Stitch Key

159 TBSS & TSS HONEYCOMB

Worked over a multiple of 2 stitches and 2 rows.

Row 1: [Tbss, Tss] rep.

Row 2: [Tss, Tbss] rep.

Repeat Rows 1 and 2.

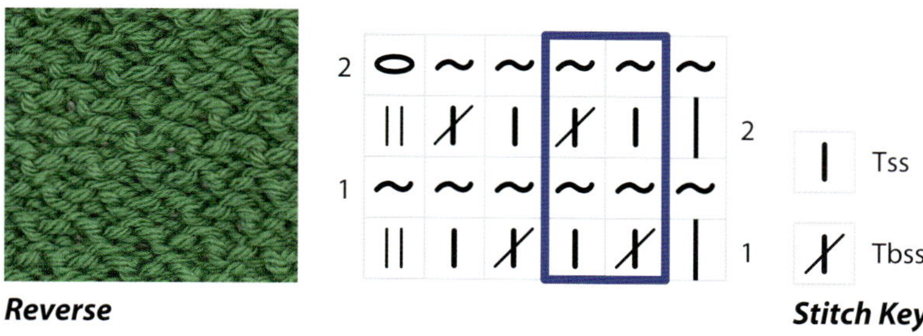

Reverse

Stitch Key

160 TBSS & TKS HONEYCOMB

Worked over a multiple of 2 stitches and 2 rows.

Row 1: [Tbss, Tks] rep.

Row 2: [Tks, Tbss] rep.

Repeat Rows 1 and 2.

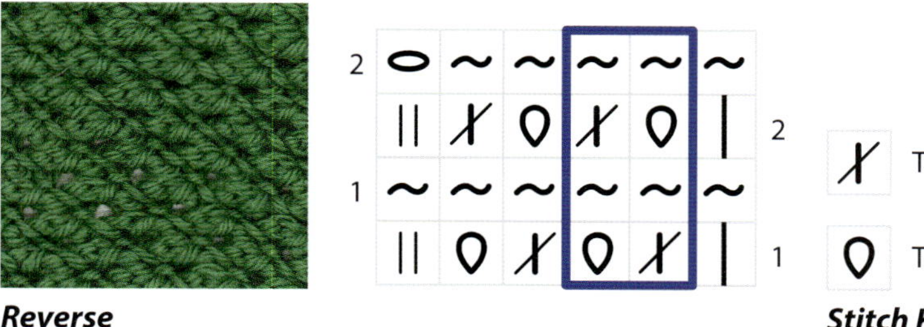

Reverse

Tbss

Tks

Stitch Key

161 TBSS & TRS HONEYCOMB

Worked over a multiple of 2 stitches and 2 rows.

Row 1: [Tbss, Trs] rep.

Row 2: [Trs, Tbss] rep.

Repeat Rows 1 and 2.

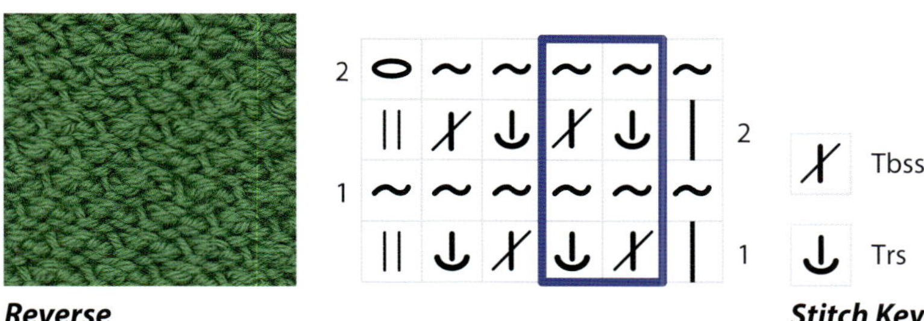

Reverse

Tbss

Trs

Stitch Key

162 TBSS & TPS HONEYCOMB

Worked over a multiple of 2 stitches and 2 rows.

Row 1: [Tbss, Tps] rep.

Row 2: [Tps, Tbss] rep.

Repeat Rows 1 and 2.

Reverse

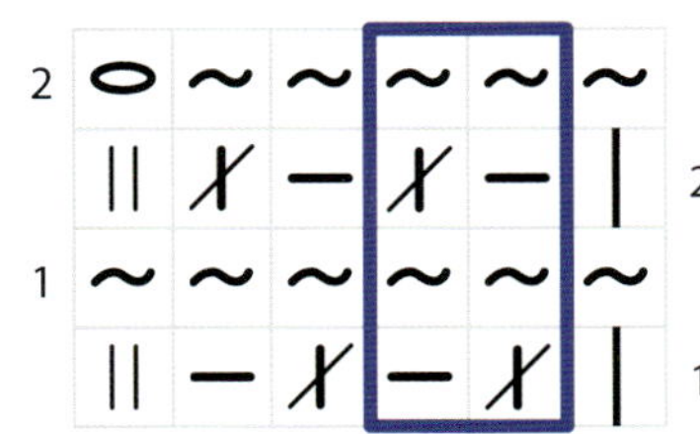

Stitch Key

163 TFRS & TSS HONEYCOMB

Worked over a multiple of 2 stitches and 2 rows.

Row 1: [Tfrs, Tss] rep.

Row 2: [Tss, Tfrs] rep.

Repeat Rows 1 and 2.

Reverse

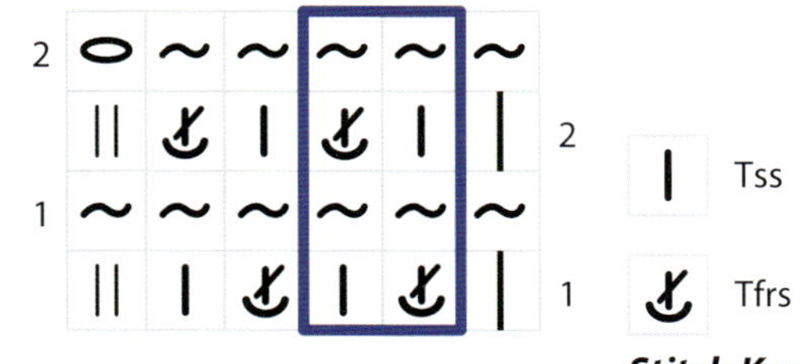

Stitch Key

164 TFRS & TKS HONEYCOMB

Worked over a multiple of 2 stitches and 2 rows.

Row 1: [Tfrs, Tks] rep.

Row 2: [Tks, Tfrs] rep.

Repeat Rows 1 and 2.

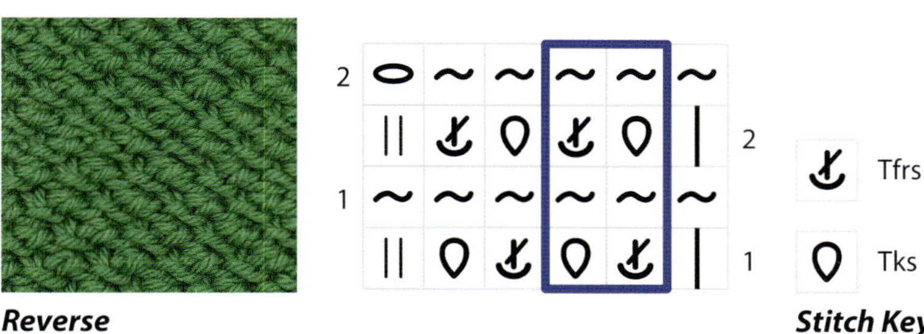

Reverse

Stitch Key

165 TFRS & TPS HONEYCOMB

Worked over a multiple of 2 stitches and 2 rows.

Row 1: [Tfrs, Tps] rep.

Row 2: [Tps, Tfrs] rep.

Repeat Rows 1 and 2.

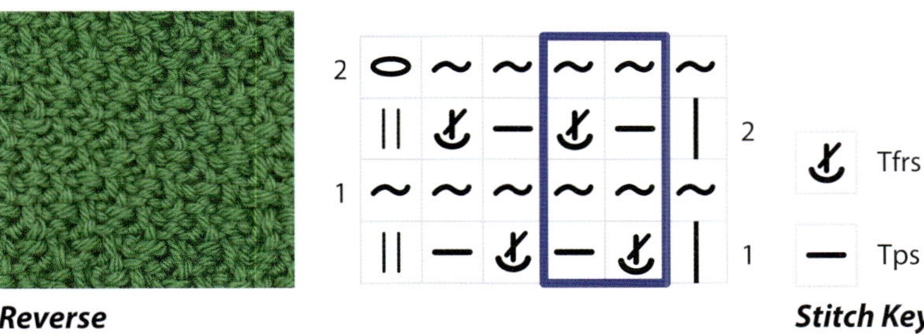

Reverse

Stitch Key

166 TFRS & TRS HONEYCOMB

Worked over a multiple of 2 stitches and 2 rows.

Row 1: [Tfrs, Trs] rep.

Row 2: [Trs, Tfrs] rep.

Repeat Rows 1 and 2.

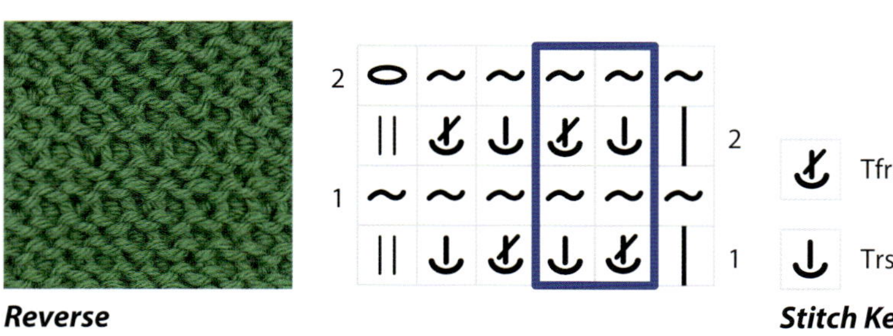

Reverse

Stitch Key

167 TKS & TWTKS HONEYCOMB

Worked over a multiple of 2 stitches and 2 rows.

Row 1: [Tks, TwTks] rep.

Row 2: [TwTks, Tks] rep.

Repeat Rows 1 and 2.

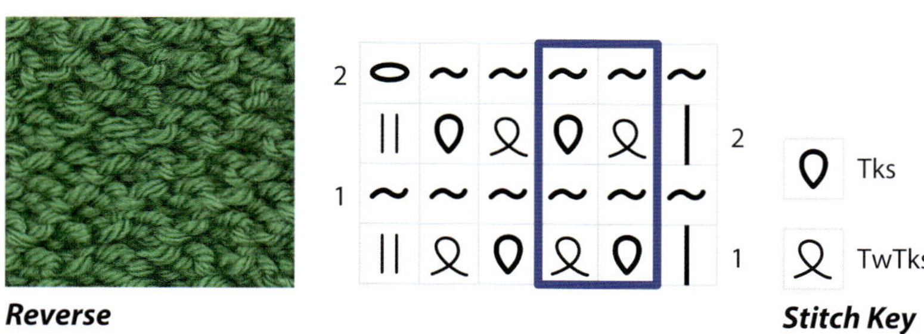

Reverse

Stitch Key

168 TSS & TWUP HONEYCOMB

Worked over a multiple of 2 stitches and 2 rows.

Row 1: [Tss, Twup] rep.

Row 2: [Twup, Tss] rep.

Repeat Rows 1 and 2.

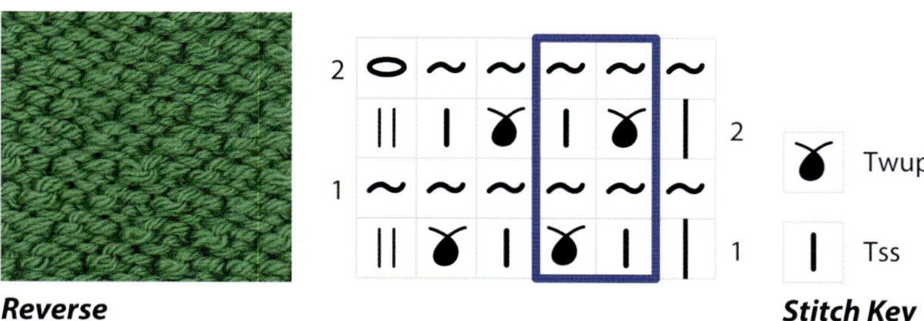

Reverse

Stitch Key

169 TDC & TPS HONEYCOMB

Worked over a multiple of 2 stitches and 2 rows.

Row 1: [Tdc, Tps] rep.

Row 2: [Tps, Tdc] rep.

Repeat Rows 1 and 2.

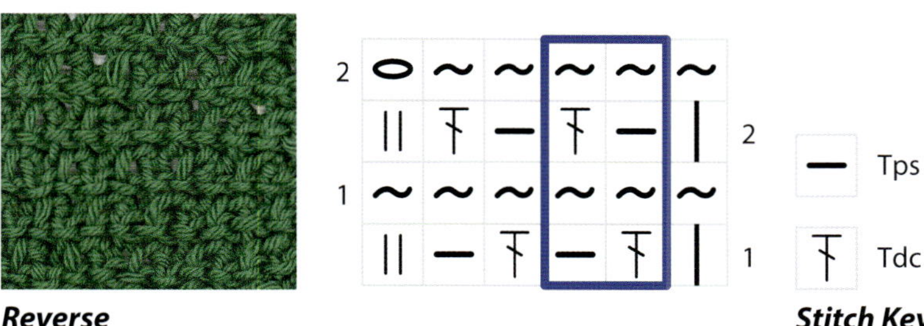

Reverse

Stitch Key

170 TFS & TTOP HONEYCOMB

Worked over a multiple of 2 stitches and 2 rows.
Row 1: [Tfs, Ttop] rep.
Row 2: [Ttop, Tfs] rep.
Repeat Rows 1 and 2.

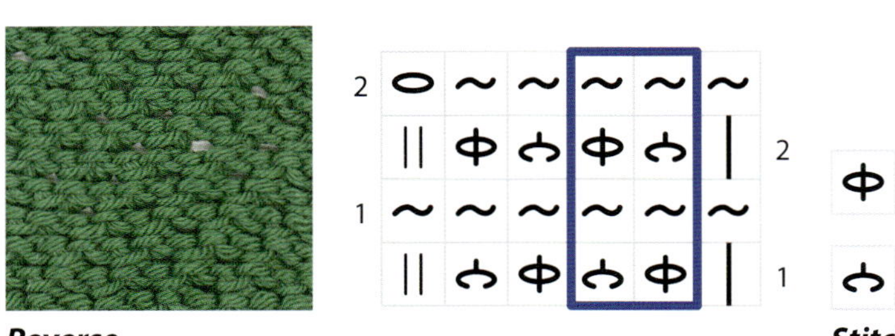

Reverse

Tfs

Ttop

Stitch Key

171 EXTKS & TPS HONEYCOMB

Worked over a multiple of 2 stitches and 2 rows.
Row 1: [ExTks, Tps] rep.
Row 2: [Tps, ExTks] rep.
Repeat Rows 1 and 2.

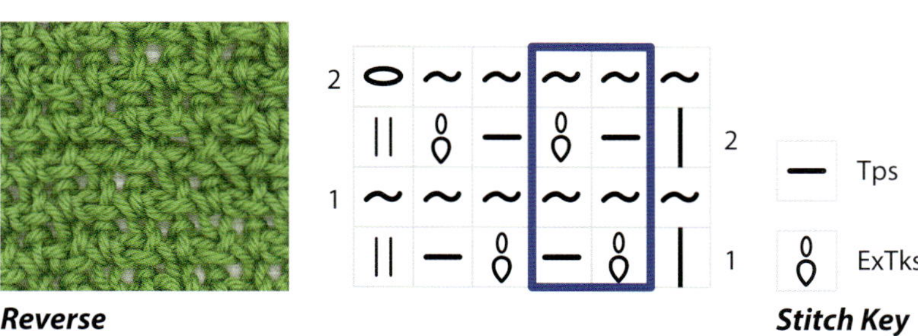

Reverse

Tps

ExTks

Stitch Key

Basketweave Stitches

172 TSS & TKS BASKETWEAVE

Reverse

Worked over a multiple of 4 stitches and 4 rows.

Rows 1 and 2: [Tss 2, Tks 2] rep.

Rows 3 and 4: [Tks 2, Tss 2] rep.

Repeat Rows 1–4.

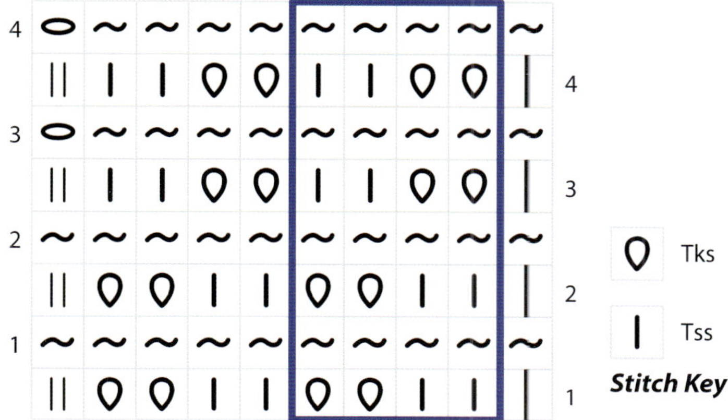

173 TSS & TPS BASKETWEAVE

Reverse

Worked over a multiple of 4 stitches and 4 rows.

Rows 1 and 2: [Tss 2, Tps 2] rep.

Rows 3 and 4: [Tps 2, Tss 2] rep.

Repeat Rows 1–4.

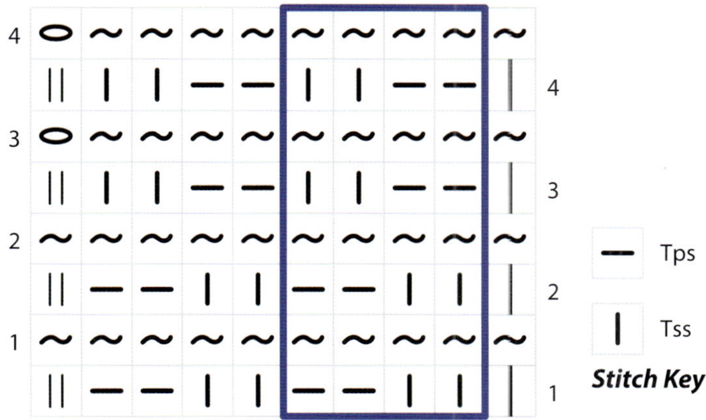

174 TSS & TRS BASKETWEAVE

Reverse

Worked over a multiple of 4 stitches and 4 rows.

Rows 1 and 2: [Tss 2, Trs 2] rep.

Rows 3 and 4: [Trs 2, Tss 2] rep.

Repeat Rows 1–4.

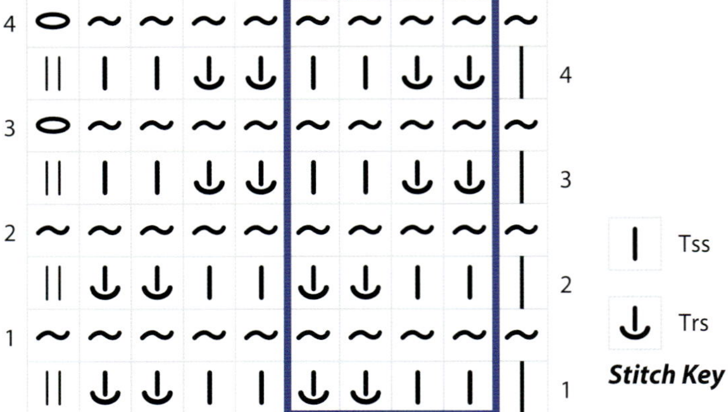

175 TKS & TRS BASKETWEAVE

Reverse

Worked over a multiple of 4 stitches and 4 rows.

Rows 1 and 2: [Tks 2, Trs 2] rep.

Rows 3 and 4: [Trs 2, Tks 2] rep.

Repeat Rows 1–4.

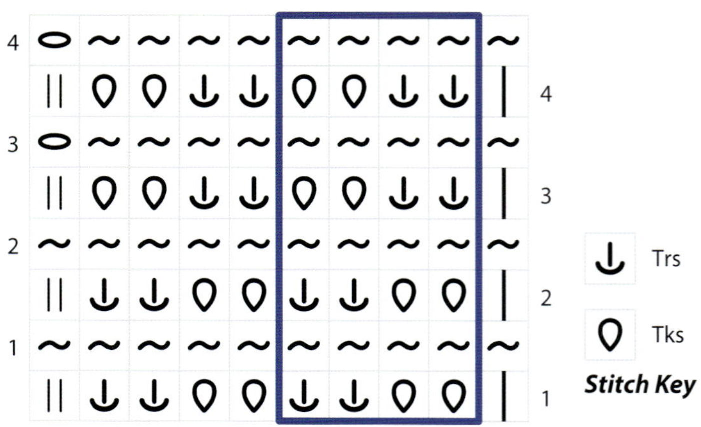

176 TKS & TPS BASKETWEAVE

Reverse

Worked over a multiple of 4 stitches and 4 rows.

Rows 1 and 2: [Tks 2, Tps 2] rep.

Rows 3 and 4: [Tps 2, Tks 2] rep.

Repeat Rows 1–4.

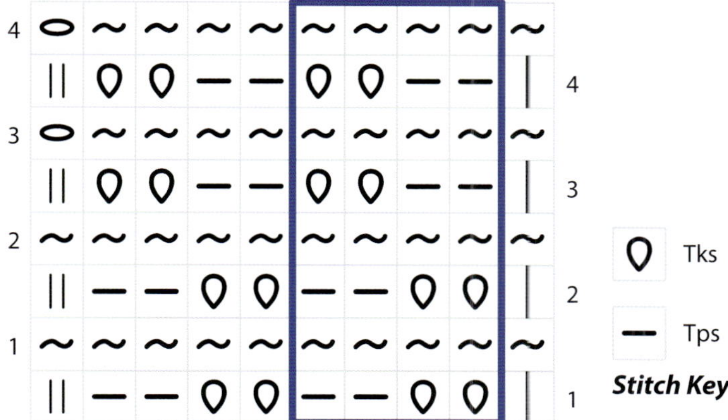

177 TPS & TRS BASKETWEAVE

Reverse

Worked over a multiple of 4 stitches and 4 rows.

Rows 1 and 2: [Tps 2, Trs 2] rep.

Rows 3 and 4: [Trs 2, Tps 2] rep.

Repeat Rows 1–4.

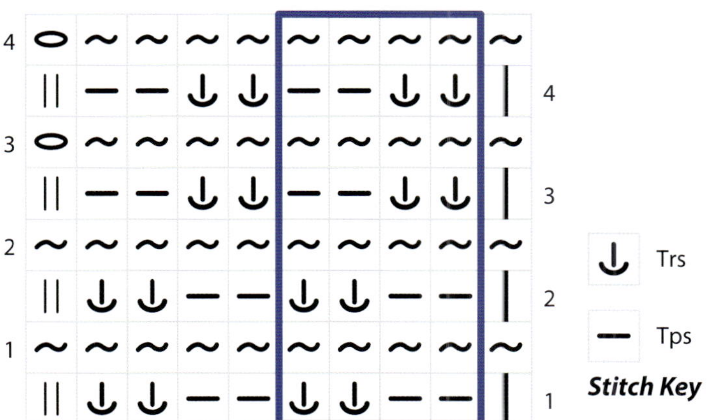

178 FPTC & BPTC BASKETWEAVE

Reverse

Worked over a multiple of 4 stitches and 4 rows.

Rows 1 and 2: [Fptc 2, Bptc 2] rep.

Rows 3 and 4: [Bptc 2, Fptc 2] rep.

Repeat Rows 1–4.

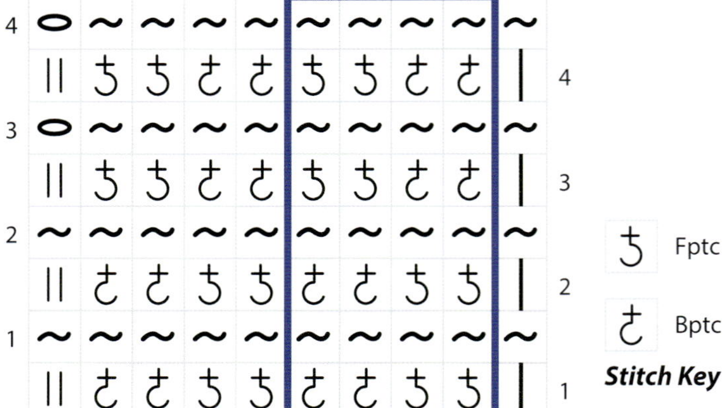

Stitch Key

179 FPTCDC & BPTCDC BASKETWEAVE

Reverse

Worked over a multiple of 4 stitches and 4 rows.

Rows 1 and 2: [FptcDc 2, BptcDc 2] rep.

Rows 3 and 4: [BptcDc 2, FptcDc 2] rep.

Repeat Rows 1–4.

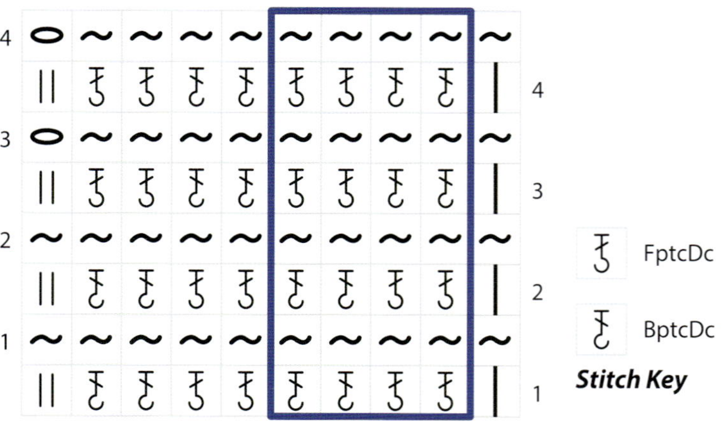

Stitch Key

Other Stitch Patterns

180 TUNISIAN CROSS STITCH (Tx)

Worked over a multiple of 2 stitches.

Tx: Skip the first stitch, Tss in second stitch (photo 1), and then Tss in the first stitch (photo 2). This stitch can also be thought of as a 1/1 F cable (see page 179).

Row 1: Tx rep.

Repeat Row 1.

Reverse

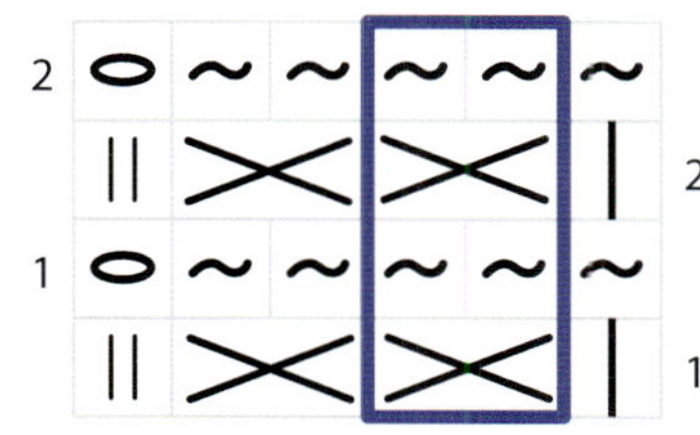

Stitch Key

181 CROSS STITCH OFFSET

Worked over a multiple of 2 + 2 stitches and 2 rows.

Row 1: Tx rep.

Row 2: Tss, Tx rep until 1 st rem, Tss.

Repeat Rows 1 and 2.

Reverse

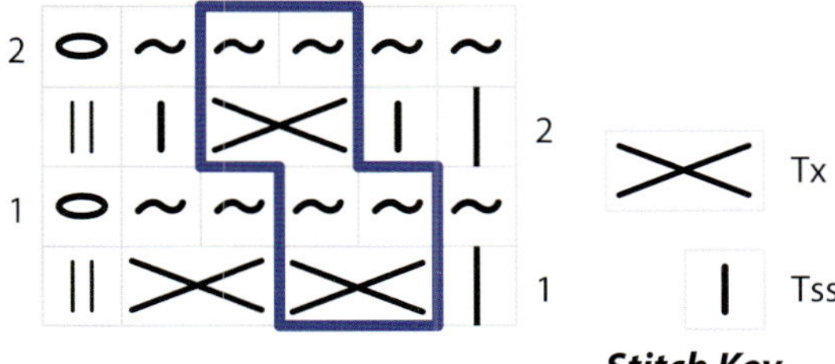

Stitch Key

182 CROSS STITCH ELONGATED

Worked over a multiple of 2 + 2 stitches and 4 rows.

Rows 1 and 2: Tx rep.

Rows 3 and 4: Tss, Tx rep until 1 st rem, Tss.

Repeat Rows 1–4.

Reverse

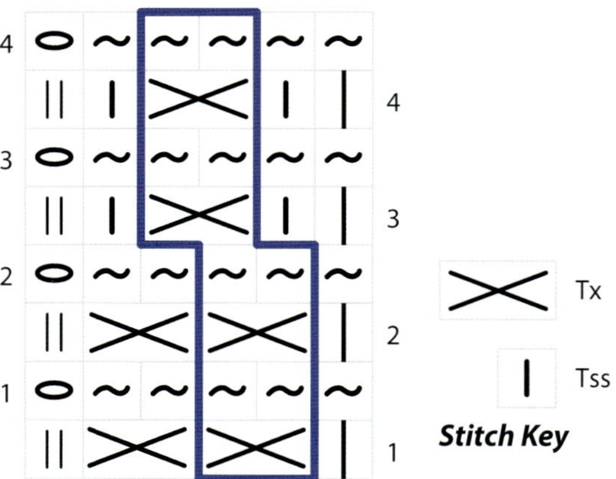

Tx

Tss

Stitch Key

183 CROSS STITCH EXTENDED (ExTx)

Worked over a multiple of 2 stitches.

ExTx: Skip the first stitch, Tss in second stitch and ch1, and then Tss in the first stitch and ch1.

Row 1: ExTx rep.

Repeat Row 1.

Reverse

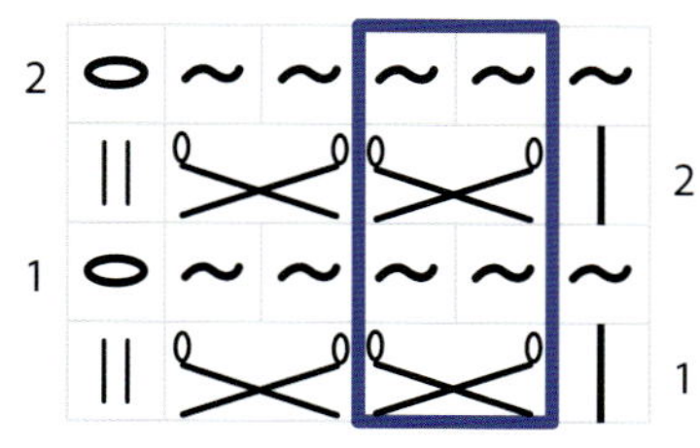

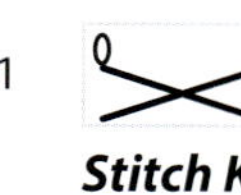

ExTx

Stitch Key

184 SLIDING CROSS STITCH

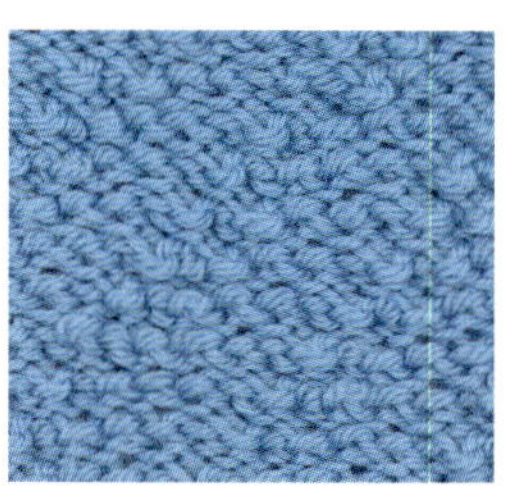

Reverse

Worked over a multiple of 6 + 6 stitches and 6 rows.

Row 1: [Tx 2, Tss 2] rep.

Row 2: [Tss, Tx 2, Tss] rep.

Row 3: [Tss 2, Tx 2] rep.

Row 4: Tss3, [Tx 2, Tss 2] rep until 3 sts rem, Tx, Tss.

Row 5: Tx, Tss, [Tss, Tx 2, Tss] rep until 3 sts rem, Tss, Tx.

Row 6: Tss, Tx [Tss 2, Tx 2] rep until 3 sts rem, Tss 3.

Repeat Rows 1–6.

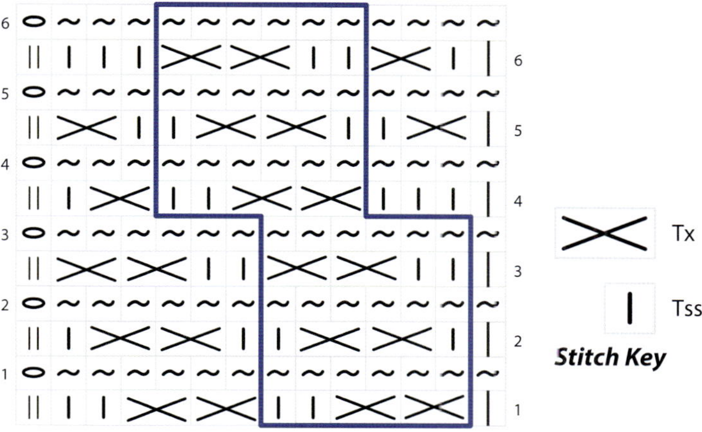

185 LATTICE STITCH (L-St)

Worked over a multiple of 2 stitches.

L-St: Tss2Tog in the next 2 stitches (photo 1), and then Tss in the first stitch (photo 2).

Row 1: L-St rep.

Repeat Row 1.

Reverse

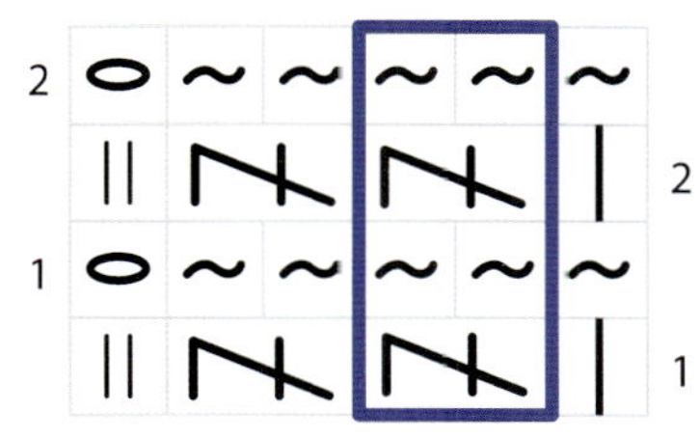

186 LATTICE STITCH OFFSET

Worked over a multiple of 2 + 2 stitches and 2 rows.

Row 1: L-St.

Row 2: Tss, L-St rep until 1 st rem, Tss.

Repeat Rows 1 and 2.

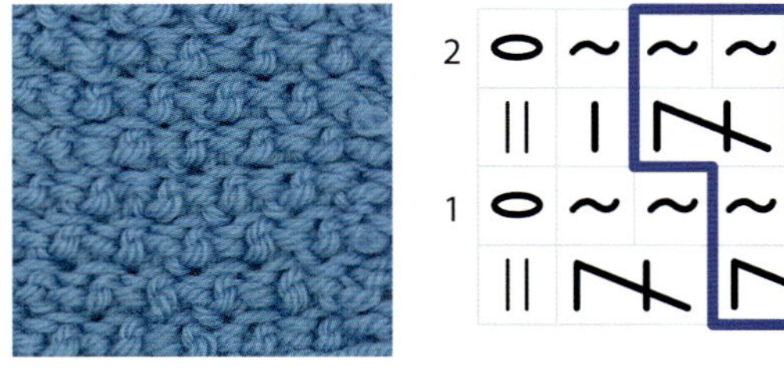

Reverse

L-St

Tss

Stitch Key

187 LATTICE STITCH ELONGATED

Worked over a multiple of 2 + 2 stitches and 4 rows.

Rows 1 and 2: L-St.

Rows 3 and 4: Tss, L-St rep until 1 st rem, Tss.

Repeat Rows 1–4.

Reverse

L-St

Tss

Stitch Key

188 LATTICE STITCH ENLARGED

Reverse

Worked over a multiple of 2 + 2 stitches and 4 rows.

Row 1: L-St rep.

Row 2: Tss.

Row 3: Tss, L-St rep until 1 st rem, Tss.

Row 4: Tss.

Repeat Rows 1–4.

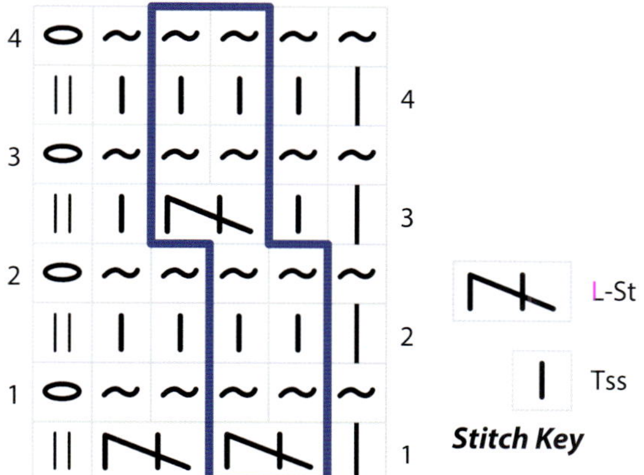

189 BAMBOO STITCH 2 (B-St2)

Worked over a multiple of 2 stitches.

B-St2: Yo (photo 1), Tss in the next 2 stitches (photo 2), pull yo over 2 loops on hook (photo 3).

Row 1: B-St2.

Repeat Row 1.

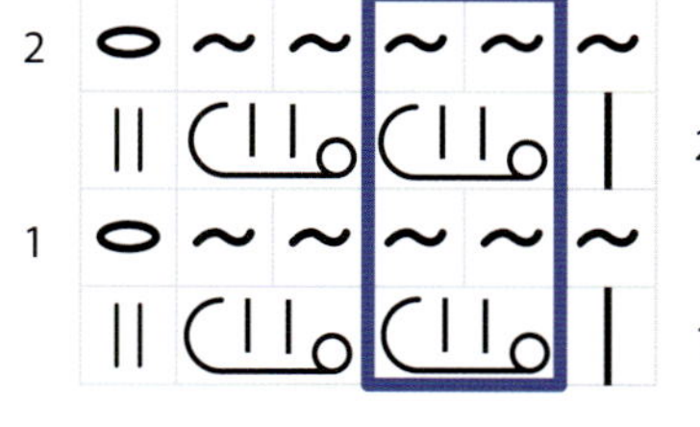

Reverse

190 BAMBOO STITCH 3 (B-St3)

Worked over 3 stitches.

B-St3: Yo, Tss in the next 3 stitches, pull yo over 3 loops on hook.

Row 1: B-St3.

Repeat Row 1.

Reverse

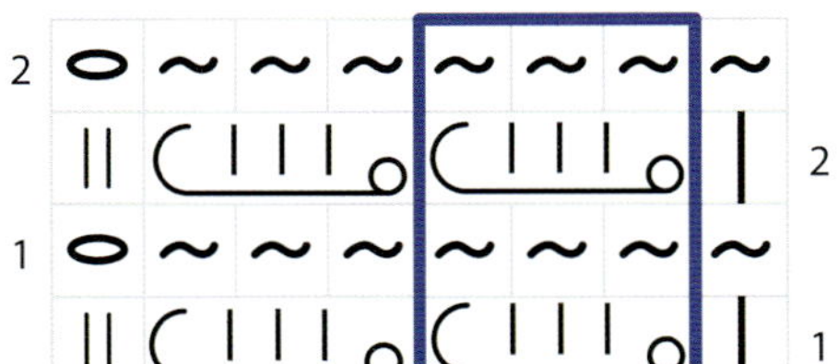

B-St3

191 BAMBOO STITCH 2 OFFSET

Worked over a multiple of 2 + 2 stitches and 2 rows.

Row 1: B-St2 rep.

Row 2: Tss, B-St2 rep until 1 st rem, Tss.

Repeat Rows 1 and 2.

Reverse

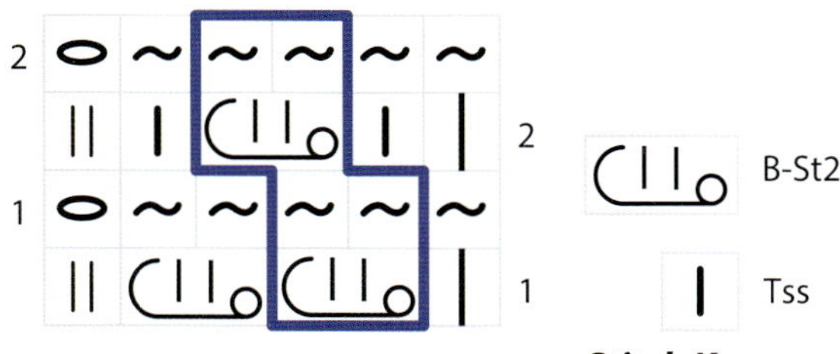

Stitch Key

192 BAMBOO STITCH 3 OFFSET

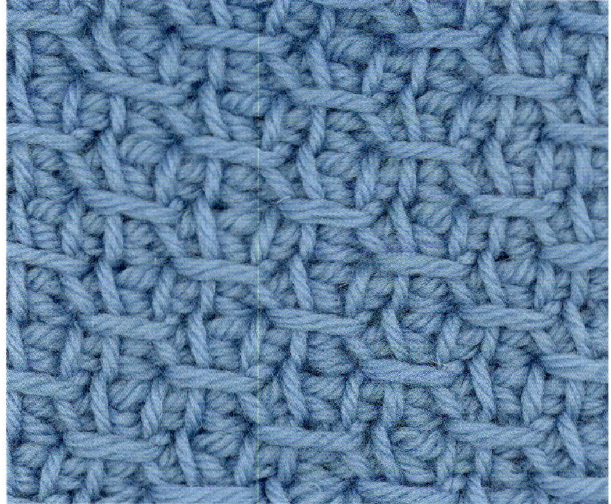

Worked over a multiple of 4 + 4 stitches and 2 rows.

Row 1: [B-St3, Tss] rep.

Row 2: Tss 2, [B-St3, Tss] rep until 2 st rem, Tss 2.

Repeat Rows 1 and 2.

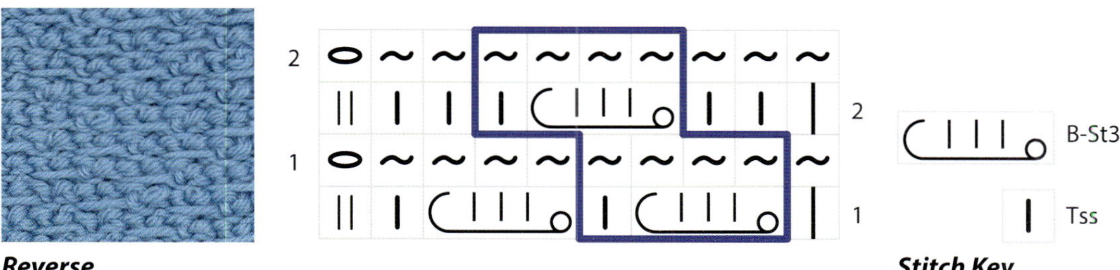

Reverse

Stitch Key

193 BAMBOO STITCH 2 WITH YARN UNDER (B-St2U)

Worked over a multiple of 2 stitches.

B-St2U: Yu, Tss in the next 2 stitches, pull yu over 2 loops on hook. *Hint:* Use your index finger to hold the yarn under in place while working the first Tss.

Row 1: B-St2U.

Repeat Row 1.

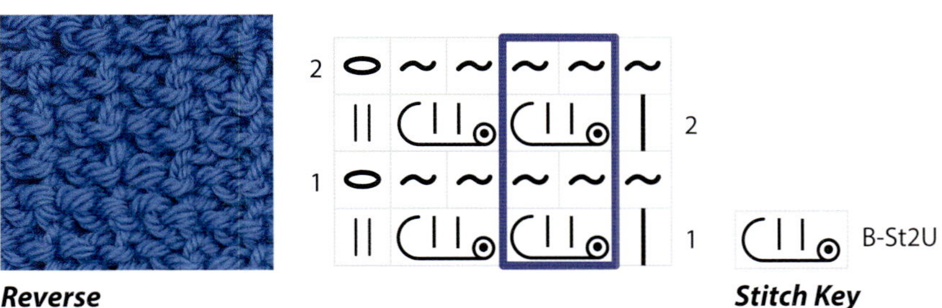

Reverse

Stitch Key

194 BAMBOO STITCH 2 WITH YARN UNDER OFFSET

Row 1: B-St2U.

Row 2: Tss, B-St2U rep until 1 st rem, Tss.

Repeat Rows 1 and 2.

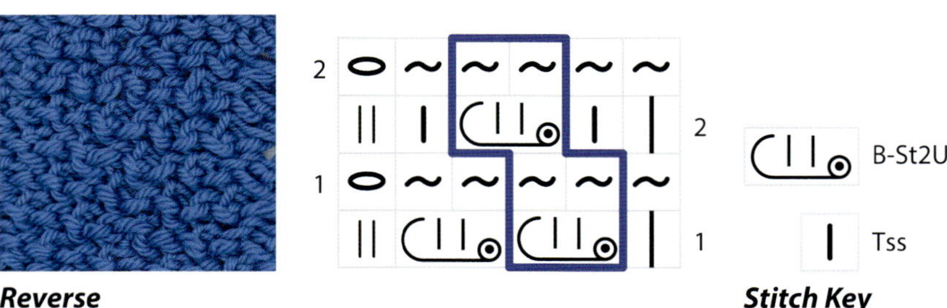

Reverse

Stitch Key

195 SMOCK STITCH

Worked over a multiple of 2 + 2 stitches and 2 rows.

Row 1: [yu, Tss2Tog] rep.

Hint: Use your index finger to hold the yarn under in place while working the Tss2Tog.

Row 2: Tss, [yu, Tss2Tog] rep until 1 st rem, Tss.

Repeat Rows 1 and 2.

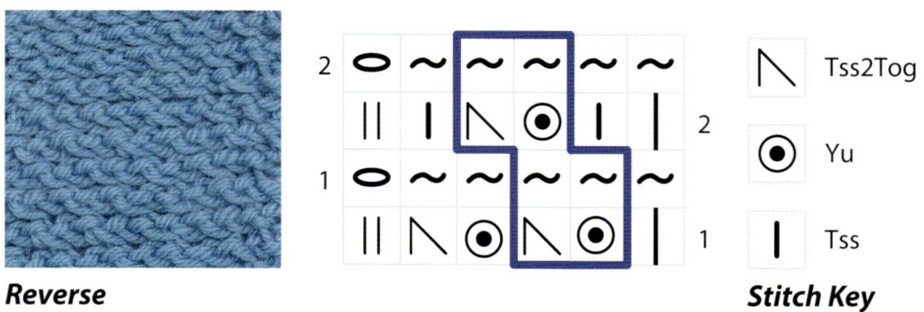

Reverse

Stitch Key

196

Worked over a multiple of 4 stitches and 2 rows.

Row 1: [Tx, Tss 2] rep.

Row 2: [Tss 2, Tx] rep.

Repeat Rows 1 and 2.

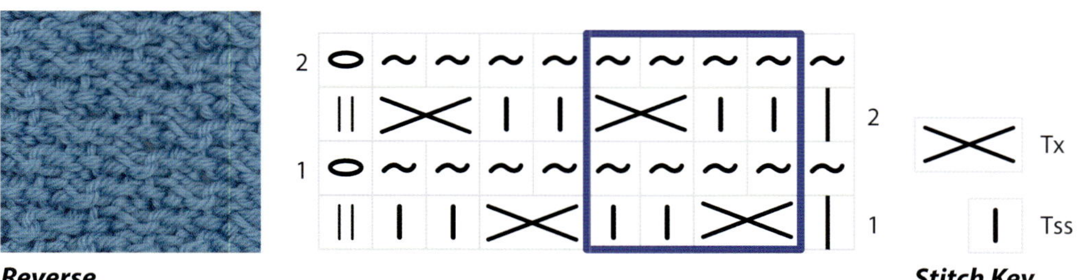

Reverse

Stitch Key

197

Worked over a multiple of 3 stitches and 2 rows.

Row 1: [Tx, Tps] rep.

Row 2: [Tx, Tss] rep.

Repeat Rows 1 and 2.

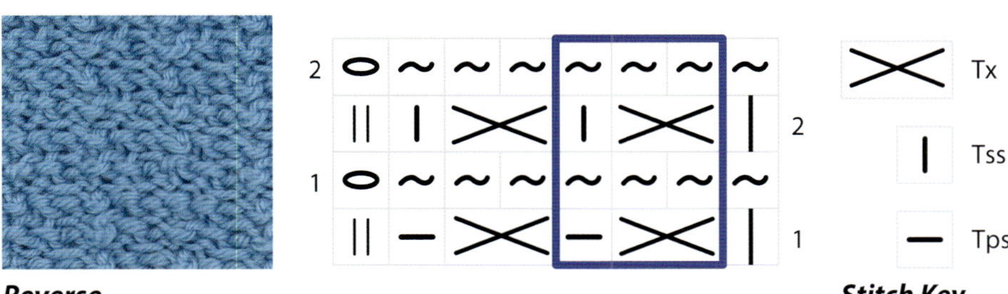

Reverse

Stitch Key

198 STAR STITCH (Star)

Reverse

Worked over a multiple of 3 stitches and 2 rows.

Star: In the next 3 sts (Tss3Tog, yo, and then Tss3Tog in the same 3 sts).

Row 1: At desired location, Star.

Row 2: At Star location, Tks 3.

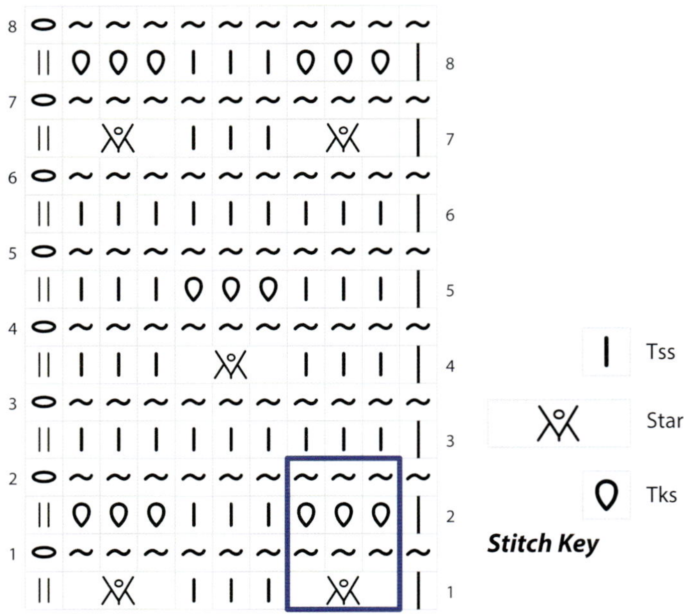

199 STAR STITCH WITH YO (Star-yo)

Reverse

Worked over a multiple of 3 stitches and 2 rows.

Star-yo: Yo, and then in the next 3 sts (Tss3Tog, yo, then Tss3Tog in the same 3 sts), pull yo over 3 loops on hook.

Row 1: At desired location, Star-yo.

Row 2: At Star-yo location, Tks 3.

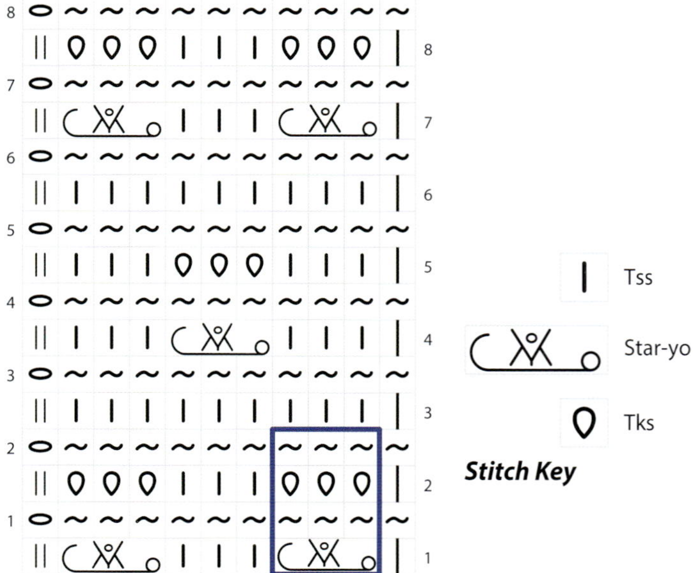

200

Worked over a multiple of 4 + 1 stitches and 2 rows.

Uses Star stitch (198).

Row 1: [Star, Tss] rep until 1 st rem, Tss.

Row 2: Tss, [Tss, Star] rep.

Repeat Rows 1 and 2.

Reverse

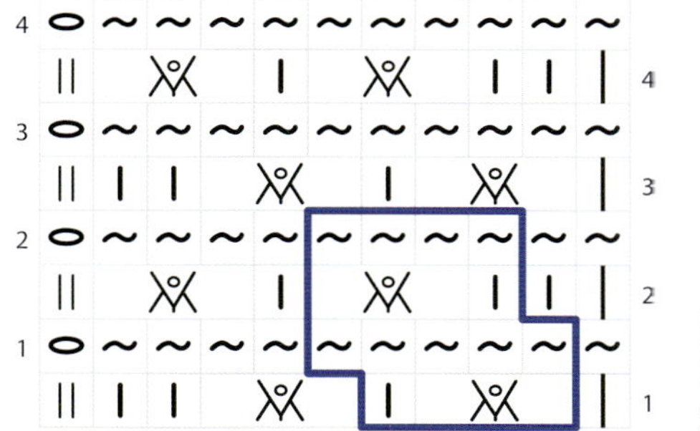

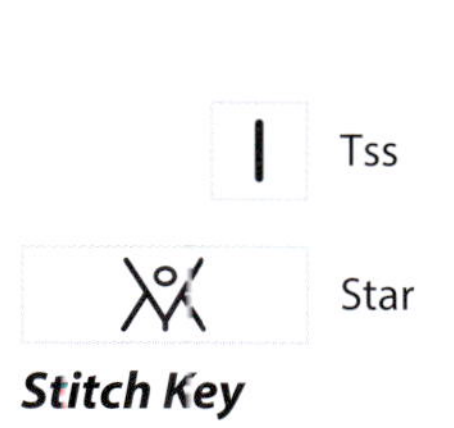

Stitch Key

201

Worked over a multiple of 2 stitches.

Stitch 201 (St-201): Tks2Tog (photo 1), Tss in the first st (photo 2), Tss in the second stitch (photo 3). Pull 1st loop (Tks2Tog) over 2 loops (photo 4).

Row 1: St-201, rep.

Repeat Row 1.

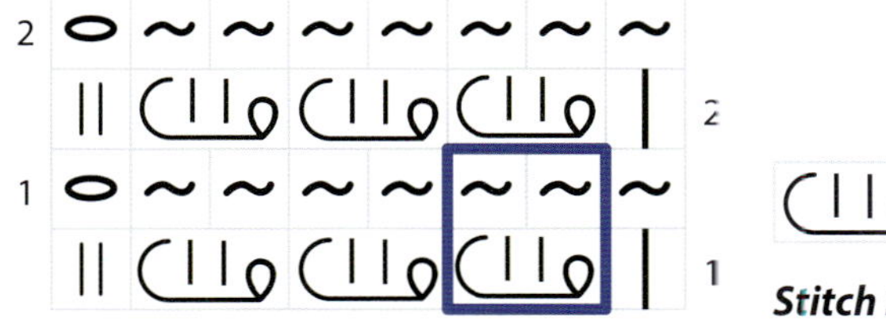

St-201

Stitch Key

Reverse

202

Worked over a multiple of 2 + 2 stitches and 2 rows.

Uses Stitch 201 (St-201).

Row 1: St-201, rep.

Row 2: Tss, St-201 rep until 1 st rem, Tss.

Repeat Rows 1 and 2.

Reverse

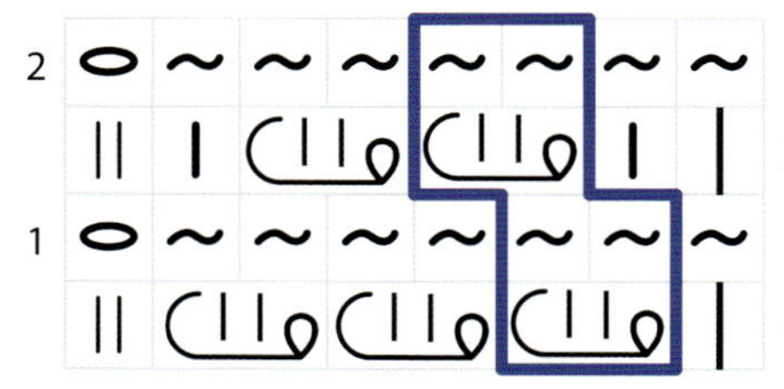

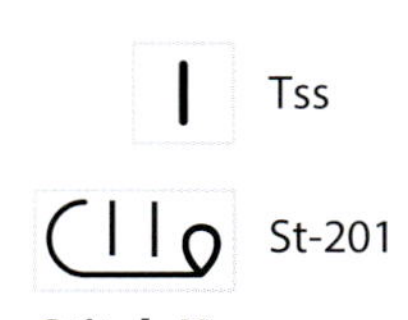

Stitch Key

203

Worked over any number of stitches.

Row 1 FP: In the next st, Ttop (photo 1) and Tfs in prior stitch space (photo 2) rep.

Row 1 RP: RP-2, RP-3 rep.

Repeat Row 1.

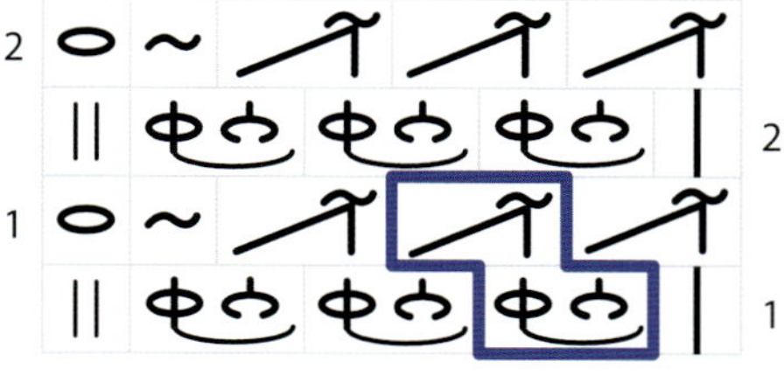

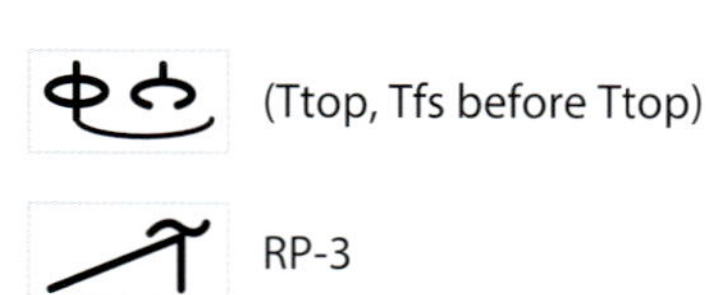

Stitch Key

Reverse

204

Worked over any number of stitches.

Row 1 FP: In the next st, Tss in next set of vertical bars (photo 1) and Tts in next set of horizontal bars (photo 2) rep.

Row 1 RP: RP-3 rep.

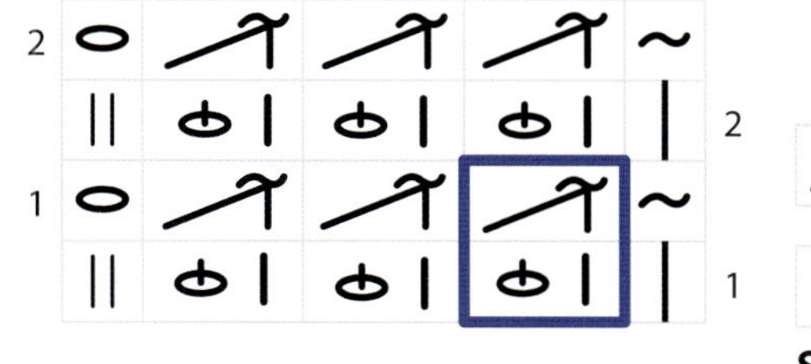

RP-3

(Tss, Tts)

Stitch Key

Reverse

2

205

Worked over any number of stitches.

Row 1 FP: In the next st, (Tks and Tfs in next st sp) rep.

Row 1 RP: RP-3 rep.

Row 2 FP: In the next st, Tks in prior row Tks only (photo 1) and Tfs in next st sp (photo 2) rep.

Row 2 RP: RP-3 rep.

Repeat Row 2.

Reverse

2

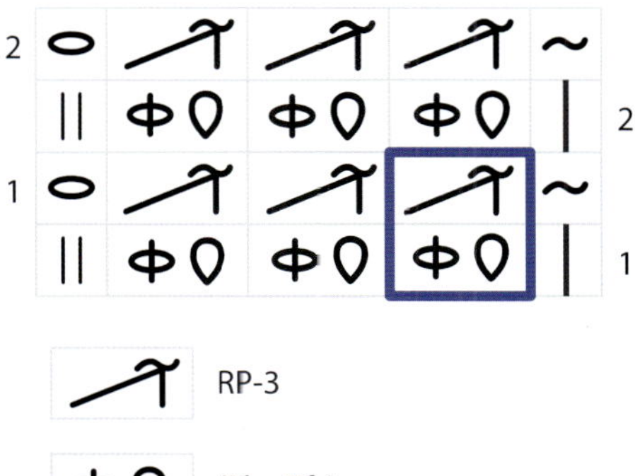

RP-3

(Tks, Tfs)

Stitch Key

206

Worked over a multiple of 2 stitches and 2 rows.

Tfs Cluster Stitch (Tfs-CS): Worked in the next 2 st sp, Tfs in first st sp (photo 1), Tfs in second st sp (photo 2), yo and pull through 2 loops (photo 3).

Row 1 FP: [Tfs-CS, yu, Tss in next st] rep.

Row 1 RP: [RP-2, RP-3] rep.

Row 2 FP: [Ttop over 2 sts closed together (photo 4), Tfs-CS, yu] rep.

Row 2 RP: [RP-3, RP-2] rep.

Row 3 FP: [Tfs-CS, yu, Ttop over 2 sts closed together] rep.

Row 3 RP: [RP-2, RP-3] rep.

Repeat Rows 2 and 3.

Reverse

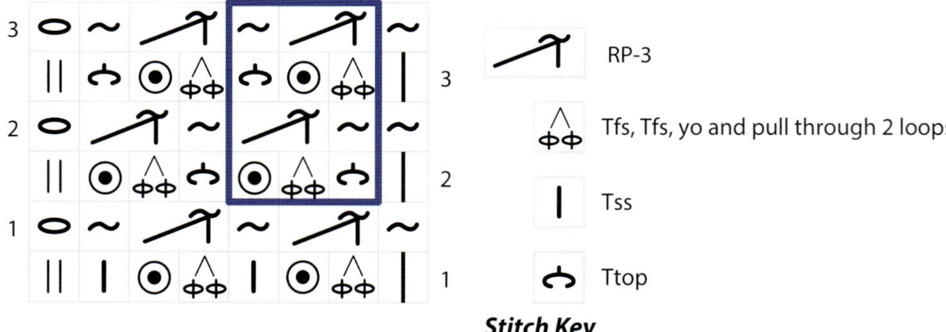

Stitch Key

207

Worked over 3 sts.

Row 1: Tss 3 (photo 1), Tfs in st sp before 3rd Tss (photo 2) and slst through 3 loops (photo 3). Yo and Tfs in same spot as prior Tfs (photo 4).

Repeat Row 1.

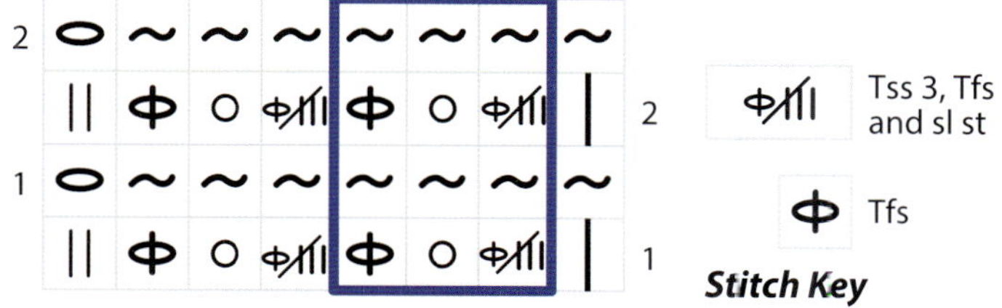

Reverse

208

Worked over a multiple of 2 stitches and 2 rows.

Row 1 FP: In the next 2 sts, (Tss2Tog, yo, Tss2Tog) rep.

Row 1 RP: [RP-2, RP-3] rep.

Row 2 FP: [Tfs in space between first Tss2Tog & yo, Tfs in space between yo & second Tss2Tog] rep.

Row 2 RP: Std RP.

Repeat Rows 1 and 2.

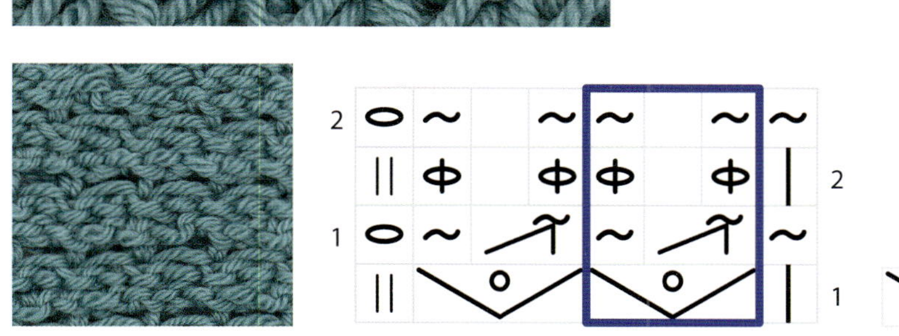

Reverse

RP-3

Tfs

Tss2Tog, yo, Tss2Tog

Stitch Key

209

Worked over a multiple of 2 stitches.

Fptc2Tog: Insert hook behind both vertical bars of the next two stitches. Yarn over and pull up a loop.

Row 1: In the next 2 sts, Fptc2Tog (photo 1), Tss in 1st st. Tss in 2nd st (photo 2). Pull first loop over 2 loops on hook (photo 3).

Repeat Row 1.

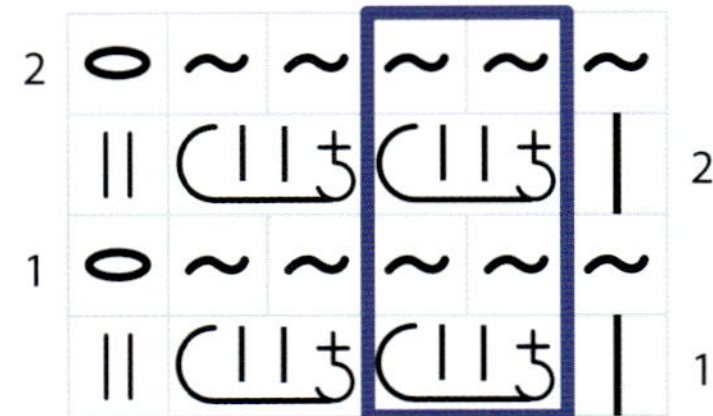

 St-209

Stitch Key

Reverse

210

Worked over a multiple of 2 stitches.

Row 1: [Tss2Tog, PTts before next set of vertical bars] rep.

Repeat Row 1.

Reverse

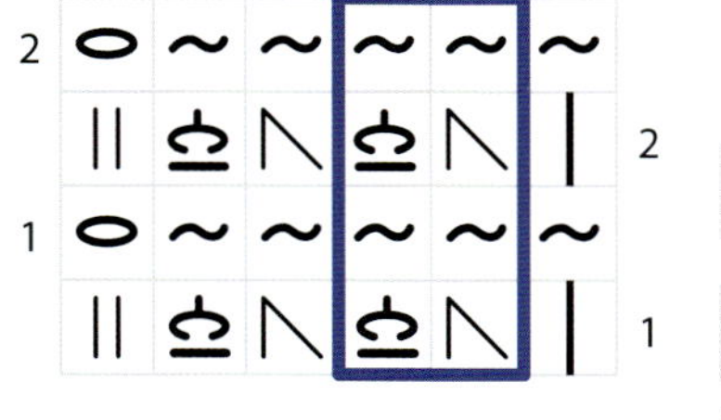

PTts

Tss2Tog

Stitch Key

211

Worked over a multiple of 2 stitches and 2 rows.

Row 1: [Tss2Tog, PTts before next set of vertical bars] rep.

Row 2: [PTts before next set of vertical bars, Tss2Tog] rep.

Repeat Rows 1 and 2.

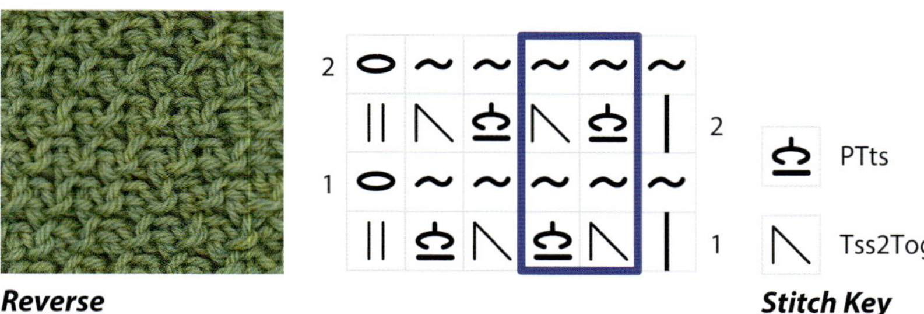

Reverse

Stitch Key

212

Worked over a multiple of 3 stitches.

Row 1: [Tps2Tog, yo, Trs] rep.

Repeat Row 1.

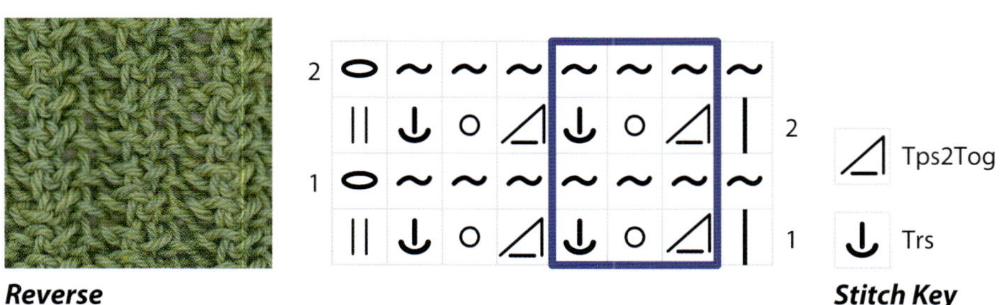

Reverse

Stitch Key

213

Worked over a multiple of 2 stitches.

Row 1 FP: [Tss, Fptc, yo] rep.

Row 1 RP: [RP-3, RP-2] rep.

Row 2 FP: [Tss, sk st (prior row Fptc), Fptc behind both bars of yo, yo] rep.

Row 2 RP: [RP-3, RP-2] rep.

Repeat Row 2.

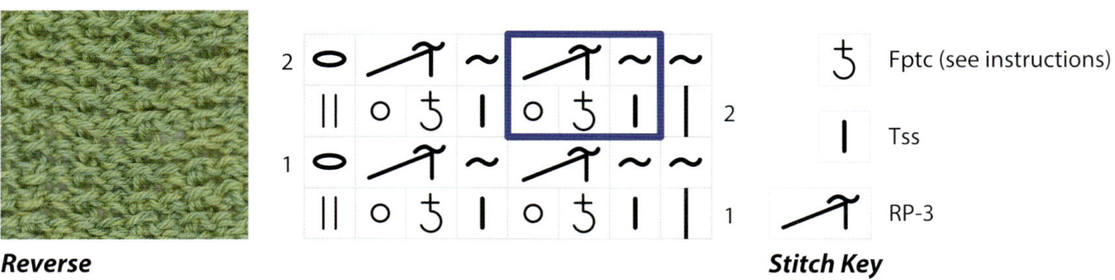

Reverse

Stitch Key

214

Worked over a multiple of 4 stitches and 2 rows.

Half Tunisian Double Crochet Cross Stitch (Txdc): Worked over 2 sts. Skip the first st, Tss in the second st. In the first st, Tdc.

Row 1: [Txdc, Tss 2] rep.

Row 2: [Tss 2, Txdc] rep.

Repeat Rows 1 and 2.

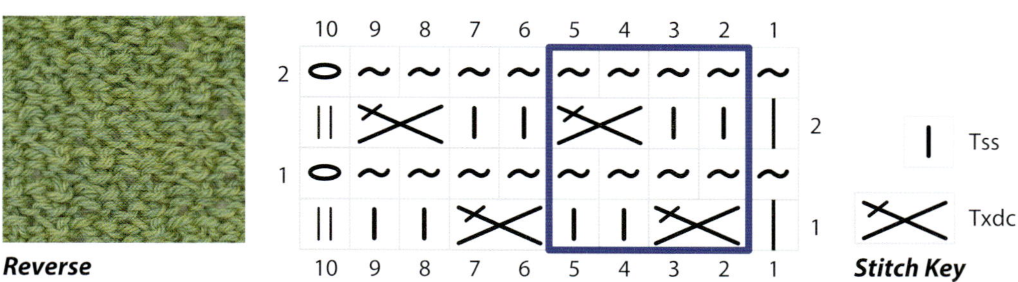

Reverse

Stitch Key

215

Worked over a multiple of 2 stitches and 2 rows.

Row 1: [Tps2Tog, PTtop] rep.

Row 2: Tss rep.

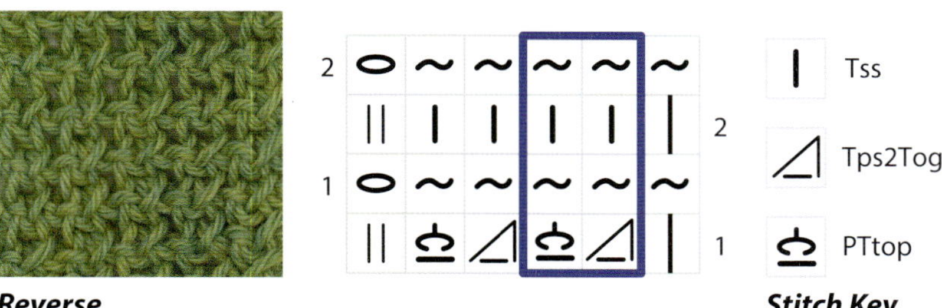

Reverse

Stitch Key

216

Worked over a multiple of 2 stitches and 2 rows.

Row 1: Tss rep.

Row 2: Tss rep.

Row 3: [In the next 2 sts, Tps2Tog in prior row (Row 1 for first rep, photo 1) and then Tps2Tog in current row (Row 2 for first rep, photo 2)] rep.

Repeat Rows 2 and 3.

Reverse

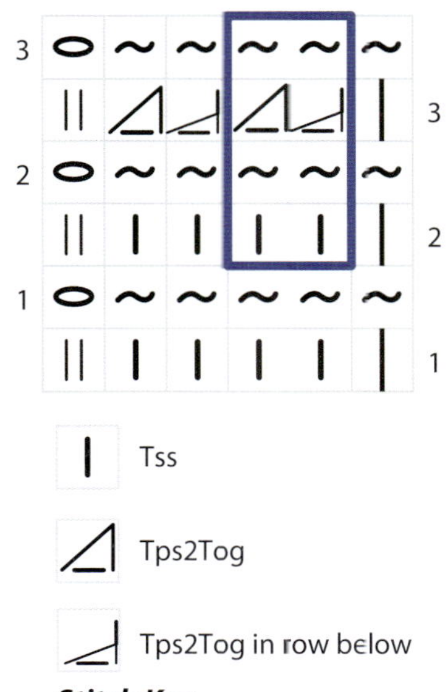

Stitch Key

217

Worked over a multiple of 2 stitches and 2 rows.

Stitch 217 (St-217): In next 2 sts, Tks in 1st st, Tss2Tog in both sts.

Row 1: St-217 rep.

Row 2: Tss, St-217 rep until 1 st rem, Tss.

Repeat Rows 1 and 2.

Reverse

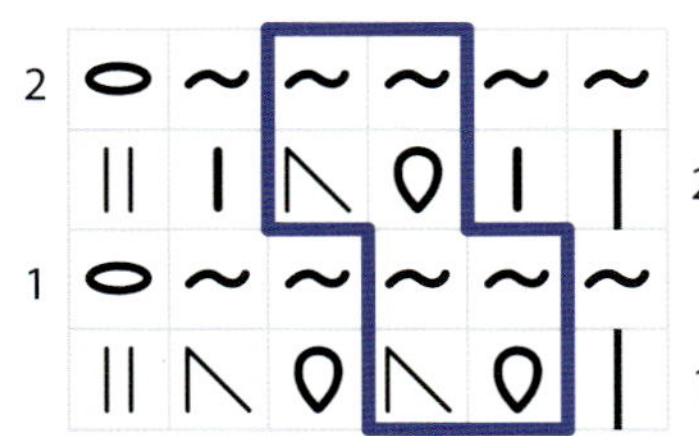

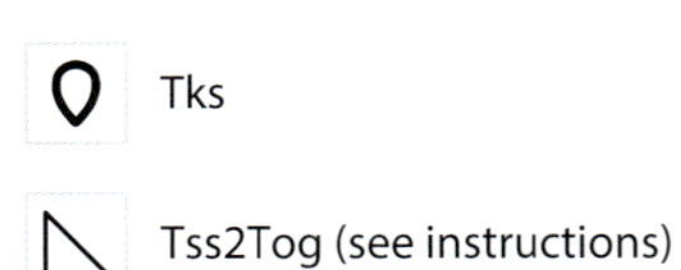

Stitch Key

218

Worked over a multiple of 3 stitches.

Row 1: In next 3 sts, (Tss3Tog, Tss in 2nd st, Tss in 1st st) rep.

Repeat Row 1.

Reverse

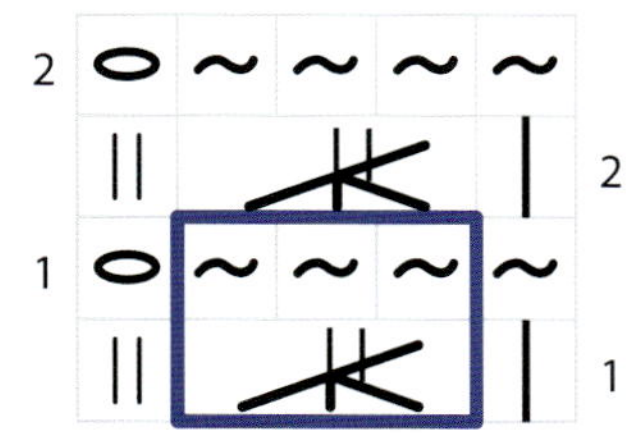

Tss3Tog, Tss in 2nd st, Tss in 1st st

Stitch Key

219

Worked over a multiple of 2 stitches.

Stitch 219 (St-219): In next 2 sts, Tss2Tog, and in the same 2 sts Tps2Tog.

Row 1: In next 2 sts, (Tss2Tog, Tps2Tog) rep.

Repeat Row 1.

Reverse

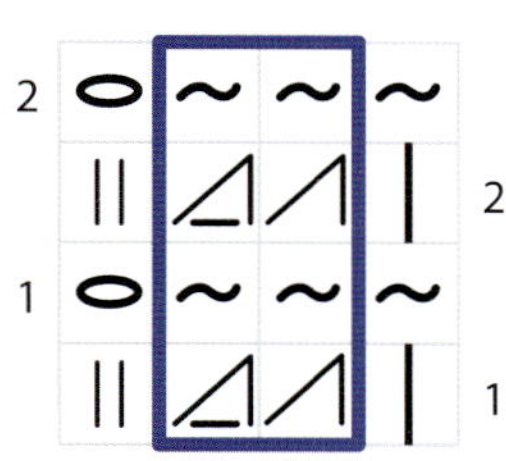

Tps2Tog (see instructions)

Tss2Tog

Stitch Key

220

Worked over a multiple of 2 stitches and 2 rows.

Uses Stitch 219 (St-219).

Row 1: St-219 rep.

Row 2: Tss, St-219 rep until 1 st rem, Tss.

Reverse

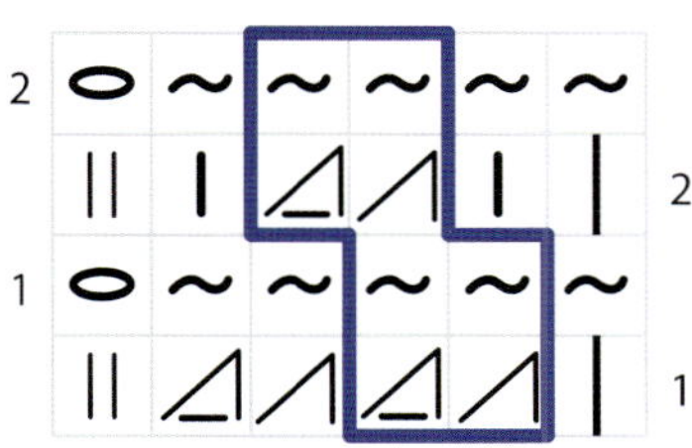

Tps2Tog (see instructions)

Tss2Tog

Tss

Stitch Key

221

Worked over any number of stitches.

Row 1: [In next st, yo, Tts (photo 1) and Tss (photo 2) in next st, slip last stitch through 2 loops (photo 3)] rep.

Repeat Row 1.

Reverse

222

Worked over a multiple of 2 stitches.

Row 1: [Tfs in the first st sp (photo 1), Tfs in the next st sp (photo 2), slip second stitch through first (photo 3)] rep with the first Tfs worked into the second space of the prior stitch (photo 4).

Repeat Row 1.

Reverse

223

Worked over a multiple of 2 stitches.

Row 1 FP: [Tss, Ttop in next set of vertical bars, Tfs in next st sp (photo 2), Tfs in st sp before Tss (photo 3)] rep.

Row 1 RP: [RP-4, RP-2] rep.

Row 2 FP: [Tss, Ttop over 3 st cluster (photo 1), Tfs in next st sp (photo 2), Tfs in st sp before Tss (photo 3)] rep.

Row 2 RP: [RP-4, RP-2] rep.

Repeat Row 2.

Reverse

1

2

3

224

Worked over a multiple of 2 stitches.

Row 1: [Fptc 2, yo and pull through 2 loops, yo] rep.

Row 2: [Fptc (photo 1), Tbss in yo (photo 2), yo and pull through 2 loops (photo 3), yo] rep.

Repeat Row 2.

Reverse

1

2

3

225

Worked over a multiple of 3 stitches.

Row 1: [sk st sp, TfsTc 2 (photos 1 and 2), in skipped sp (yo, Tfs) 3 times (photo 3), yo and pull through 6 (photo 4)] (3 loops on hook) rep.

Repeat Row 1.

Reverse

226

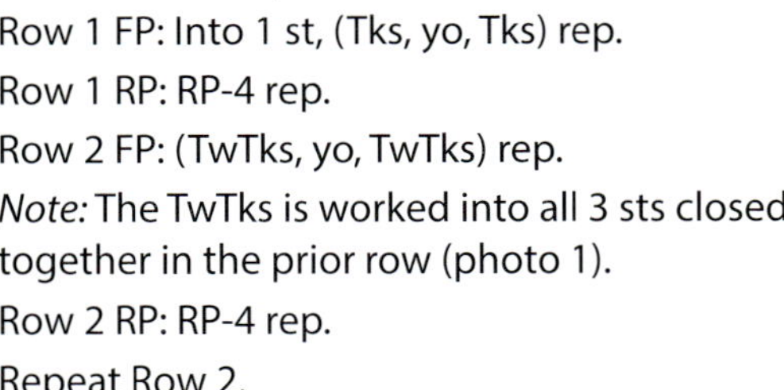

Worked over any number of stitches.

Row 1 FP: Into 1 st, (Tks, yo, Tks) rep.

Row 1 RP: RP-4 rep.

Row 2 FP: (TwTks, yo, TwTks) rep.

Note: The TwTks is worked into all 3 sts closed together in the prior row (photo 1).

Row 2 RP: RP-4 rep.

Repeat Row 2.

Reverse

227

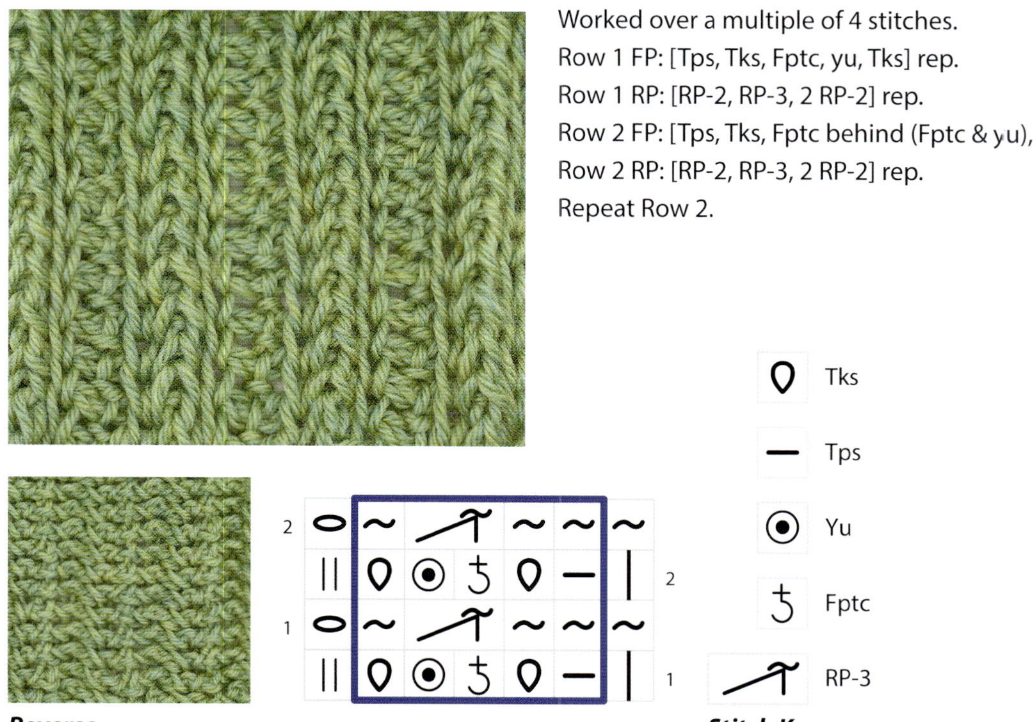

Worked over a multiple of 4 stitches.
Row 1 FP: [Tps, Tks, Fptc, yu, Tks] rep.
Row 1 RP: [RP-2, RP-3, 2 RP-2] rep.
Row 2 FP: [Tps, Tks, Fptc behind (Fptc & yu), yu, Tks] rep.
Row 2 RP: [RP-2, RP-3, 2 RP-2] rep.
Repeat Row 2.

Reverse

Stitch Key

228

Worked over 6 sts.
Row 1 FP: [Tss 6] rep.
Row 1 RP: [3 RP-2, ch 1, RP-4, ch 1] rep.
Row 2 FP: [Ttop, Tss, Ttop, Tss 3] rep.
Row 1 RP: [3 RP-2, ch 1, RP-4, ch 1] rep.
Repeat Row 2.

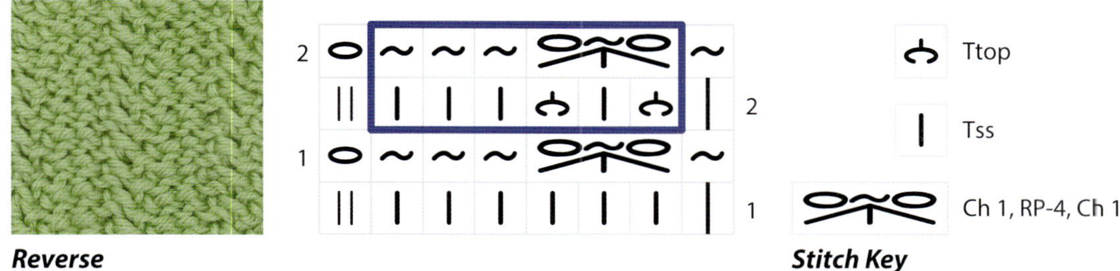

Reverse

Stitch Key

229

Worked over 2 sts and 2 rows.

Row 1 FP: Tfs in next st sp, (Tss, Tfs in next st sp) rep.

Row 1 RP: RP-2, [RP-4, RP-2] rep.

Row 2 FP: Tfs in next st sp, Tss, Tfs in next st sp, [Ttop, Tfs in next st sp, Tss, Tfs in next st sp] rep.

Row 2 RP: [RP-4, RP-2] rep.

Row 3 FP: [Ttop, Tfs in next st sp, Tss, Tfs in next st sp] rep until 1 st rem, Ttop.

Row 3 RP: RP-2, [RP-4, RP-2] rep.

Repeat Rows 2 and 3.

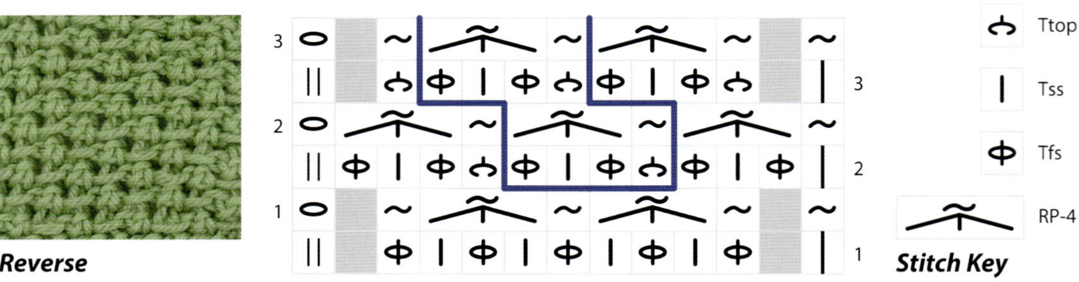

Reverse

230

Worked over 1 stitch space and 2 rows.

Row 1 FP: Tss.

Row 1 RP: [RP-3, ch1] rep.

Row 2 FP: In the same stitch space, (Tfs, Tts).

Row 2 RP: [ch1, RP-3] rep.

Row 3 FP: In the same stitch space, (Tfs, Tts).

Row 3 RP: [RP-3, ch1] rep.

Repeat Rows 2 and 3.

Reverse

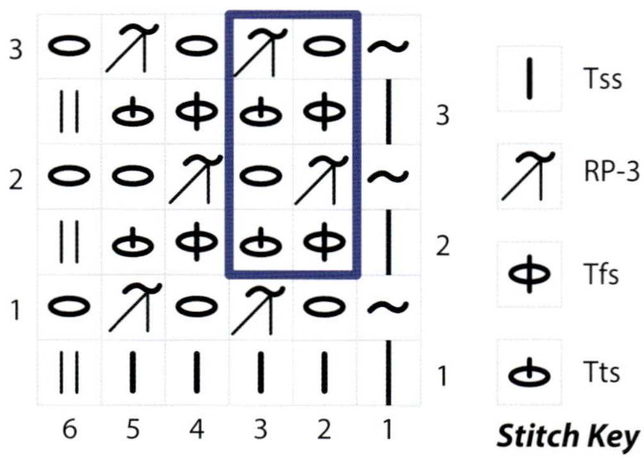

231

Worked over a multiple of 2 stitches.

Row 1 FP: (Tfs in next st sp, Tss) rep.

Row 1 RP: RP-2, [RP-4, RP-2] rep.

Repeat Row 1.

Reverse

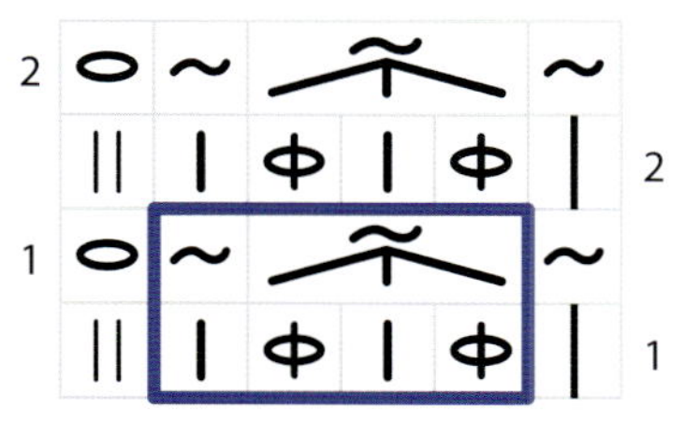

Tss

Tfs

RP-4

Stitch Key

232

Worked over a multiple of 2 stitches and 4 rows.

Rows 1–3: Tks.

Row 4: Tx.

Repeat Rows 1–4.

Reverse

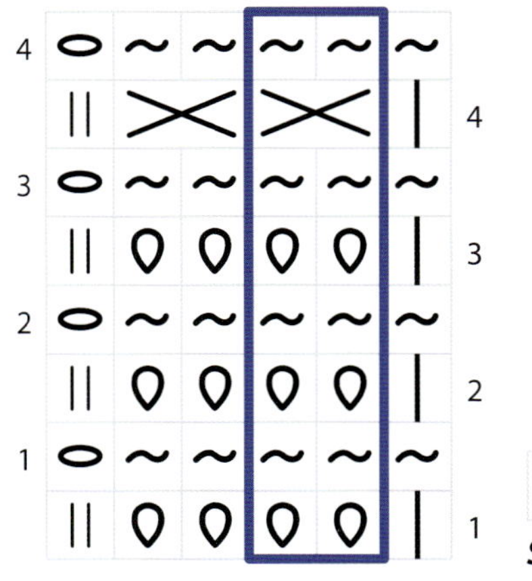

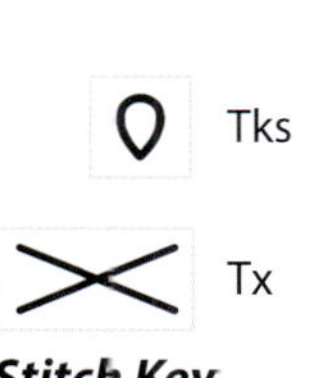

Stitch Key

233

Worked over any number of stitches.

Row 1 FP: [yo, Tss] rep.

Row 1 RP: [RP-3] rep.

Repeat Row 1.

Note: The Tss in subsequent rows goes into both the yo and the Tss of the prior row (photo 1).

Reverse

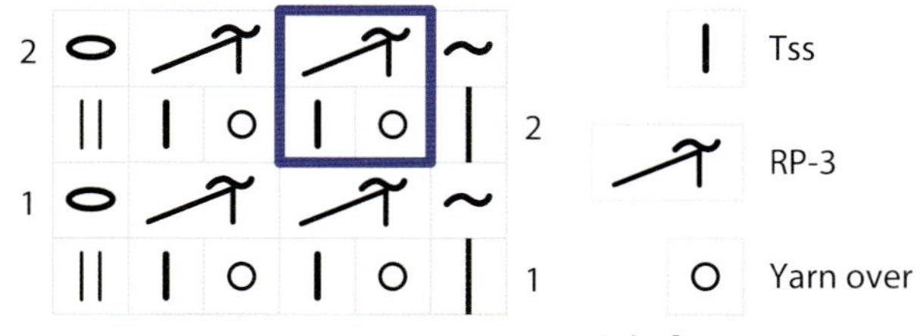

Stitch Key

234

Worked over a multiple of 2 stitches and 2 rows.

TssSC2Tog: Tss in next 2 sts, yo and pull through 2 loops. 1 loop on hook.

Row 1: [TssSC2Tog, yo] rep.

Row 2: [yo, TssSC2Tog] rep.

Repeat Rows 1 and 2.

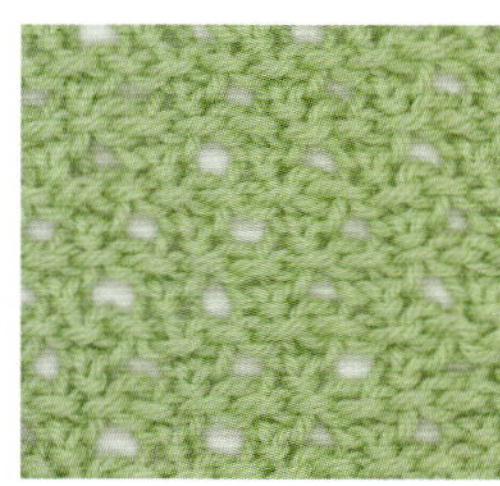

Reverse

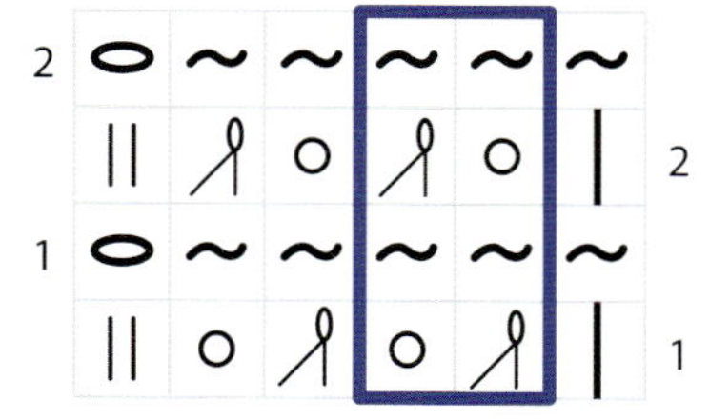

Stitch Key

235

Worked over any number of stitches.

Row 1 FP: Tss.

Row 1 RP: [RP-3, ch1] rep.

Row 2 FP: (Ttop in top of cluster and Tfs in next st sp) rep.

Row 2 RP: [RP-3, ch1] rep.

Repeat Row 2.

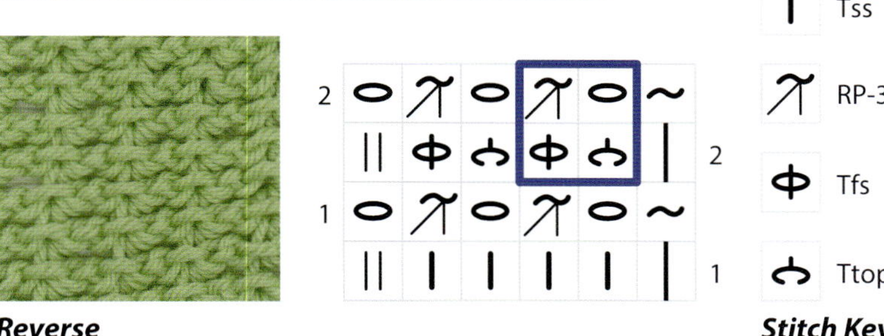

Reverse

Stitch Key

236

Worked over a multiple of 2 stitches.

Row 1 FP: [In next st sp (Tmfs, yo, Tmfs) twice, yo and pull through 6 loops, ch 1] rep.

Row 1 RP: [ch 1, RP-2, ch 1] rep.

Row 2 FP: [(Tmfs, yo, Tmfs) into chain before the vertical bars (photo 1), (Tmfs, yo, Tmfs) into the chain after the vertical bars (photo 2), yo and pull through 6 loops (photo 3), ch 1 (photo 4)] rep.

Row 2 RP: [ch 1, RP-2, ch 1] rep.

Repeat Row 2.

Reverse

1

2

3

4

237

Worked over a multiple of 2 stitch spaces.

Row 1 FP: [ExTfs in 1st st sp, in next st sp [yo, Tfs] 4 times, and then pull ExTfs loop over 8 loops] rep.

Row 1 RP: Ch 1, [RP-5, ch 1] rep.

Row 2 FP: In the space in the middle of the cluster [ExTfs (photo 1), [yo, Tfs] 4 times (photo 2), pull ExTfs loop over 8 loops (photo 3)] rep.

Row 2 RP: Ch 1, [RP-5, ch 1] rep.

Repeat Row 2.

Reverse

1

2

3

238

Worked over a multiple of 2 stitches and 2 rows.

Row 1 FP: [Tps, in next st sp (Tfs, yo, Tfs) twice] rep.

Row 1 RP: ch1, [RP-7, RP-2] rep.

Row 2 FP: [Tps, (Tfs, yo, Tfs) in middle of the 6 st cluster] rep.

Row 2 RP: ch1, [RP-4, RP-2 loops] rep.

Row 3 FP: [Tps, (Tfs, yo, Tfs) in stitch space before cluster (photo 1) and in stitch space after cluster (photo 2)] rep.

Row 3 RP: ch1, [RP-7, RP-2] rep.

Repeat Rows 2 and 3.

Reverse

1

2

239 BOBBLE STITCH

A Bobble Stitch is worked over 1 stitch. At desired Bobble Stitch location, Tdc in next stitch. Tdc in the same stitch until desired fullness of Bobble Stitch, and then yo and pull through all loops of Bobble Stitch. Shown with a total of 5 Tdc (main), 3 Tdc (photo 1), and 4 Tdc (photo 2).

Reverse

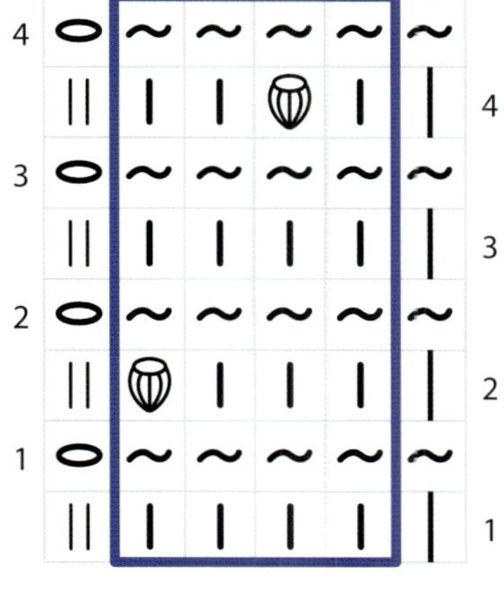

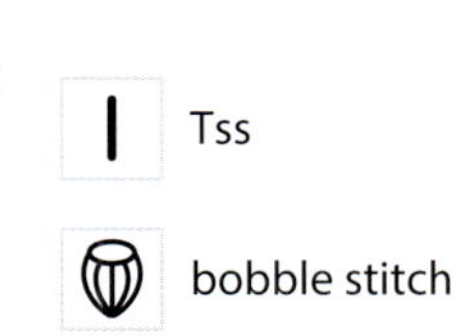

Stitch Key

240 PUFF STITCH

A Puff Stitch is worked over 1 stitch. At desired Puff Stitch location, yo, and Tks. Repeat [Yo, Tks] in the same stitch location until the desired fullness of Puff Stitch, and then yo and pull through all loops of the Puff Stitch.

Shown with a total of 5 (Main), 3 (photo 1), and 4 (photo 2) repeats of [yo, Tks].

Reverse

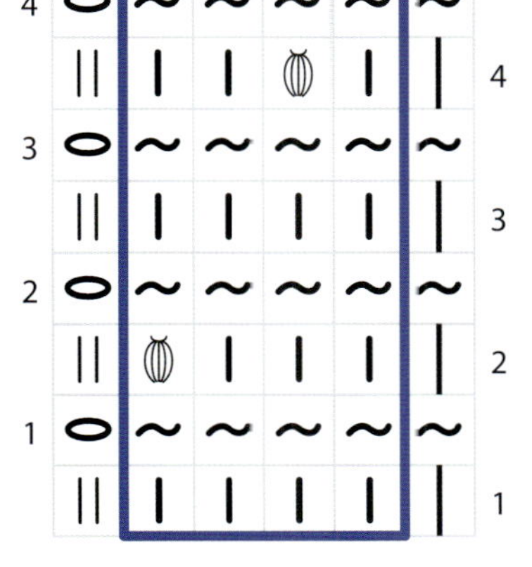

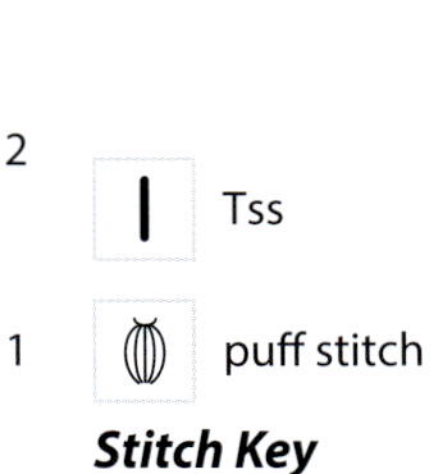

Stitch Key

241 PEBBLE STITCH

The Pebble Stitch is worked over 1 stitch and is created by adding chains during the return pass. Work the forward pass with any stitch. On the return pass, at the desired Pebble Stitch location, chain 3 and then continue the return pass.

Reverse

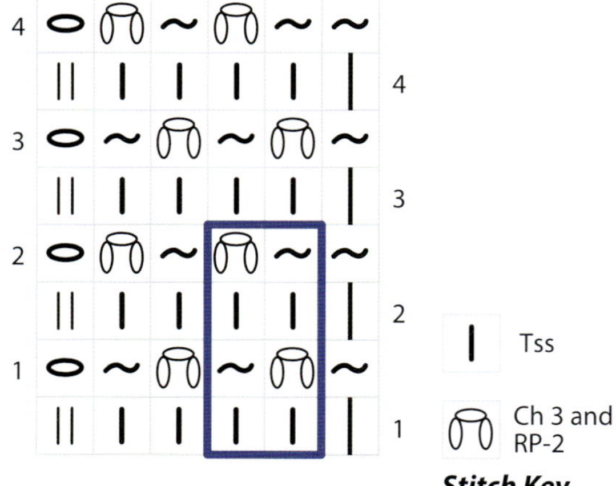

Stitch Key

242

Worked over a multiple of 4 + 3 stitches and 2 rows.

In this stitch variation, the Puff Stitch is closed on the return pass.

Row 1 FP: Tps 3, [in next st sp (Tfs, yo, Tfs, yo, Tfs, yo, Tfs), Tps 3] rep.

Row 1 RP: RP-2 3 times, [RP-8, RP-2 3 times] rep.

Row 2 FP: Tps 3, [(Tfs, yo, Tfs, yo, Tfs, yo, Tfs) in st sp after prior row Puff Stitch (photo 1), Tps 3] rep.

Row 2 RP: RP-2 3 times, [RP-8, RP-2 3 times] rep.

Row 3 FP: Tps 3, [(Tfs, yo, Tfs, yo, Tfs, yo, Tfs) in st sp before prior row Puff Stitch (photo 2), Tps 3] rep.

Row 3 RP: RP-2 3 times, [RP-8, RP-2 3 times] rep.

Repeat Rows 2 and 3.

Reverse

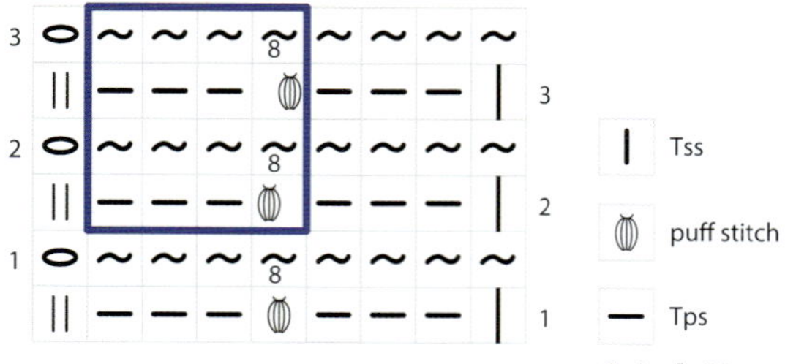

Stitch Key

243

Reverse

Worked over a multiple of 3 stitches.

Row 1 FP: [Tss 2, in next stitch space [yo, Tfs] 4 times] rep.

Row 1 RP: [RP-5 twice, RP-2 twice] rep.

Row 2 FP: [Tss 2, in the space in the middle of the cluster (photo 1) [yo, tfs] 4 times] rep.

Row 2 RP: [RP-5 twice, RP-2 loops twice] rep.

Repeat Row 2.

244

Reverse

Worked over a multiple of 2 stitches and 2 rows.

Long Double Crochet (LDC): Yo and insert hook behind front vertical bar of stitch in prior row (photo 1). Yo and pull up a loop, yo and pull through 2 loops.

Rows 1 and 2: Tss.

Row 3: [Tss, LDC] rep.

Row 4: [LDC, Tss] rep.

Repeat Rows 3 and 4.

245

Worked over any number of stitches.

Tdc4B: Tdc in next stitch 4 times, yo and pull through 4 loops.

Row 1 FP: Tdc4B across.

Row 1 RP: [Ch 1, RP-2] rep.

Repeat Row 1.

Reverse

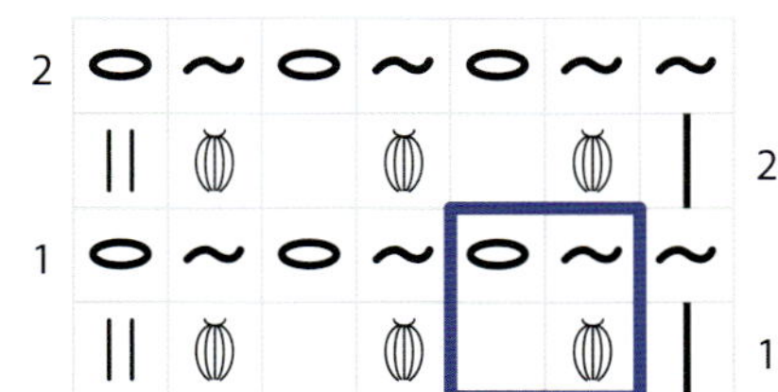

TdcBobble/Tdc4B

Stitch Key

246

Worked over any number of stitches and 2 rows.

Tdc2B: Tdc in next twice, yo and pull through 2 loops. 1 loop on hook.

Row 1 FP: [Tdc2B, Tps] rep.

Row 1 RP: [Ch 1, RP-2] rep.

Row 2 FP: [Tps, Tdc2B] rep.

Row 2 RP: [RP-2, Ch 1] rep.

Repeat Rows 1 and 2.

Reverse

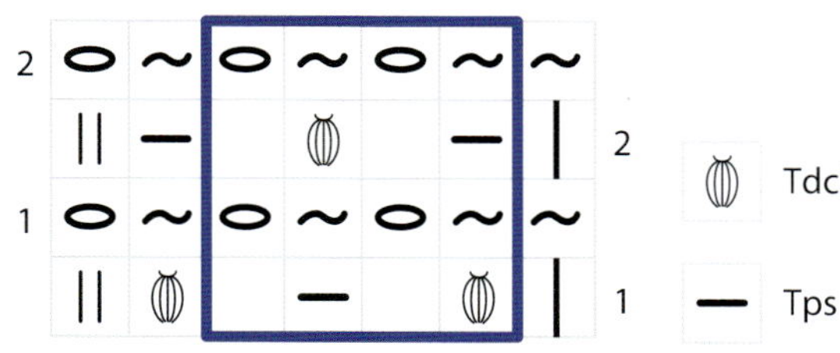

Tdc2B

Tps

Stitch Key

247

Worked over a multiple of 3 stitches.
Row 1 FP: Tss.
Row 1 RP: [Ch 1, RP-4, ch 1] rep.
Row 2 FP: [Tts, Ttop, Tts] rep.
Row 2 RP: [Ch 1, RP-4, ch 1] rep.
Repeat Row 2.

Reverse

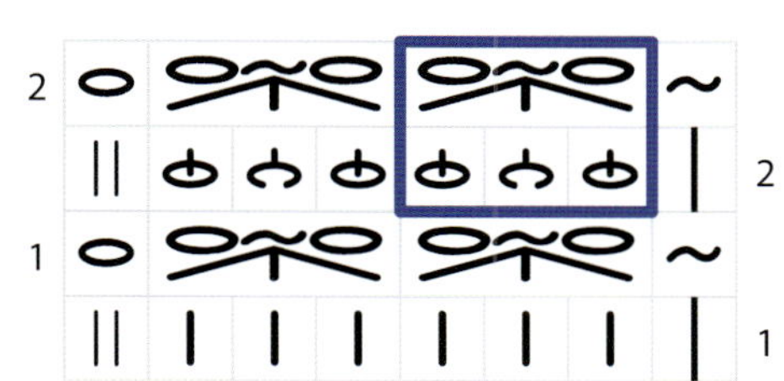

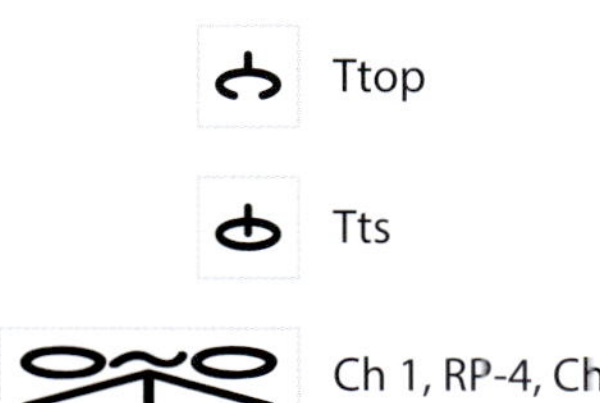

Stitch Key

248

Worked over a multiple of 3 stitches.
ExTtop: Work a Ttop stitch, ch 1.
Row 1 FP: [Tss 3] rep.
Row 1 RP: [Ch 1, RP-4, ch 1] rep.
Row 2 FP: [ExTtop 3] rep.
Row 2 RP: [Ch 1, RP-4, ch 1] rep.
Repeat Row 2.

Reverse

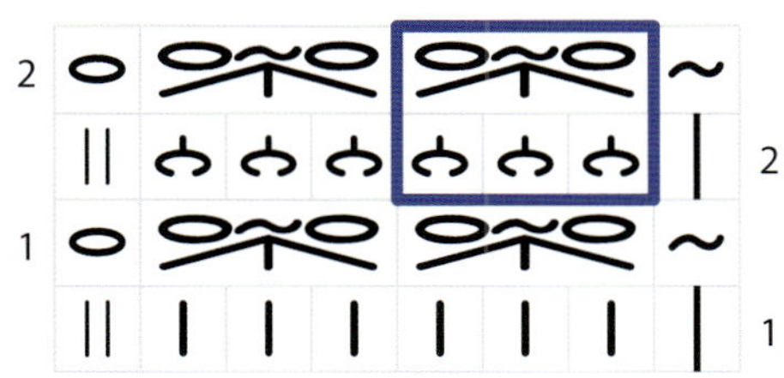

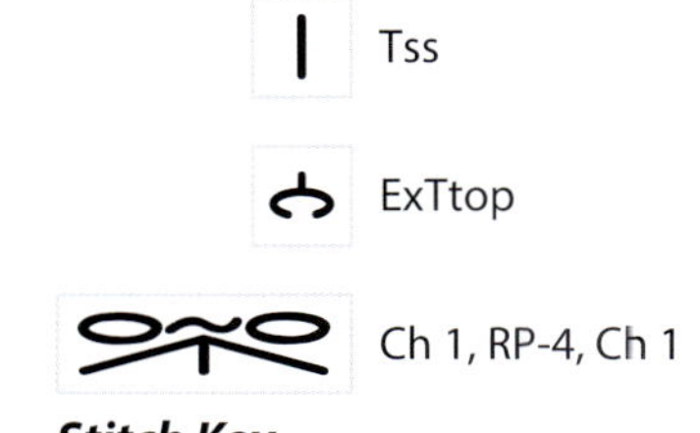

Stitch Key

249

Worked over a multiple of 5 stitches and 2 rows.

Row 1 FP: [Tss 5] rep.

Row 1 RP: [ch 2, RP-6, ch 2] rep.

Row 2 FP: [Ttop 5] rep.

Row 2 RP: Std RP.

Repeat Rows 1 and 2.

Reverse

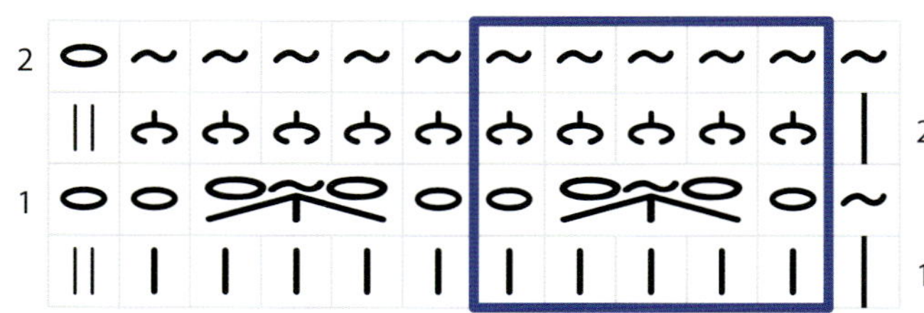

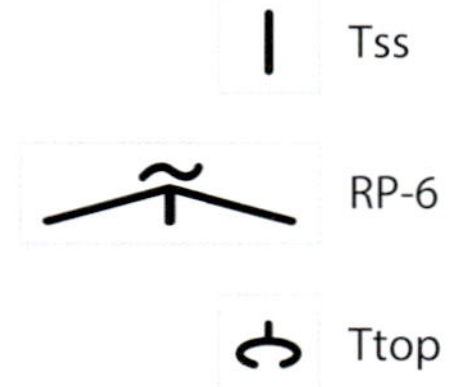

Stitch Key

250

Worked over a multiple of 6 + 3 stitches and 2 rows.

TtopDC: Yarn over and insert hook for Ttop. Yarn over and pull up a loop. Yarn over and pull through 2 loops. Leave loop on hook.

Row 1 FP: Tdc 2, [Tss 3, Tdc 3] rep until 1 st rem, Tss.

Row 1 RP: RP-4, ch 2, RP-2, [ch 2, RP-6, ch 2, RP-2] rep.

Row 2 FP: [Tss, Tfs, in top of cluster (TtopDC 3), Tfs] rep until 1 st rem, (TtopDC 2).

Row 2 RP: RP-2, [ch 2, RP-6, ch 2, RP-2] rep until 3 loops on hook, ch 2, RP-4.

Row 3 FP: In first st, (TtopDC 2), Tfs, [Tss, Tfs, in top of cluster (TtopDC 3), Tfs] rep.

Row 3 RP: RP-4, ch 2, RP-2, [ch 2, RP-6, ch 2, RP-2] rep.

Repeat Rows 2 and 3.

Reverse

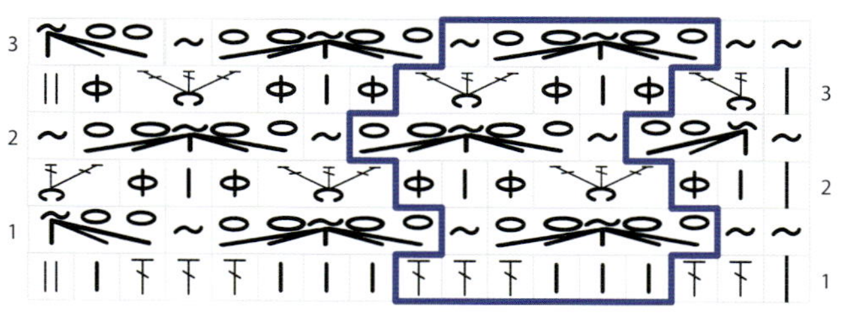

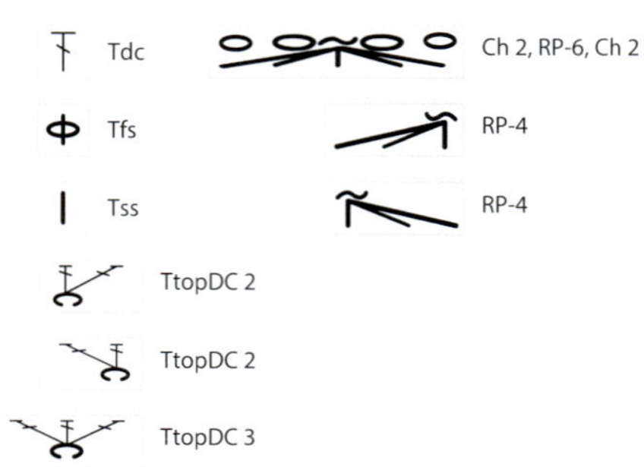

Stitch Key

251 GRANNY STITCH

Worked over a multiple of 2 + 4 stitches and 2 rows

Row 1: Ch 1, TksDc, yo sk st, [TksDc 2, yo sk st] rep, TksDc, exTe.

Row 2: Ch 1, TksDc, [in next yo space: TksDc 2 (photo 1), sk 2 sts, yo] rep across, TksDc, exTe.

Row 3: Ch 1, TksDc, [yo, sk 2 sts, in next yo space TksDc 2] rep across, TksDc, exTe.

Repeat Rows 2 and 3.

Reverse

252

Worked over a multiple of 2 stitches and 2 rows.

Row 1: [Tss2Tog, yo] rep.

Row 2: Tss.

Repeat Rows 1 and 2.

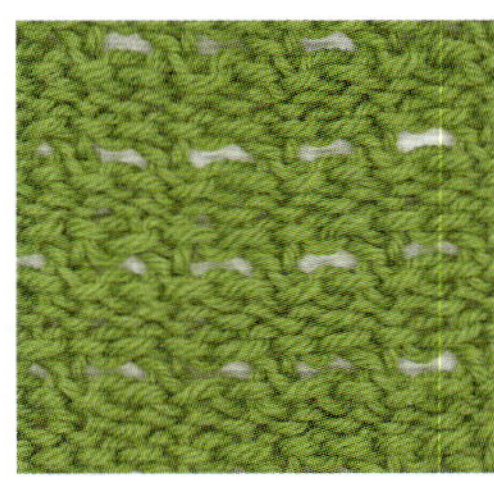

Reverse

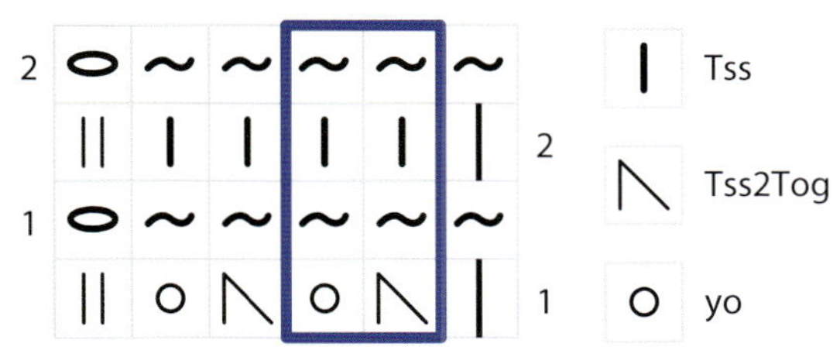

Stitch Key

253

Worked over a multiple of 2 stitches and 2 rows.

Row 1: [Tss2Tog, yo] rep.

Row 2: Tks.

Repeat Rows 1 and 2.

Reverse

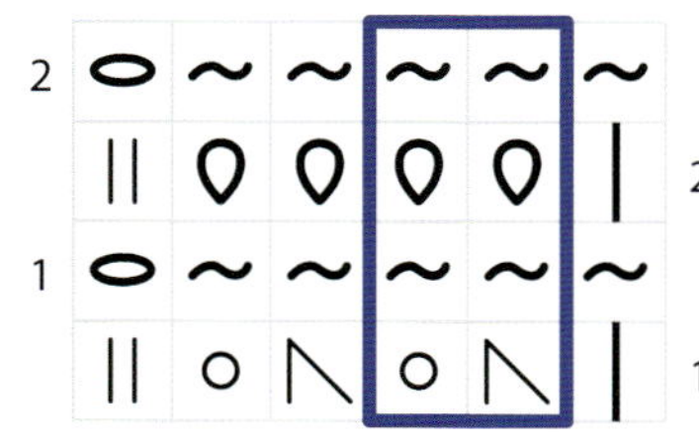

Tss2Tog

yo

Tks

Stitch Key

254

Worked over a multiple of 2 stitches and 2 rows.

Row 1: [Tss2Tog, yo] rep.

Row 2: Trs.

Repeat Rows 1 and 2.

Reverse

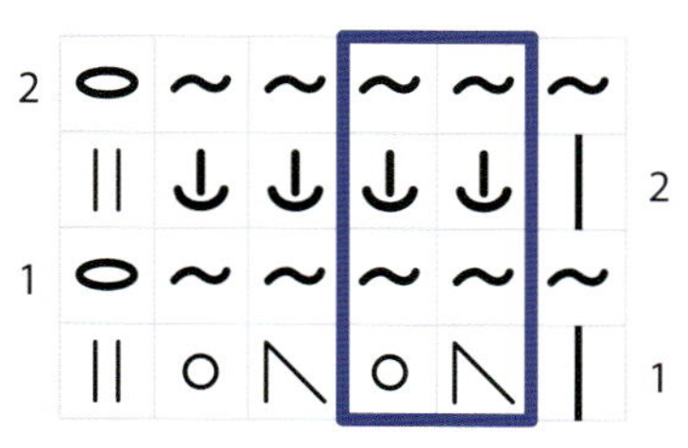

Stitch Key

255

Worked over a multiple of 2 stitches and 2 rows.

Row 1: [Tss2Tog, yo] rep.

Row 2: Tps.

Repeat Rows 1 and 2.

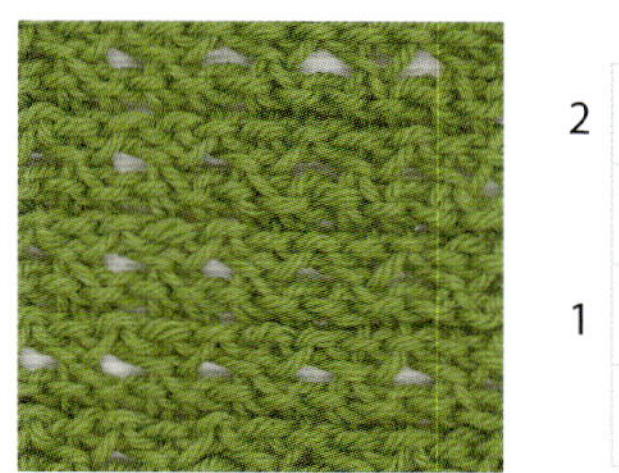

Reverse

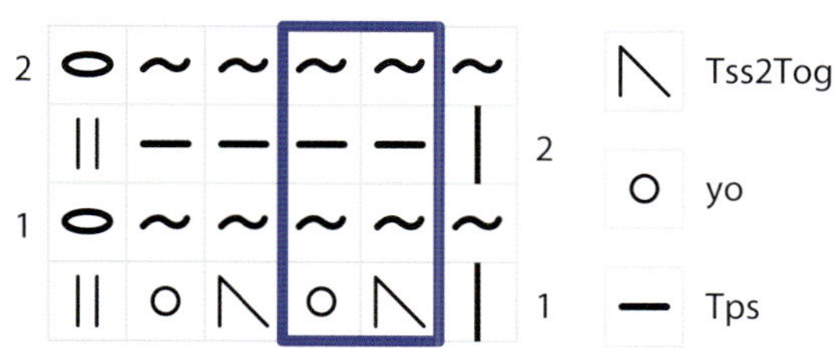

Tss2Tog

yo

Tps

Stitch Key

256

Worked over a multiple of 2 stitches and 2 rows.

Row 1: [Tss2Tog, yo] rep.

Row 2: Tfs.

Repeat Rows 1 and 2.

Reverse

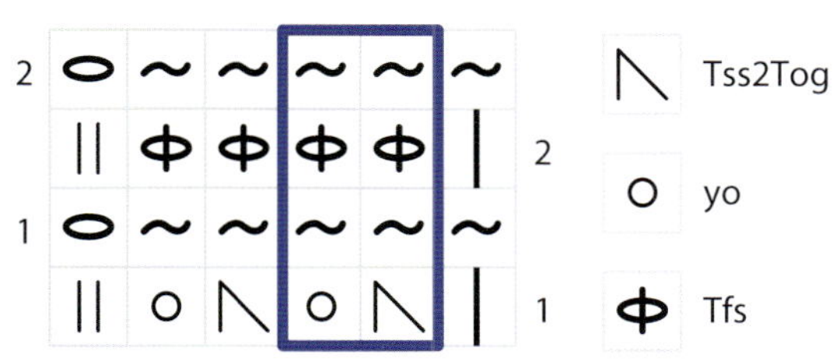

Tss2Tog

yo

Tfs

Stitch Key

257

Worked over a multiple of 2 stitches and 2 rows.

Row 1: [Tps2Tog, yo] rep.

Row 2: Tss.

Repeat Rows 1 and 2.

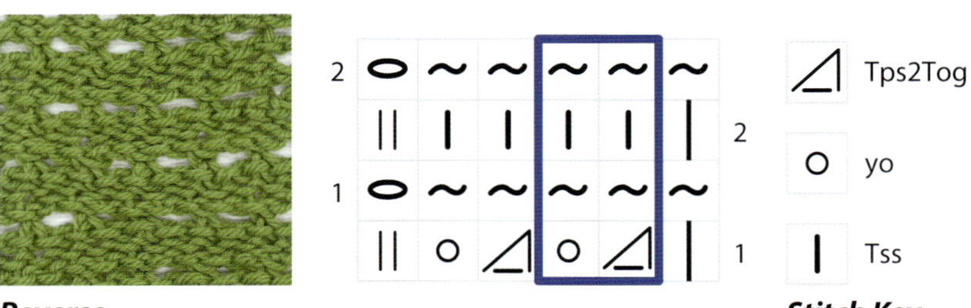

Reverse

Tps2Tog

yo

Tss

Stitch Key

258

Worked over a multiple of 2 stitches and 2 rows.

Row 1: [Tps2Tog, yo] rep.

Row 2: Tks.

Repeat Rows 1 and 2.

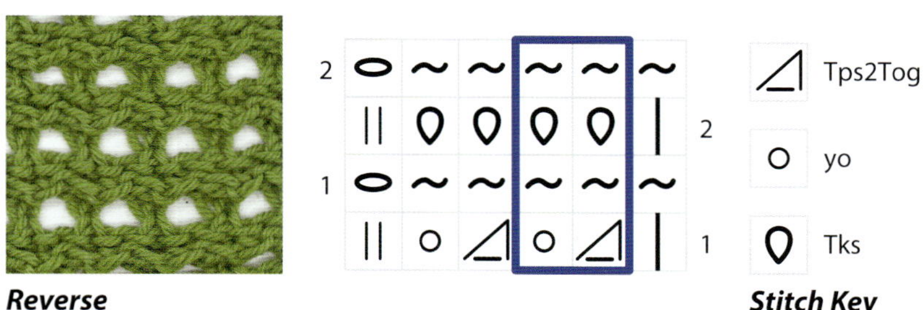

Reverse

Tps2Tog

yo

Tks

Stitch Key

259

Worked over a multiple of 2 stitches and 2 rows.

Row 1: [Tps2Tog, yo] rep.

Row 2: Trs.

Repeat Rows 1 and 2.

Reverse

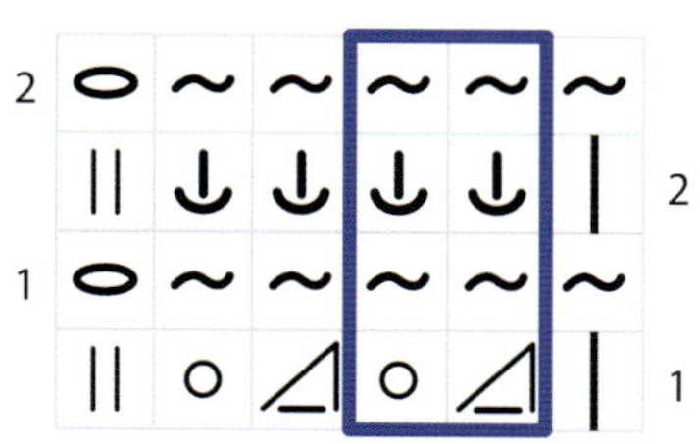

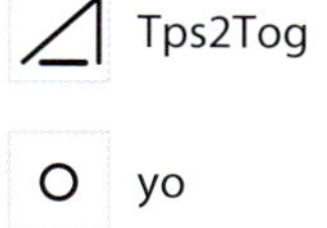

Tps2Tog

yo

Trs

Stitch Key

260

Worked over a multiple of 2 stitches and 2 rows.

Row 1: [Tps2Tog, yo] rep.

Row 2: Tps.

Repeat Rows 1 and 2.

Reverse

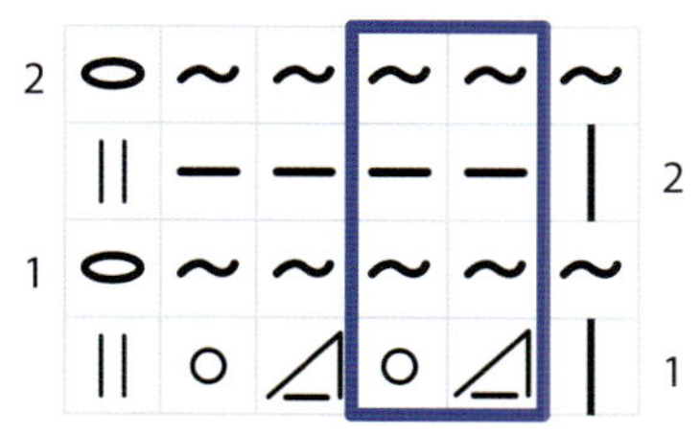

Tps2Tog

yo

Tps

Stitch Key

261

Worked over a multiple of 2 stitches and 2 rows.

Row 1: [Tps2Tog, yo] rep.

Row 2: Tfs.

Repeat Rows 1 and 2.

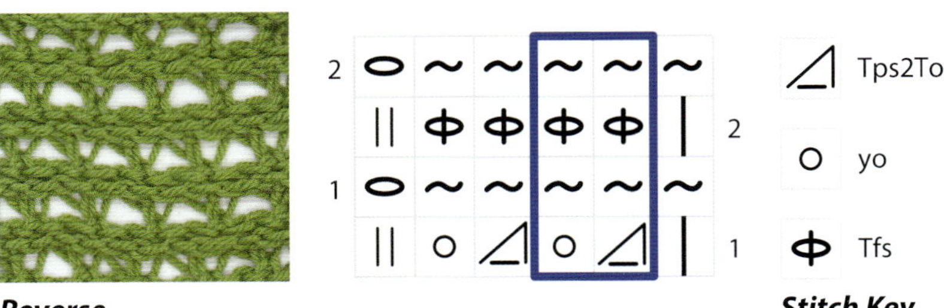

Reverse

Stitch Key

262

Worked over a multiple of 2 stitches and 2 rows.

Stitch 262 (St-262): Into the next 2 sts [Tss2Tog (photo 1), insert hook behind first vertical bar, grab second bar with hook (photo 2) and pull through first (photo 3), ch 1 (photo 4)].

Row 1: St-262 rep.

Row 2: Tss, St-262 rep until 1 st rem, Tss.

Repeat Rows 1 and 2.

Reverse

263

Worked over a multiple of 2 stitches and 2 rows.

Row 1: [Tss 2] rep.

Row 2: Worked over next 2 sts, [Tss2Tog (photo 1), and then Tss2Tog in prior row (photo 2), Tfs in the next st sp (photo 3) and pull through 2 loops on hook (photo 4), yo] rep.

Row 3: [Tss, Tks] rep.

Repeat Rows 2 and 3.

Reverse

264

Worked over a multiple of 2 stitches.

Stitch 264 (St-264): Worked over next 2 sts, insert hook behind first vertical bar, grab second bar with hook (photo 1), and pull through first (photo 2), ch 1 (photo 3), Tss in first bar (photo 4).

Row 1: St-264 rep.

Repeat Row 1.

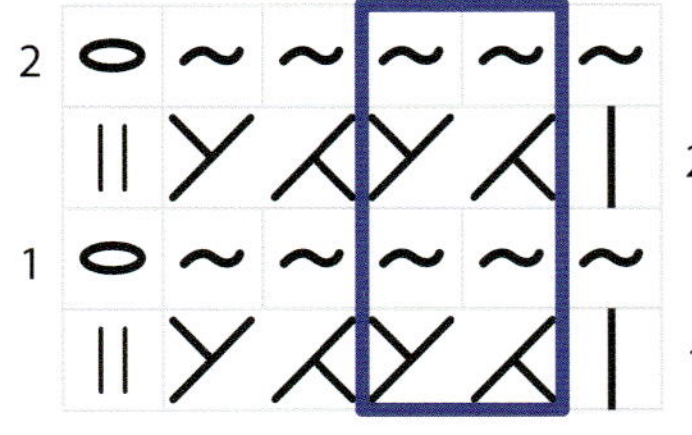

Stitch Key

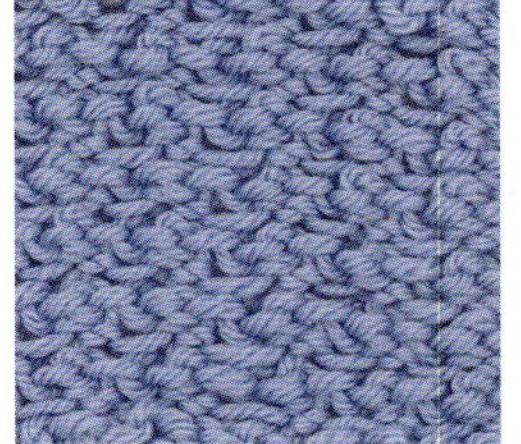

Reverse

265

Worked over a multiple of 4 stitches and 2 rows.

Uses Stitch 264 (St-264).

Row 1: St-264 rep.

Row 2: Tss, St-264 rep until 1 st rem, Tss.

Repeat Rows 1 and 2.

Reverse

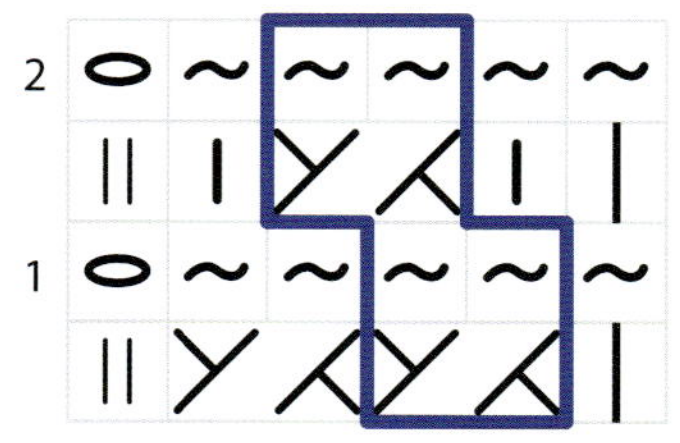

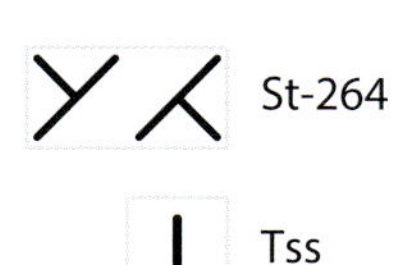

Stitch Key

266

Worked over a multiple of 8 stitches and 2 rows.

Stitch 266 (St-266): In the next 4 sts, Tss 4 (photo 1), slip sts 3 and 4 under sts 1 and 2 (photo 2). Tss in st 1 (photo 3), Tss in st 2 (photo 4).

Row 1: St-266 rep.

Row 2: Tss 2, St-266 rep until 2 sts rem, Tss 2.

Repeat Rows 1 and 2.

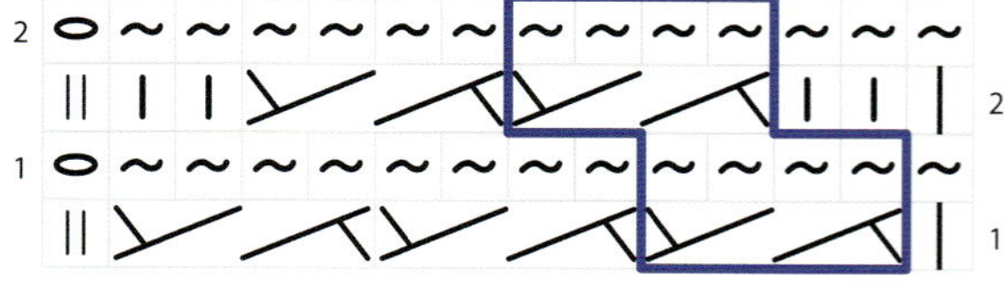

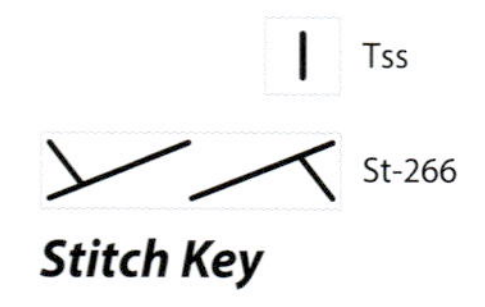

Stitch Key

Reverse

1

2

3

4

267

Worked over a multiple of 2 stitches and 2 rows.

Row 1 FP: [Tps, Tss] rep.

Row 1 RP: Std RP.

Row 2 FP: [yo, Tslst, Tps] rep.

Row 2 RP: [RP-2, RP-3] rep.

Row 3 FP: [Tps (photo 2), yo, Tslst (photo 2)] rep.

Row 3 RP: [RP-3, RP-2] rep.

Repeat Rows 2 and 3.

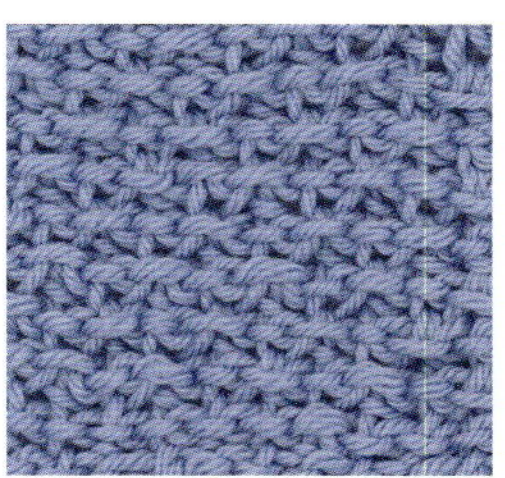

Reverse

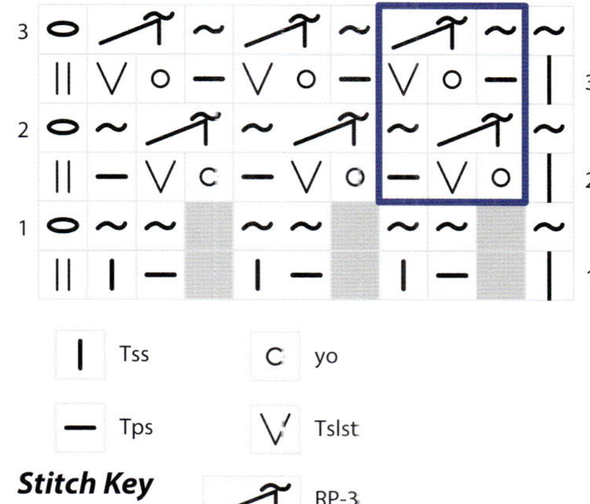

Stitch Key

268

Worked over a multiple of 2 stitches and 2 rows.

Txks: In next 2 sts [Tks in st 1, Tss2Tog in sts 1 and 2].

Row 1: Txks rep.

Row 2: Tss, Txks rep until 1 st rem, Tss.

Repeat Rows 1 and 2.

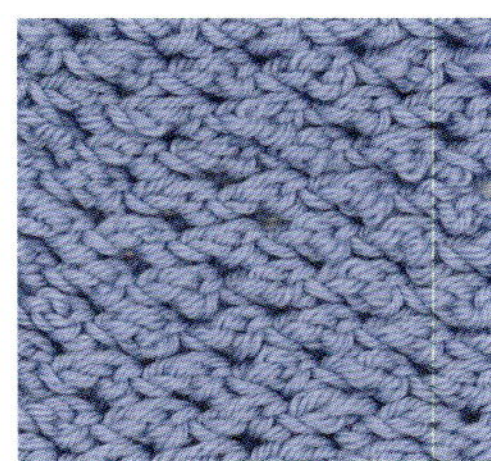

Reverse

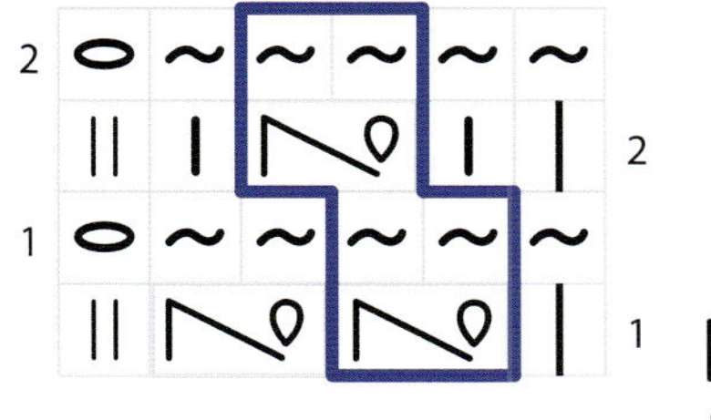

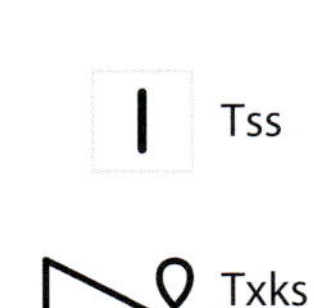

Stitch Key

269

Worked over 4 sts.

4x4Tss: [Tss in st 1, Tss2Tog in sts 1 and 2, Tss3Tog in st 1–3, Tss4Tog in sts 1–4].

Row 1: [Tps, Tss 4] rep.

Row 2: [Tps, 4x4Tss] rep.

Row 3: [Tps, Tss 4] rep.

Repeat Rows 1–3.

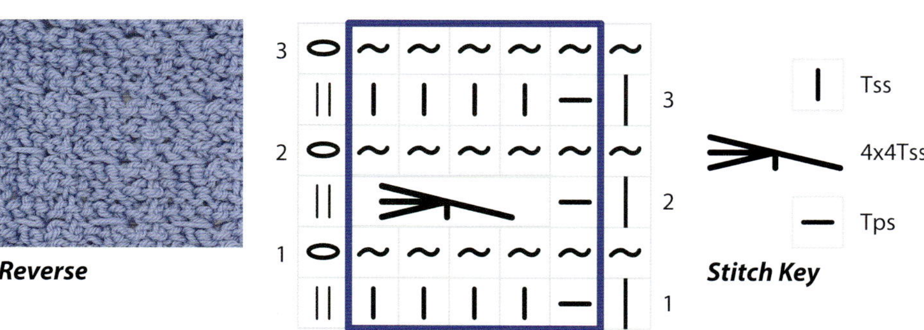

Reverse

Stitch Key

270 BACK CROSSED TSSDC

Worked over 2 stitches.

Row 1: In the next 2 sts [skip the first st, TrsDc in the second st, TssDc in the first st] rep.

Repeat Row 1.

Reverse

271 BACK CROSSED TSSTC

Worked over 2 stitches.

Row 1: In next 2 sts [skip the first st, TrsTc in the second st, TssTc in the first st] rep.

Repeat Row 1.

Reverse

272

Worked over 2 stitches.

PFptc2Tog: Move yarn to front of fabric. Insert hook behind both vertical bars in the next 2 sts. Yarn over and pull up a loop.

Row 1: In next 2 sts, [PFptc2Tog (photos 1 and 2), Tfs between st 1 and st 2 (photo 3)] rep.

Repeat Row 1.

Reverse

273

Worked over a multiple of 2 + 2 stitches and 2 rows.

Stitch 273 (St-273): In next 2 sts [Tss2Tog, ExTfs in st sp before st 1].

Row 1: St-273 rep.

Row 2: Tss, St-273 rep until 1 st rem, Tss.

Repeat Rows 1 and 2.

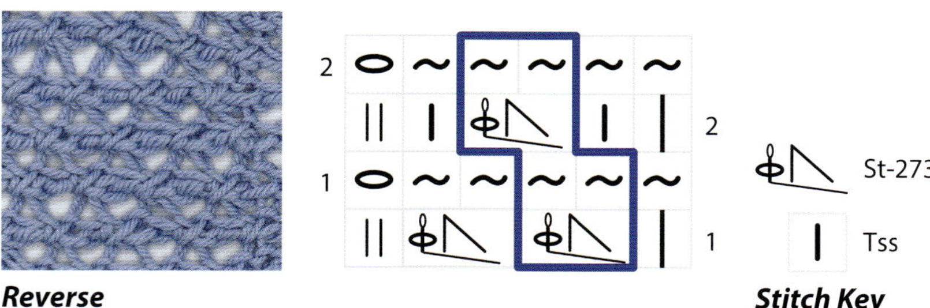

Reverse

Stitch Key

274

Worked over a multiple of 2 stitches and 2 rows.

Row 1: [Tss2Tog, yo] rep.

Row 2: Ttop rep.

Repeat Rows 1 and 2.

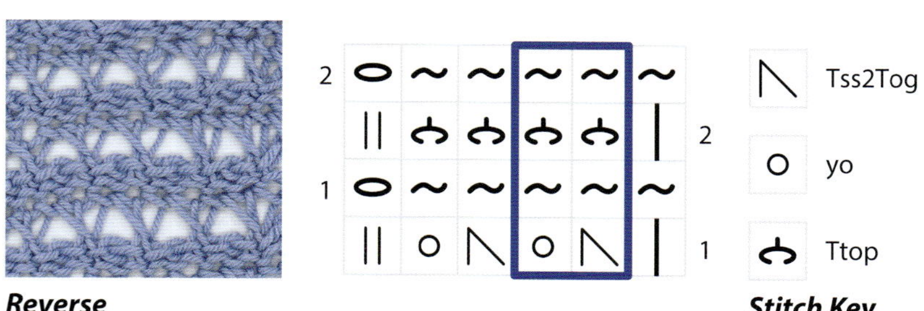

Reverse

Stitch Key

275

Worked over a multiple of 3 stitches and 2 rows.

St-275: Yo, in the next 3 sts, Tss3Tog, and then Tss in the first st.

Row 1: St-275 rep.

Row 2: Tss rep.

Repeat Rows 1 and 2.

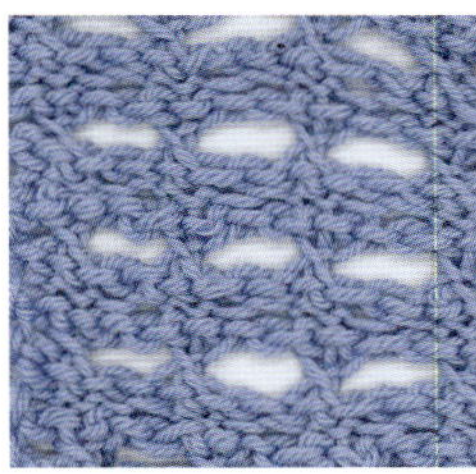

Reverse

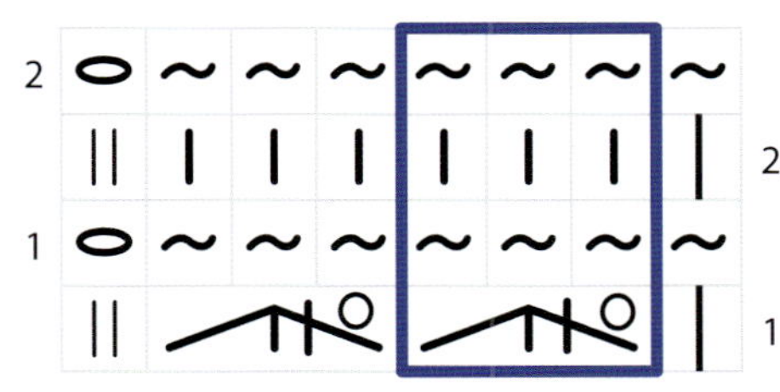

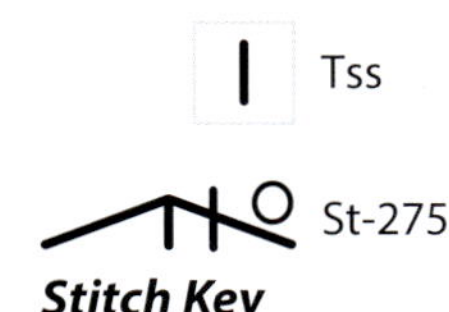

Stitch Key

276

Worked over a multiple of 3 stitches.

St-276: In the next 3 sts, Tss in first st (photo 1), yo, Tss3Tog in all 3 sts (photo 2).

Row 1: St-276 rep.

Repeat Row 1.

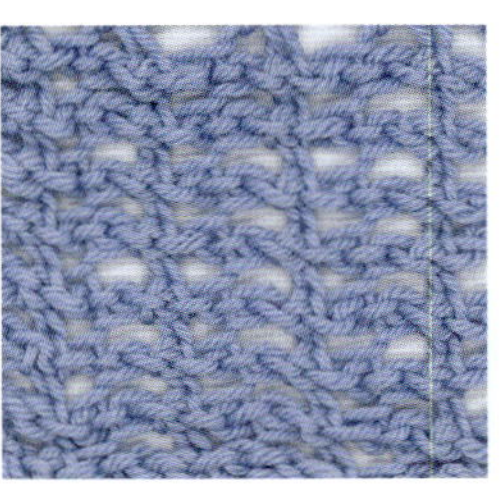

Reverse

277

Worked over a multiple of 2 stitches.

Row 1: *In next st [Tks, Tfs (photo 1), yo and pull through 2 loops (photo 2)], Tps, rep from *.

Repeat Row 1.

Reverse

278

Worked over any number of stitches.

Row 1: In next stitch, (Ttop (photo 1), Tps (photo 2) & slst) rep.

Repeat Row 1.

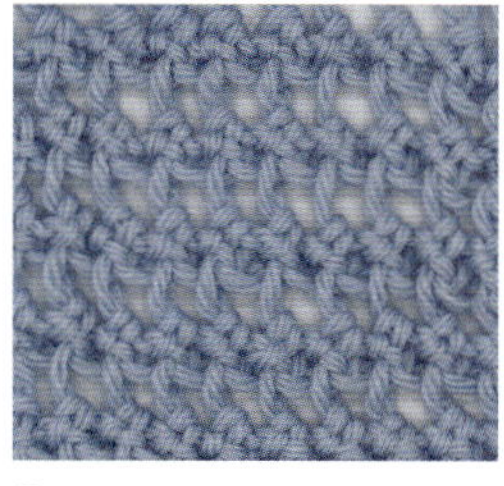

Reverse

279

Worked over a multiple of 2 stitches.
Row 1: [Tps2Tog, Ttop in next back bump] rep.
Repeat Row 1.

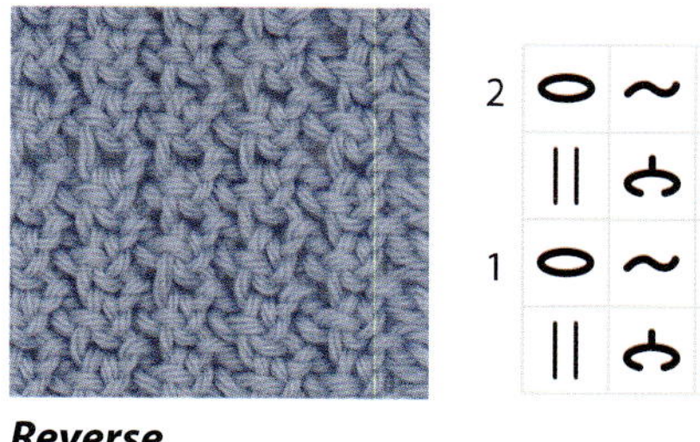

Reverse

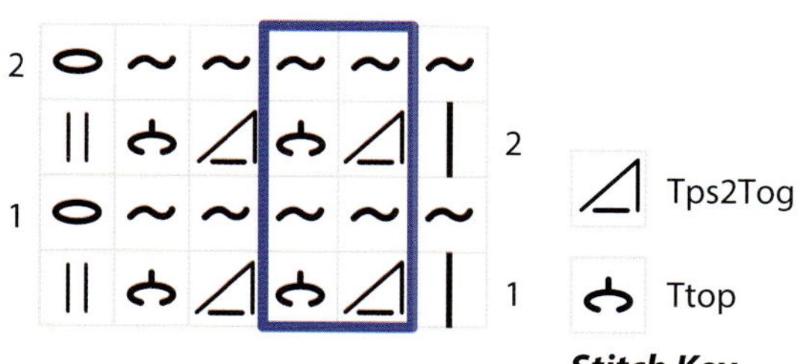

Stitch Key

280

Worked over a multiple of 2 stitches.
Row 1: [TwTks 2, Tfs in next st sp (photo 1) and sl st (photo 2), yo] rep.
Repeat Row 1.

Reverse

281 DROP STITCH

Worked over any number of stitches.

Row 1 FP: [Tss, yo] rep.

Row 1 RP: [remove loop from hook (photo 1), drop yo st off hook (photo 2), place loop back on hook, yo and pull through 2 loops] rep.

Repeat Row 1.

Reverse

282

Worked over a multiple of 2 stitches.

Row 1: [skip st, Ttop in 2nd st (photo 1), Tss2Tog in sts 1 and 2 (photo 2)] rep.

Repeat Row 1.

Reverse

283

Worked over a multiple of 2 stitches.

Row 1: [Ttop, Tss2Tog] rep.

Repeat Row 1.

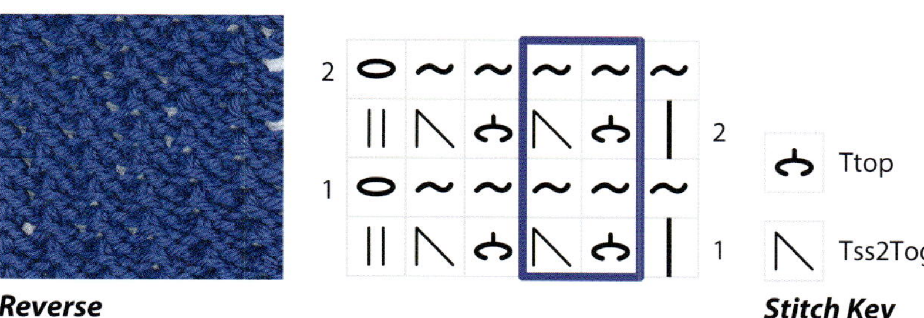

Reverse

Ttop

Tss2Tog

Stitch Key

284

Worked over a multiple of 2 stitches and 2 rows.

Row 1: [Ttop, Tss2Tog] rep.

Row 2: [Tss2Tog, Ttop] rep.

Repeat Rows 1 and 2.

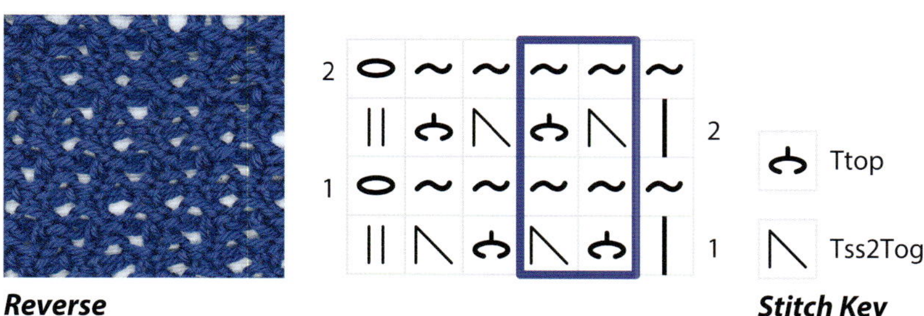

Reverse

Ttop

Tss2Tog

Stitch Key

285

Worked over a multiple of 2 stitches.

Row 1: [Tss2Tog, Ttop] rep.

Repeat Row 1.

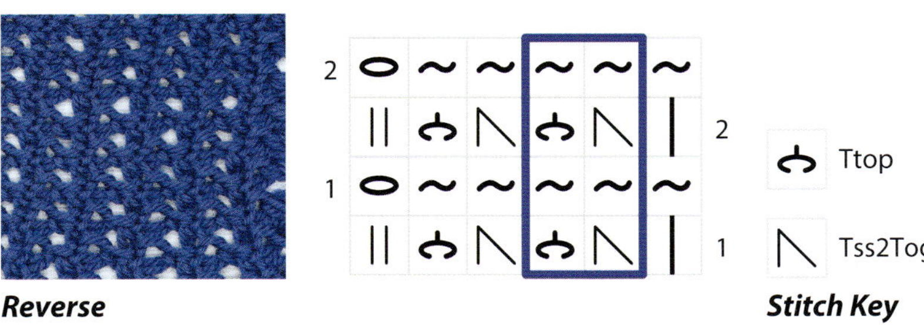

Reverse

Ttop

Tss2Tog

Stitch Key

286

Worked over a multiple of 2 stitches and 2 rows.

Row 1: [yo, Tss2Tog] rep.

Row 2: [Tss2Tog, yo] rep.

Repeat Rows 1 and 2.

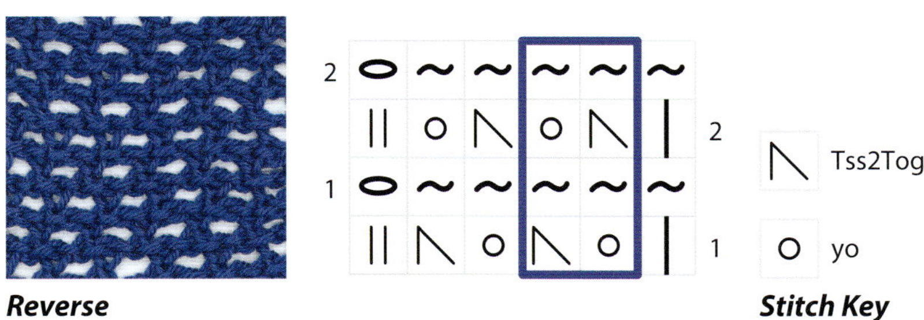

Reverse

Tss2Tog

yo

Stitch Key

287

Worked over a multiple of 2 stitches.

Row 1: [Tss2Tog, yo] rep.

Repeat Row 1.

Reverse

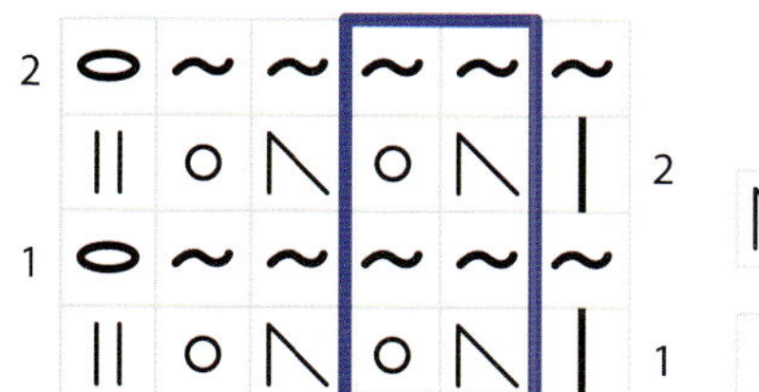

Tss2Tog

yo

Stitch Key

288

Worked over a multiple of 2 stitches.

Row 1: [yo, Tss2Tog] rep.

Repeat Row 1.

Reverse

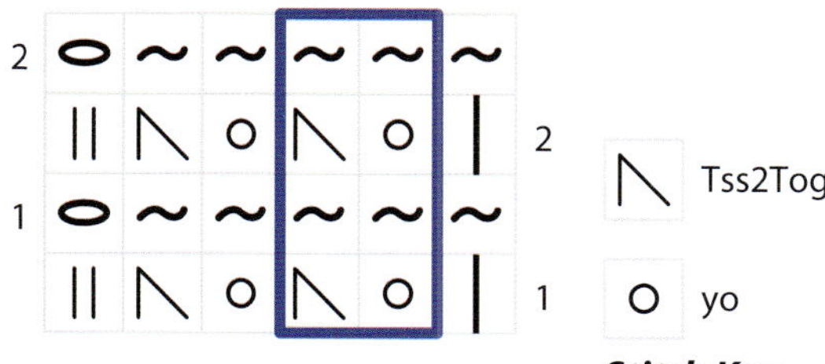

Tss2Tog

yo

Stitch Key

289

Worked over a multiple of 2 stitches and 2 rows.

Row 1: [Tfs, Tss2Tog] rep.

Row 2: [Tss2Tog, Tfs] rep.

Repeat Rows 1 and 2.

Reverse

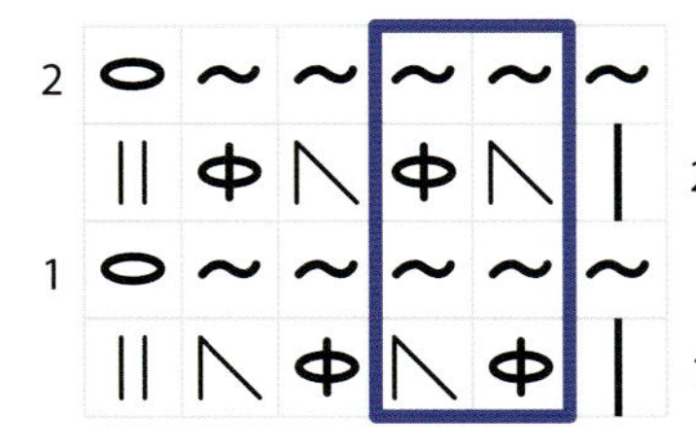

Tss2Tog

Tfs

Stitch Key

290

Worked over a multiple of 2 stitches.

Row 1: [Tss2Tog, Tfs] rep.

Repeat Row 1.

Reverse

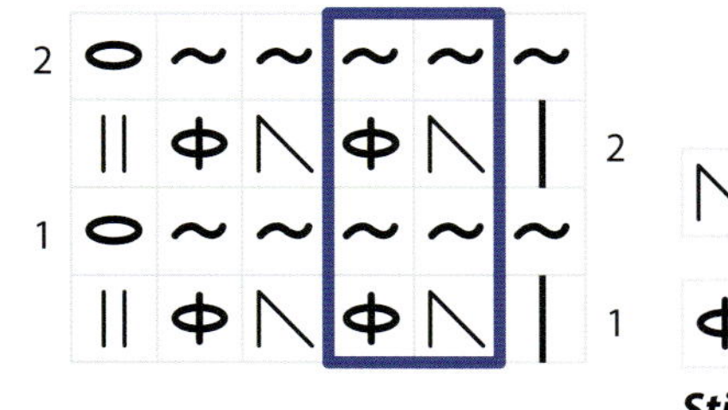

Tss2Tog

Tfs

Stitch Key

291

Worked over a multiple of 2 stitches.

Row 1: [Tks2Tog, yo] rep.

Repeat Row 1.

Reverse

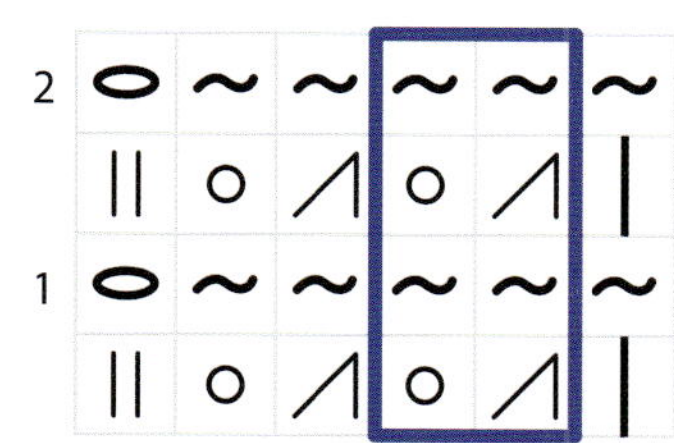

Tks2Tog

yo

Stitch Key

292

Worked over a multiple of 2 stitches and 2 rows.

Row 1: [yo, Tks2Tog] rep.

Row 2: [Tks2Tog, yo] rep.

Repeat Rows 1 and 2.

Reverse

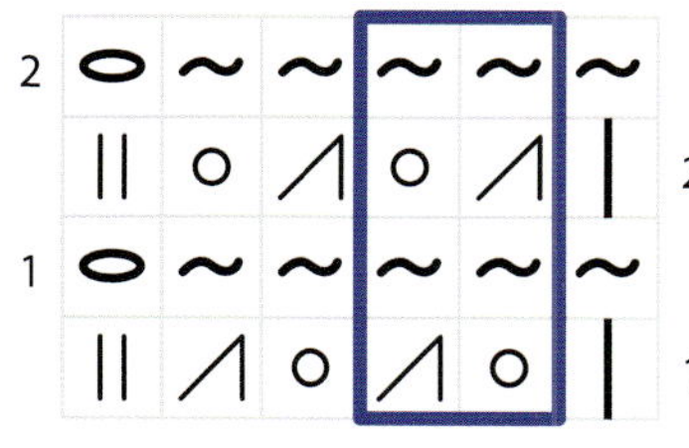

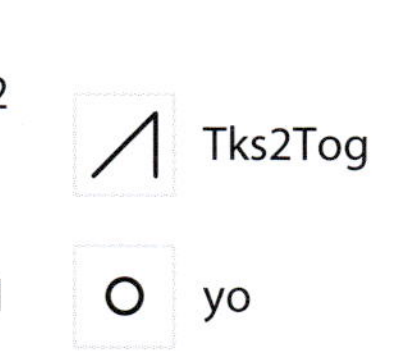

Stitch Key

293

Worked over a multiple of 2 stitches.

Row 1: [Tks2Tog, Tfs] rep.

Repeat Row 1.

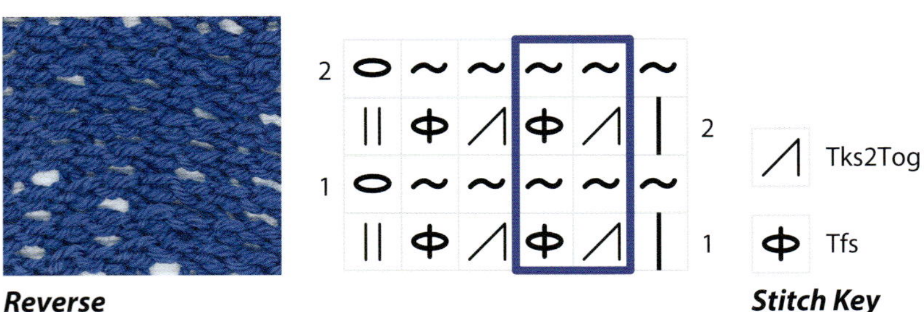

Reverse

Stitch Key

294

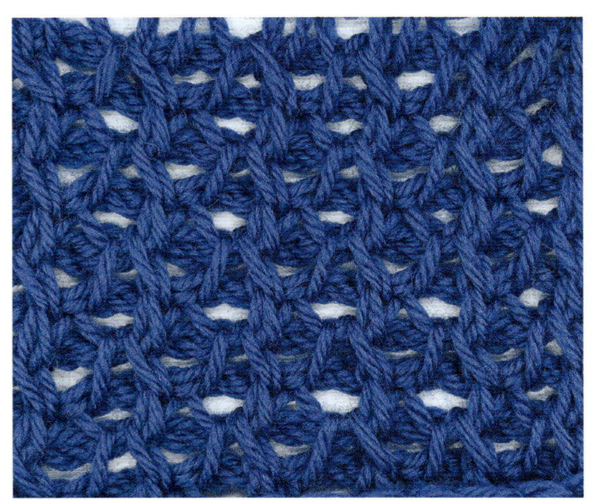

Worked over a multiple of 2 stitches and 2 rows.

Row 1: [Tfs, Tks2Tog] rep.

Row 2: [Tks2Tog, Tfs] rep.

Repeat Rows 1 and 2.

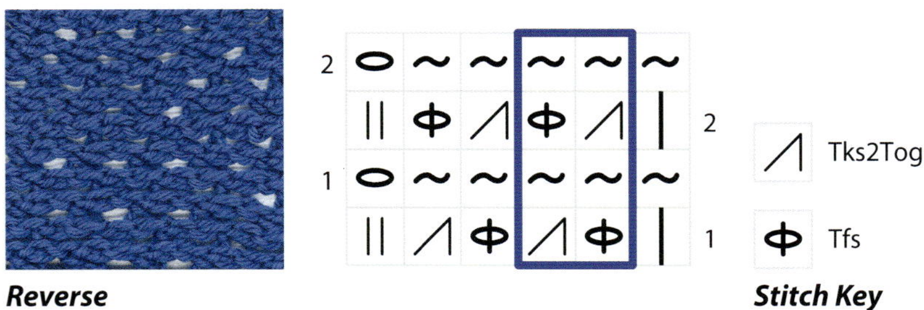

Reverse

Stitch Key

295

Worked over a multiple of 2 stitches and 2 rows.

Row 1: [Tfs, Trs2Tog] rep.

Row 2: [Trs2Tog, Tfs] rep.

Repeat Rows 1 and 2.

Reverse

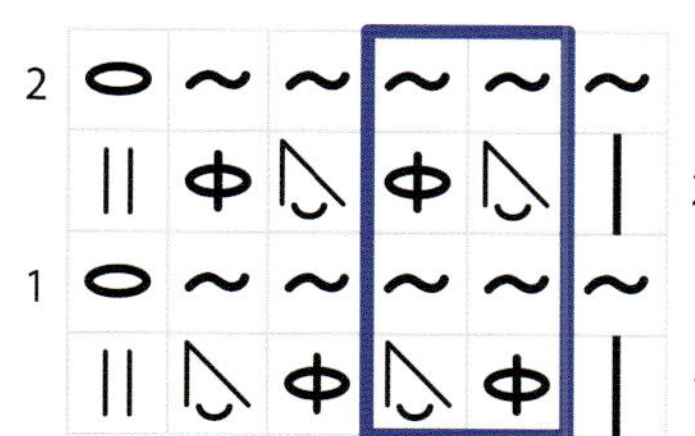

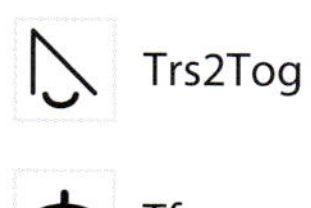

Stitch Key

296

Worked over a multiple of 2 stitches.

Row 1: [Trs2Tog, Tfs] rep.

Repeat Row 1.

Reverse

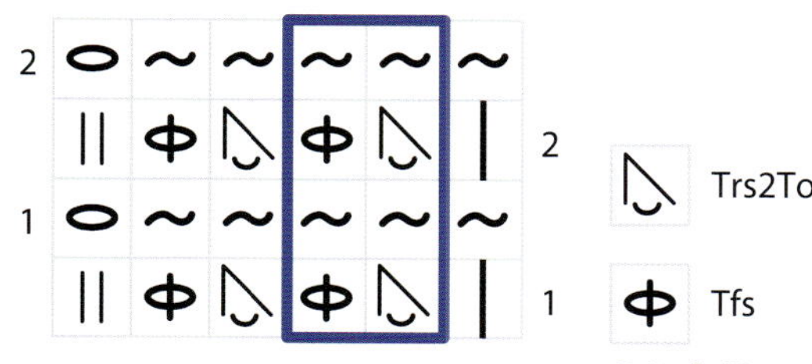

Stitch Key

297

Worked over a multiple of 2 stitches and 2 rows.

Row 1: [Tfs, Tps2Tog] rep.

Row 2: [Tps2Tog, Tfs] rep.

Repeat Rows 1 and 2.

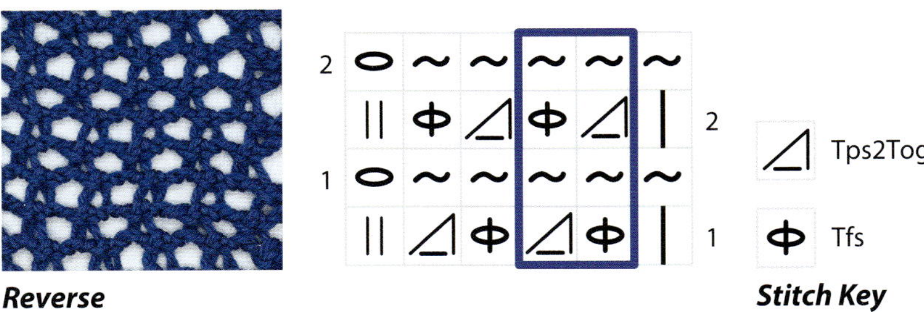

Reverse

Tps2Tog

Tfs

Stitch Key

298

Worked over a multiple of 2 stitches.

Row 1: [Tfs, Tps2Tog] rep.

Repeat Row 1.

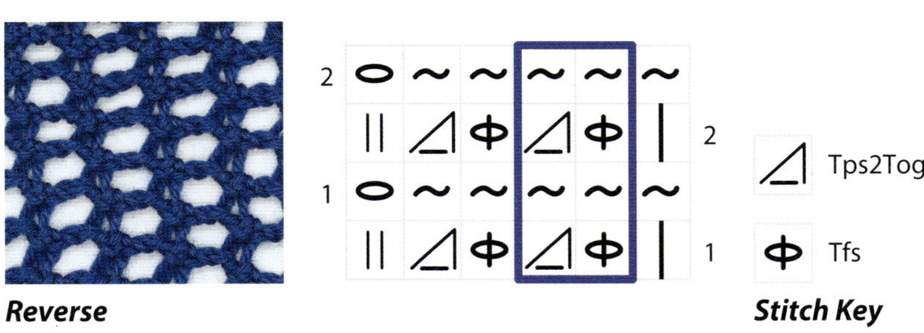

Reverse

Tps2Tog

Tfs

Stitch Key

299

Worked over a multiple of 2 stitches.

Row 1: [Tps2Tog, Tfs] rep.

Repeat Row 1.

Reverse

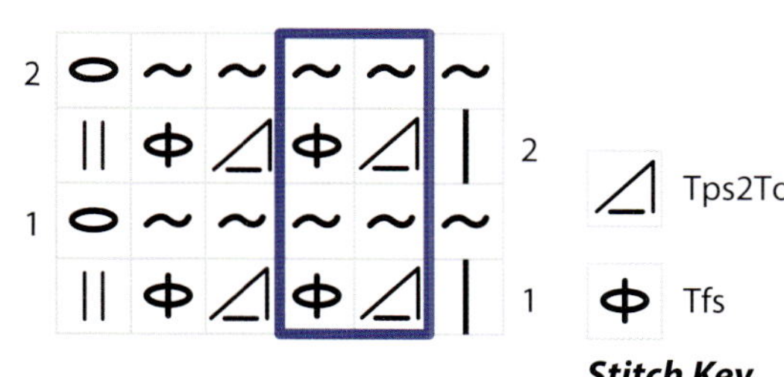

Stitch Key

Tps2Tog

Tfs

300

Worked over a multiple of 2 stitches and 2 rows.

Row 1: [Tps, Ttop] rep.

Row 2: [Ttop, Tps] rep.

Repeat Rows 1 and 2.

Reverse

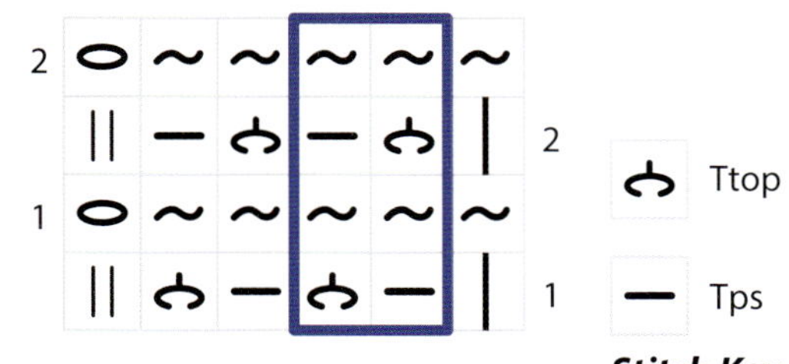

Stitch Key

Ttop

Tps

301

Worked over a multiple of 2 stitches and 2 rows.

Row 1: [Tss, Ttop] rep.

Row 2: [Ttop, Tss] rep.

Repeat Rows 1 and 2.

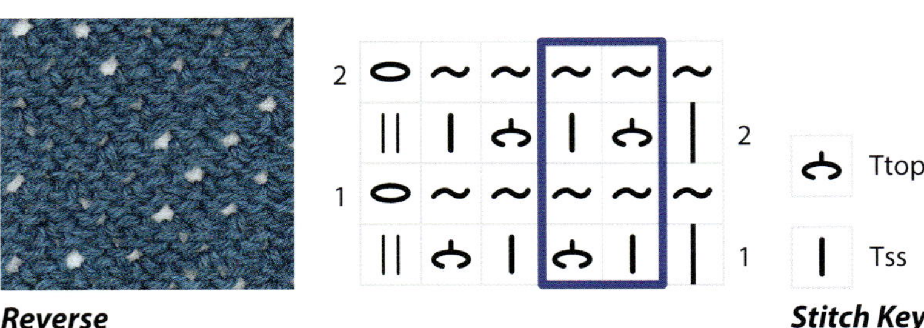

Reverse

Stitch Key

302

Worked over a multiple of 2 stitches.

ExTss2Tog: Tss2Tog, ch 1.

Row 1: [ExTss2Tog, yo] rep.

Repeat Row 1.

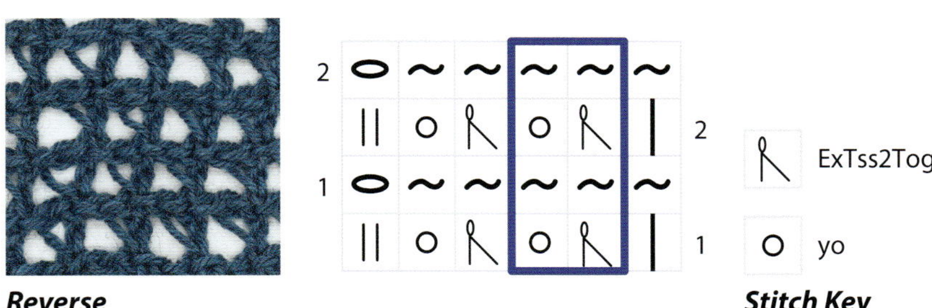

Reverse

Stitch Key

303

Worked over a multiple of 2 + 2 stitches and 2 rows.

Tdc2Tog: Yo, insert hook behind next 2 vertical bars, yo and pull up a loop, [yo and pull through 2 loops] twice.

Row 1: In next 2 sts, (Tdc2Tog twice) rep.

Row 2: Tdc, in next 2 sts (Tdc2Tog twice) rep until 1 st rem, Tdc.

Repeat Rows 1 and 2.

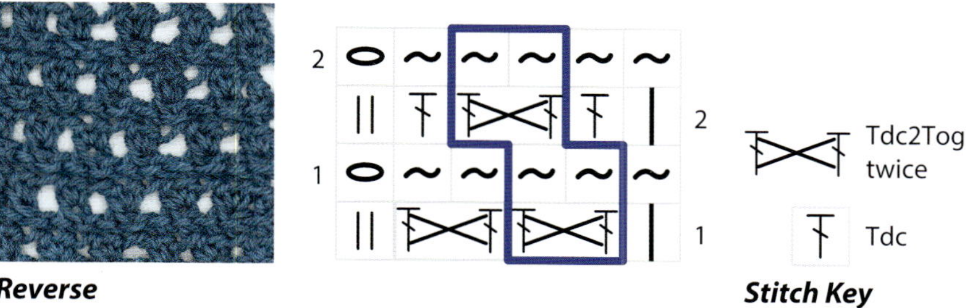

Reverse

Stitch Key

304

Worked over a multiple of 2 stitches and 2 rows.

Row 1: [yo sk st, Tmss] rep.

Row 2: [Tmss, yo sk st] rep.

Repeat Rows 1 and 2.

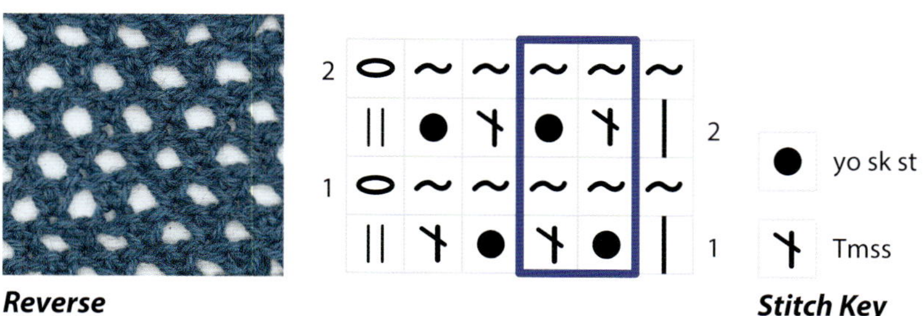

Reverse

Stitch Key

305

Worked over a multiple of 2 stitches and 2 rows.

Row 1: [yo sk st, Tks] rep.

Row 2: [Tks, yo sk st] rep.

Repeat Rows 1 and 2.

Reverse

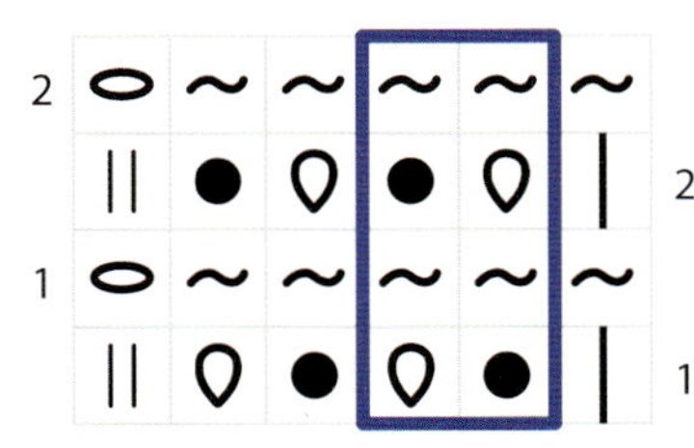

yo sk st

Tks

Stitch Key

306

Worked over a multiple of 2 stitches.

Row 1: [yu, Tps2Tog] rep.

Repeat Row 1.

Reverse

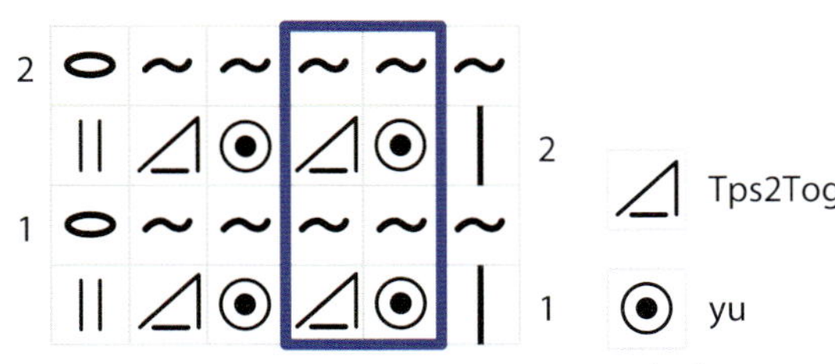

Stitch Key

307

Worked over a multiple of 2 stitches and 2 rows.

Row 1: [Tps2Tog, yu] rep.

Row 2: [yu, Tps2Tog] rep.

Repeat Rows 1 and 2.

Reverse

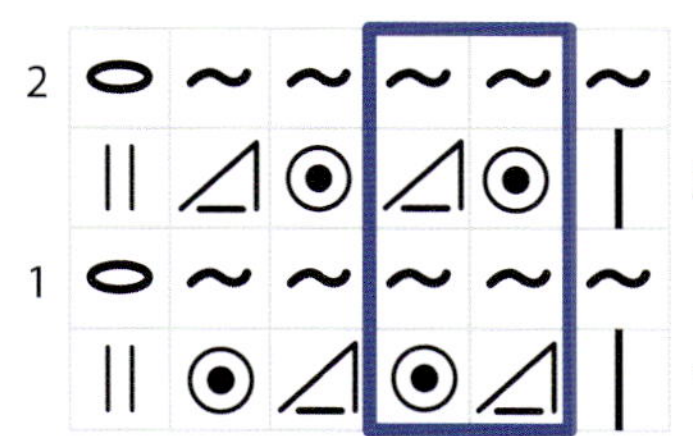

Tps2Tog

yu

Stitch Key

308

Worked over a multiple of 2 stitches.

Row 1: [Tps2Tog, yu] rep.

Repeat Row 1.

Reverse

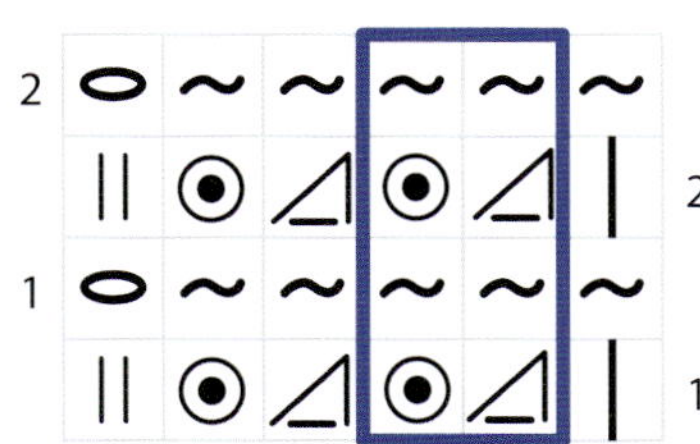

Tps2Tog

yu

Stitch Key

309

Worked over a multiple of 2 stitches and 2 rows.

Row 1: [Tks, Ttop] rep.

Row 2: [Ttop, Tks] rep.

Repeat Rows 1 and 2.

Reverse

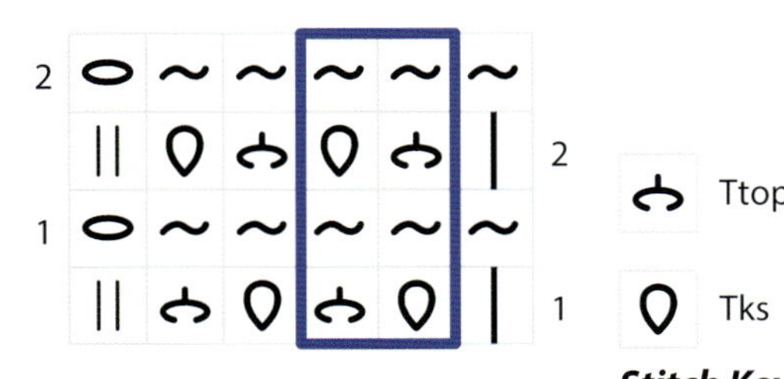

Stitch Key

310

Worked over a multiple of 2 stitches.

Row 1: [Tps, TwTks, yo and Tfs in next st sp (photo 1), yo and pull through 3 (photo 2)] rep.

Repeat Row 1.

Reverse

311

Worked over a multiple of 3 stitches and 2 rows.

Row 1: [Tfs in next st sp (photo 1), Tss3Tog (photo 2) and slst, ch1 (photo 3)] rep.

Row 2: [Tss, Ttop in next 2 ch] rep.

Repat Rows 1 and 2.

Reverse

1

2

3

312

Worked over a multiple of 4 stitches and 2 rows.

ExTss3Tog: Insert hook behind next 3 front vertical bars from right to left*. Yarn over and pull up a loop. Ch 1.

**Left-handed makers: Insert hook from left to right.*

Row 1: [ExTss3Tog (photo 1), in next st ExTks 3 times (photo 2)] rep.

Row 2: [In next st (ExTks 3 times), ExTss3Tog] rep.

Repeat Rows 1 and 2.

1

2

CHAPTER 3

Lace Stitches

313 EYELET RIGHT WITH SKIP STITCH

Reverse

Worked over 1 stitch and 2 rows.
Row 1: At eyelet location, yo sk st.
Row 2: At eyelet location, Tks.

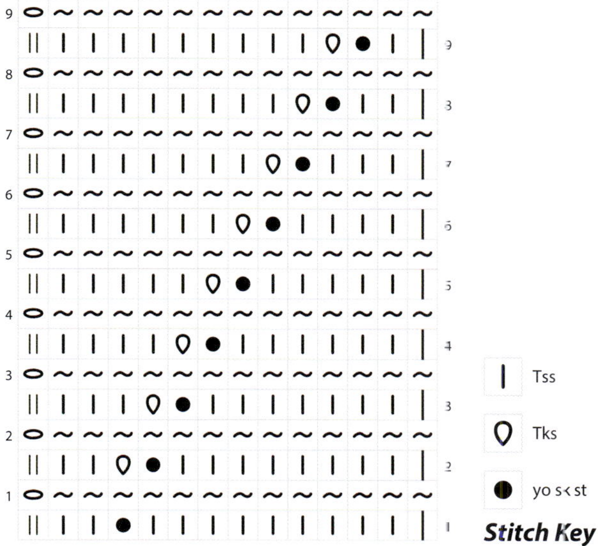

Stitch Key

314 EYELET RIGHT WITH TSS2TOG

Reverse

Worked over 2 stitches and 2 rows.
Row 1: At eyelet location, Tss2Tog, yo.
Row 2: At yo location, Tks.

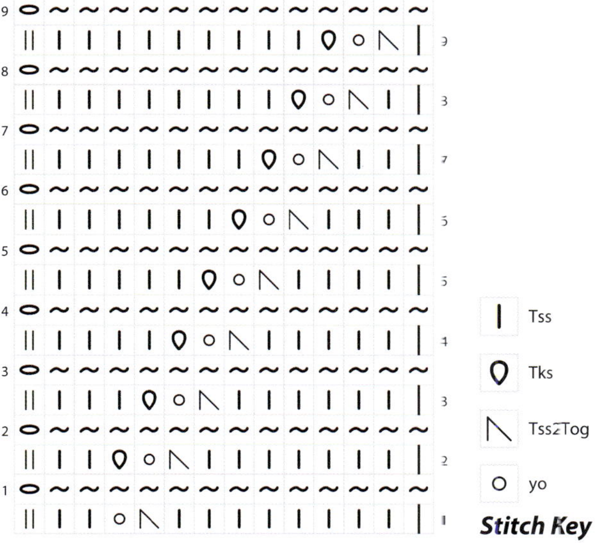

Stitch Key

315 EYELET LEFT WITH SKIP STITCH

Reverse

Worked over 1 stitch and 2 rows.
Row 1: At eyelet location, yo, skst.
Row 2: At eyelet location, Tks.

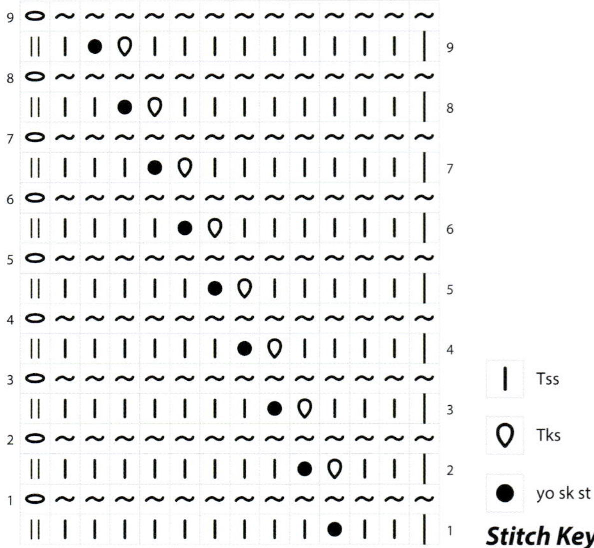

Stitch Key

316 EYELET LEFT WITH TSS2TOG

Reverse

Worked over 2 stitches and 2 rows.
Row 1: At eyelet location, yo, Tss2Tog.
Row 2: At yo location, Tss.

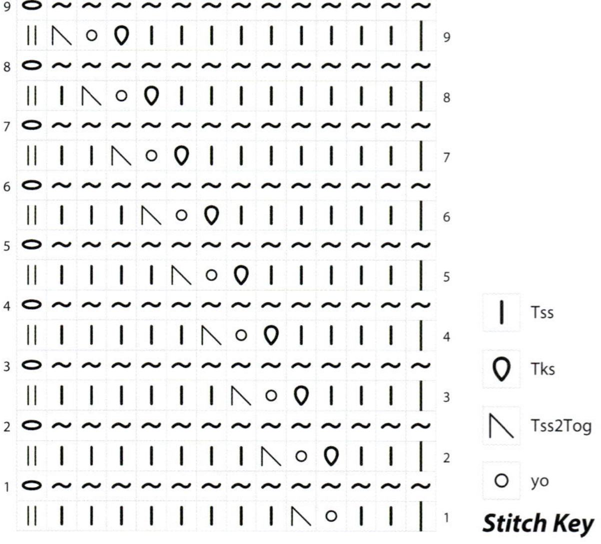

Stitch Key

317

Worked over a multiple of 3 stitches and 2 rows.

Row 1 FP: [Tss 3] rep.

Row 1 RP: [ch 1, RP-4, ch 1] rep.

Row 2 FP: [Skip the first ch, into the back bump of the 3 sts closed together, (Ttop, yo, Ttop), skip next ch] rep.

Row 2 RP: Std RP.

Repeat Rows 1 and 2.

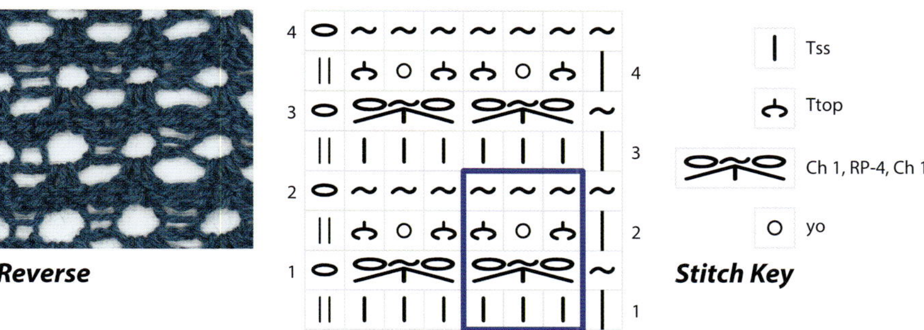

Reverse

Stitch Key

318

Worked over a multiple of 6 stitches and 2 rows.

Row 1 FP: [Tss 3] rep.

Row 1 RP: [RP-2 three times, ch 1, RP-4, ch 1] rep.

Row 2 FP: [Skip the next ch, into the back bump of the 3 sts closed together, (Ttop, yo, Ttop), skip next ch, Tss 3] rep.

Row 2 RP: [ch 1, RP-4, ch 1, RP-2 three times] rep.

Row 3 FP: [Tss 3, Skip the next ch, into the back bump of the 3 sts closed together, (Ttop, yo, Ttop), skip next ch] rep.

Row 3 RP: [RP-2 three times, ch 1, RP-4, ch 1] rep.

Repeat Rows 2 and 3.

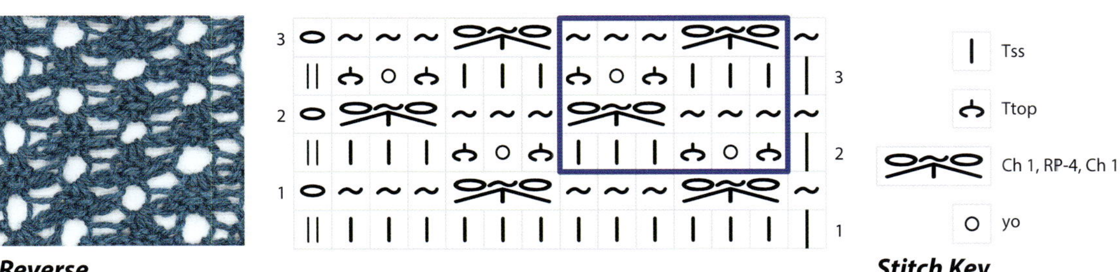

Reverse

Stitch Key

319

Worked over a multiple of 7 stitches and 2 rows.
Row 1: [Tss 3, yo, Tss3Tog, yo, Tss] rep.
Row 2: [Tss 2, Tks2Tog, yo, Tss, yo, Tss2Tog] rep.
Repeat Rows 1 and 2.

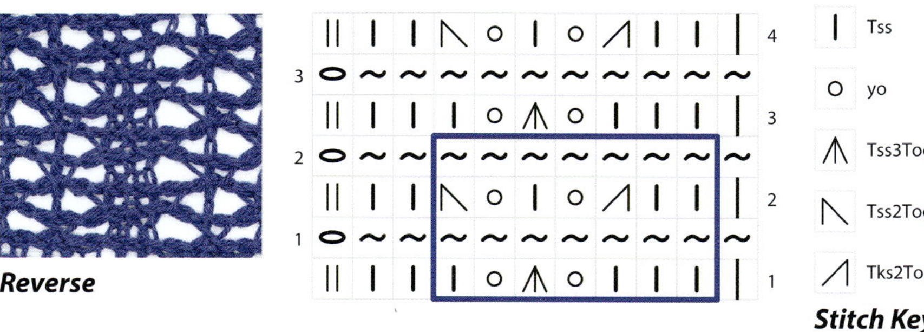

320

Worked over a multiple of 8 stitches and 2 rows.
Row 1: [Tss 3, Tss2Tog, yo 2, Tss2Tog, Tss] rep.
Row 2: [Tss 2, Tss2Tog, yo, Tks, Tss, yo, Tss2Tog] rep.
Row 3: [Tss 3, Tss2Tog, yo 2, Tks2Tog, Tss] rep.
Repeat Rows 2 and 3.

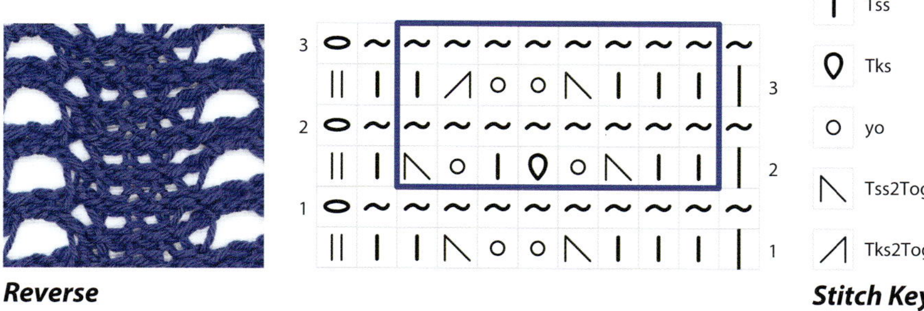

321

Worked over a multiple of 4 stitches and 1 row.

Row 1: [Tss2Tog, yo 2, Tss2Tog] rep.

Row 2: [Tks2Tog, yo 2, Tss2Tog] rep.

Repeat Row 2.

Reverse

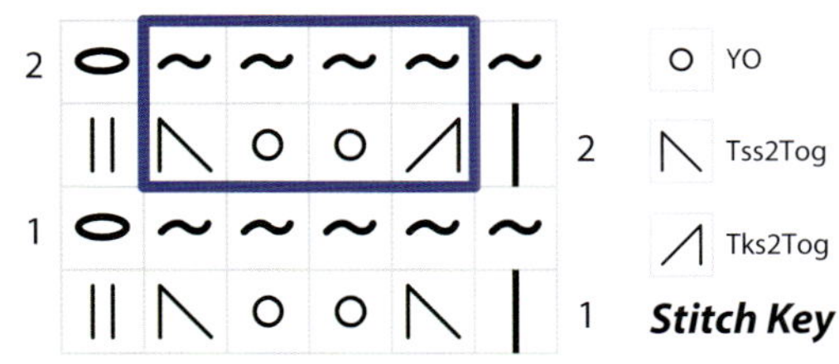

YO

Tss2Tog

Tks2Tog

Stitch Key

322

Worked over a multiple of 4 stitches and 4 rows.

Row 1: [yo, Tss2Tog 2, yo] rep.

Row 2: Tks, [Tx, Tks, Tss] rep until 3 st rem, Tx, Tks.

Row 3: [Tss2Tog, yo 2, Tss2Tog] rep.

Row 4: Tss, [Tks, Tss, Tx] rep until 3 st rem, Tks, Tss 2.

Repeat Rows 1–4.

Reverse

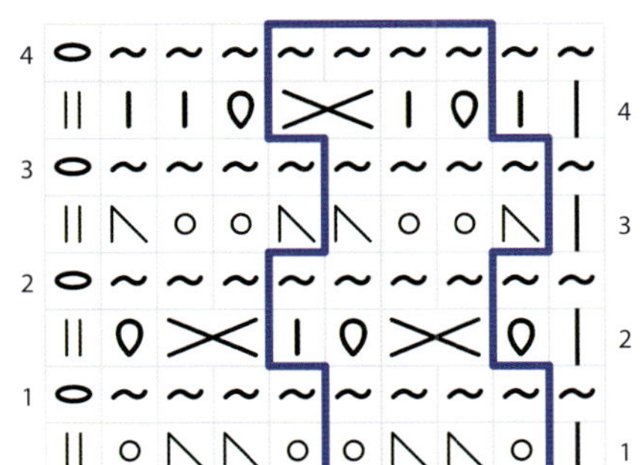

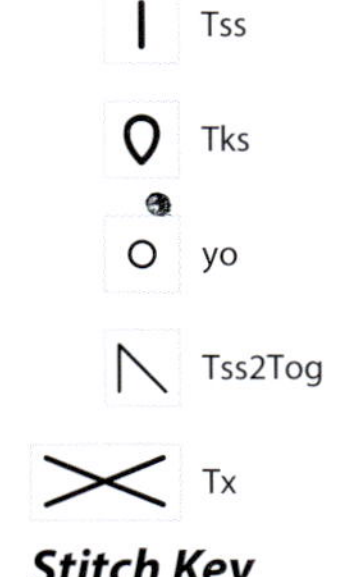

Stitch Key

323

Worked over a multiple of 4 stitches and 2 rows.
Row 1: [yo, Tss2Tog, Tss 2] rep.
Row 2: [Tks, Tss, yo, Tss2Tog] rep.
Row 3: [yo, Tss2Tog, Tks, Tss] rep.
Repeat Rows 2 and 3.

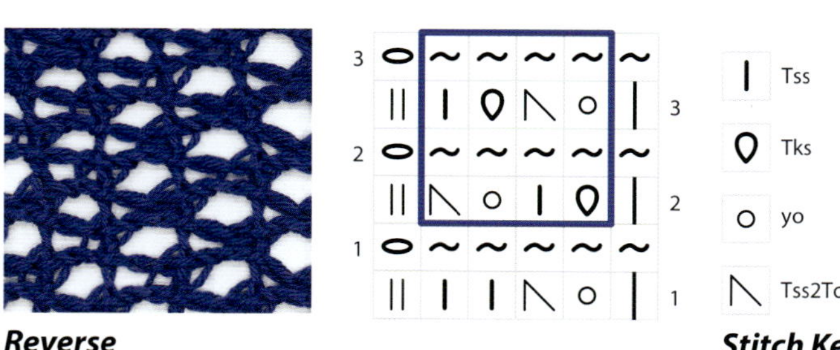

Reverse

Tss

Tks

yo

Tss2Tog

Stitch Key

324

Worked over a multiple of 5 stitches and 4 rows.
Row 1: [Tss, yo, Tss2Tog 2, yo] rep.
Row 2: [Tss, Tks, Tss 2, Tks] rep.
Row 3: [Tss, Tss2Tog, yo 2, Tss2Tog] rep.
Row 4: [Tss 2, Tks, Tss 2] rep.
Repeat Rows 1–4.

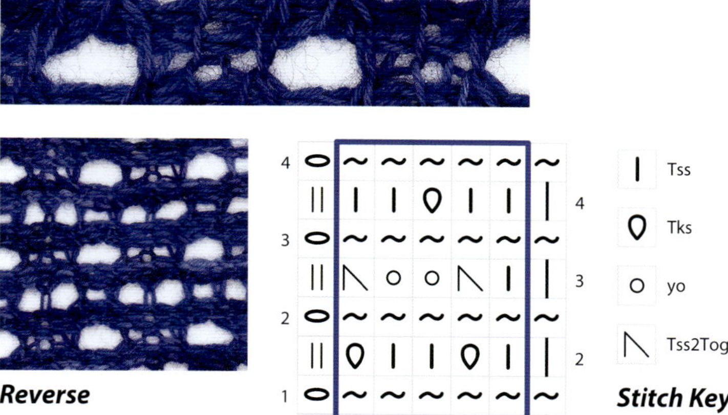

Reverse

Tss

Tks

yo

Tss2Tog

Stitch Key

325

Reverse

Worked over a multiple of 4 + 2 stitches and 4 rows.

Row 1: Tss, [Tss 2, Tss2Tog, yo] rep until 1 st rem, Tss.

Row 2: Tss, [yo, Tss3Tog, yo, Tks] rep until 1 st rem, Tss.

Row 3: Tss, [Tss2Tog, yo, Tks, Tss] rep until 1 st rem, Tss.

Row 4: Tss2Tog, [yo, Tks, yo, Tss3Tog] rep, yo.

Row 5: Tss, [Tks, Tss, Tss2Tog, yo] rep until 1 st rem, Tks.

Repeat Rows 2–5.

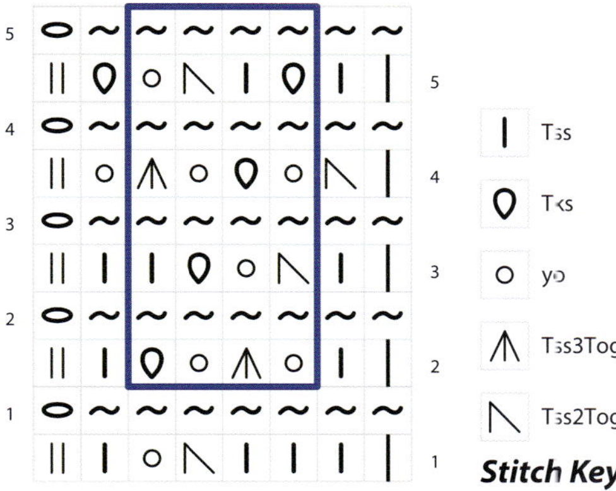

326

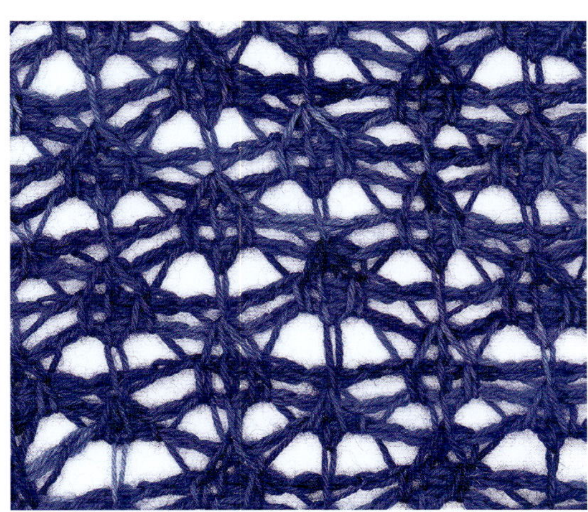

Reverse

Worked over a multiple of 6 + 2 stitches and 4 rows.

Row 1: Tss, [yo, Tss2Tog, Tss, Tss2Tog yo, Tss] rep until 1 st rem, Tss.

Row 2: Tss, [Tks, yo, Tss3Tog, yo, Tks, Tss] rep until 1 st rem, Tss.

Row 3: Tss, [Tks2Tog, yo, Tss, yo, Tss2Tog, Tss] rep until 1 st rem, Tss.

Row 4: Tss2Tog, [yo, Tks, Tss, Tks, yo, Tss3Tog] rep, yo.

Row 5: Tss, [yo, Tss2Tog, Tss, Tss2Tog, Tss] rep until 1 st rem, Tks.

Repeat Rows 2–5.

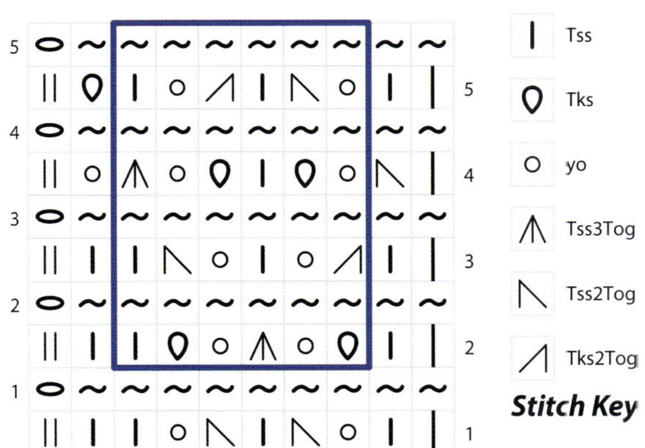

327

Worked over a multiple of 7 + 5 stitches and 6 rows.

Row 1: Tss 2, [Tss 4, yo, Tss2Tog, Tss] rep until 3 st rem, Tss 3.

Row 2: Tss 2, [Tss 2, Tss2Tog, yo, Tks, yo, Tss2Tog] rep until 3 st rem, Tss 3.

Row 3: Tss 2, [Tss 3, Tks, yo sk st, Tks, Tss] rep until 3 st rem, Tss 3.

Row 4: Tss 2, [yo, Tss2Tog, Tss 2, Tks, Tss 2] rep until 3 st rem, yo, Tss2Tog, Tss.

Row 5: Tss2Tog, yo, [Tks, yo, Tss2Tog, Tss 2, Tss2Tog, yo] rep until 3 st rem, Tks, yo, Tss2Tog.

Row 6: Tss, Tks, [yo sk st, Tks, Tss 4, Tks] rep until 3 st rem, yo sk st, Tks, Tss.

Row 7: Tss 2, [Tks, Tss 3, yo, Tss2Tog, Tss] rep until 3 st rem, Tks, Tss 2.

Repeat Rows 2–7.

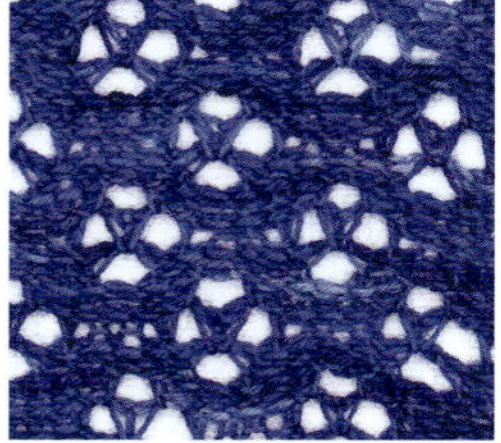

Reverse

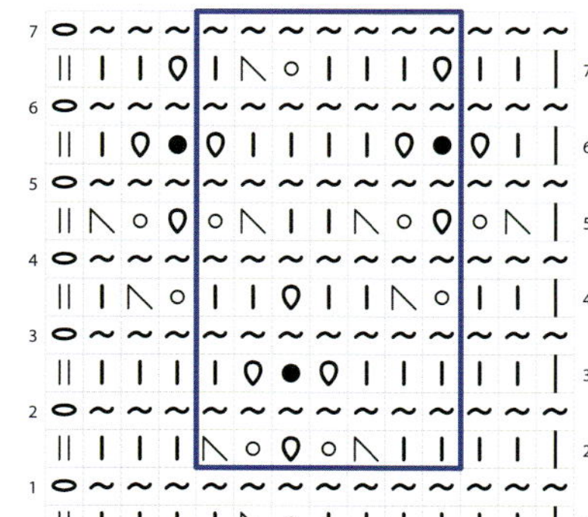

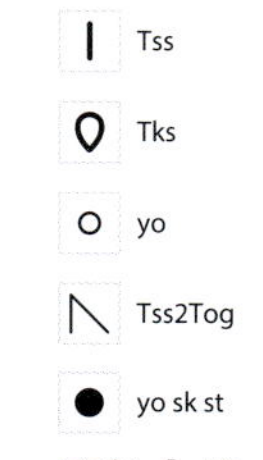

Stitch Key

328

Worked over a multiple of 8 stitches and 5 rows.

Row 1: [Tss, yo, Tss2Tog, Tss 3, Tss2Tog, yo] rep.

Row 2: [Tss, Tks, yo, Tss2Tog, Tss, Tss2Tog, yo, Tks] rep.

Row 3: [Tss 2, Tks, yo, Tss3Tog, yo, Tks, Tss] rep.

Row 4: [Tss 3, Tks, Tss, Tks, Tss 2] rep.

Row 5: [Tss 8] rep.

Repeat Rows 1–5.

Reverse

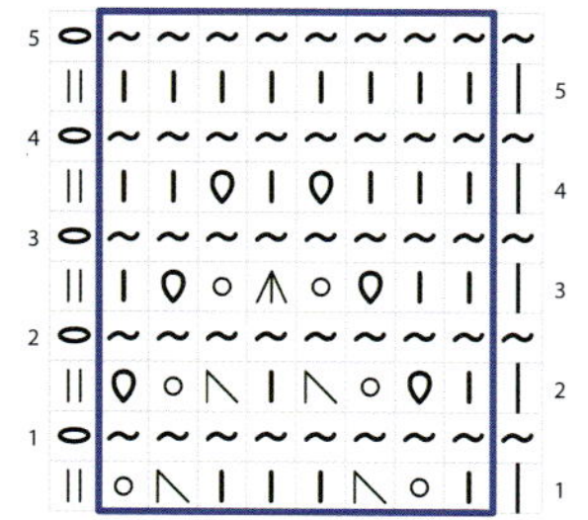

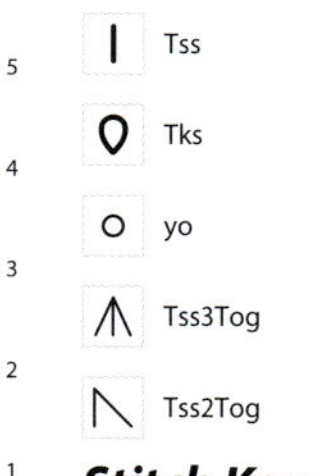

Stitch Key

329

Worked over a multiple of 10 stitches and 8 rows.

Row 1: [Tss 3, Tss2Tog, yo, Tss, yo, Tss2Tog, Tss 2] rep

Row 2: [Tss 4, Tks, Tss, Tks, Tss 3] rep.

Row 3: [Tss, Tss2Tog, Tss 2, yo, Tss, yo, Tss 2, Tss2Tog] rep.

Row 4: [Tss, yo, Tss2Tog, Tss, Tks, Tss, Tks, Tss, Tss2Tog, yo] rep.

Row 5: [Tss, Tks, yo, Tss2Tog, Tss 3, Tss2Tog, yo, Tks] rep.

Row 6: [Tss 2, Tks, yo, Tss2Tog, Tss, Tss2Tog, yo, Tks, Tss] rep.

Row 7: [Tss 3, Tks, yo, Tss3Tog, yo, Tks, Tss 2] rep.

Row 8: [Tss 4, Tks, Tss, Tks, Tss 3] rep.

Repeat Rows 1–8.

Reverse

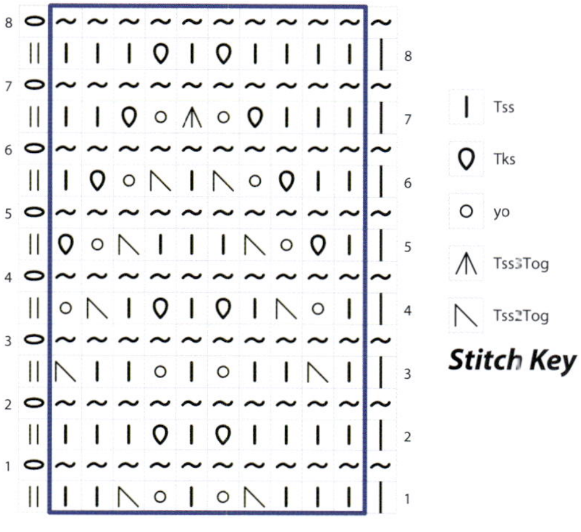

Stitch Key

330

Worked over a multiple of 11 stitches and 8 rows.

Row 1: [Tps, Tss 10] rep.

Row 2: [Tps, yo, Tss 3, Tss2Tog, Tss 5] rep.

Row 3: [Tps, Tks, yo, Tss 3, Tss2Tog, Tss 4] rep.

Row 4: [Tps, Tss, Tks, yo, Tss 3, Tss2Tog, Tss 3] rep.

Row 5: [Tps, Tss 2, Tks, yo, Tss 3, Tss2Tog, Tss 2] rep.

Row 6: [Tps, Tss 3, Tks, yo, Tss 3, Tss2Tog, Tss] rep.

Row 7: [Tps, Tss 4, Tks, yo, Tss 3, Tss2Tog] rep.

Row 8: [Tps, Tss 5, Tks, Tss 4] rep.

Repeat Rows 1–8.

Reverse

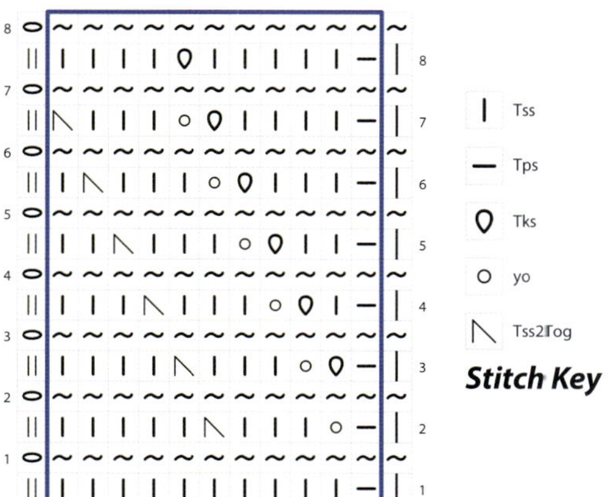

Stitch Key

CHAPTER 4

Cable Stitches

Cable Terminology

A Tunisian crochet cable is one or more stitches crossing over one or more neighboring stitches (to either the immediate left or right). The return pass closes the stitches in their new order. The following row also works the stitches in their new order. Working Tunisian crochet cables requires a second hook, but the second hook needs to hold only a few loops temporarily while working the cable (a regular crochet hook will work well for this purpose). The most common stitches used to create Tunisian crochet cables are Tss and Tks.

Cable stitches are labeled with numbers and letters. The numbers describe how many stitches are being worked and the letter(s) describe how the cable is created. For example, a 3/2 F cable is worked over 5 stitches. The first 3 stitches are worked on a second hook and held to the front, while the next 2 stitches are worked on the main hook.

Front Cables

With front cables, the loops on the second hook are held to the front. Front cables lean to the left if right-handed and to the right if left-handed.

To work a 3/3Ft cable:

1. With the second hook (shown in black), Tss in the next 3 stitches. Hold hook in front of fabric.

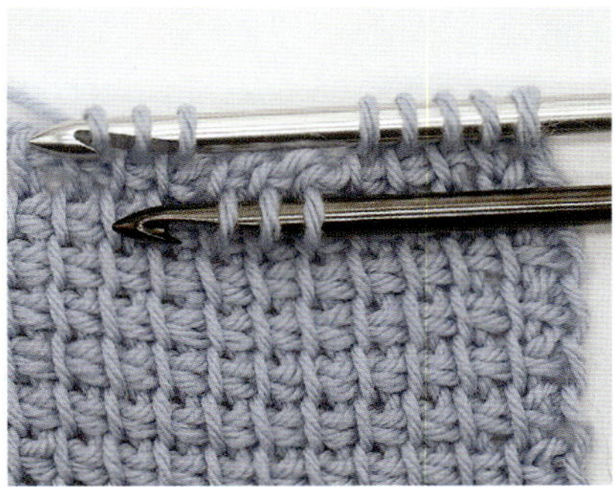

2. With the main hook, Tss in next 3 stitches.

3. Keeping the second hook in front of the main hook, move the second hook so that the stitches can be transferred onto the main hook.

4. Slip the stitches on the second hook to the main hook in the order they were originally worked.

5. Remove the second hook.

6. All loops are now on main hook. Continue forward pass. On the return pass, close the stitches in this new order.

Back Cables

With back cables, the stitches on the second hook are held to the back. Back cables lean to the right if right-handed and to the left if left-handed.

To work a 3/3Bt cable:

1. With the second hook (shown in black), Tss in the next 3 stitches.

2. Move second hook to back of fabric and Tss in the next 3 stitches with main hook.

3. Keeping the second hook behind the main hook, move the second hook so that the stitches can be transferred onto the main hook.

4. Slip the stitches on the second hook to the main hook in the order they were originally worked.

5. Continue the forward pass. On the return pass, close the loops in their new order.

6. In the next forward pass, work the stitches in their new order.

331 2/1 FRONT CABLE WITH TKS (2/1Fk)

Reverse

Worked over 3 stitches.

2/1Fk: With a second hook, Tks in the next 2 stitches and hold to the front. Tss in stitch 3. Move the held stitches to the main hook.

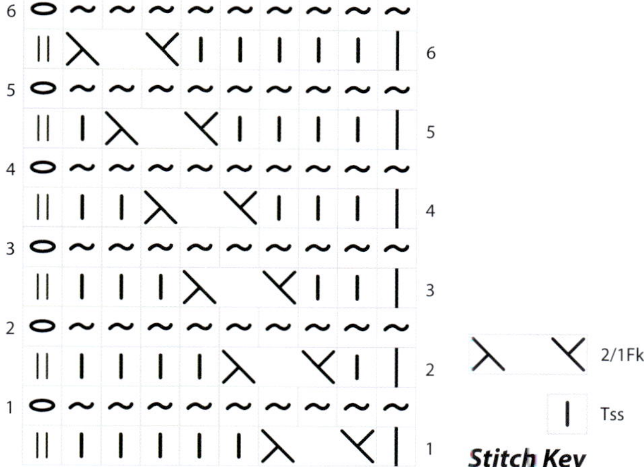

332 2/1 BACK CABLE WITH TKS (2/1Bk)

Reverse

Worked over 3 stitches.

2/1Bk: With a second hook, Tss in first stitch and hold to the back. Tks in next 2 stitches. Move the held stitches to the main hook.

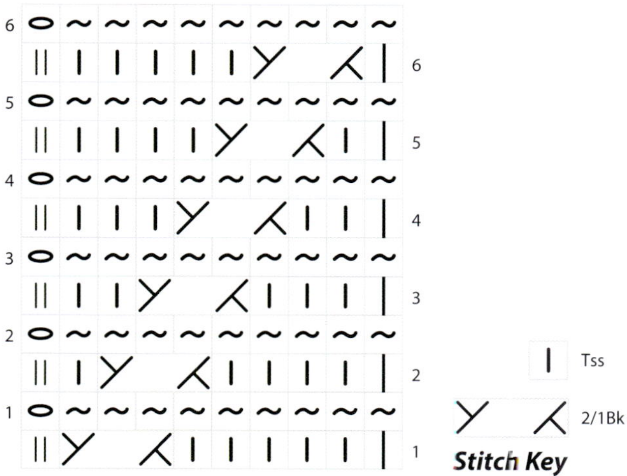

333 2/2 FRONT CABLE WITH TKS (2/2Fk)

Reverse

Worked over 4 stitches and 3 rows.

2/2Fk: With a second hook, Tks in the next 2 stitches and hold to the front. Tks in next 2 stitches. Move the held stitches to the main hook.

Row 1: 2/2Fk.

Rows 2 and 3: Tks 4.

Repeat Rows 1–3.

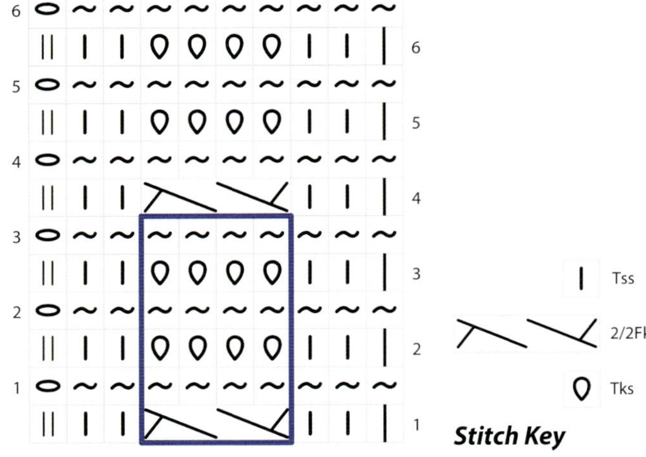

334 2/2 BACK CABLE WITH TKS (2/2Bk)

Reverse

Worked over 4 stitches and 3 rows.

2/2Bk: With a second hook, Tks in the next 2 stitches and hold to the back. Tks in next 2 stitches. Move the held stitches to the main hook.

Row 1: 2/2Bk.

Rows 2 and 3: Tks 4.

Repeat Rows 1–3.

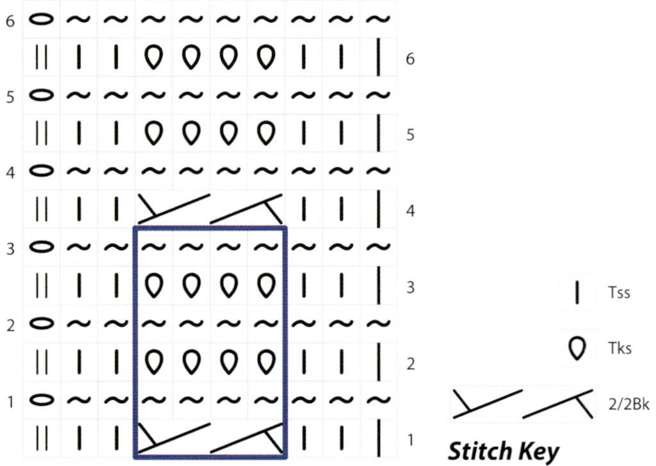

335 3/3 FRONT CABLE WITH TKS (3/3Fk)

Reverse

Worked over 6 stitches and 4 rows.

3/3Fk: With a second hook, Tks in the next 3 stitches and hold to the front. Tks in next 3 stitches. Move the held stitches to the main hook.

Row 1: 3/3Fk.

Rows 2–4: Tks 6.

Repeat Rows 1–4.

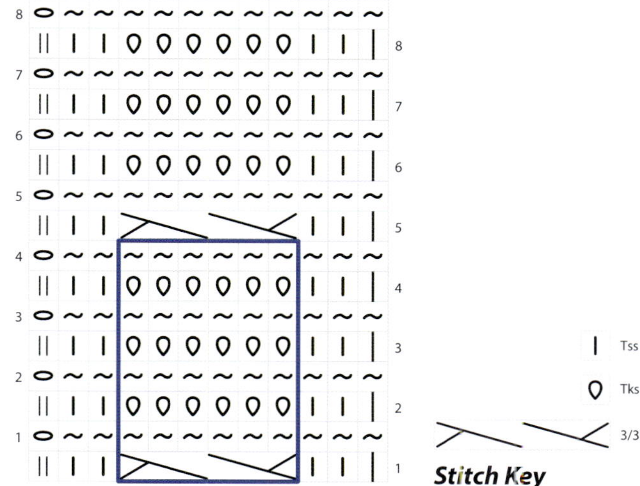

Stitch Key

336 3/3 BACK CABLE WITH TKS (3/3Bk)

Reverse

Worked over 6 stitches and 4 rows.

3/3Bk: With a second hook, Tks in the next 3 stitches and hold to the back. Tks in next 3 stitches. Move the held stitches to the main hook.

Row 1: 3/3Bk.

Rows 2–4: Tks 6.

Repeat Rows 1–4.

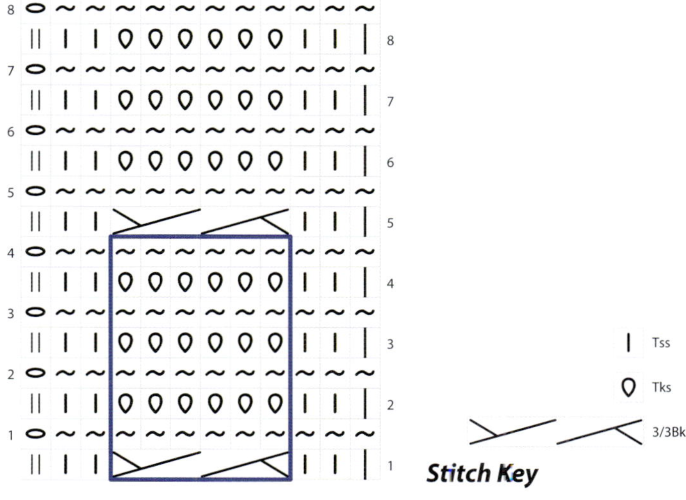

Stitch Key

337 2/1 FRONT CABLE WITH TSS (2/1Ft)

Reverse

Worked over 3 stitches.

2/1Ft: With a second hook, Tss in the next 2 stitches and hold to the front. Tss in stitch 3. Move the held stitches to the main hook.

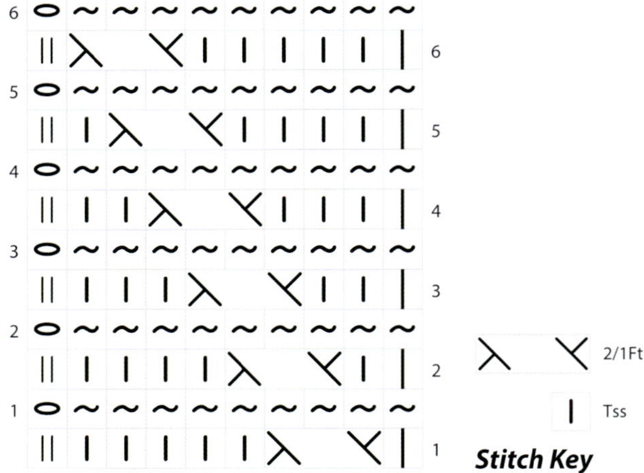

338 2/1 BACK CABLE WITH TSS (2/1Bt)

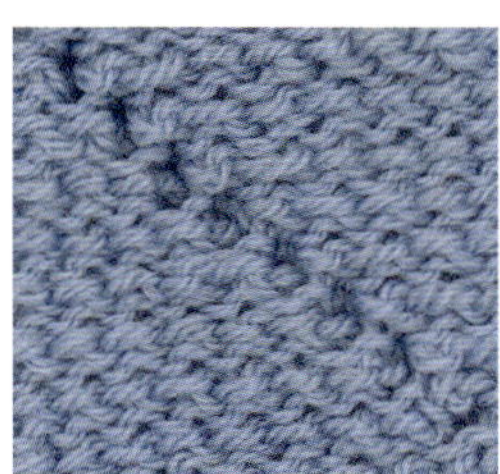

Reverse

Worked over 3 stitches.

2/1Bt: With a second hook, Tss in first stitch and hold to the back. Tss in next 2 stitches. Move the held stitch to the main hook.

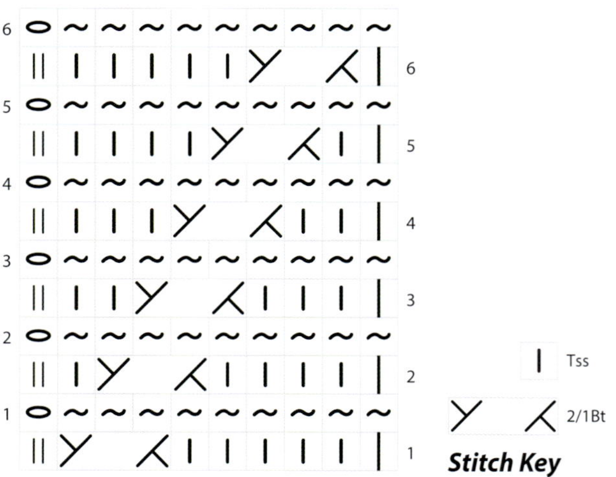

339 2/2 FRONT CABLE WITH TSS (2/2Ft)

Worked over 4 stitches and 3 rows.

2/2Ft: With a second hook, Tss in the next 2 stitches and hold to the front. Tss in next 2 stitches. Move the held stitches to the main hook.

Row 1: 2/2Ft.

Rows 2 and 3: Tss 4.

Repeat Rows 1–3.

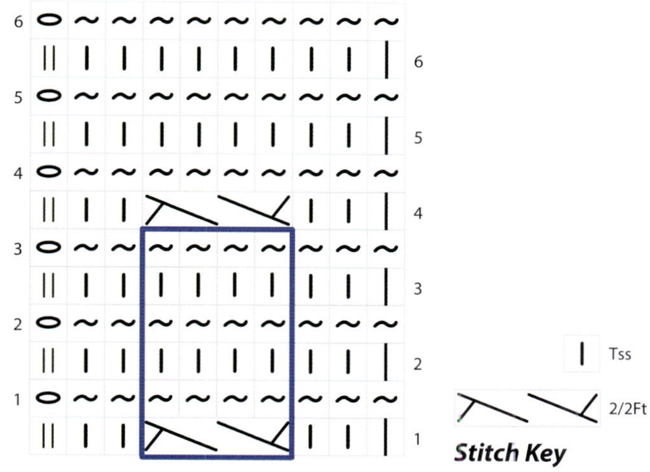

340 2/2 BACK CABLE WITH TSS (2/2Bt)

Worked over 4 stitches and 3 rows.

2/2Bt: With a second hook, Tss in the next 2 stitches and hold to the back. Tss in next 2 stitches. Move the held stitches to the main hook.

Row 1: 2/2Bt.

Rows 2 and 3: Tss 4.

Repeat Rows 1–3.

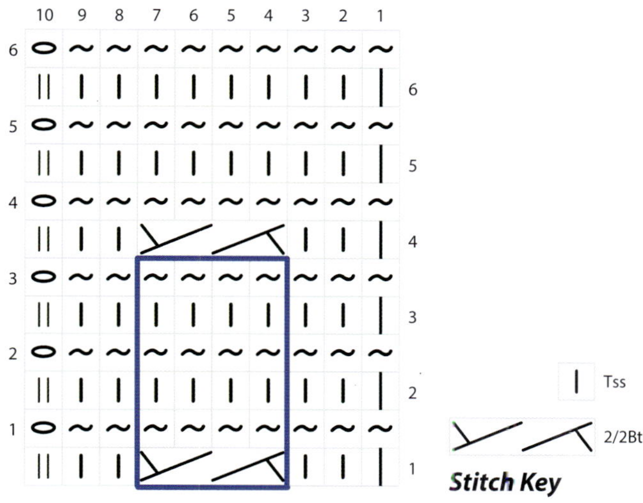

341 3/3 FRONT CABLE WITH TSS (3/3Ft)

Worked over 6 stitches and 4 rows.

3/3Ft: With a second hook, Tss in the next 3 stitches and hold to the front. Tss in next 3 stitches. Move the held stitches to the main hook.

Row 1: 3/3Ft.

Rows 2–4: Tss 6.

Repeat Rows 1–4.

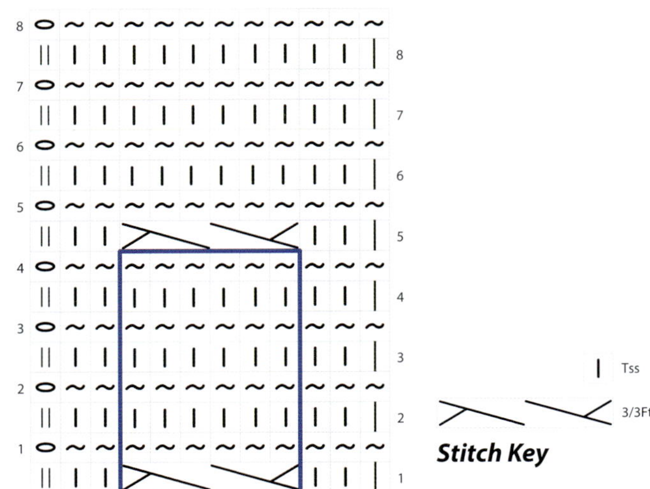

342 3/3 BACK CABLE WITH TSS (3/3Bt)

Worked over 6 stitches and 4 rows.

3/3Bt: With a second hook, Tss in the next 3 stitches and hold to the back. Tss in next 3 stitches. Move the held stitches to the main hook.

Row 1: 3/3Bt.

Rows 2–4: Tss 6.

Repeat Rows 1–4.

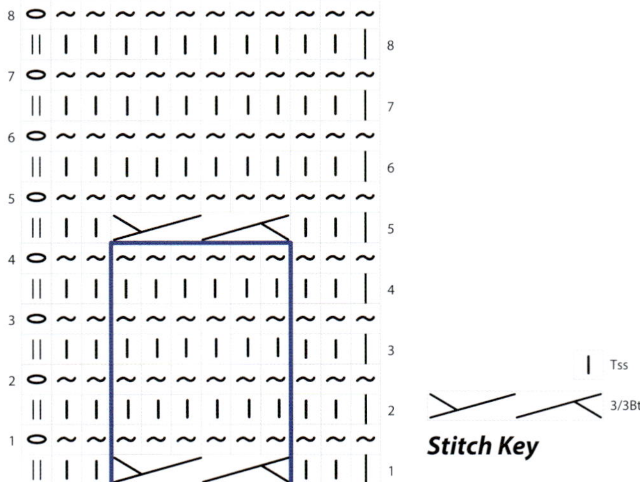

343

Worked over 12 stitches and 4 rows.
Row 1: 3/3Fk, 3/3Bk.
Rows 2–4: Tks 12.
Repeat Rows 1–4.

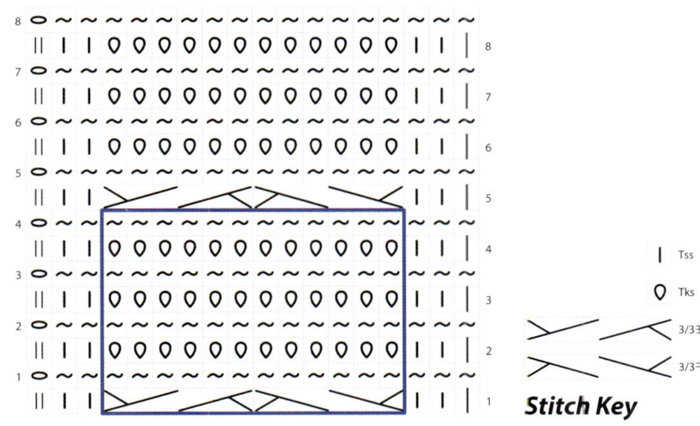

344

Worked over 12 stitches and 4 rows.
Row 1: 3/3Bk, 3/3Fk.
Rows 2–4: Tks 12.
Repeat Rows 1–4.

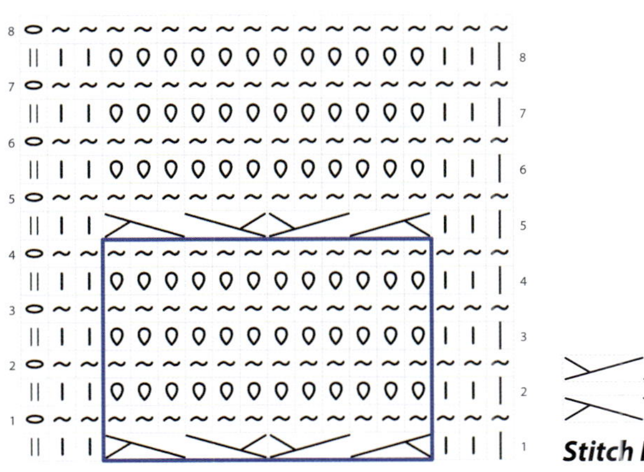

345

Worked over 4 stitches and 8 rows.
Row 1: 2/2Bk.
Rows 2–4: Tks 4.
Row 5: 2/2Fk.
Rows 6–8: Tks 4.
Repeat Rows 1–8.

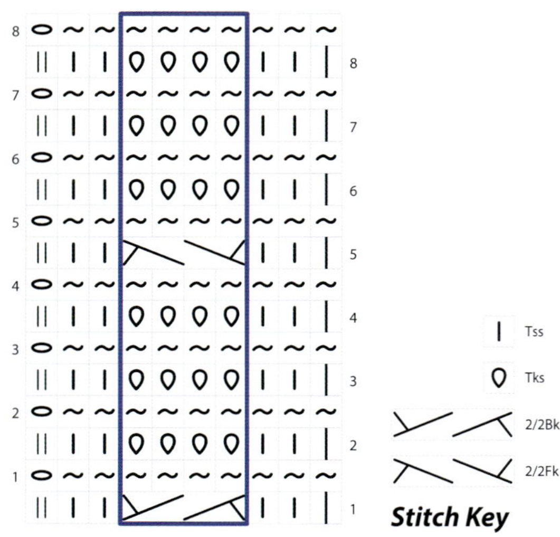

346

Worked over 12 stitches and 8 rows.
Row 1: 3/3Bk, 3/3Fk.
Rows 2–4: Tks 12.
Row 5: 3/3Fk, 3/3Bk.
Rows 6–8: Tks 12.
Repeat Rows 1–8.

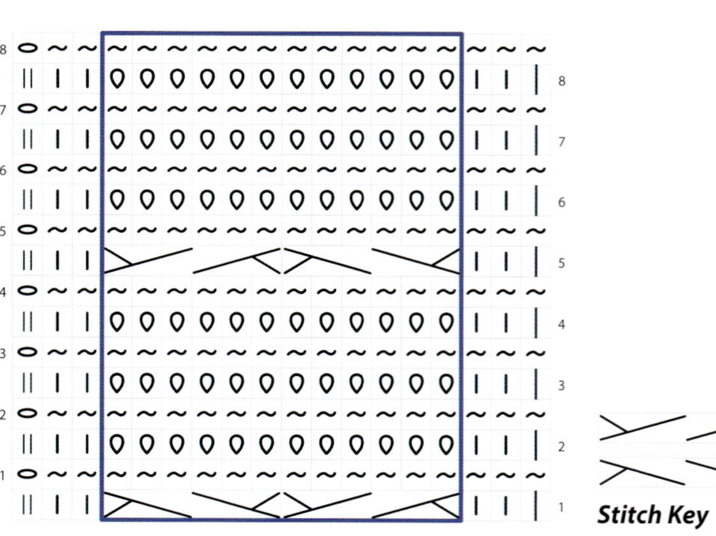

347

Worked over 4 stitches and 8 rows.

Row 1: 2/2Bt.

Rows 2–4: Tss 4.

Row 5: 2/2Ft.

Rows 6–8: Tss 4.

Repeat Rows 1–8.

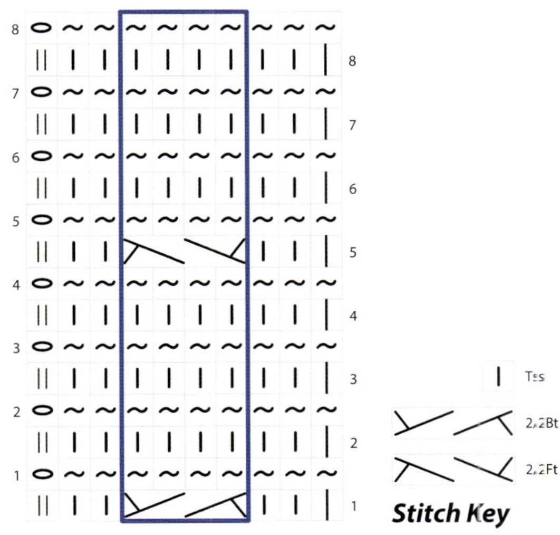

348

Worked over 12 stitches and 4 rows.

Row 1: 3/3Bt, 3/3Ft.

Rows 2–4: Tss 12.

Repeat Rows 1–4.

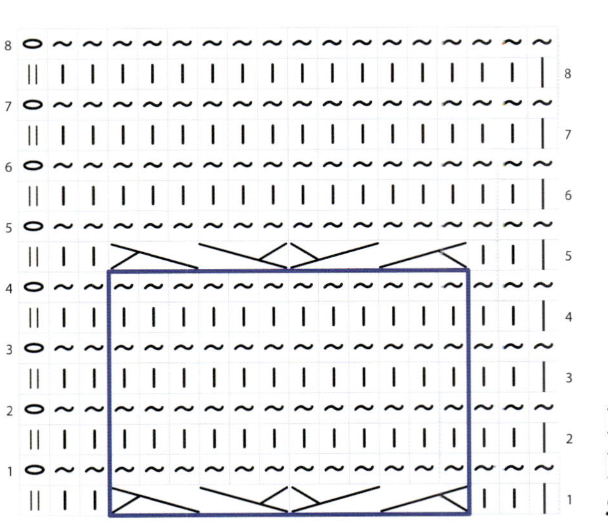

349

Worked over 9 stitches and 6 rows.

Row 1: Tks 9.

Row 2: 3/3Fk, Tks 3.

Rows 3 and 4: Tks 9.

Row 5: Tks 3, 3/3Bk.

Rows 6 and 7: Tks 9.

Repeat Rows 2–7.

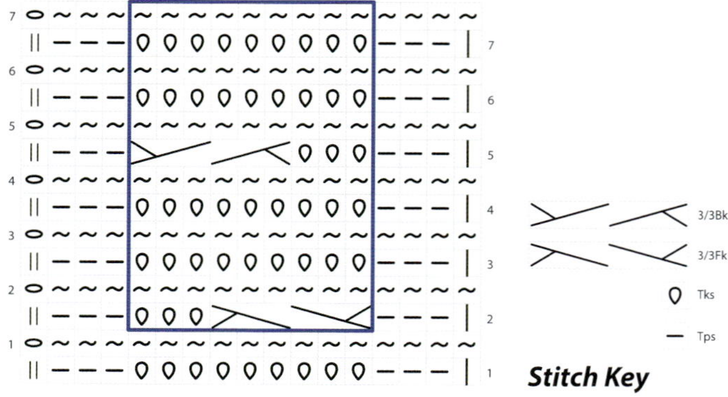

350

Worked over 6 stitches and 5 rows.

Rows 1 and 2: Tks 2, Tps 2, Tks 2.

Row 3: 2/1Fk, 2/1Bk.

Row 4: Tps, 2/2Bk, Tps.

Row 5: 2/1Bk, 2/1Fk.

Repeat Rows 1–5.

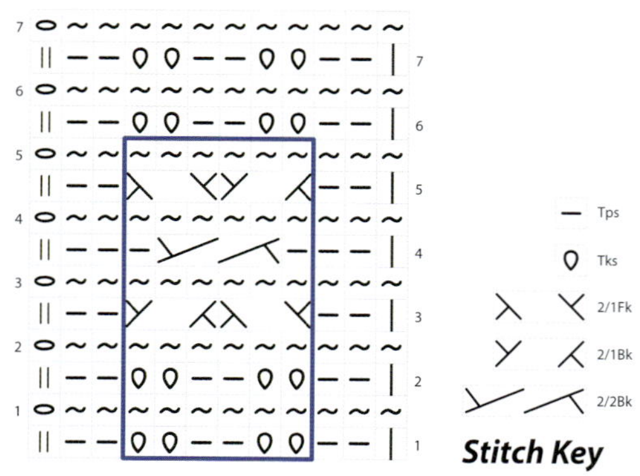

351

Worked over 10 stitches and 10 rows.

Row 1: Tps 2, 2/1Fk, Tps, 2/1Fk, Tps.

Row 2: Tps 3, 2/1Fk, Tps, 2/1Fk.

Row 3: Tps 4, Tks 2, Tps 2, Tks 2.

Row 4: Tps 3, 2/1Bk, Tps, 2/1Bk.

Row 5: Tps 2, 2/1Bk, Tps, 2/1Bk, Tps.

Row 6: Tps, 2/1Bk, Tps, 2/1Bk, Tps 2.

Row 7: 2/1Bk, Tps, 2/1Bk, Tps 3.

Row 8: Tks 2, Tps 2, Tks 2, Tps 4.

Row 9: 2/1Fk, Tps, 2/1Fk, Tps 3.

Row 10: Tps, 2/1Fk, Tps, 2/1Fk, Tps 2.

Repeat Rows 1–10.

Tps

Tks

2/1Fk

2/1Bk

2/2Bk

Stitch Key

352

Worked over 12 stitches and 10 rows.

Row 1: Tks 2, Tps 8, Tks 2.

Row 2: 2/1Fk, Tps 6, 2/1Bk.

Row 3: Tps, 2/1Fk, Tps 4, 2/1Bk, Tps.

Row 4: Tps 2, 2/1Fk, Tps 2, 2/1Bk, Tps 2.

Row 5: Tps 3, 2/1Fk, 2/1Bk, Tps 3.

Row 6: Tps 4, 2/2Bk, Tps 4.

Row 7: Tps 3, 2/1Bk, 2/1Fk, Tps 3.

Row 8: Tps 2, 2/1Bk, Tps 2, 2/1Fk, Tps 2.

Row 9: Tps, 2/1Bk, Tps 4, 2/1Fk, Tps.

Row 10: 2/1Bk, Tps 6, 2/1Fk.

Repeat Rows 1–10.

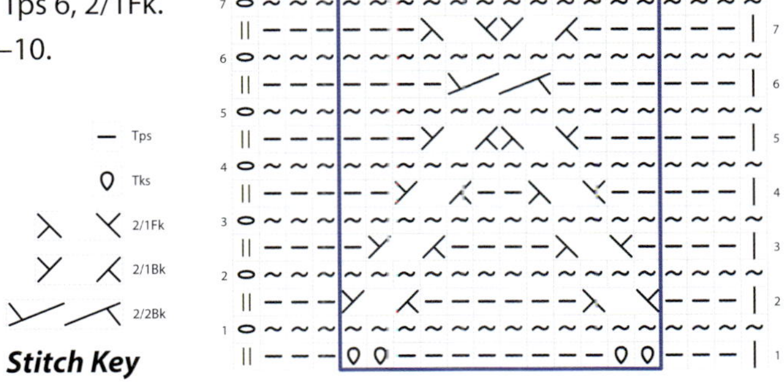

353

Worked over 10 stitches and 2 rows.

Row 1: Tks 2, 2/2Bk 2.

Row 2: 2/2Fk 2, Tks 2.

Repeat Rows 1 and 2.

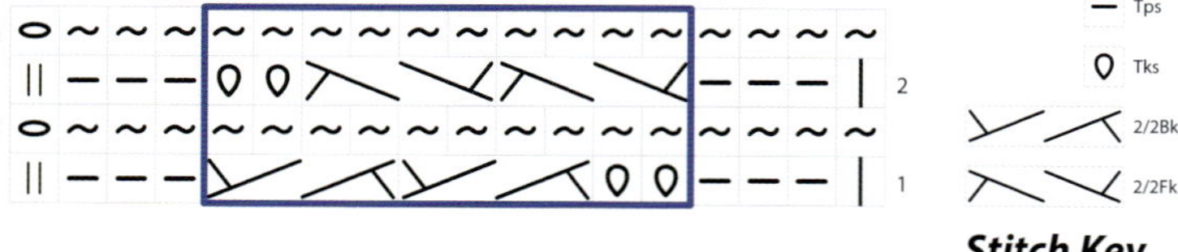

354

Worked over 9 stitches and 4 rows.

Row 1: 2/1Fk, 2/1Bk, 2/1Fk.

Row 2: Tps, 2/2Bk, Tps 2, Tks 2.

Row 3: 2/1Bk, 2/1Fk, 2/1Bk.

Row 4: Tks 2, Tps 2, 2/2Fk, Tps.

Repeat Rows 1–4.

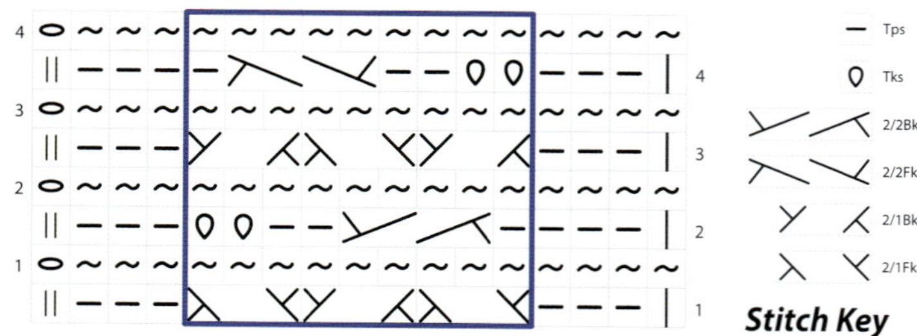

355

Worked over 12 stitches and 8 rows.

Row 1: Tks 2, Tps 2, 2/2Fk, Tps 2, Tks 2.

Row 2: 2/1Fk, 2/1Bk, 2/1Fk, 2/1Bk.

Row 3: Tps, 2/2Bk, Tps 2, 2/2Fk, Tps.

Row 4: 2/1Bk, 2/1Fk, 2/1Bk, 2/1Fk.

Row 5: Tks 2, Tps 2, 2/2Bk, Tps 2, Tks 2.

Row 6: 2/1Fk, 2/1Bk, 2/1Fk, 2/1Bk.

Row 7: Tps, 2/2Bk, Tps 2, 2/2Fk, Tps.

Row 8: 2/1Bk, 2/1Fk, 2/1Bk, 2/1Fk.

Repeat Rows 1–8.

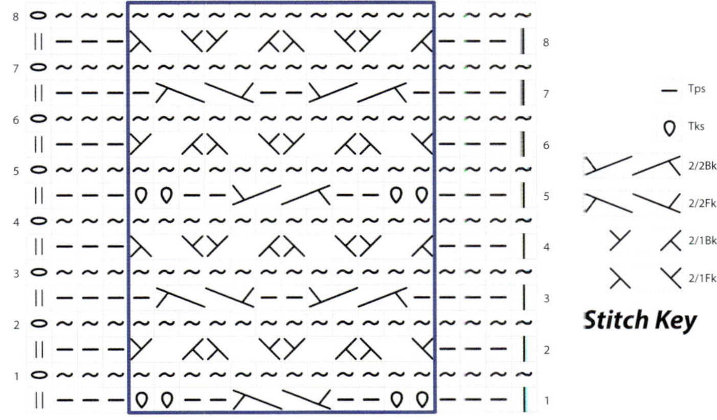

356

Worked over 6 stitches and 6 rows.

Row 1: 2/1Bk, 2/1Fk.

Rows 2 and 3: Tks 2, Tps 2, Tks 2.

Row 4: 2/1Fk, 2/1Bk.

Rows 5 and 6: Tps, Tks 4, Tps.

Repeat Rows 1–6.

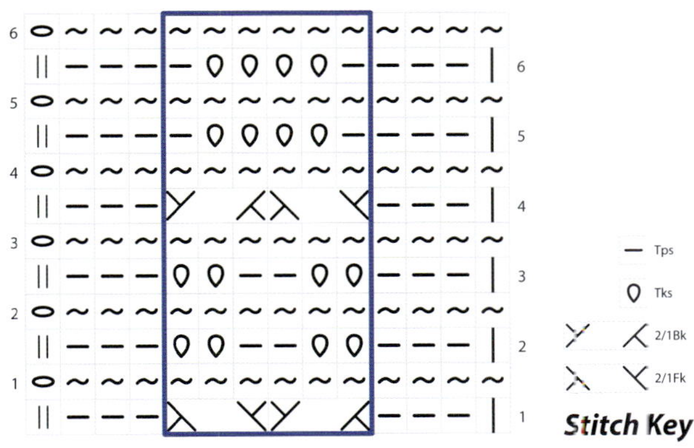

357

Worked over a multiple of 6 stitches and 6 rows.

Row 1: [2/1Bk, 2/1Fk] rep.

Rows 2 and 3: [Tks 2, Tps 2, Tks 2] rep.

Row 4: [2/1Fk, 2/1Bk] rep.

Rows 5 and 6: [Tps, Tks 4, Tps] rep.

Repeat Rows 1–6.

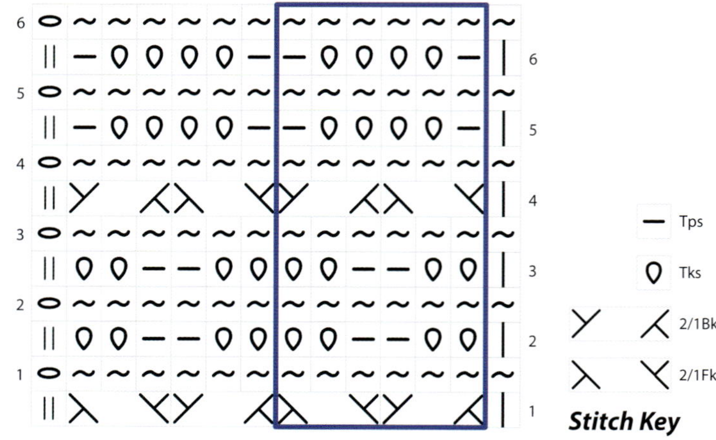

358

Worked over a multiple of 4 stitches and 4 rows.

1/1Fk: Worked over 2 stitches. With a second hook, Tks in the next stitch and hold to the front. Tss in second stitch. Move the held stitch to the main hook.

1/1Bk: Worked over 2 stitches. With a second hook, Tss in the next stitch and hold to the back. Tks in second stitch. Move the held stitch to the main hook.

Row 1: [1/1Fk, 1/1Bk] rep.

Row 2: [Tps, Tks 2, Tps] rep.

Row 3: [1/1Bk, 1/1Fk] rep.

Row 4: [Tks, Tps 2, Tks] rep.

Repeat Rows 1–4.

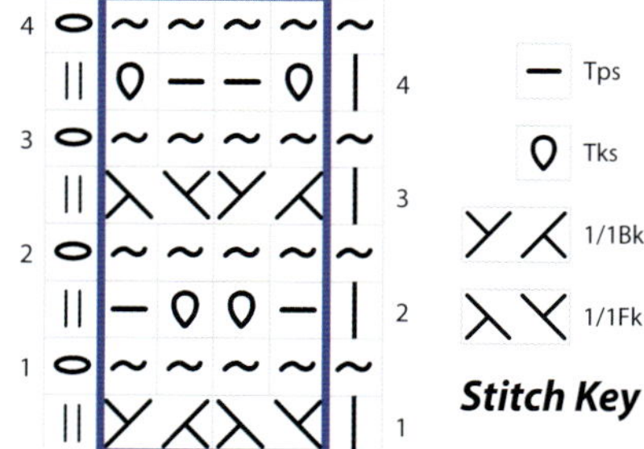

359

Reverse

Worked over 12 stitches and 9 rows.

Row 1: 2/1Fk, Tss 6, 2/1Bk.

Row 2: Tss, 2/1Fk, Tss 4, 2/1Bk, Tss.

Row 3: Tss 2, 2/1Fk, Tss 2, 2/1Bk, Tss 2.

Row 4: Tss 3, 2/1Fk, 2/1Bk, Tss 3.

Row 5: Tss 4, 2/2Bk, Tss 4.

Row 6: Tss 3, 2/1Bk, 2/1Fk, Tss 3.

Row 7: Tss 2, 2/1Bk, Tss 2, 2/1Fk, Tss 2.

Row 8: Tss, 2/1Bk, Tss 4, 2/1Fk, Tss.

Row 9: 2/1Bk, Tss 6, 2/1Fk.

Repeat Rows 1–9.

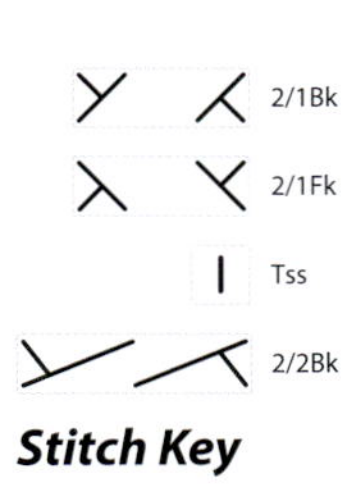

Stitch Key

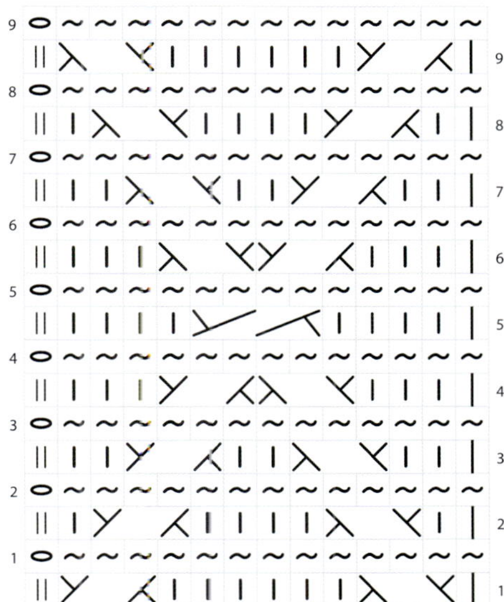

360

Worked over 12 stitches and 4 rows.

Row 1: Tss 3, 2/1Bk, 2/1Fk, Tss 3.

Row 2: Tss 2, 2/1Bk, Tss 2, 2/1Fk, Tss 2.

Row 3: Tss, 2/1Bk, Tss 4, 2/1Fk, Tss.

Row 4: 2/1Bk, Tss 6, 2/1Fk.

Repeat Rows 1–4.

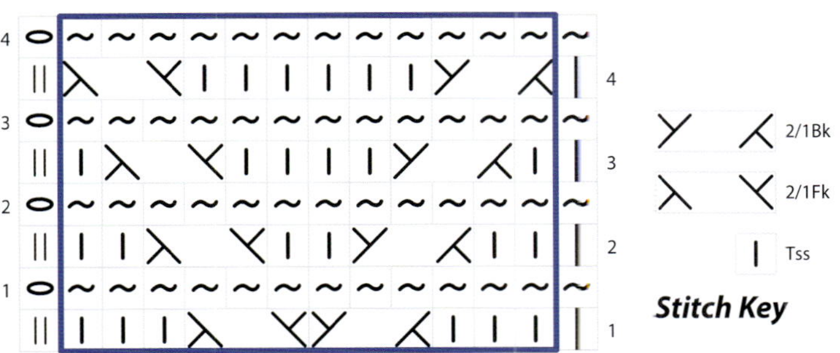

Stitch Key

361

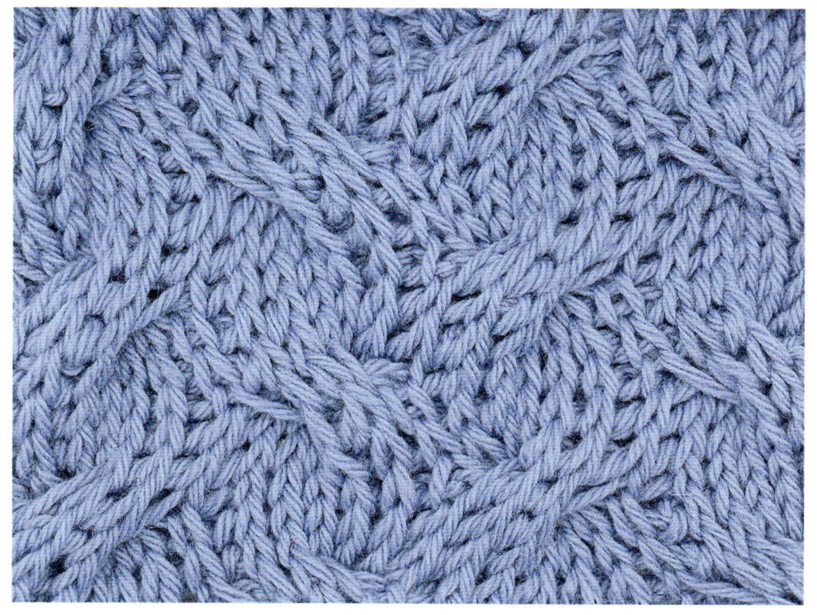

Worked over a multiple of 12 stitches and 6 rows.

Row 1: [3/3Fk, Tks 6] rep.

Rows 2 and 3: Tks 12.

Row 4: [Tks 6, 3/3Bk] rep.

Rows 5 and 6: Tks 12.

Repeat Rows 1–6.

Reverse

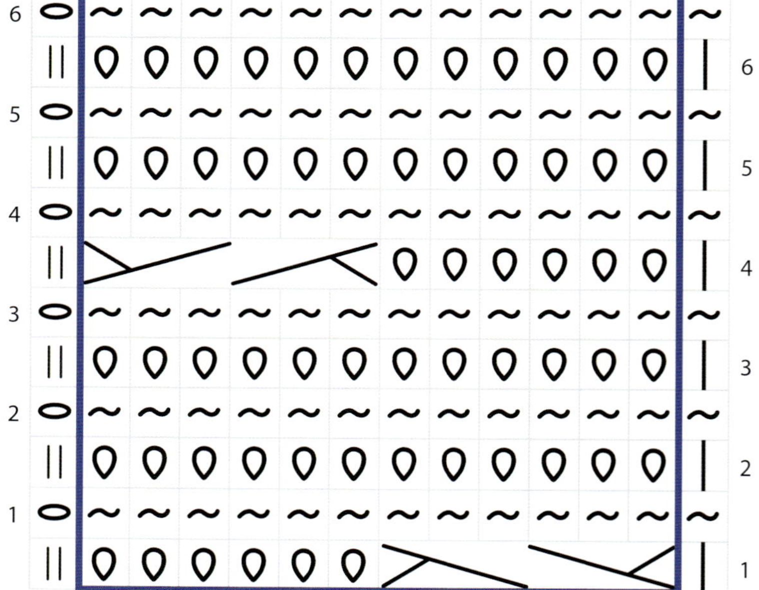

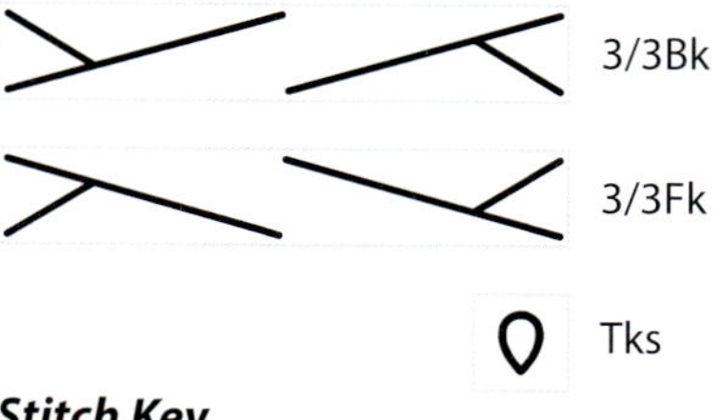

Stitch Key

362

Worked over 9 stitches and 6 rows.

Row 1: 3/3Bk, Tks 3.

Rows 2 and 3: Tks 9.

Row 4: Tks 3, 3/3Fk.

Rows 5 and 6: Tks 9.

Repeat Rows 1–6.

Reverse

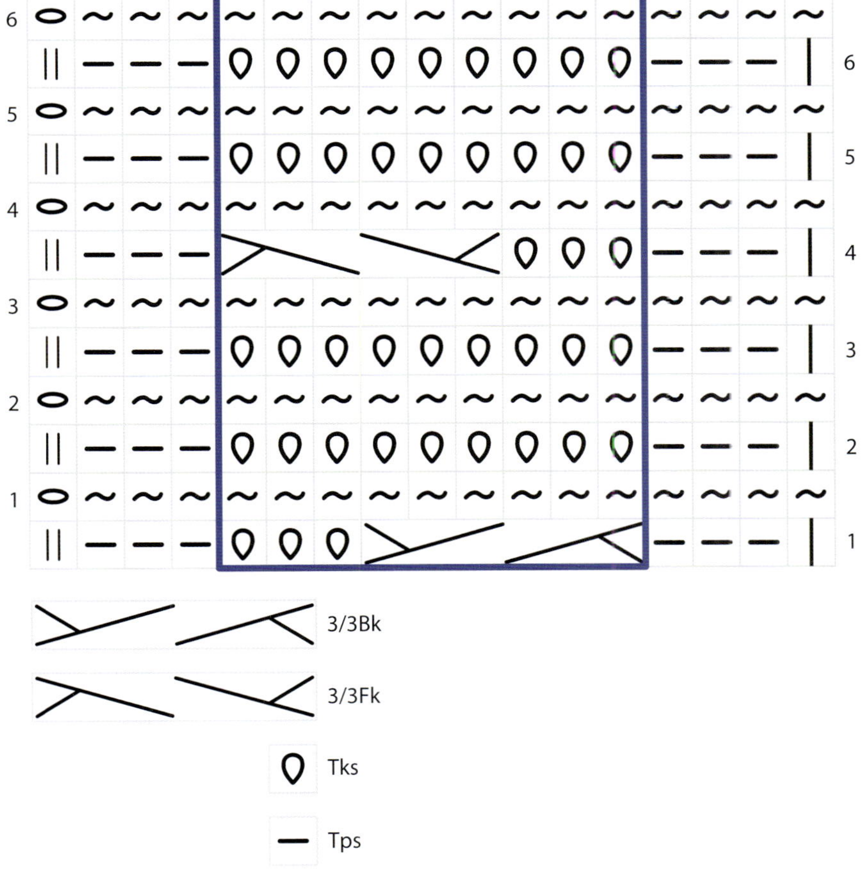

Stitch Key

363

Worked over 6 stitches and 10 rows.

Row 1: 3/3Fk.

Rows 2 and 3: Tks 6.

Row 4: 3/3Fk.

Rows 5–10: Tks 6.

Repeat Rows 1–10.

Reverse

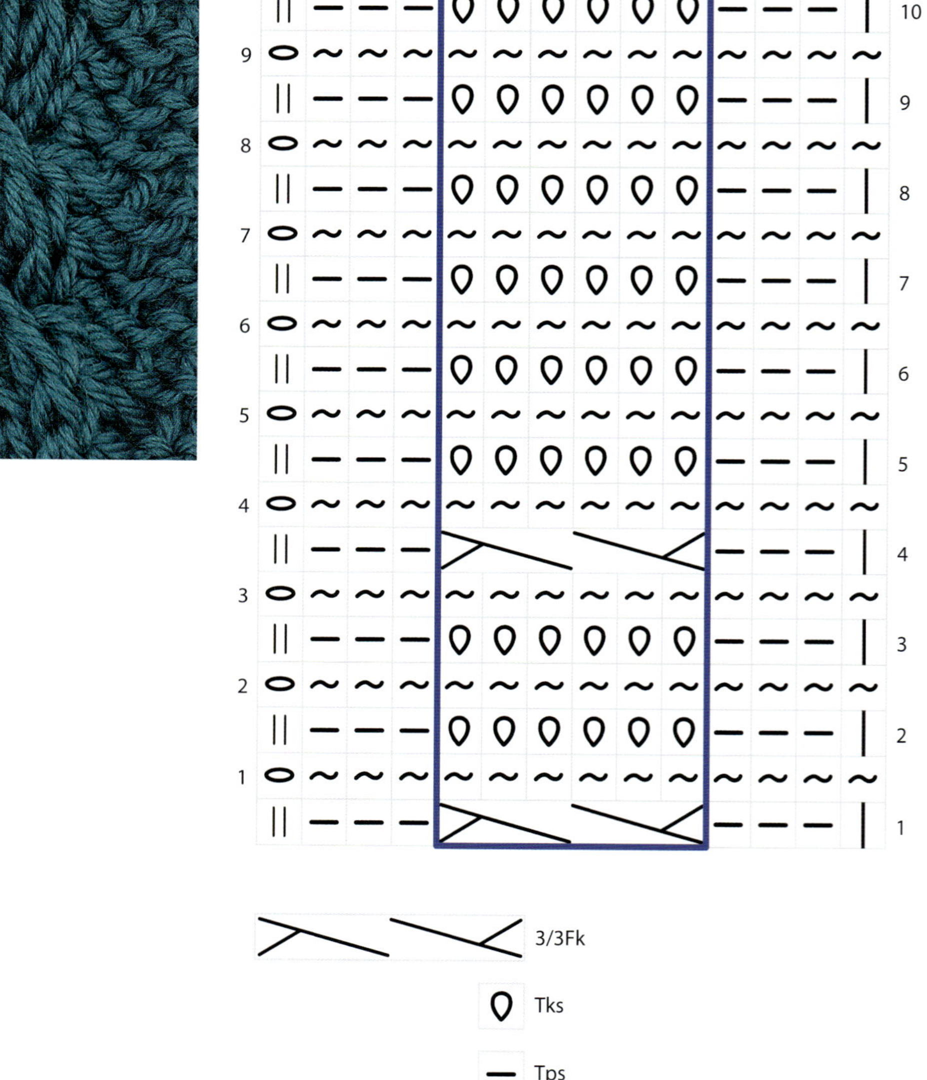

Stitch Key

364

Worked over a multiple of 4 stitches and 8 rows.
Row 1: 2/2Bk rep.
Rows 2–4: [Tks 2, Tps 2] rep.
Row 5: 2/2Fk rep.
Rows 6–8: [Tps 2, Tks 2] rep.
Repeat Rows 1–8.

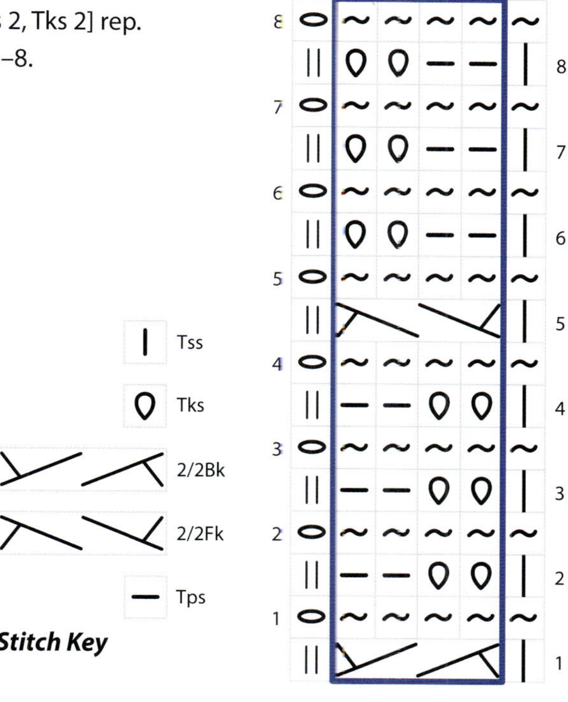

365

Worked over 6 stitches and 4 rows.
Row 1: Tps, 1/1Fk, Tks 3.
Row 2: Tps, Tks, 1/1Fk, Tks 2.
Row 3: Tps, Tks 2, 1/1Fk, Tks.
Row 4: Tps, Tks 3, 1/1Fk.
Repeat Rows 1–4.

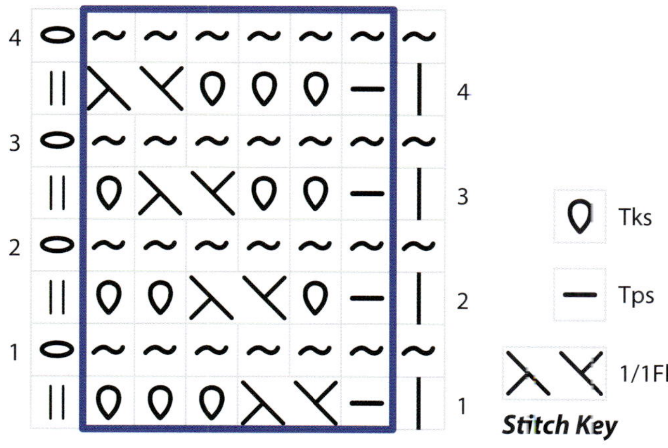

366

Worked over a multiple of 8 stitches and 3 rows.

Row 1: Tps, 1/1Fk, Tps 2, 1/1Bk, Tps.

Rows 2 and 3: Tps, Tks 2, Tps 2, Tks 2, Tps.

Repeat Rows 1–3.

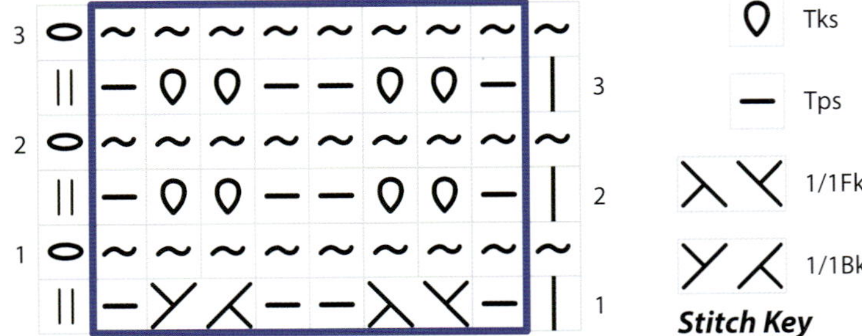

367 2/1/2FK

Worked over 5 stitches and 3 rows.

2/1/2Fk: Tks in the first 2 stitches, move to cable needle and hold in front. Tps in next stitch, move to second cable needle and hold in back. Tks in the last 2 stitches, move Tps to hook, move 2 Tks stitches to hook.

Row 1: 2/1/2Fk.

Rows 2 and 3: Tks 2, Tps, Tks 2.

Repeat Rows 1–3.

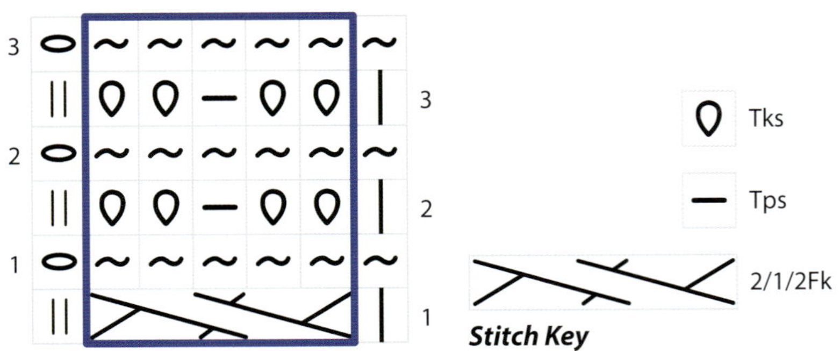

368

Worked over 8 stitches and 12 rows.
Row 1: 2/2Bk, 2/2Fk.
Rows 2 and 3: Tks 8.
Row 4: 2/2Bk, 2/2Fk.
Rows 5 and 6: Tks 2, Tps 4, Tks 2.
Row 7: 2/2Fk, 2/2Bk.
Rows 8 and 9: Tks 8.
Row 10: 2/2Fk, 2/2Bk.
Rows 11 and 12: Tks 8.
Repeat Rows 1–12.

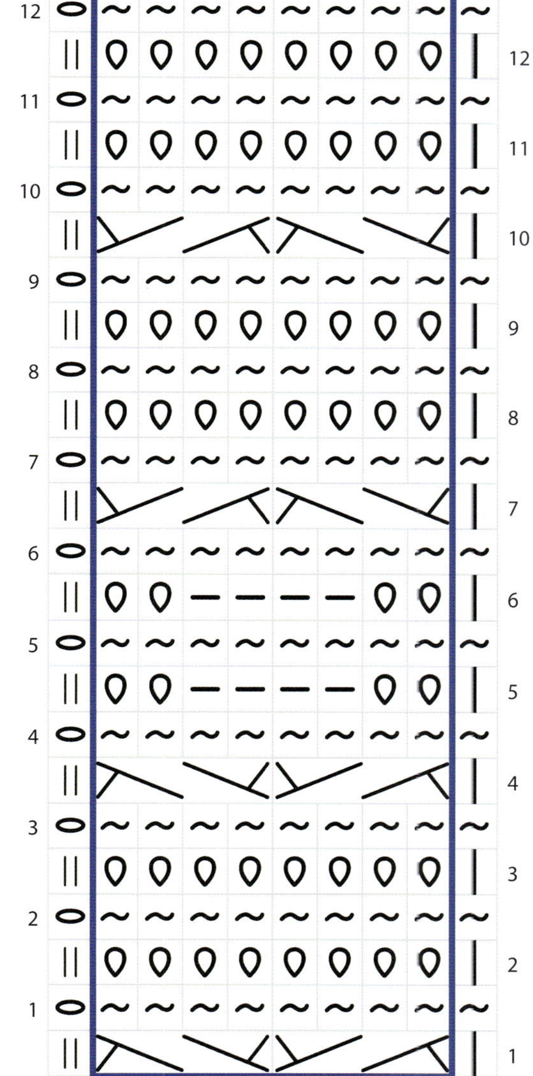

Reverse

Tks
Tps
2/2Fk
2/2Bk
Stitch Key

369

Worked over 12 stitches and 4 rows.

Row 1: Tps 3, 2/1Bk, 2/1Fk, Tps 3.

Row 2: Tps 2, 2/1Bk, Tks 2, 2/1Fk, Tps 2.

Row 3: Tps, 2/1Bk, Tks 4, 2/1Fk, Tps.

Row 4: 2/1Bk, Tps, 2/2Bk, Tps, 2/1Fk.

Repeat Rows 1–4.

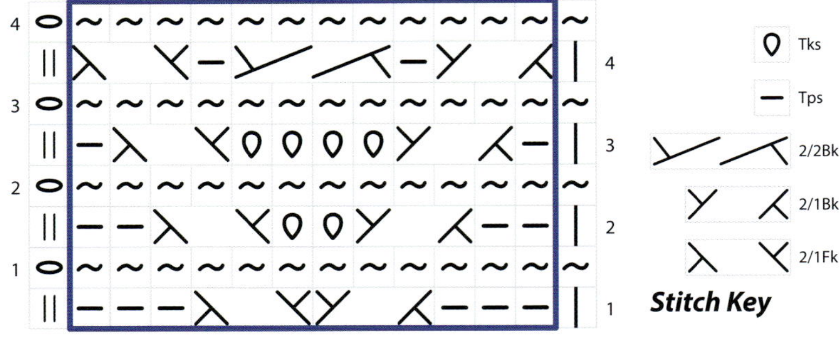

370

Worked over 8 stitches and 5 rows.

Rows 1–3: Tks 2, Tps 4, Tks 2.

Row 4: 2/2Fk, 2/2Bk.

Row 5: Tks 8.

Repeat Rows 1–5.

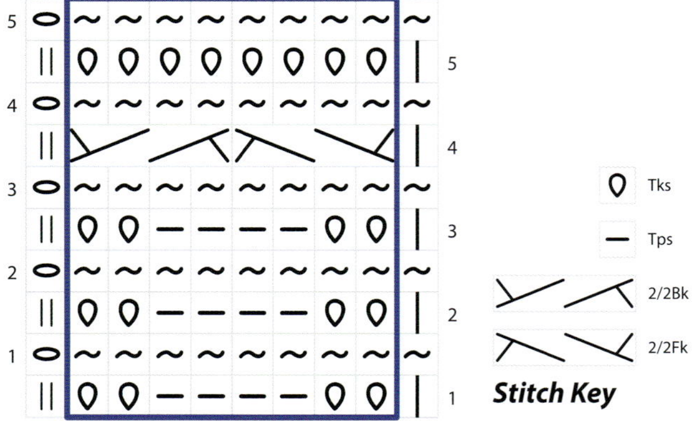

371

Worked over 12 stitches and 4 rows.

Row 1: 2/2Bk, Tks 4, 2/2Fk.

Row 2: Tks 12.

Row 3: Tks 2, 2/2Fk, 2/2Bk, Tks 2.

Row 4: Tks 12.

Repeat Rows 1–4.

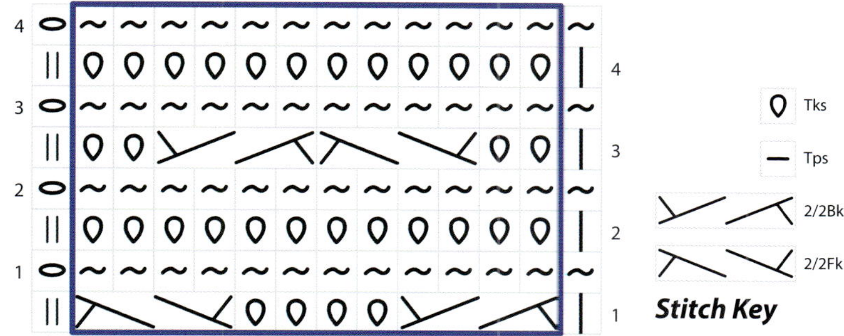

372 4/4BK

Worked over 8 stitches and 5 rows.

4/4Bk: With a second hook, Tks in the next 4 stitches and hold to the back. Tks in next 4 stitches. Move the held stitches to the main hook.

Row 1: 4/4Bk.

Rows 2–5: Tks 8.

Repeat Rows 1–5.

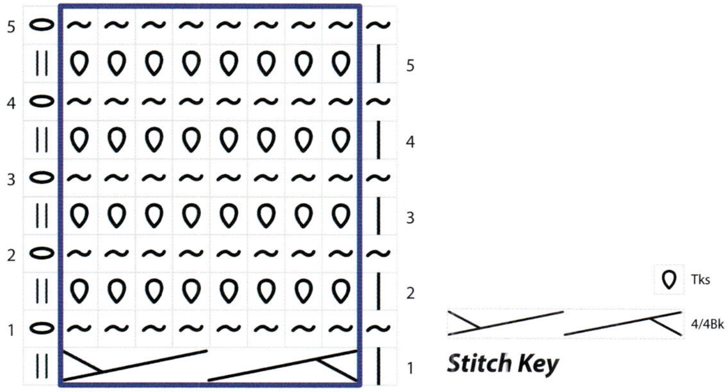

CHAPTER 5

Colorwork Stitches

Changing Colors

Tunisian crochet is unique in that each row has two passes. This method creates noticeably different effects depending on where the color change occurs.

Creating Stripes

If the desired result is stripes, the swap between yarn colors occurs at the end of the return pass. In order to create a row with loops all the same color, the color change happens just before the last "yarn over and pull through 2 loops" of the return pass.

1. Stop the return pass when there are two loops on the hook. Drop the current color and pick up the next color. Yarn over.

2. Pull through two loops. Loop on hook is in the new color. Continue working the next forward pass.

3. Repeat steps 1 and 2 whenever a color change is required.

Fading

Having a forward pass and a return pass allows for very smooth color transitions as well as fun colorwork. If the colors are swapped at the end of the forward pass, both colors contribute to the row, and the result is a mixing of the two colors. This method of blending yarn makes skein transitions not noticeable and can create a smoother fade compared to knit or crochet.

1. Work the entire forward pass until the last stitch.

2. Insert the hook for the edge stitch. Drop the current color and pick up the next color.

3. Yarn over with next color and pull up a loop. Continue the return pass with the new color.

4. Repeat steps 1–3 whenever a color change is required.

373 TSS STRIPES

Worked over 2 rows.
Row 1: With MC, Tss.
Row 2: With CC, Tss.
Repeat Rows 1 and 2.

Reverse

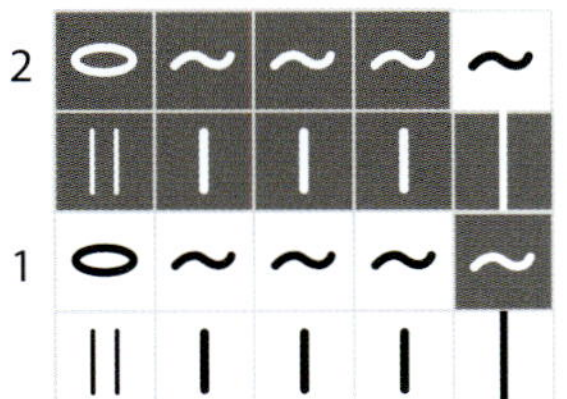

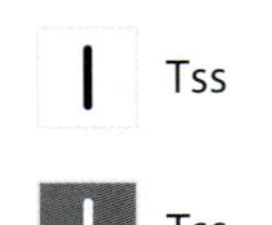

Stitch Key

374 TSS FADE

Worked over 2 rows.
Row 1 FP: With MC, Tss.
Row 1 RP: With CC, Std RP.
Row 2 FP: With CC, Tss.
Row 2 RP: With MC, Std RP.
Repeat Rows 1 and 2.

Reverse

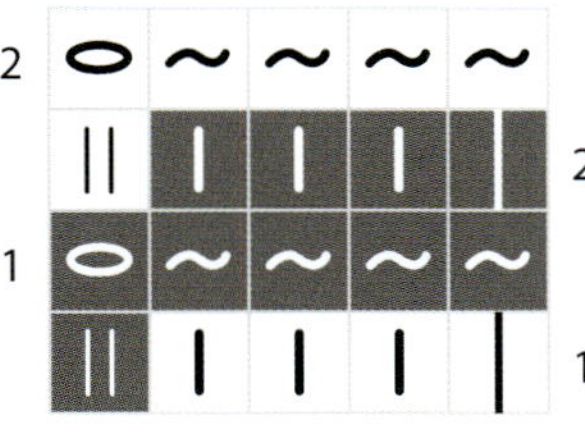

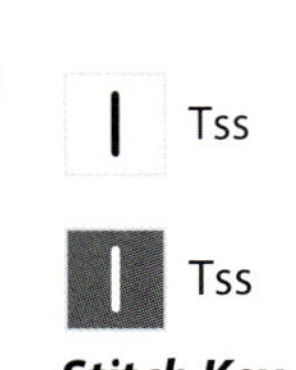

Stitch Key

375 TKS STRIPES

Worked over 2 rows.

Row 1: With MC, Tks.

Row 2: With CC, Tks.

Repeat Rows 1 and 2.

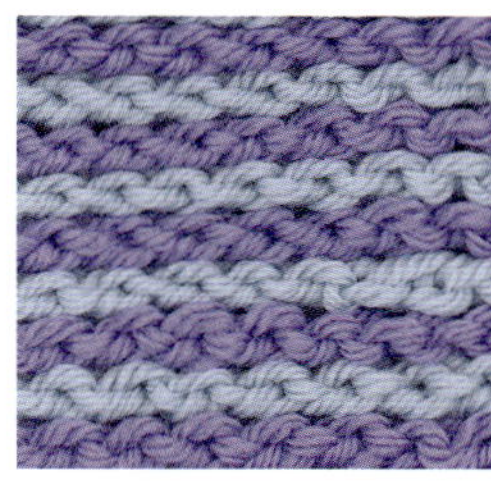

Reverse

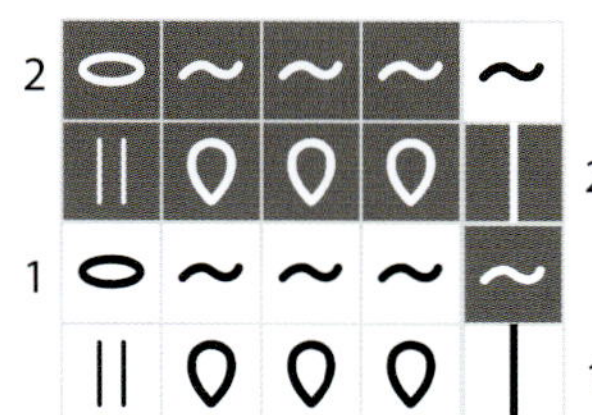

 Tks

 Tks

Stitch Key

376 TKS FADE

Worked over 2 rows.

Row 1 FP: With MC, Tks.

Row 1 RP: With CC, Std RP.

Row 2 FP: With CC, Tks.

Row 2 RP: With MC, Std RP.

Repeat Rows 1 and 2.

Reverse

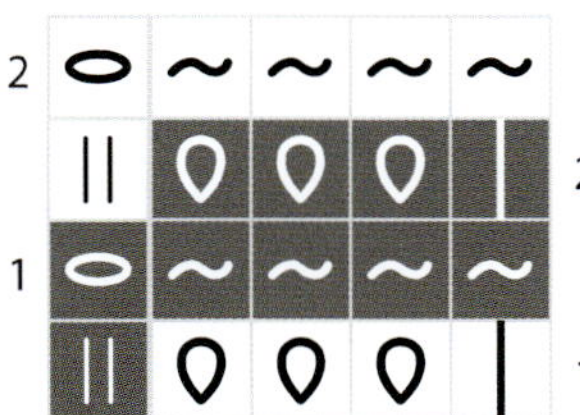

 Tks

Tks

Stitch Key

377 TRS STRIPES

Worked over 2 rows.
Row 1: With MC, Trs.
Row 2: With CC, Trs.
Repeat Rows 1 and 2.

Reverse

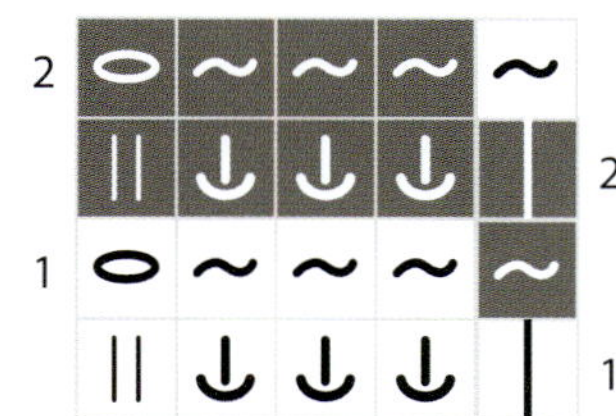

Stitch Key

378 TRS FADE

Worked over 2 rows.
Row 1 FP: With MC, Trs.
Row 1 RP: With CC, Std RP.
Row 2 FP: With CC, Trs.
Row 2 RP: With MC, Std RP.
Repeat Rows 1 and 2.

Reverse

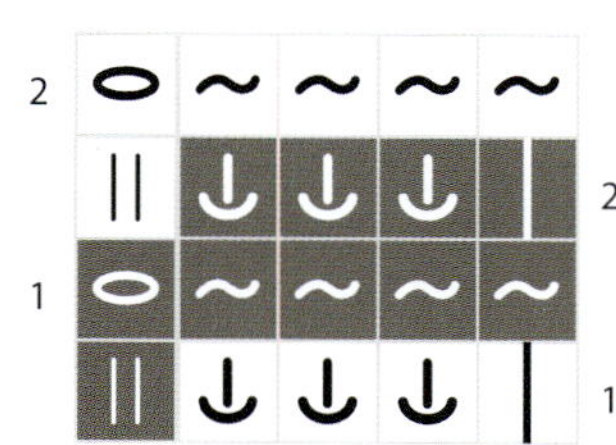

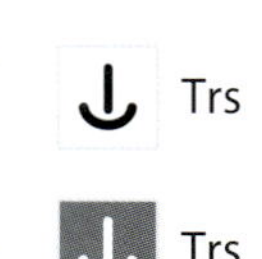

Stitch Key

379 TPS STRIPES

Worked over 2 rows.
Row 1: With MC, Tps.
Row 2: With CC, Tps.
Repeat Rows 1 and 2.

Reverse

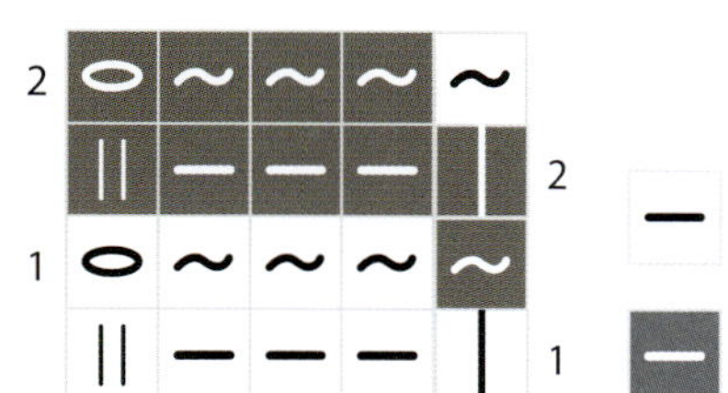

— Tps

— Tps

Stitch Key

380 TPS FADE

Worked over 2 rows.
Row 1 FP: With MC, Tps.
Row 1 RP: With CC, Std RP.
Row 2 FP: With CC, Tps.
Row 2 RP: With MC, Std RP.
Repeat Rows 1 and 2.

Reverse

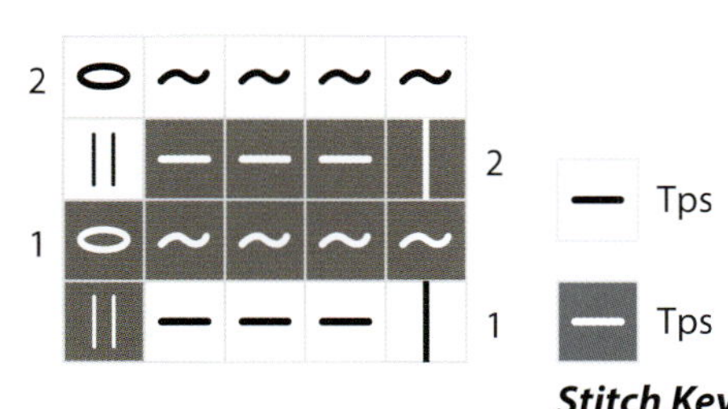

— Tps

— Tps

Stitch Key

381 TFS STRIPES

Worked over 2 rows.
Row 1: With MC, Tfs.
Row 2: With CC, Tfs.
Repeat Rows 1 and 2.

Reverse

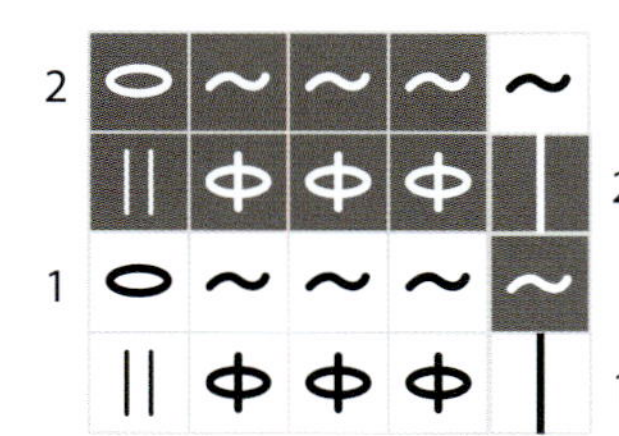

Tfs

Tfs

Stitch Key

382 TFS FADE

Worked over 2 rows.
Row 1 FP: With MC, Tfs.
Row 1 RP: With CC, Std RP.
Row 2 FP: With CC, Tfs.
Row 2 RP: With MC, Std RP.
Repeat Rows 1 and 2.

Reverse

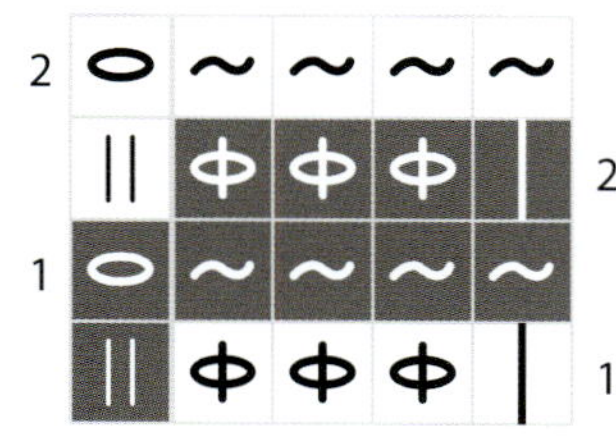

Stitch Key

383 TWD FADE

Worked over 2 rows.

Row 1 FP: With MC, Twd.

Row 1 RP: With CC, Std RP.

Row 2 FP: With CC, Twd.

Row 2 RP: With MC, Std RP.

Repeat Rows 1 and 2.

Reverse

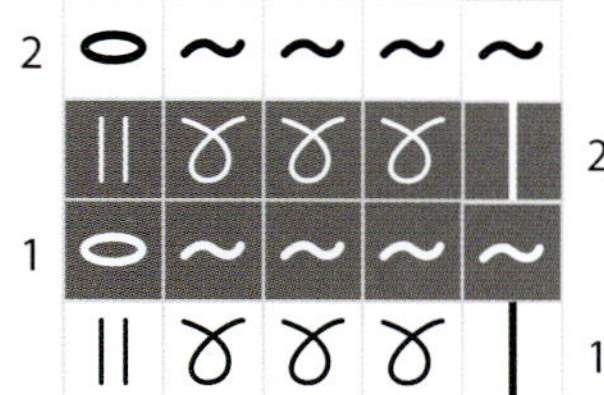

Stitch Key

384 TMSS FADE

Worked over 2 rows.

Row 1 FP: With MC, Tmss.

Row 1 RP: With CC, Std RP.

Row 2 FP: With CC, Tmss.

Row 2 RP: With MC, Std RP.

Repeat Rows 1 and 2.

Reverse

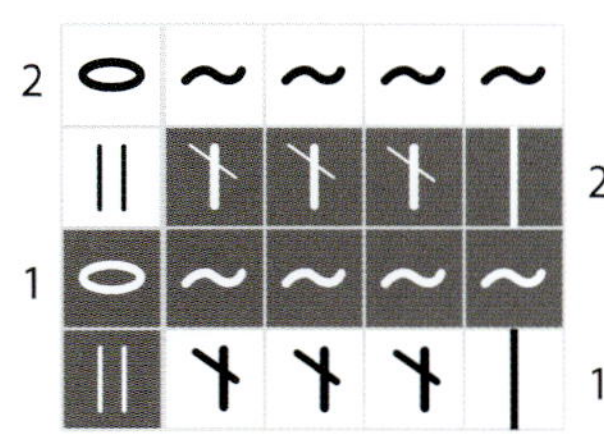

Stitch Key

385 TMKS STRIPES

Worked over 2 rows.
Row 1: With MC, Tmks.
Row 2: With CC, Tmks.
Repeat Rows 1 and 2.

Reverse

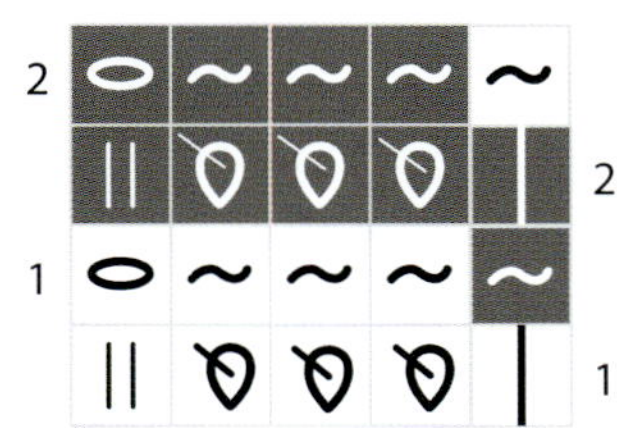

Tmks

Tmks

Stitch Key

386 TMKS FADE

Worked over 2 rows.
Row 1 FP: With MC, Tmks.
Row 1 RP: With CC, Std RP.
Row 2 FP: With CC, Tmks.
Row 2 RP: With MC, Std RP.
Repeat Rows 1 and 2.

Reverse

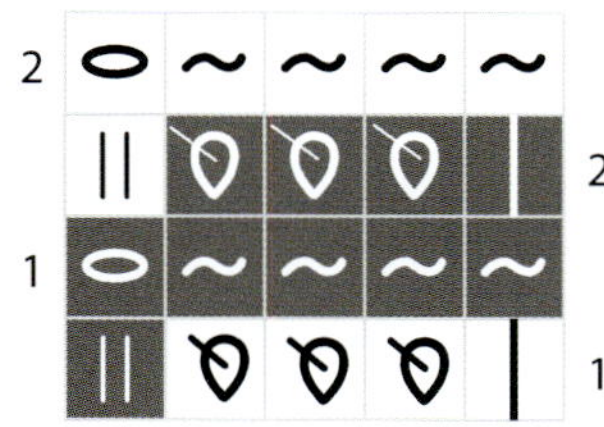

Tmks

Tmks

Stitch Key

387 PTRS STRIPES

Worked over 2 rows.
Row 1: With MC, PTrs.
Row 2: With CC, PTrs.
Repeat Rows 1 and 2.

Reverse

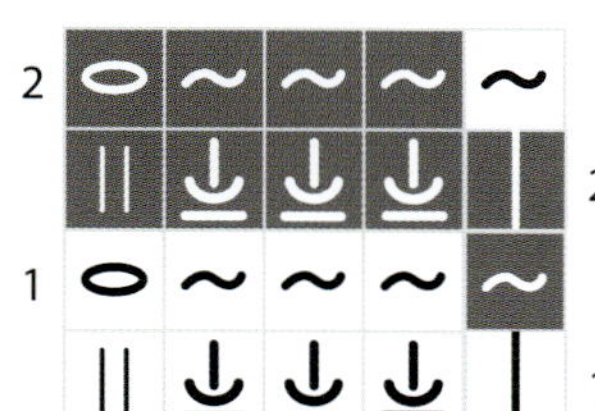

Stitch Key

388 PTRS FADE

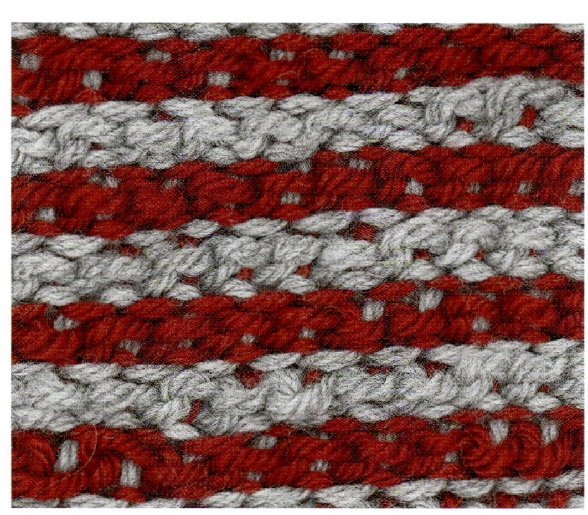

Worked over 2 rows.
Row 1 FP: With MC, PTrs.
Row 1 RP: With CC, Std RP.
Row 2 FP: With CC, PTrs.
Row 2 RP: With MC, Std RP.
Repeat Rows 1 and 2.

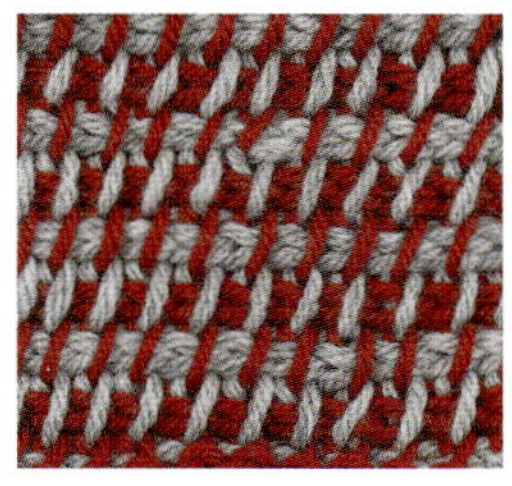

Reverse

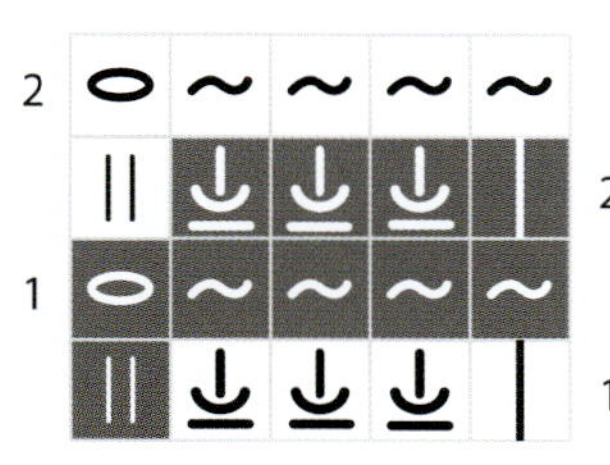

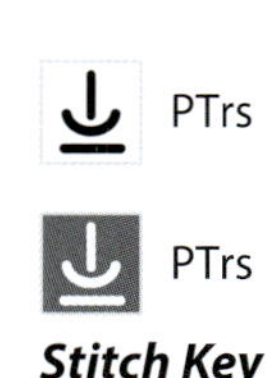

Stitch Key

389 TMFS STRIPES

Worked over 2 rows.
Row 1: With MC, Tmfs.
Row 2: With CC, Tmfs.
Repeat Rows 1 and 2.

Reverse

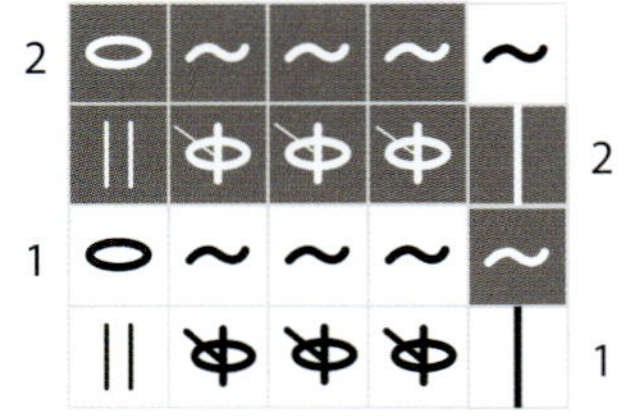

Stitch Key

390 TMFS FADE

Worked over 2 rows.
Row 1 FP: With MC, Tmfs.
Row 1 RP: With CC, Std RP.
Row 2 FP: With CC, Tmfs.
Row 2 RP: With MC, Std RP.
Repeat Rows 1 and 2.

Reverse

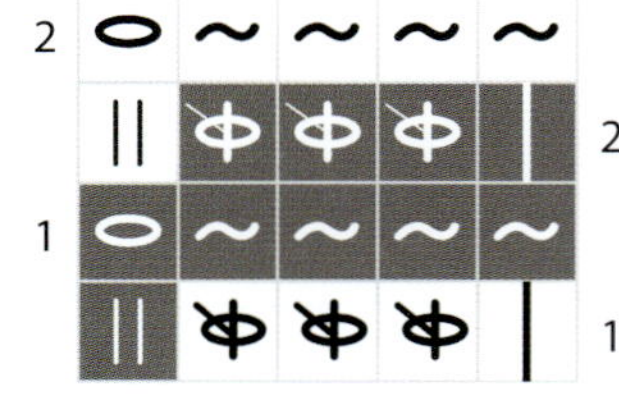

Stitch Key

391 TTOP STRIPES

Worked over 2 rows.
Row 1: With MC, Ttop.
Row 2: With CC, Ttop.
Repeat Rows 1 and 2.

Reverse

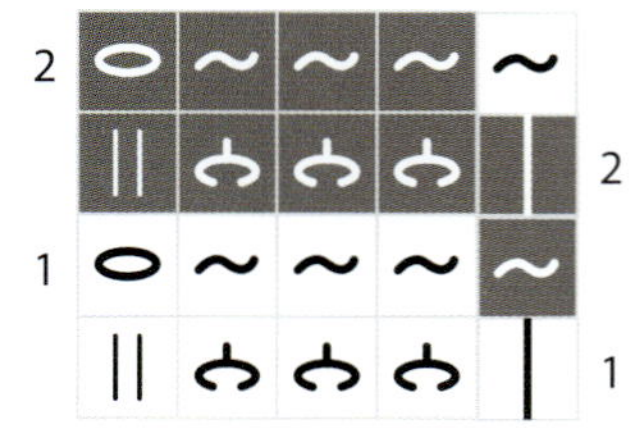

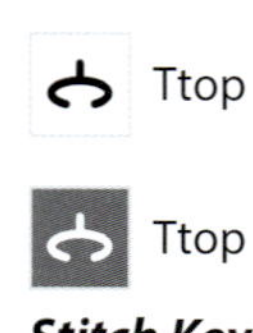

Stitch Key

392 TTOP FADE

Worked over 2 rows.
Row 1 FP: With MC, Ttop.
Row 1 RP: With CC, Std RP.
Row 2 FP: With CC, Ttop.
Row 2 RP: With MC, Std RP.
Repeat Rows 1 and 2.

Reverse

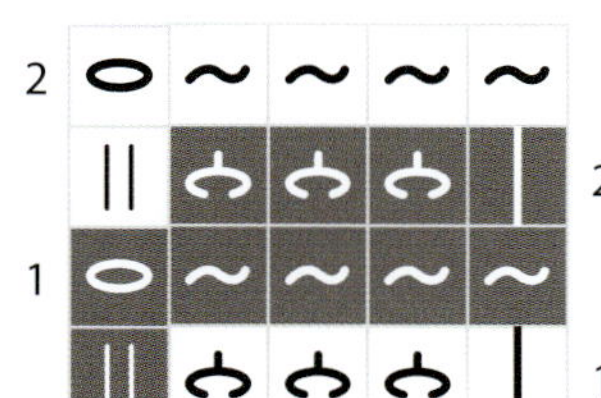

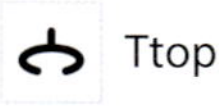

Stitch Key

393 FPTC STRIPES

Worked over 2 rows.
Row 1: With MC, Fptc.
Row 2: With CC, Fptc.
Repeat Rows 1 and 2.

Reverse

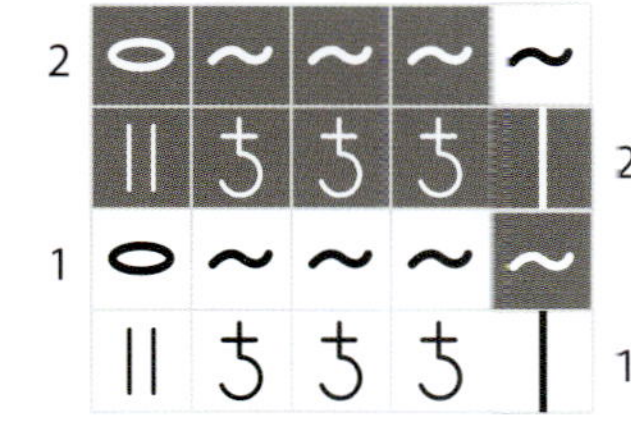

Stitch Key

Mosaic Stitches

Mosaic colorwork charts are different from standard charts. The return pass is omitted. Each row uses a single color, and the colors alternate every row. Only the Tunisian Mosaic (Tmos) stitches are labeled, and they are worked into the prior row (which is the same color). Boxes with no stitch labeled are Tss.

394 TUNISIAN MOSAIC STITCH (Tmos) using ExTmss

Reverse

Worked over any number of stitches.

Tmos: Insert hook as for Tmss in the prior row (photo 1). Yo and pull up a loop, chain 1 and leave loop on hook. *Note:* The chain 1 is very important; otherwise the fabric will be too tight and will curl.

Swatch shown is:

Row 1: With MC, Tss 11.

Row 2: With CC, Tss 11.

Row 3: With MC, Tmos, Tss 9, Tmos.

Row 4: With CC, Tss, Tmos, Tss 7, Tmos, Tss.

Row 5: With MC, Tmos, Tss, Tmos, Tss 5, Tmos, Tss, Tmos.

Row 6: With CC, Tss, Tmos, Tss, Tmos, Tss 3, Tmos, Tss, Tmos, Tss.

Row 7: With MC, Tmos, [Tss, Tmos] rep.

Row 8: With CC, Tss, Tmos, Tss, Tmos, Tss 3, Tmos, Tss, Tmos, Tss.

Row 9: With MC, Tmos, Tss, Tmos, Tss 5, Tmos, Tss, Tmos.

Row 10: With CC, Tss, Tmos, Tss 7, Tmos, Tss.

Row 11: With MC, Tss 11.

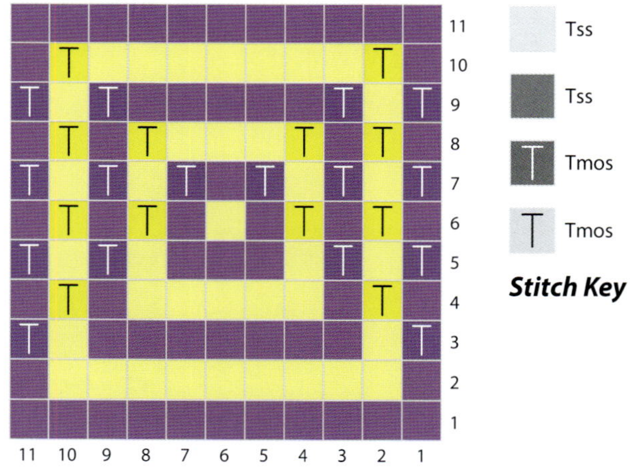

395 TUNISIAN MOSAIC STITCH (Tmos) using ExFptc

Reverse

Tmos: Insert hook as for Fptc in the prior row (photo 1). Yo and pull up a loop, chain 1 and leave loop on hook. *Note:* The chain 1 is very important; otherwise the fabric will be too tight and will curl.

Swatch shown is:

Row 1: With MC, Tss 11.

Row 2: With CC, Tss 11.

Row 3: With MC, Tmos, Tss 9, Tmos.

Row 4: With CC, Tss, Tmos, Tss 7, Tmos, Tss.

Row 5: With MC, Tmos, Tss, Tmos, Tss 5, Tmos, Tss, Tmos.

Row 6: With CC, Tss, Tmos, Tss, Tmos, Tss 3, Tmos, Tss, Tmos, Tss.

Row 7: With MC, Tmos, [Tss, Tmos] rep.

Row 8: With CC, Tss, Tmos, Tss, Tmos, Tss 3, Tmos, Tss, Tmos, Tss.

Row 9: With MC, Tmos, Tss, Tmos, Tss 5, Tmos, Tss, Tmos.

Row 10: With CC, Tss, Tmos, Tss 7, Tmos, Tss.

Row 11: With MC, Tss 11.

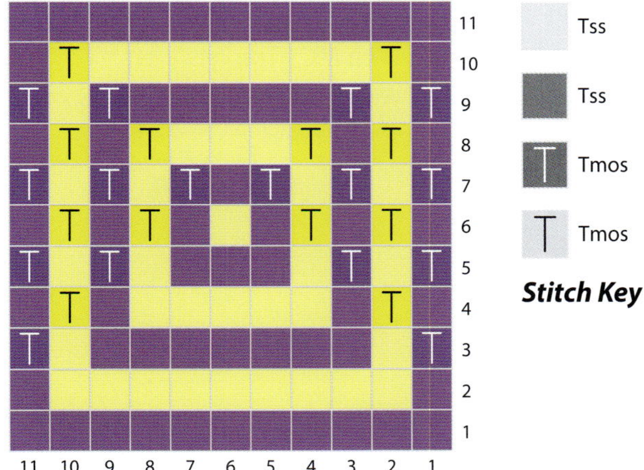

396 TSLST WITH TSS

Worked over a multiple of 2 stitches and 2 rows.

Row 1: With MC, [Tss, Tslst] rep.

Row 2: With CC, [Tslst, Tss] rep.

Repeat Rows 1 and 2.

Reverse

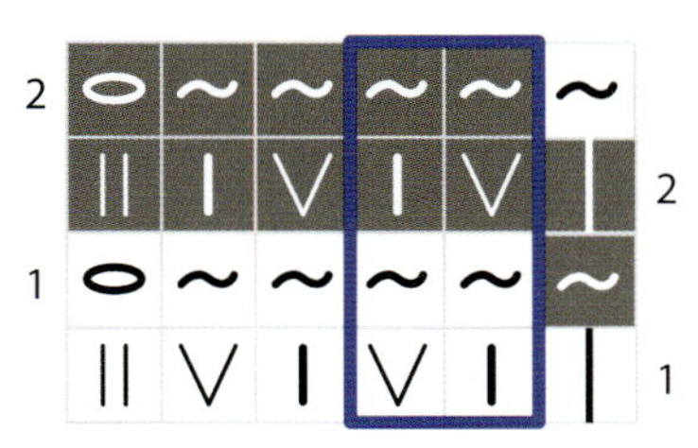

Tslst

Tslst

Tss

Tss

Stitch Key

397 TSLST WITH TKS

Worked over a multiple of 2 stitches and 2 rows.

Row 1: With MC, [Tks, Tslst] rep.

Row 2: With CC, [Tslst, Tks] rep.

Repeat Rows 1 and 2.

Reverse

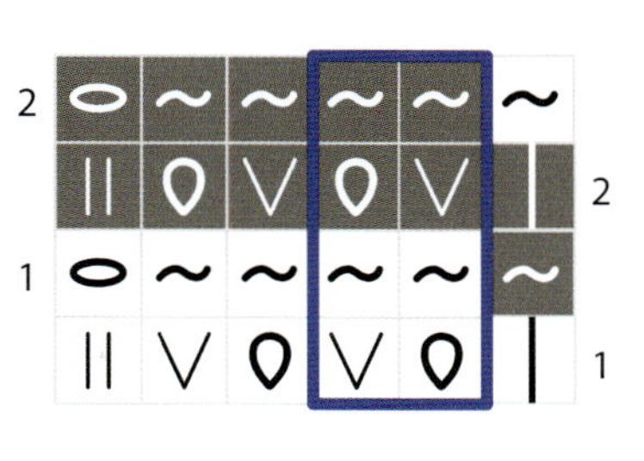

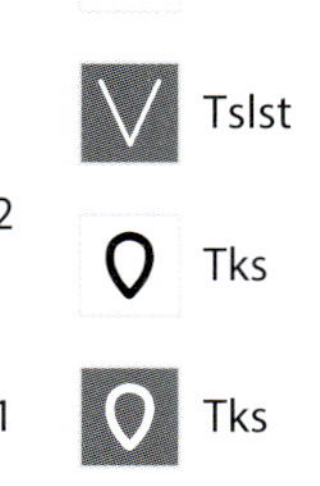

Stitch Key

398 TSLST WITH TRS

Worked over a multiple of 2 stitches and 2 rows.

Row 1: With MC, [Trs, Tslst] rep.

Row 2: With CC, [Tslst, Trs] rep.

Repeat Rows 1 and 2.

Reverse

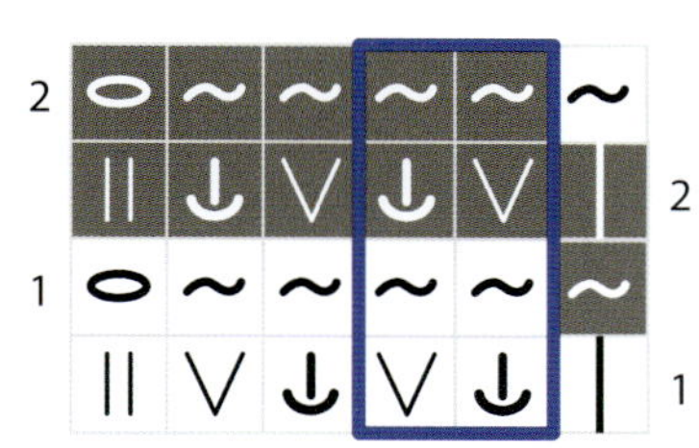

Tslst

 Tslst

 Trs

 Trs

Stitch Key

399 TSLST WITH TPS

Worked over a multiple of 2 stitches and 2 rows.

Row 1: With MC, [Tps, Tslst] rep.

Row 2: With CC, [Tslst, Tps] rep.

Repeat Rows 1 and 2.

Reverse

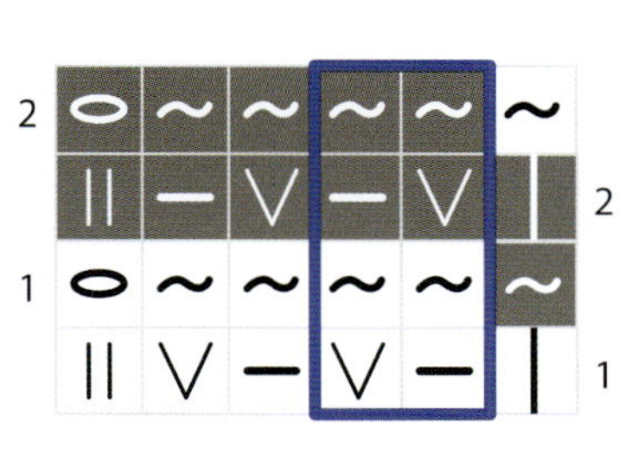

 Tslst

 Tslst

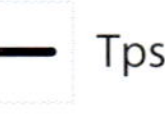 Tps

 Tps

Stitch Key

400 TSLST WITH TTOP

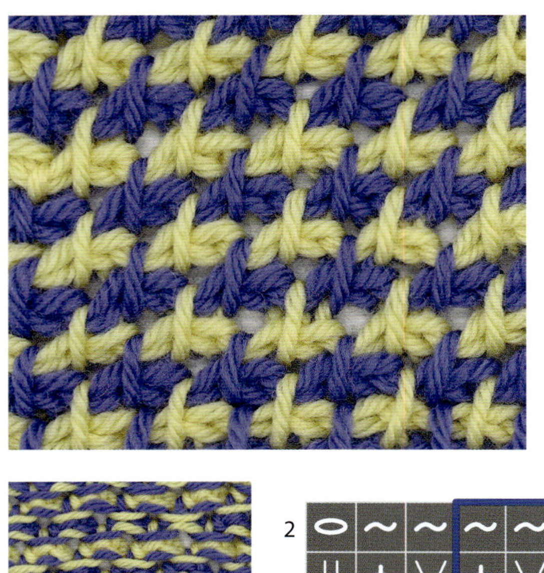

Worked over a multiple of 2 stitches and 2 rows.

Row 1: With MC, [Ttop, Tslst] rep.

Row 2: With CC, [Tslst, Ttop] rep.

Repeat Rows 1 and 2.

Reverse

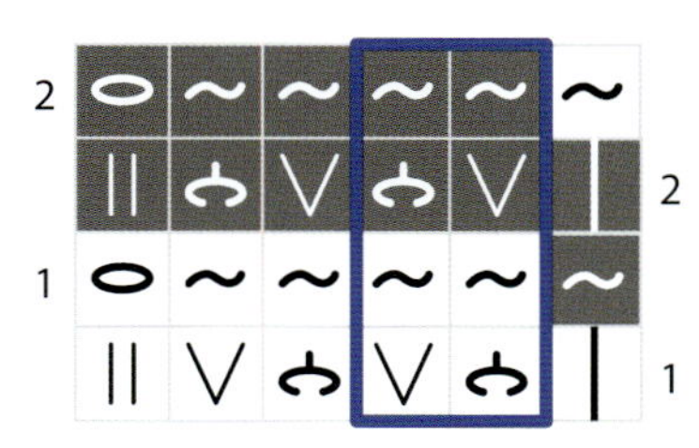

Tslst

Tslst

Ttop

Ttop

Stitch Key

401 PTSLST WITH TSS

Worked over a multiple of 2 stitches and 2 rows.

Row 1: With MC, [Tss, PTslst] rep.

Row 2: With CC, [PTslst, Tss] rep.

Repeat Rows 1 and 2.

Reverse

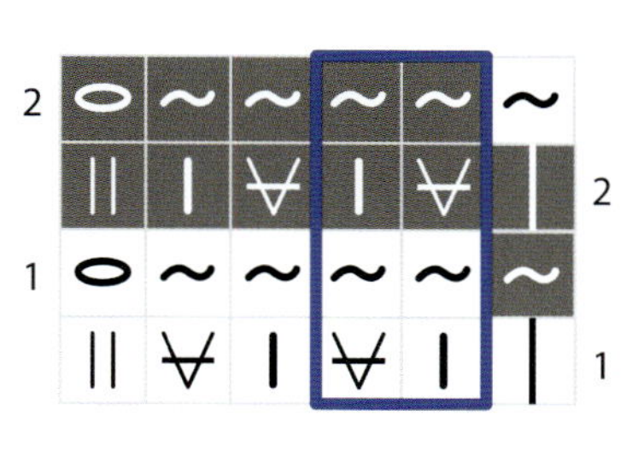

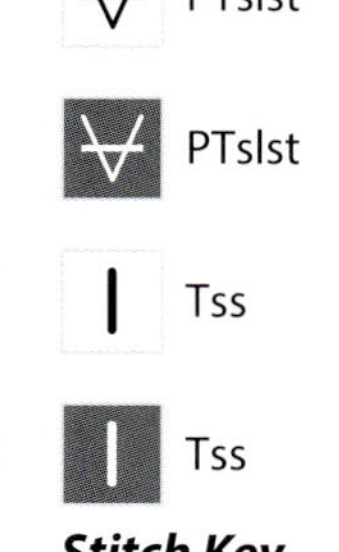

Stitch Key

402 PTSLST WITH TKS

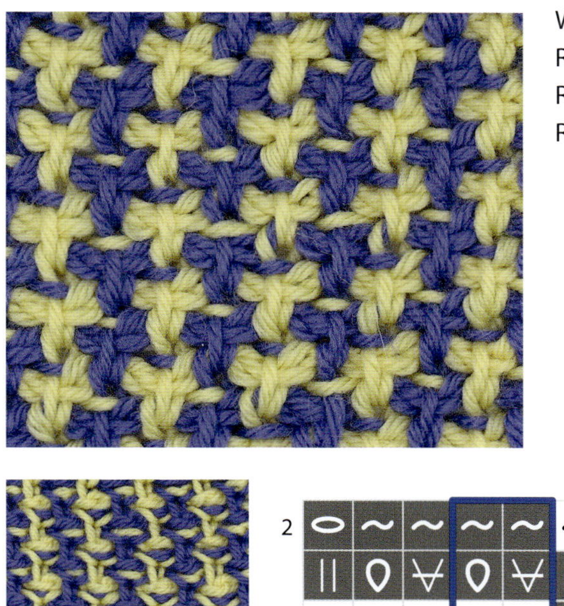

Worked over a multiple of 2 stitches and 2 rows.

Row 1: With MC, [Tks, PTslst] rep.

Row 2: With CC, [PTslst, Tks] rep.

Repeat Rows 1 and 2.

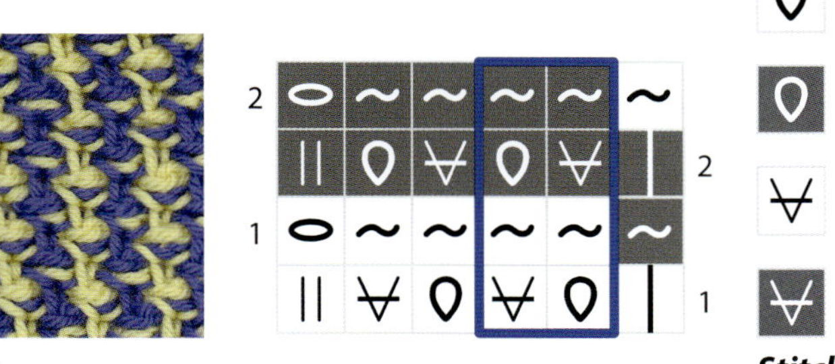

Reverse

Tks

Tks

PTslst

PTslst

Stitch Key

403 PTSLST WITH TRS

Worked over a multiple of 2 stitches and 2 rows.

Row 1: With MC, [Trs, PTslst] rep.

Row 2: With CC, [PTslst, Trs] rep.

Repeat Rows 1 and 2.

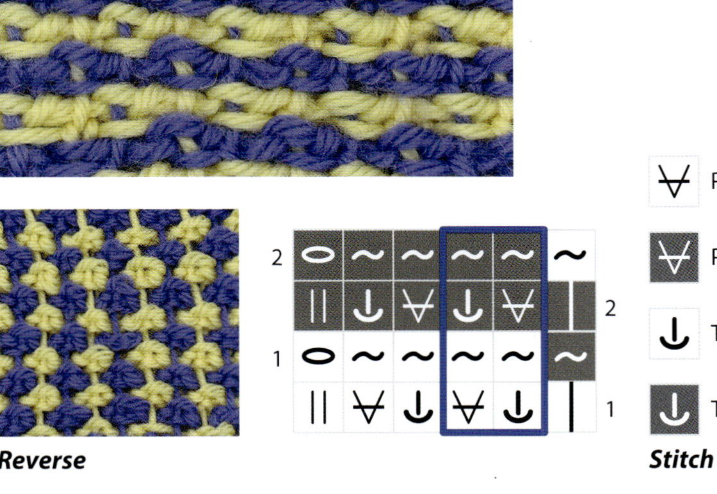

Reverse

PTslst

PTslst

Trs

Trs

Stitch Key

404 PTSLST WITH TPS

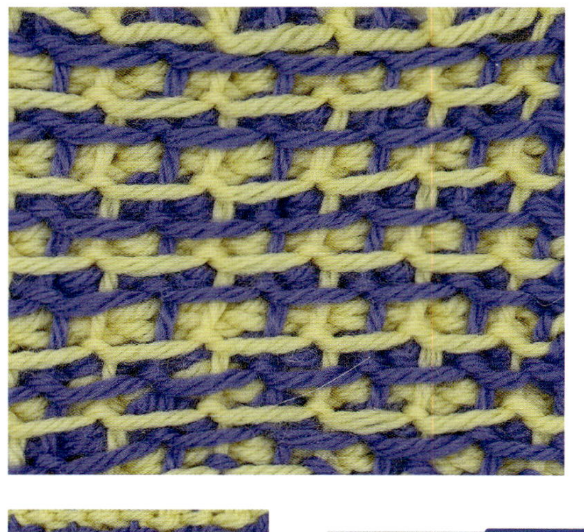

Worked over a multiple of 2 stitches and 2 rows.
Row 1: With MC, [Tps, PTslst] rep.
Row 2: With CC, [PTslst, Tps] rep.
Repeat Rows 1 and 2.

Reverse

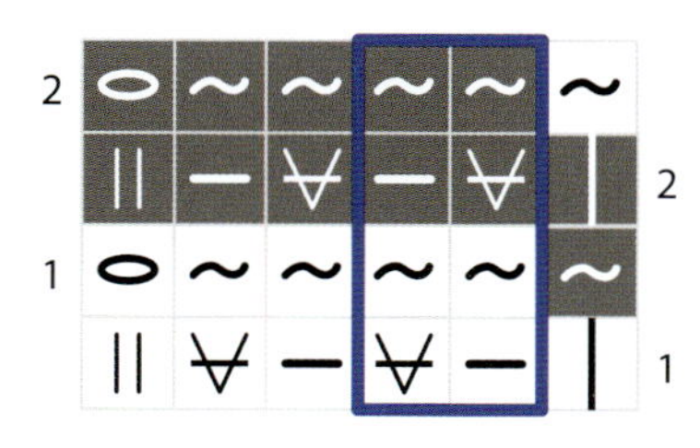

PTslst

PTslst

Tps

Tps

Stitch Key

405 TFS WIDE STRIPES

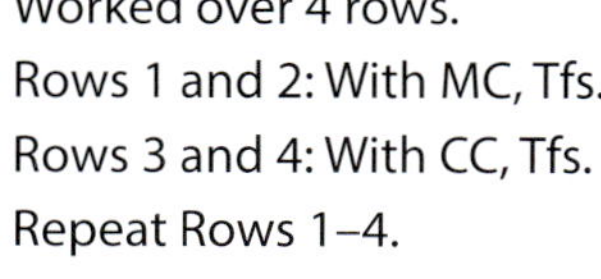

Worked over 4 rows.
Rows 1 and 2: With MC, Tfs.
Rows 3 and 4: With CC, Tfs.
Repeat Rows 1–4.

Reverse

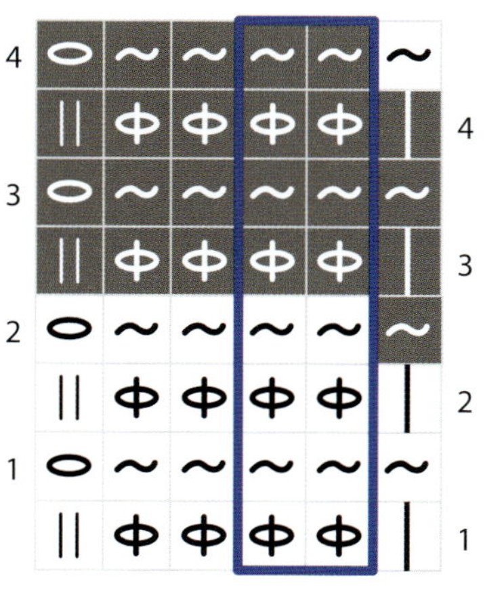

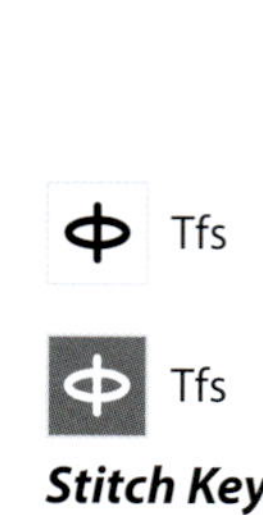

Stitch Key

406 TFS EXTRA WIDE STRIPES

Worked over 6 rows.

Rows 1–3: With MC, Tfs.

Rows 4–6: With CC, Tfs.

Repeat Rows 1–6.

Reverse

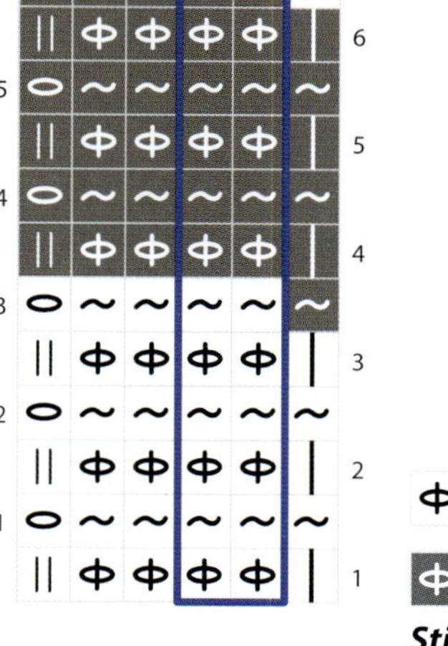

Tfs

Tfs

Stitch Key

407 WAVE STITCH

Worked over a multiple of 6 stitches and 2 rows.

Row 1: With MC, [Tss 3, Tdc 3] rep.

Row 2: With CC, Tss.

Row 3: With MC, [Tdc 3, Tss 3] rep.

Row 4: With CC, Tss.

Repeat Rows 1–4.

Reverse

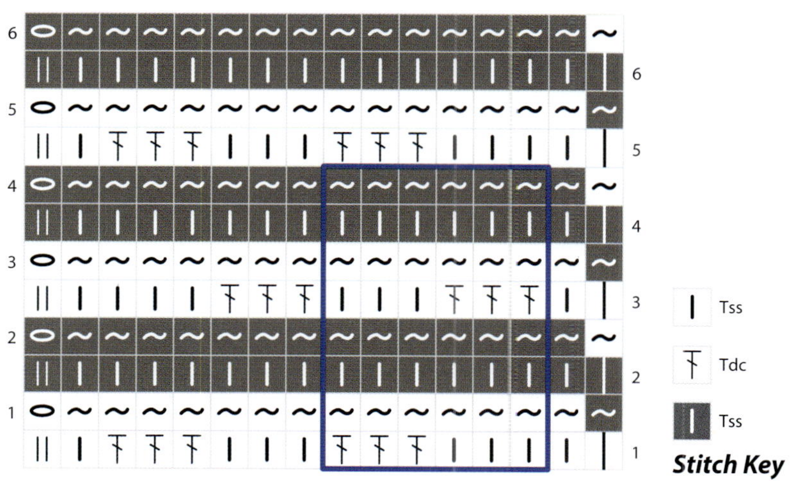

Tss

Tdc

Tss

Stitch Key

408

Reverse

Worked over a multiple of 2 + 2 stitches and 8 rows.

Row 1 FP: With MC, Tss.

Row 1 RP: With CC, Std RP.

Row 2 FP: With CC, [Tss2Tog, yu] rep.

Row 2 RP: With MC, Std RP.

Row 3 FP: With MC, Tss.

Row 3 RP: With CC, Std RP.

Row 4 FP: With CC, Tss, [yu, Tss2Tog] rep until 1 st rem, Tss.

Row 4 RP: With MC, Std RP.

Row 5 FP: With MC, Tss.

Row 5 RP: With CC, Std RP.

Row 6 FP: With CC, Tss, [Tss2Tog, yu] rep until 1 st rem, Tss.

Row 6 RP: With MC, Std RP.

Row 7 FP: With MC, Tss.

Row 7 RP: With CC, Std RP.

Row 8 FP: With CC, [yu, Tss2Tog] rep.

Row 8 RP: With MC, Std RP.

Repeat Rows 1–8.

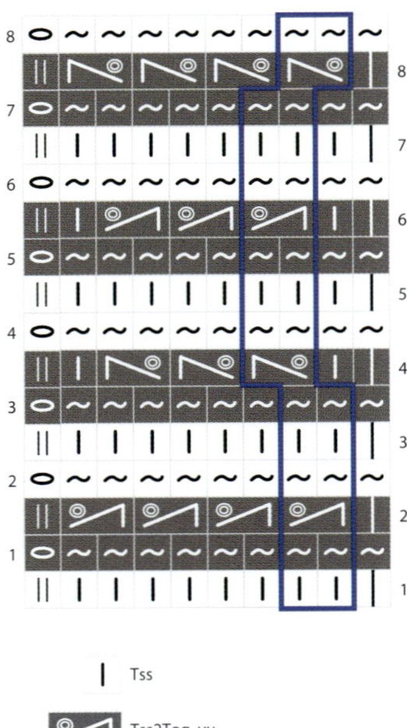

Stitch Key

409

Reverse

Worked over multiples of 2 stitches and 4 rows.

Row 1 FP: With MC, [Tss, Tps] rep.

Row 1 RP: With CC, Std RP.

Row 2 FP: With CC, [Tps, Tslst] rep.

Row 2 RP: With MC, Std RP.

Row 3 FP: With MC, [Tps, Tss] rep.

Row 3 RP: With CC, Std RP.

Row 4 FP: With CC, [Tslst, Tps] rep.

Row 4 RP: With MC, Std RP.

Repeat Rows 1–4.

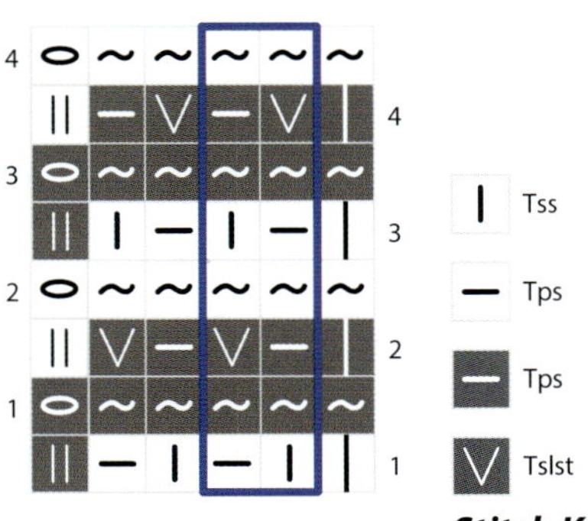

Tss

Tps

Tps

Tslst

Stitch Key

410

Worked over a multiple of 3 stitches and 2 rows.

Row 1 FP: With MC, Tss.

Row 1 RP: With CC, Std RP.

Row 2 FP: With CC, in next 3 sts (Tss3Tog, yo, Tss3Tog) rep.

Row 2 RP: With MC, Std RP.

Repeat Rows 1 and 2.

Reverse

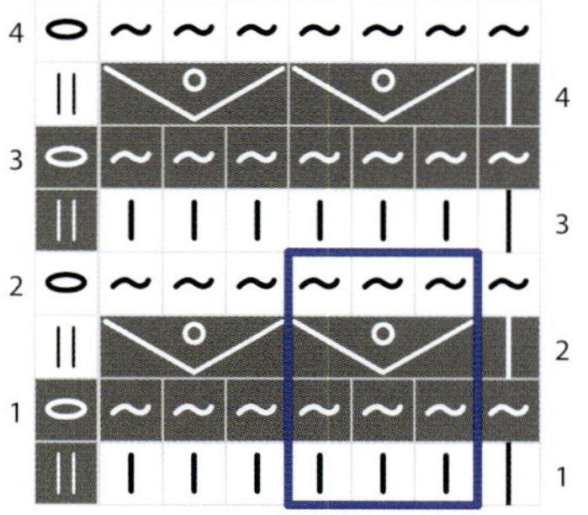

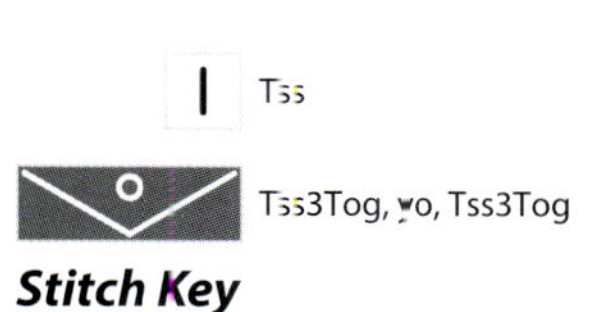

Stitch Key

411

Worked over a multiple of 4 + 3 stitches and 2 rows.

Row 1 FP: With MC, Tss.

Row 1 RP: [Ch 1, RP-4, ch 1, RP-2] rep.

Row 2 FP: With CC, [Tfs, Ttop, Tfs, Tss] rep.

Row 2 RP: RP-2 twice, [ch 1, RP-4, ch 1, RP-2] rep until 3 loops rem on hook, RP-2 twice.

Row 3 FP: With MC, Tss, [Tss, Tfs, Ttop, Tfs] rep until 2 sts rem, Tss 2.

Row 3 RP: [Ch 1, RP-4, Ch 1, RP-2] rep.

Repeat Rows 2 and 3.

Reverse

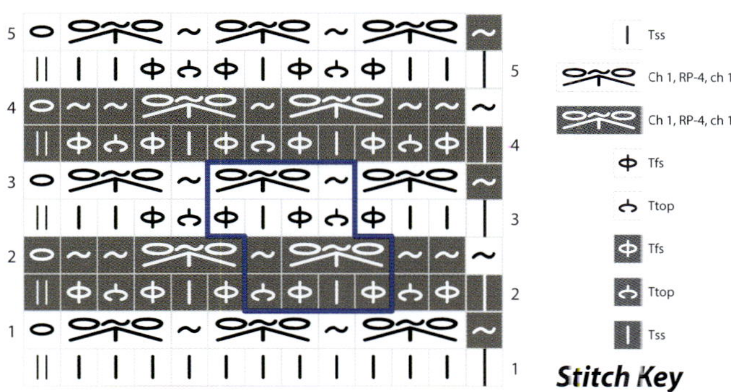

Stitch Key

412

Worked over 2 sts and 2 rows.

Long Tunisian Double Crochet (LTdc): Tdc worked in the prior row.

Row 1: With MC, Tss.

Row 2: With CC, Tss.

Row 3: With MC, [Tss, LTdc] rep.

Row 4: With CC, [LTdc, Tss] rep.

Repeat Rows 3 and 4.

Reverse

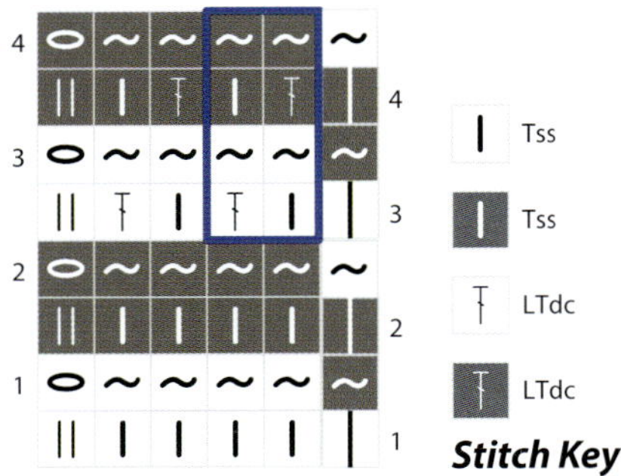

Tss

Tss

LTdc

LTdc

Stitch Key

413

Worked over a multiple of 3 + 2 stitches and 2 rows.

Row 1 FP: With MC, Tss, [worked over 3 sts: Tss 3, pull 1st loop over loops 2 and 3] rep until 1 st rem, Tss.

Row 1 RP: RP-2, [ch1, RP-2 twice] rep.

Row 2 FP: With CC, [worked over next 2 sts: Tss, Tfs in next st sp, Tss, pull 1st loop over loops 2 and 3] rep.

Row 2 RP: [RP-2, ch 1] rep.

Row 3 FP: With MC, Tss, [worked over next 2 sts: Tss, Tfs in next st sp, Tss, pull 1st loop over loops 2 and 3] rep until 1 st rem, Tss.

Row 3 RP: RP-2, [ch1, RP-2 twice] rep.

Repeat Rows 2 and 3.

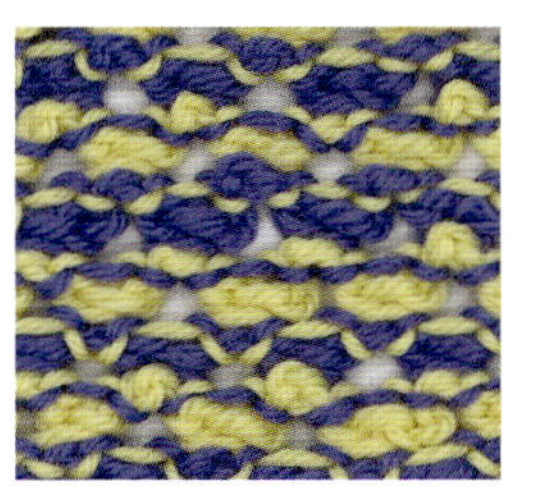

Reverse

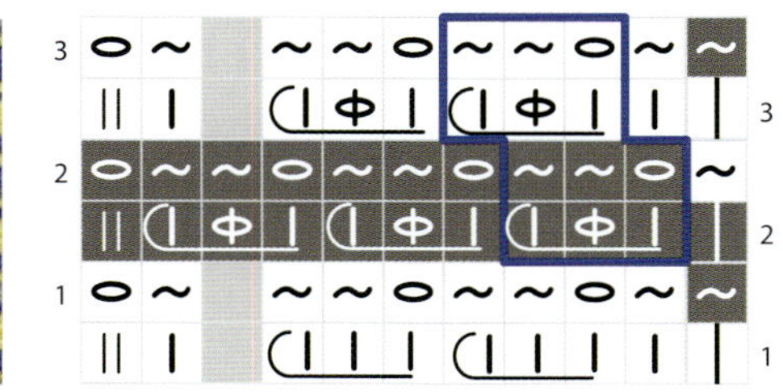

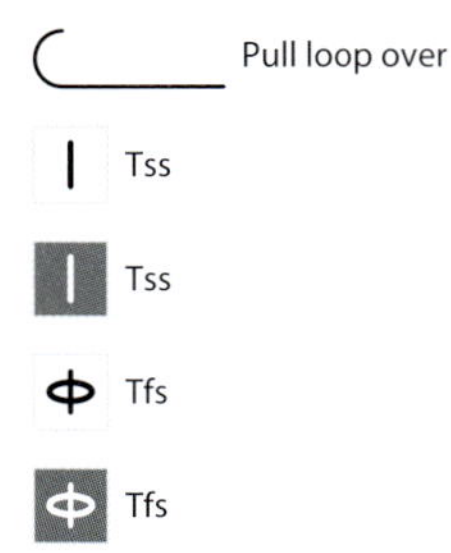

Pull loop over

Tss

Tss

Tfs

Tfs

Stitch Key

414

Worked over a multiple of 2 stitches and 2 rows.

Row 1 FP: With MC, [Tss, Tfs in the second stitch space] rep.

Row 1 RP: With CC, Std RP.

Row 2 FP: With CC, [Skip stitch space, Tfs, Tss] rep.

Row 2 RP: With MC, Std RP.

Repeat Rows 1 and 2.

Reverse

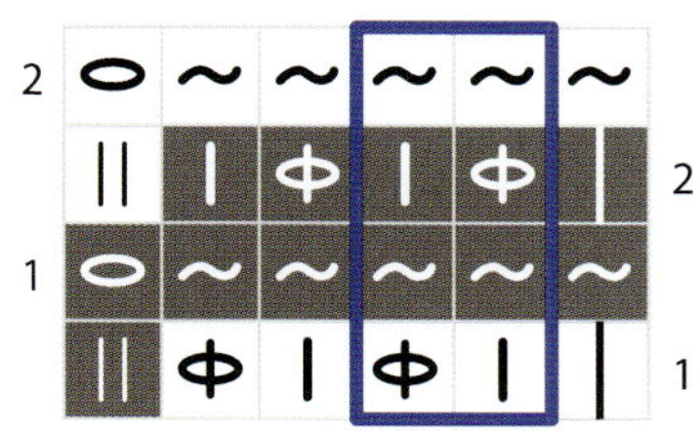

Tss

Tss

Tfs in second st sp

Tfs

Stitch Key

415

Worked over a multiple of 2 stitches and 2 rows.

Row 1 FP: With MC, [Tss, Twup] rep.

Row 1 RP: With CC, Std RP.

Row 2 FP: With CC, [Twup, Tss] rep.

Row 2 RP: With MC, Std RP.

Repeat Rows 1 and 2.

Reverse

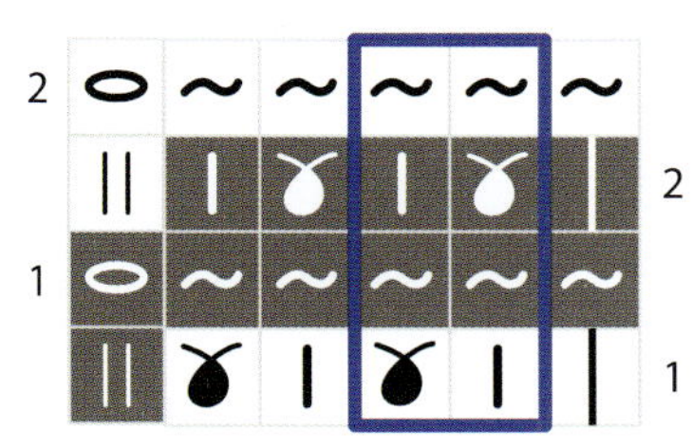

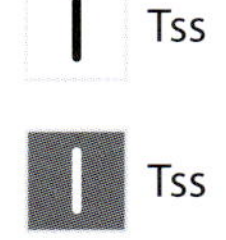

Tss

Tss

Twup

Twup

Stitch Key

416

Worked over a multiple of 2 stitches and 2 rows.

Row 1 FP: With MC, [Tss, Twup] rep.

Row 1 RP: With CC, Std RP.

Row 2 FP: With CC, [Tss, Twup] rep.

Row 2 RP: With MC, Std RP.

Repeat Rows 1 and 2.

Reverse

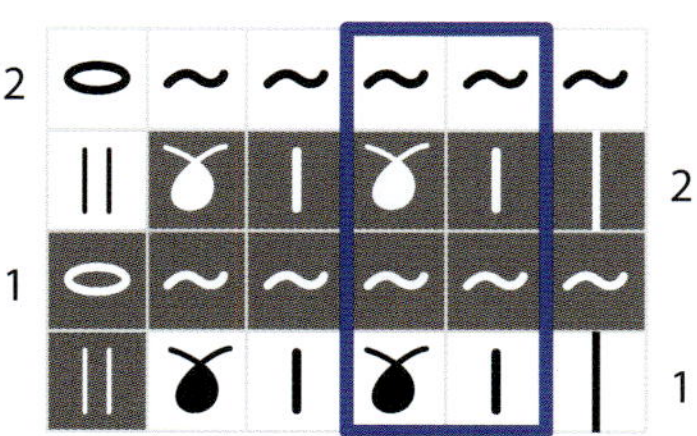

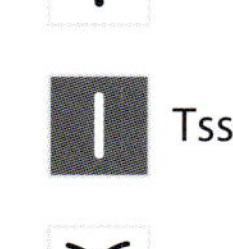

Tss

Tss

Twup

Twup

Stitch Key

417

Worked over a multiple of 2 stitches and 2 rows.

Row 1 FP: With MC, [Tss2Tog, yo] rep.

Row 1 RP: With CC, Std RP.

Row 2 FP: With CC, [Tss2Tog, yo] rep.

Row 2 RP: With MC, Std RP.

Repeat Rows 1 and 2.

Reverse

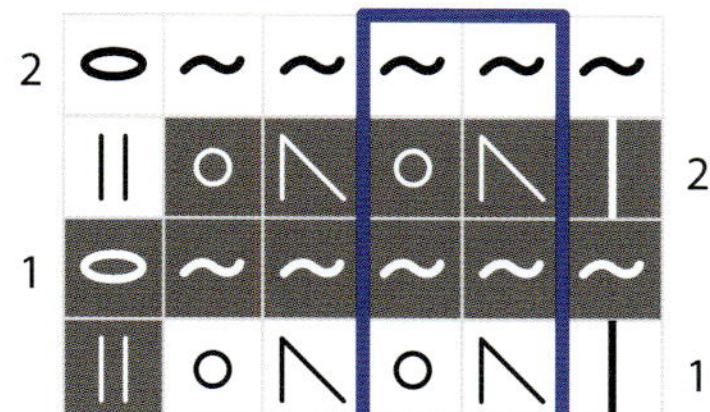

Tss2Tog

Tss2Tog

Stitch Key

418

Worked over 2 rows.
Row 1 FP: With MC, Tks.
Row 1 RP: With CC, Std RP.
Row 2 FP: With CC, Tfs.
Row 2 RP: With MC, Std RP.
Repeat Rows 1 and 2.

Reverse

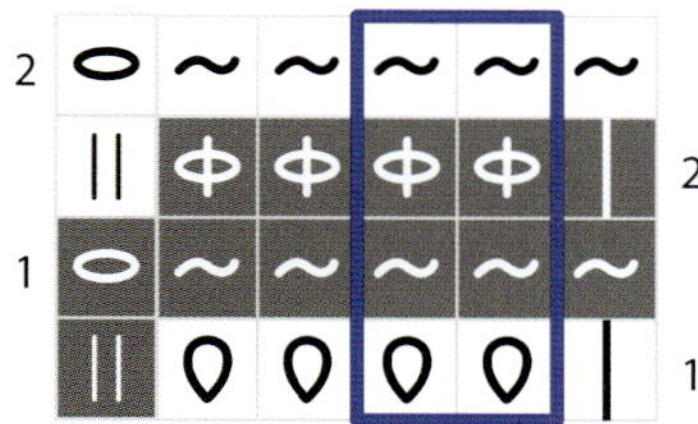

Tks

Tfs

Stitch Key

419

Worked over a multiple of 2 stitches and 2 rows.
Row 1 FP: With MC, Tps2Tog.
Row 1 RP: With CC, [Ch1, RP-2] rep.
Row 2 FP: With CC, [Tps, Tfs under chain] rep.
Row 2 RP: With MC, Std RP.
Repeat Rows 1 and 2.

Reverse

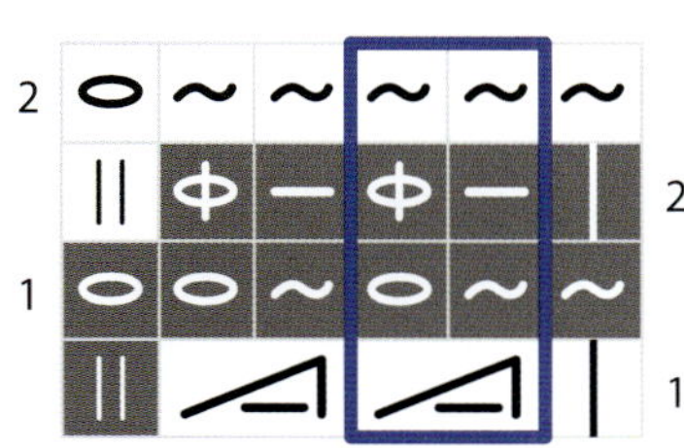

Tfs

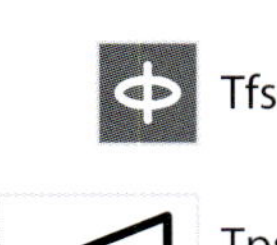

Tps2Tog

Tps

Stitch Key

420

Worked over a multiple of 2 stitches and 2 rows.

Row 1 FP: With MC, Tx.

Row 1 RP: With CC, Std RP.

Row 2 FP: With CC, [Tks, Twd] rep.

Row 2 RP: With MC, Std RP.

Repeat Rows 1 and 2.

Reverse

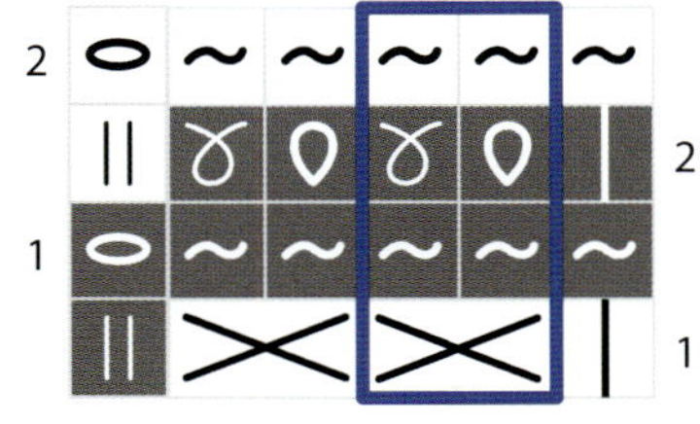

Tx

Twd

Tks

Stitch Key

421

Worked over a multiple of 2 stitches and 2 rows.

Row 1 FP: With MC, Tss.

Row 1 RP: [RP-3, ch 1] rep.

Row 2 FP: With CC, [Tfs and ch 3, Tss] rep.

Row 2 RP: [RP-3, ch 1] rep.

Row 3 FP: With MC, [Tfs, ch 3, Tss] rep.

Row 3 RP: [RP-3, ch 1] rep.

Repeat Rows 2 and 3.

Reverse

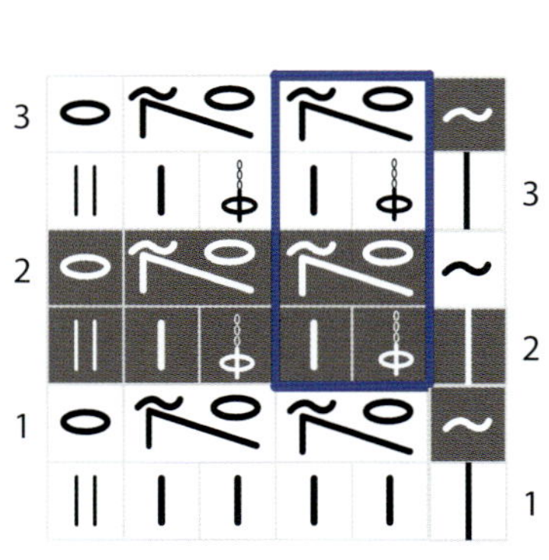

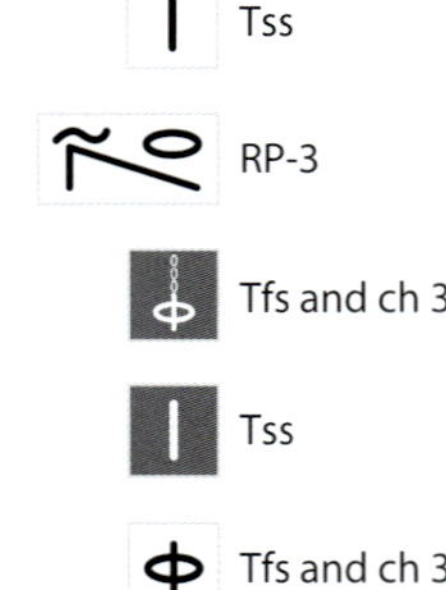

Stitch Key

422

Worked over a multiple of 2 stitches and 2 rows.

Row 1 FP: With MC, Tss.

Row 1 RP: With CC, Std RP.

Row 2 FP: With CC, [Tss and ch 2, Tslst] rep.

Row 2 RP: With MC, Std RP.

Repeat Rows 1 and 2.

Reverse

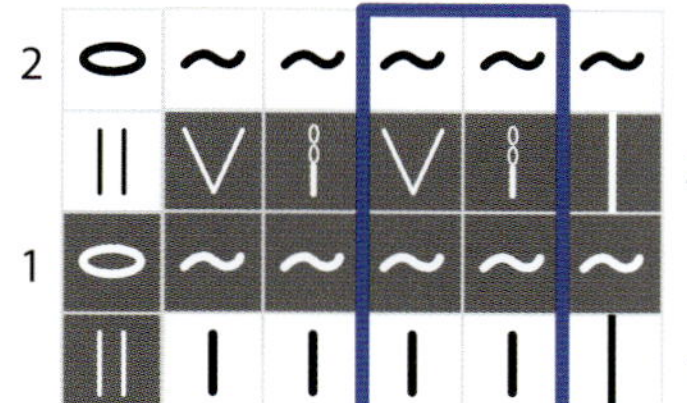

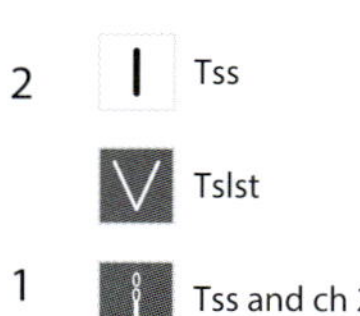

Stitch Key

423

Worked over a multiple of 3 stitches and 4 rows.

FptcDc Mosaic Stitch (FptcDCTmos): Yarn over and insert hook for Fptc in the prior row. Yarn over and pull up a loop. Yarn over and pull through 2 loops. Leave loop on hook.

Rows 1 and 2: With MC, Tss.

Row 3: With CC, [FptcDCTmos, Tss 2] rep.

Row 4: With CC, Tss.

Row 5: With MC, [FptcDCTmos, Tss 2] rep.

Row 6: With MC, Tss.

Repeat Rows 3–6.

Reverse

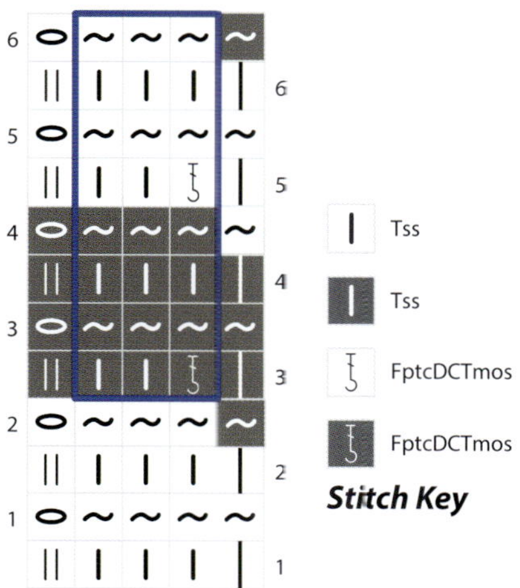

Stitch Key

424

Reverse

Worked over a multiple of 2 stitches and 4 rows.

Row 1: With MC, Tss.

Row 2: With CC, [Tslst, PTslst] rep.

Row 3: With MC, Tts.

Row 4: With CC, [PTslst, Tslst] rep.

Row 5: With MC, Tts.

Repeat Rows 2–5.

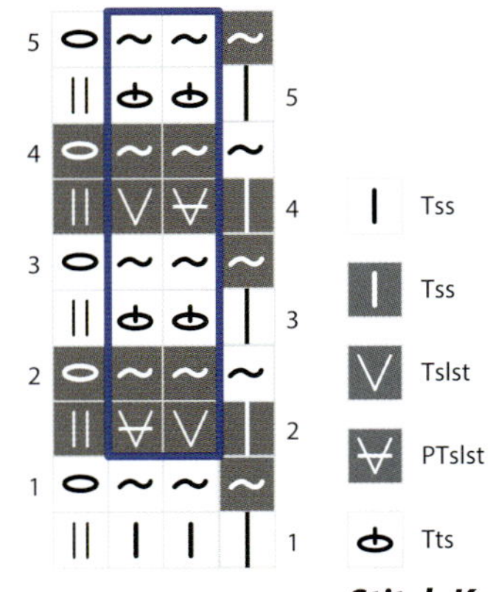

Stitch Key

425

Worked over a multiple of 2 stitches and 2 rows.

Row 1 FP: With MC, [Tss2Tog, Ttop] rep.

Row 1 RP: With CC, Std RP.

Row 2 FP: With CC, [Tss2Tog, Ttop] rep.

Row 2 RP: With MC, Std RP.

Repeat Rows 1 and 2.

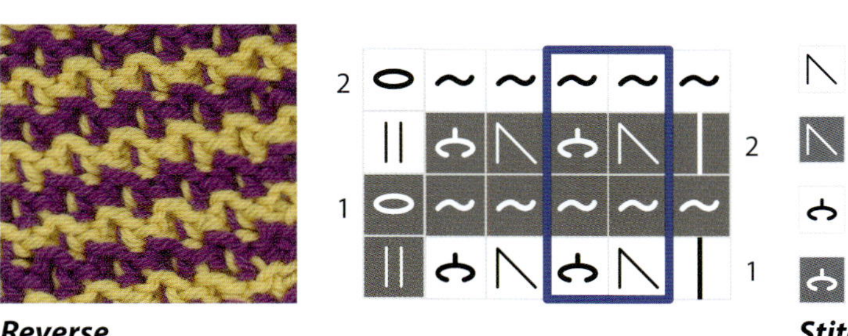

Reverse

Tss2Tog

Tss2Tog

Ttop

Ttop

Stitch Key

426

Worked over a multiple of 2 stitches and 2 rows.

Double ExTss2Tog (DExTss2Tog): Worked in the next 2 sts, (Tss2Tog, ch 1) twice.

Row 1 FP: With MC, DExTss2Tog.

Row 1 RP: With CC, Std RP.

Row 2 FP: With CC, DExTss2Tog.

Row 2 RP: With MC, Std RP.

Repeat Rows 1 and 2.

Reverse

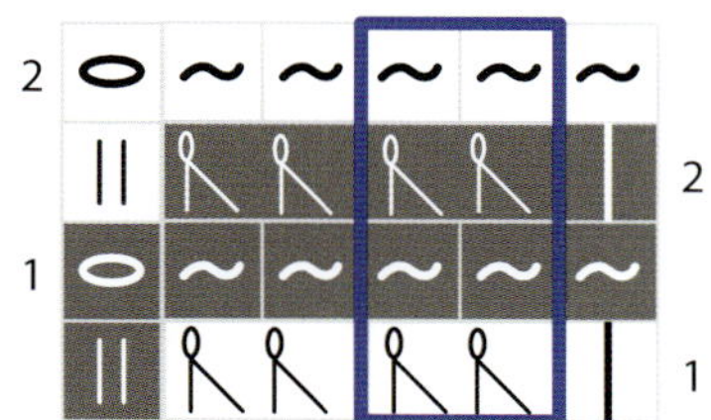

DExTss2Tog

Stitch Key

427

Worked over a multiple of 2 stitches and 2 rows.

Row 1: With MC, [Tks, Trs].

Row 2: With CC, [Tks, Trs].

Repeat Rows 1 and 2.

Reverse

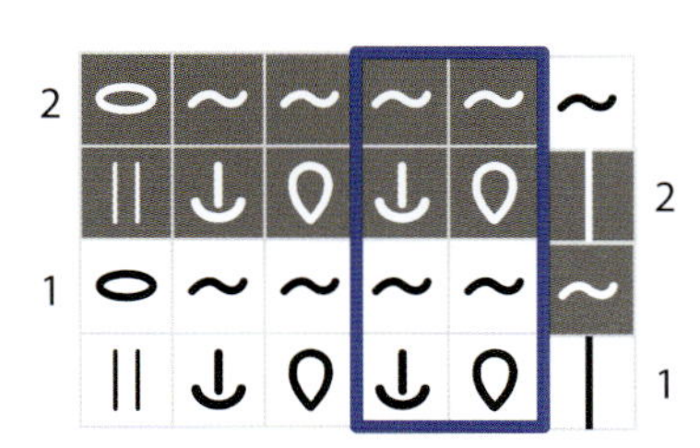

Tks

Trs

Tks

Trs

Stitch Key

428

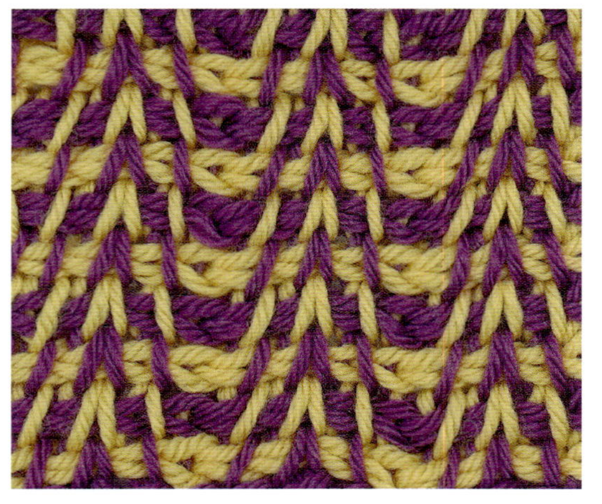

Worked over a multiple of 4 stitches and 2 rows.

Row 1 FP: With MC, [Tss 2, Twup 2] rep.

Row 1 RP: With CC, Std RP.

Row 2 FP: With CC, [Twup 2, Tss 2] rep.

Row 2 RP: With MC, Std RP.

Repeat Rows 1 and 2.

Reverse

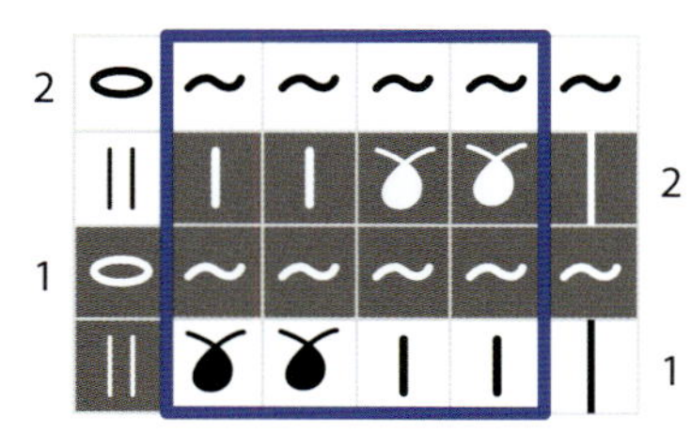

Tss

Tss

Twup

Twup

Stitch Key

429

Worked over a multiple of 3 stitches and 2 rows.

Uses Bamboo Stitch B-St3 (Stitch 190, page 106).

Row 1 FP: With MC, B-St3 rep.

Row 1 RP: With CC, Std RP.

Row 2 FP: With CC, Tss.

Row 2 RP: With MC, Std RP.

Repeat Rows 1 and 2.

Reverse

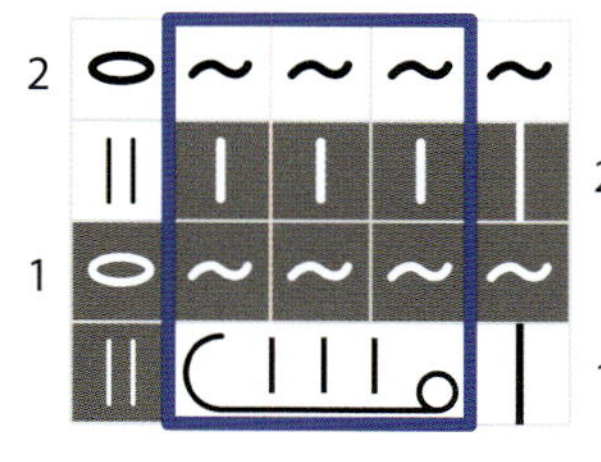

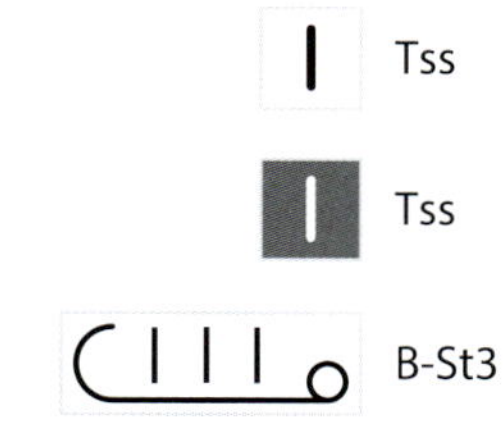

Stitch Key

430

Worked over a multiple of 2 stitches and 2 rows.

Row 1 FP: With MC, Tx.

Row 1 RP: With CC, Std RP.

Row 2 FP: With CC, Tx.

Row 2 RP: With MC, Std RP.

Repeat Rows 1 and 2.

Reverse

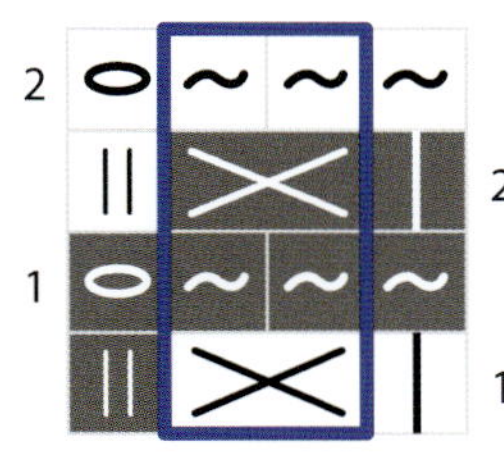

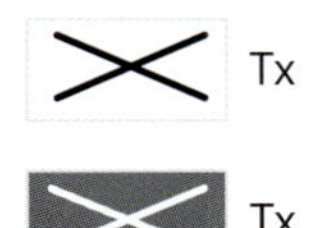

Stitch Key

431

Worked over a multiple of 2 + 2 stitches and 2 rows.

Row 1 FP: With MC, Tx.

Row 1 RP: With CC, Std RP.

Row 2 FP: With CC, Tss, Tx until 1 st rem, Tss.

Row 2 RP: With MC, Std RP.

Repeat Rows 1 and 2.

Reverse

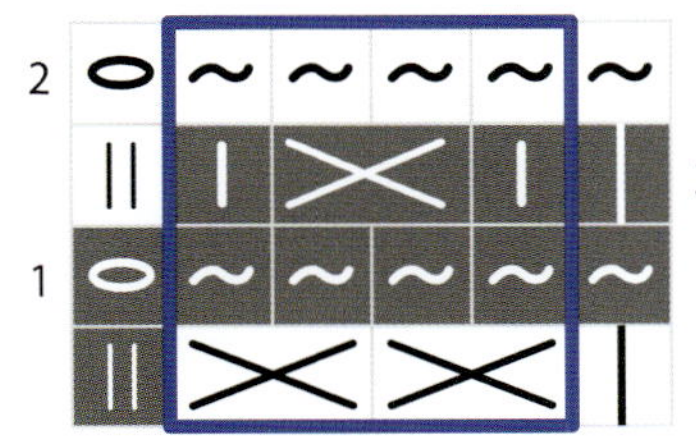

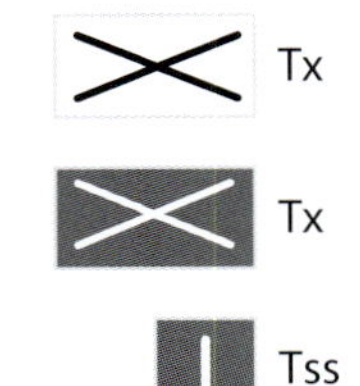

Stitch Key

432

Reverse

Worked over 4 rows.

Row 1: With MC, Tss.

Row 2: With CC, Tps.

Row 3: With CC, Tss.

Row 4: With MC, Tps.

Repeat Rows 1–4.

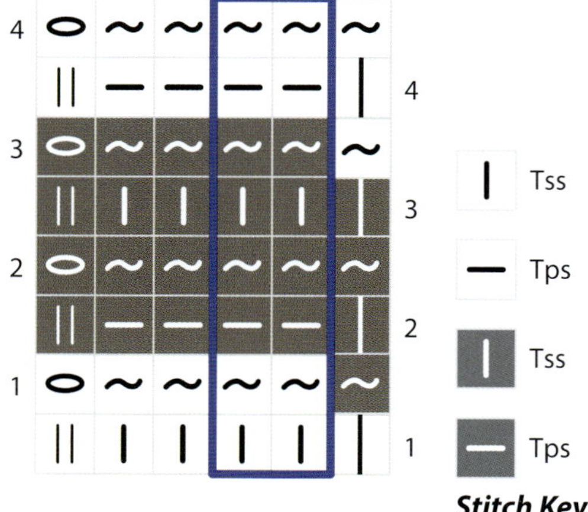

433

Reverse

Worked over 4 rows.

Row 1: With MC, Tss.

Row 2: With MC, Tps.

Row 3: With CC, Tss.

Row 4: With CC, Tps.

Repeat Rows 1–4.

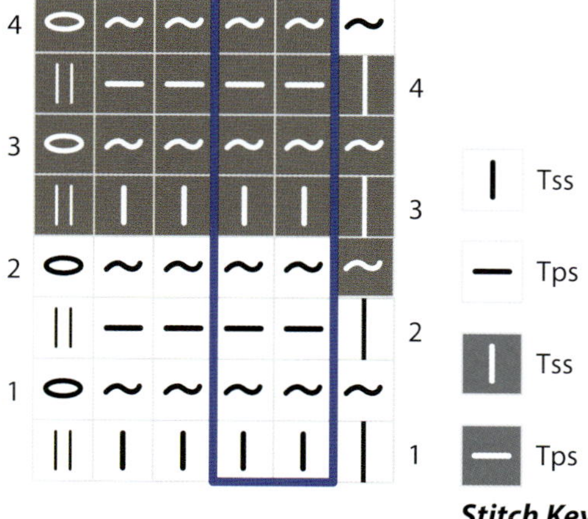

434

Reverse

Worked over a multiple of 2 stitches and 2 rows.

See Stitch 216.

Row 1: With MC, Tss rep.

Row 2: With CC, Tss rep.

Row 3: With MC, [in the next 2 sts, Tps2Tog in prior row and then Tps2Tog in current row] rep.

Repeat Rows 2 and 3.

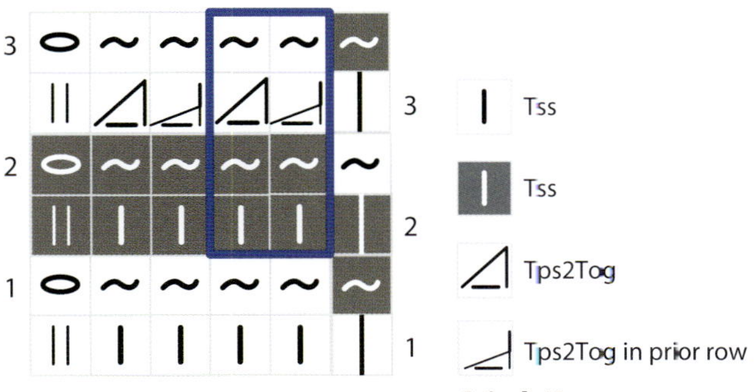

Stitch Key

435

Reverse

Worked over a multiple of 2 stitches.

Row 1 FP: With MC, Tss.

Row 1 RP: With CC, Std RP.

Row 2 FP: With CC, in the next 2 stitches (Tss2Tog, yo, Tss2Tog again) rep.

Row 2 RP: With MC, [RP-2, RP-3] rep.

Row 3 FP: With MC, [work into the 2 sts closed together (Tss2Tog, yo, Tss2Tog), sk st] rep.

Row 3 RP: With CC, [RP-2, RP-3] rep.

Repeat Row 3, alternating colors after the forward pass.

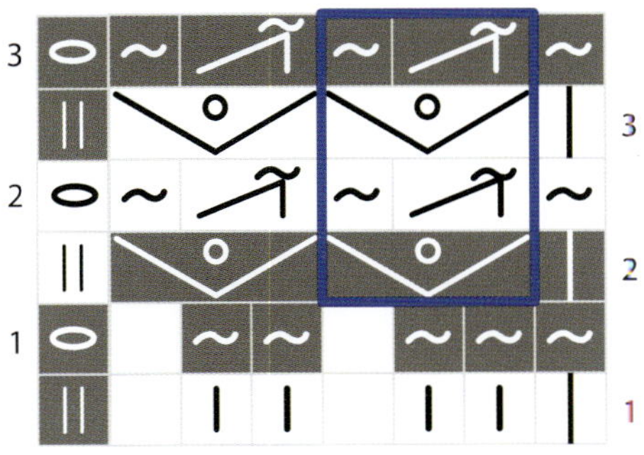

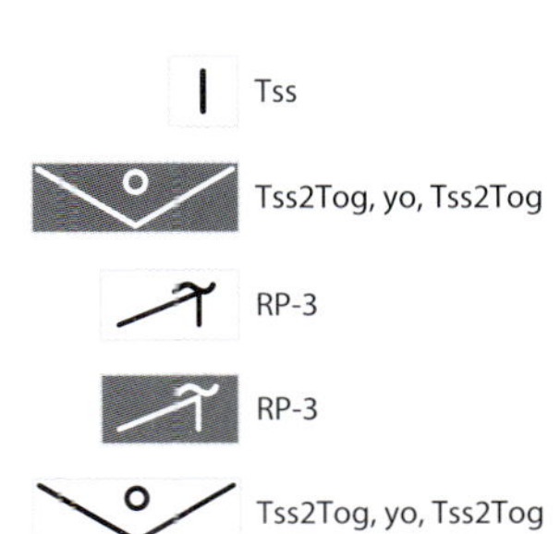

Stitch Key

436

Reverse

Worked over any number of stitches and 2 rows.

Row 1 FP: With MC, Tss.

Row 1 RP: With CC, Std RP.

Row 2 FP: With CC, in the next st (Ttop, Tss) rep.

Row 2 RP: With MC, RP-3 across.

Row 3 FP: With MC, TwTks into prior row (Ttop, Tss) rep.

Row 3 RP: With CC, Std RP.

Repeat Rows 2 and 3.

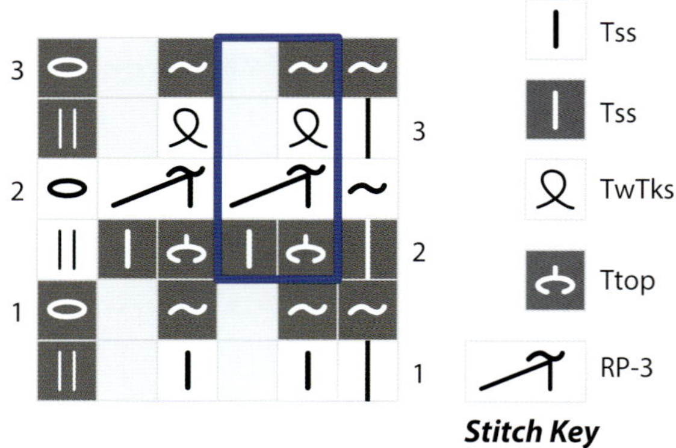

Stitch Key

437

Reverse

Worked over any number of stitches and 2 rows.

Row 1 FP: With MC, Tss.

Row 1 RP: With CC, Std RP.

Row 2 FP: With CC, [Tss, Tfs in next st sp] rep.

Row 2 RP: With MC, RP-3 across.

Row 3 FP: With MC, [Tfs in next st sp, Tss] rep. *Note:* The Tss is worked into the 2 stitches closed together in the prior return pass.

Row 3 RP: With CC, RP-3 across.

Repeat Rows 2 and 3.

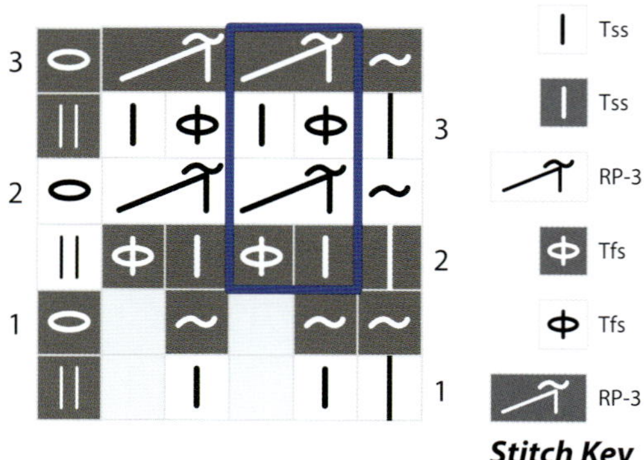

Stitch Key

438

Worked over any number of stitches and 2 rows.

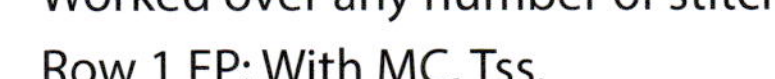

Row 1 FP: With MC, Tss.

Row 1 RP: With CC, Std RP.

Row 2 FP: With CC, (Tks, Tss) rep.

Row 2 RP: With MC, ch 1, RP-2, RP-3 across.

Row 3 FP: With MC, [Tss in the prior row Tss only] rep.

Row 3 RP: With CC, Std RP.

Repeat Rows 2 and 3.

Reverse

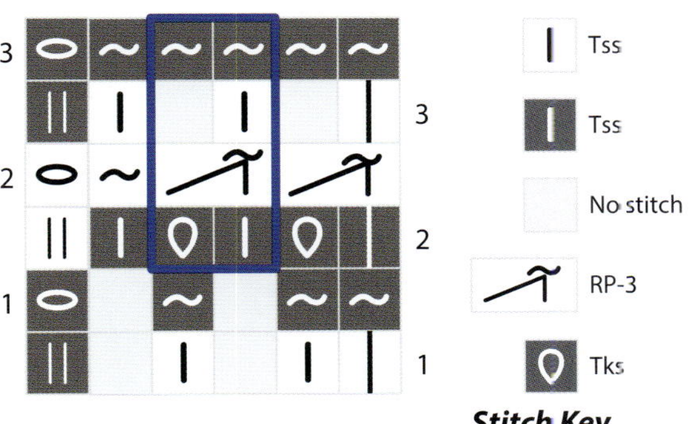

Stitch Key

439

Worked over a multiple of 2 stitches and 2 rows.

Row 1 FP: With MC, [Tss, TwTks] rep.

Row 1 RP: With CC, Std RP.

Row 2 FP: With CC, [TwTks, Tss] rep.

Row 2 RP: With MC, Std RP.

Repeat Rows 1 and 2.

Reverse

2

1

2

1

Tss

Tss

TwTks

TwTks

Stitch Key

440

Worked over a multiple of 2 stitches and 2 rows.

Row 1: With MC, [Tss, Tks] rep.

Row 2: With CC, [Tks, Tss] rep.

Repeat Rows 1 and 2.

Reverse

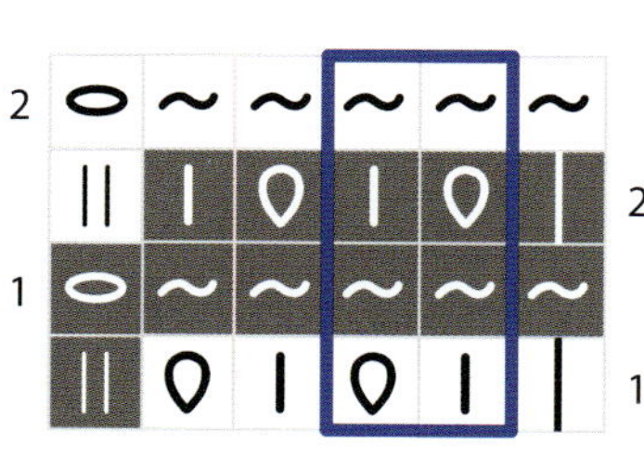

Stitch Key

441

Worked over any number of stitches and 2 rows.

Row 1 FP: With MC, in next st (Tss, yo, Tss) rep.

Row 1 RP: With MC, RP-4 rep.

Row 2 FP: With CC, Tps. *Note:* The Tps st is worked into all 3 sts closed together in the prior return pass.

Row 2 RP: With CC, Std RP.

Repeat Rows 1 and 2.

Reverse

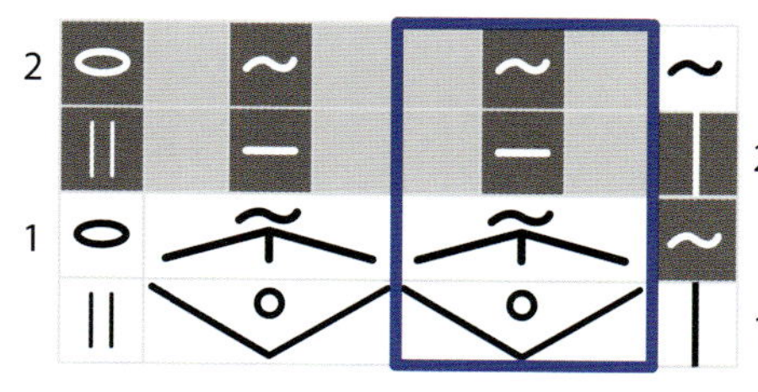

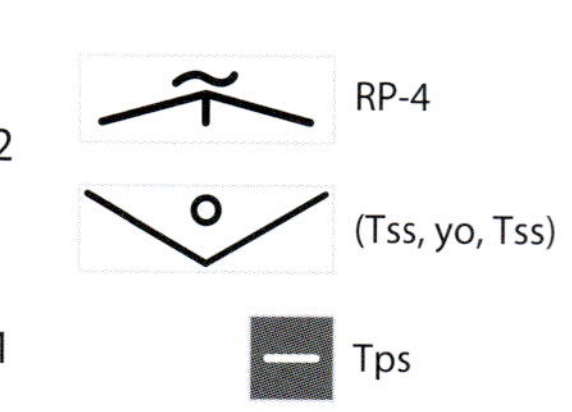

Stitch Key

442

Reverse

Worked over a multiple of 2 stitches and 3 rows.

Row 1: With MC, [PTslst, Tps] rep.

Row 2: With MC, [Tss, Tps] rep.

Row 3: With CC, Tss.

Repeat Rows 1–3.

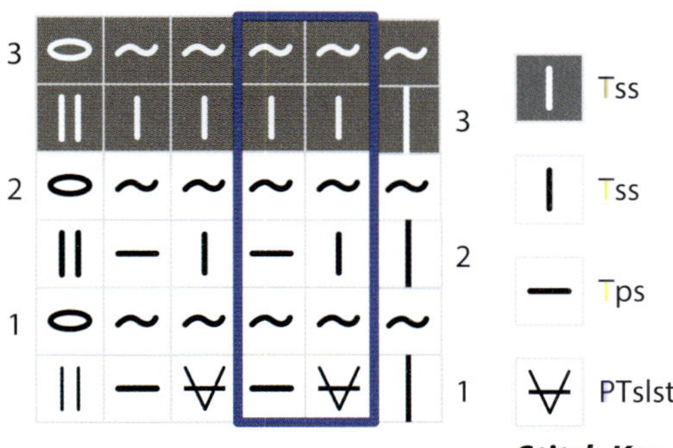

Stitch Key

443

Worked over a multiple of 2 stitches and 2 rows.

Row 1 FP: With MC, (Tss2Tog, yu, Tss in first st) rep.

Row 1 RP: With CC, [ch 1, RP-4] rep.

Row 2 FP: With CC, [Tss into the yu only, Tts] rep.

Row 2 RP: With MC, Std RP.

Repeat Rows 1 and 2.

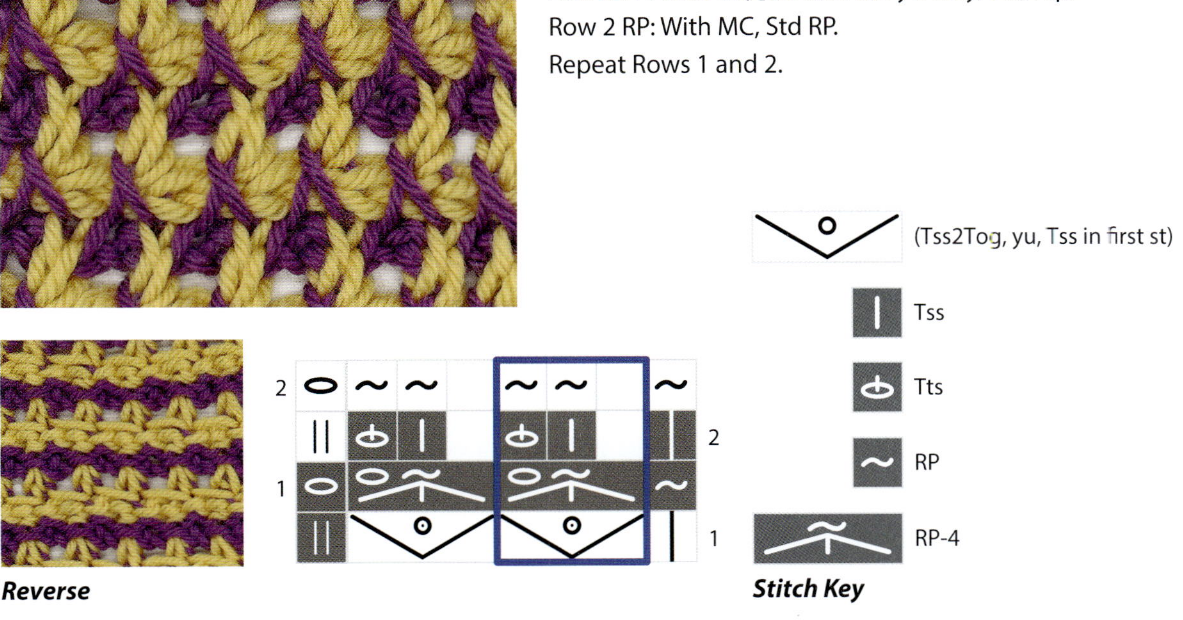

Reverse

Stitch Key

444

Worked over a multiple of 2 stitches and 4 rows.

Row 1 FP: With MC, [Tss, Tps] rep.

Row 1 RP: With CC, Std RP.

Row 2 FP: With CC, [Tps, Tslst] rep.

Row 2 RP: With MC, Std RP.

Row 3 FP: With MC, [Tps, Tss] rep.

Row 3 RP: With CC, Std Rp.

Row 4 FP: With CC, [Tslst, Tps] rep.

Row 4 RP: With MC, Std RP.

Repeat Rows 1–4.

Reverse

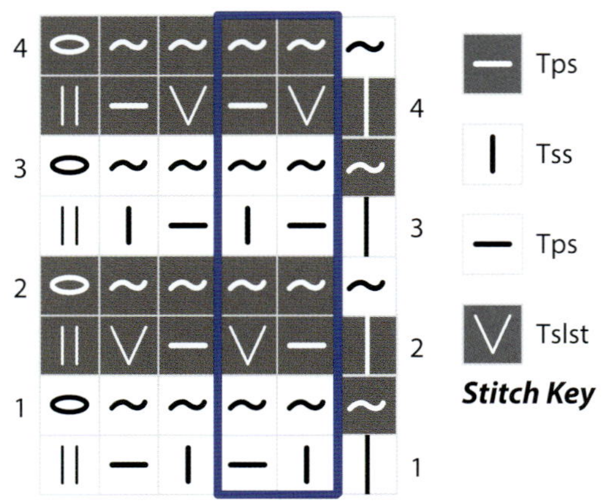

Stitch Key

445

Worked over a multiple of 2 stitches and 2 rows.

Tdc2Tog: Yo, insert hook behind next 2 front vertical bars, yo and pull up a loop, [yo and pull through 2 loops] twice.

Long Tts Double Crochet (LTtsDC): Yo and insert hook for Tts in the prior row. Yo and pull up a loop, yo and pull through 2 loops.

Row 1: With MC, [Tdc2Tog, yo] rep.

Row 2: With CC, [Tss, LTtsDC] rep.

Repeat Rows 1 and 2.

Reverse

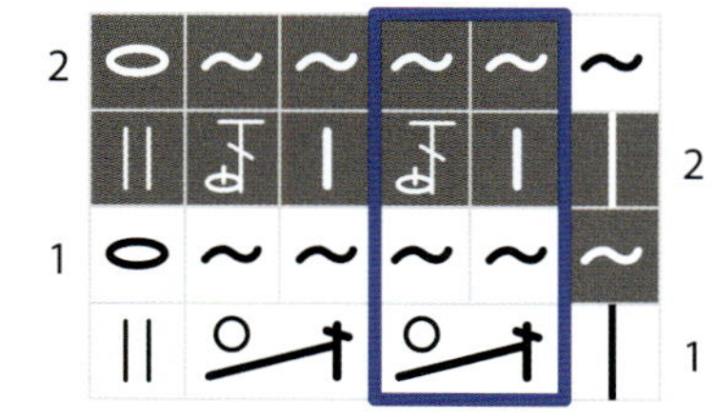

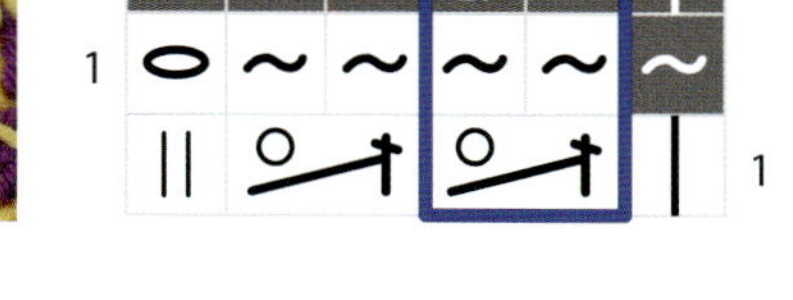

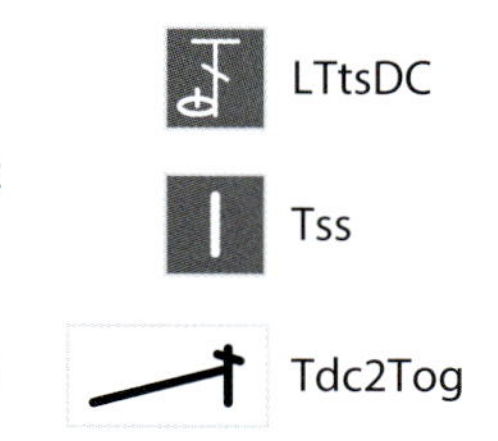

Stitch Key

446

Worked over a multiple of 2 stitches and 2 rows.

Row 1 FP: With MC, [Tss2Tog, Tfs in next st sp] rep.

Row 1 RP: With CC, Std RP.

Row 2 FP: With CC, [Tss, Tps] rep.

Row 2 RP: With MC, Std RP.

Repeat Rows 1 and 2.

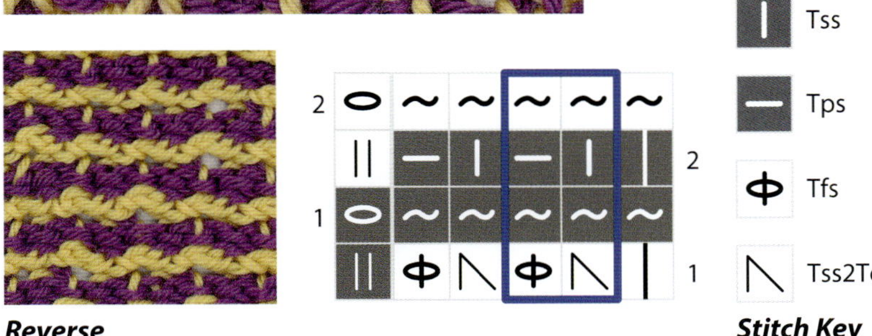

Reverse

Stitch Key

CHAPTER 6

Tunisian Crochet in the Round Stitches

Tunisian crochet in the round uses a double-ended hook and two strands of yarn. On all rounds, the MC is used for the forward pass and the CC is used for the return pass. For Tunisian crochet in the round charts, both the forward pass and the return pass are read from right to left.

447 TUNISIAN SIMPLE STITCH IN THE ROUND

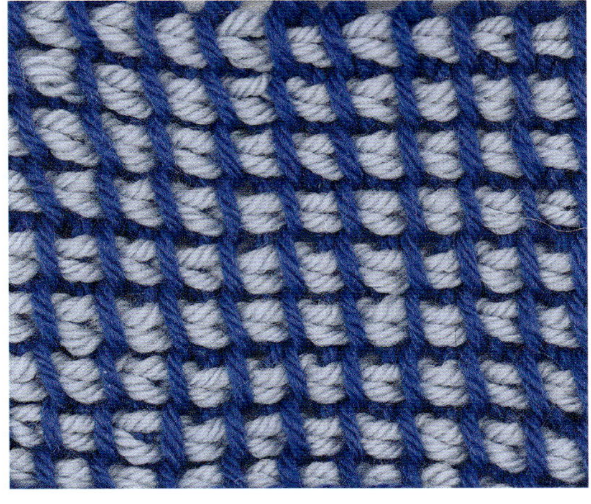

Worked over any number of stitches.
Round 1 FP: With MC, Tss.
Round 1 RP: With CC, Std RP.
Repeat Round 1.

Reverse

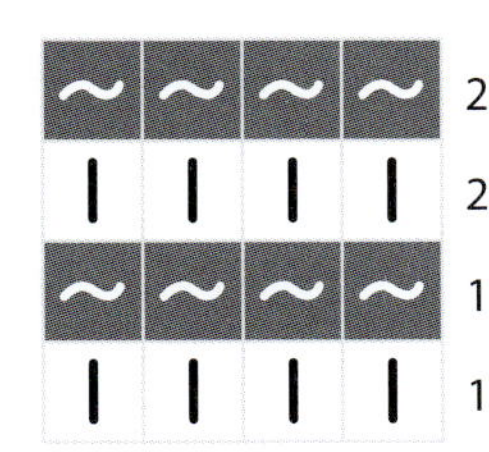

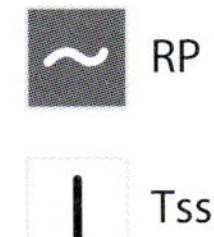

RP

Tss

Stitch Key

448 TUNISIAN KNIT STITCH IN THE ROUND

Worked over any number of stitches.
Round 1 FP: With MC, Tks.
Round 1 RP: With CC, Std RP.
Repeat Round 1.

Reverse

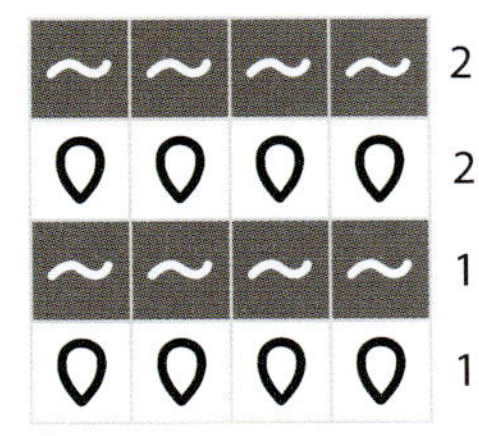

RP

Tks

Stitch Key

449 TUNISIAN REVERSE STITCH IN THE ROUND

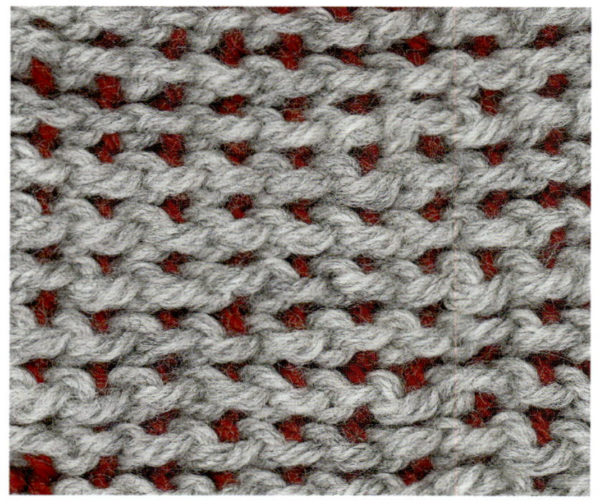

Worked over any number of stitches.
Round 1 FP: With MC, Trs.
Round 1 RP: With CC, Std RP.
Repeat Round 1.

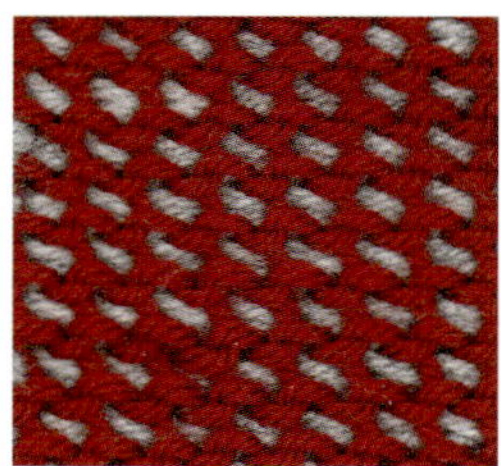

Reverse

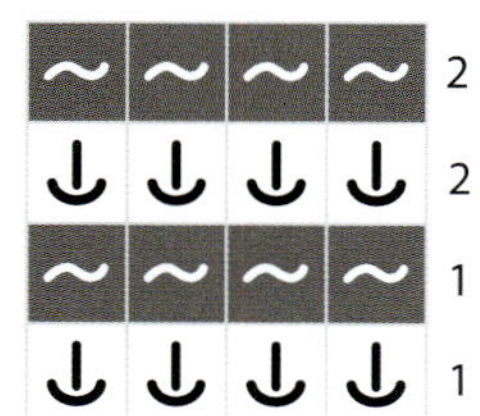

Stitch Key

450 TUNISIAN PURL STITCH IN THE ROUND

Worked over any number of stitches.
Round 1 FP: With MC, Tps.
Round 1 RP: With CC, Std RP.
Repeat Round 1.

Reverse

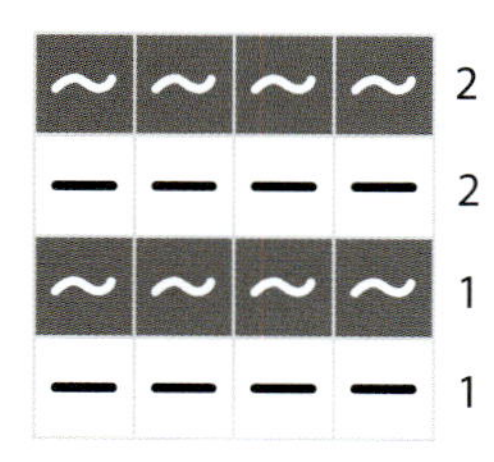

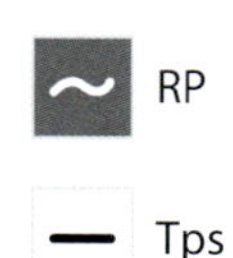

Stitch Key

451 TUNISIAN FULL STITCH IN THE ROUND

Worked over any number of stitches. *Note:* When working the Tunisian full stitch in the round, there is no need to skip any stitch spaces.

Round 1 FP: With MC, Tfs.

Round 1 RP: With CC, Std RP.

Repeat Round 1.

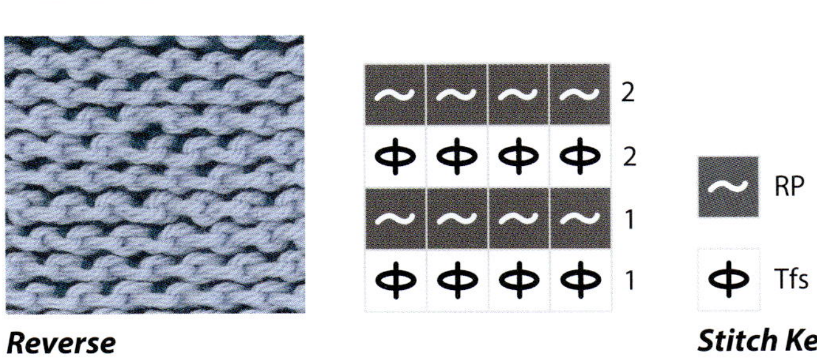

Reverse

Stitch Key

452 TSS & TPS VERTICAL STRIPE

Worked over a multiple of 2 stitches.

Round 1 FP: With MC, [Tss, Tps] rep.

Round 1 RP: With CC, Std RP.

Repeat Round 1.

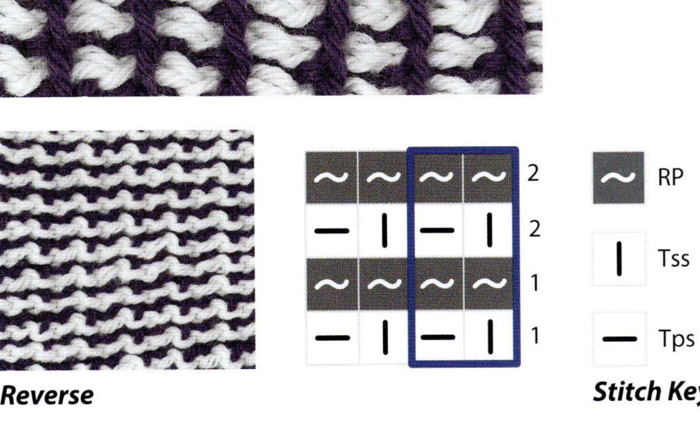

Reverse

Stitch Key

453 TSS & TKS VERTICAL STRIPE

Worked over a multiple of 2 stitches.
Round 1 FP: With MC, [Tss, Tks] rep.
Round 1 RP: With CC, Std RP.
Repeat Round 1.

Reverse

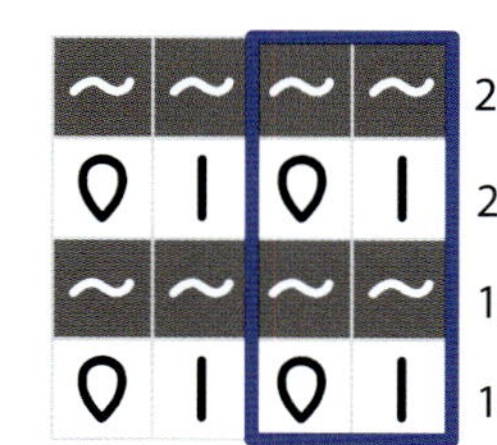

Stitch Key

454 TSS & TRS VERTICAL STRIPE

Worked over a multiple of 2 stitches.
Round 1 FP: With MC, [Tss, Trs] rep.
Round 1 RP: With CC, Std RP.
Repeat Round 1.

Reverse

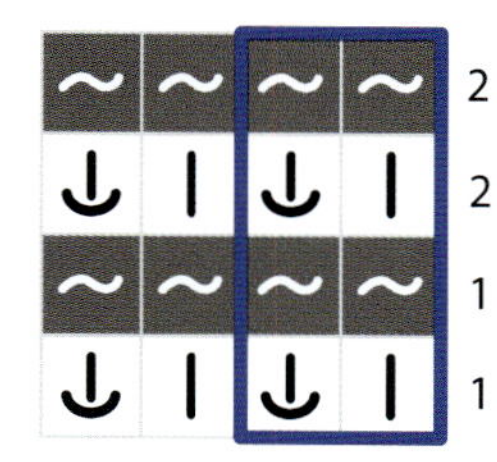

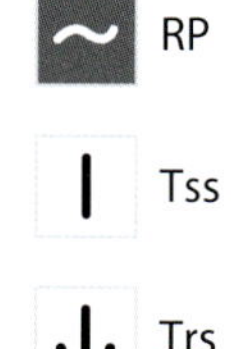

Stitch Key

455 TKS & TRS VERTICAL STRIPE

Worked over a multiple of 2 stitches.
Round 1 FP: With MC, [Tks, Trs] rep.
Round 1 RP: With CC, Std RP.
Repeat Round 1.

Reverse

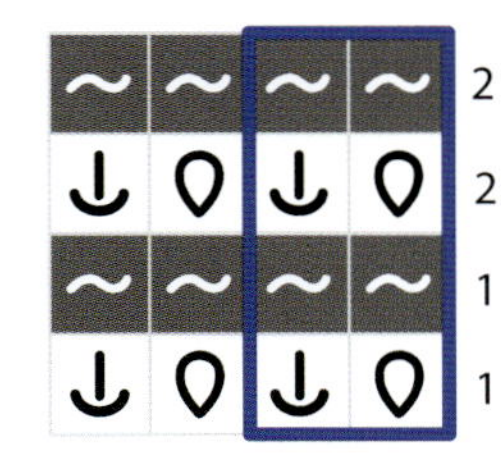

Stitch Key

456 TKS & TPS VERTICAL STRIPE

Worked over a multiple of 2 stitches.
Round 1 FP: With MC, [Tks, Tps] rep.
Round 1 RP: With CC, Std RP.
Repeat Round 1.

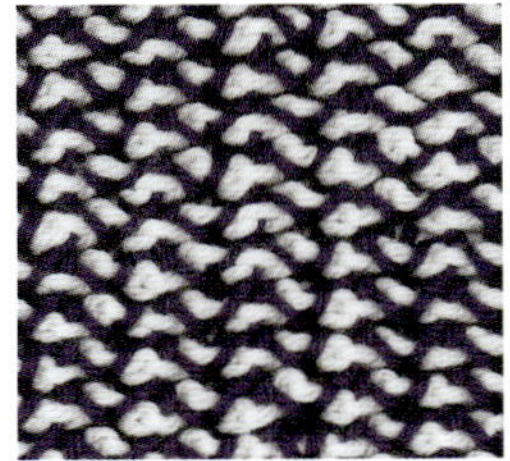

Reverse

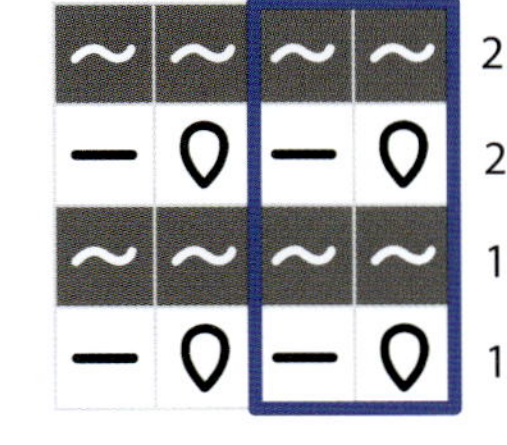

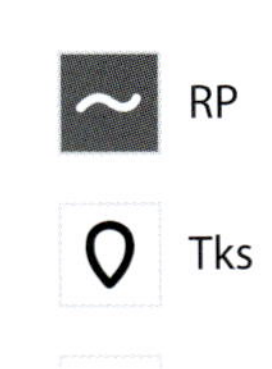

Stitch Key

457 TRS & TPS VERTICAL STRIPE

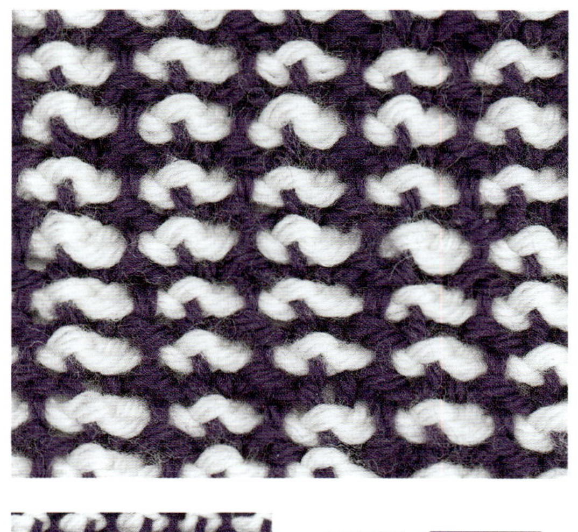

Worked over a multiple of 2 stitches.
Round 1 FP: With MC, [Trs, Tps] rep.
Round 1 RP: With CC, Std RP.
Repeat Round 1.

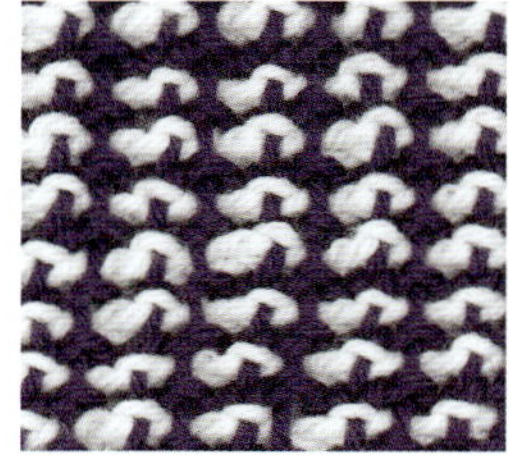

Reverse

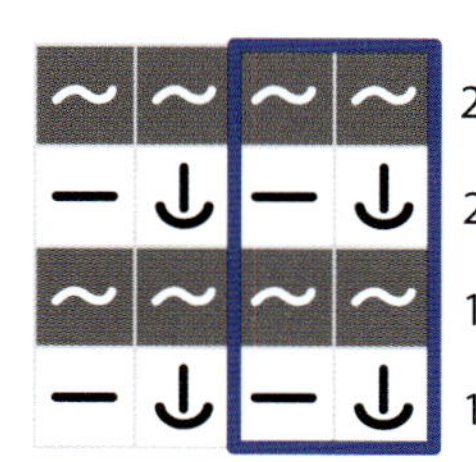

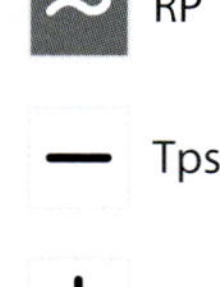

Stitch Key

458 TWD & TSS VERTICAL STRIPE

Worked over a multiple of 2 stitches.
Round 1 FP: With MC, [Twd, Tss] rep.
Round 1 RP: With CC, Std RP.
Repeat Round 1.

Reverse

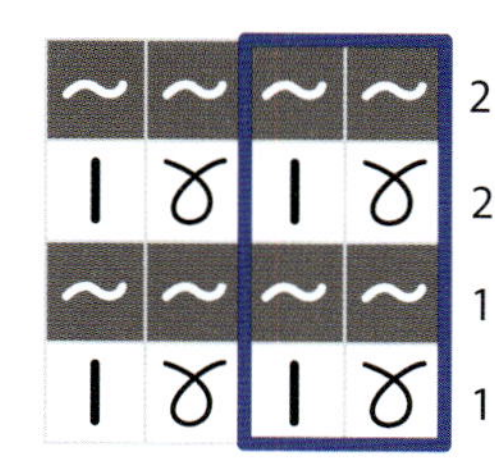

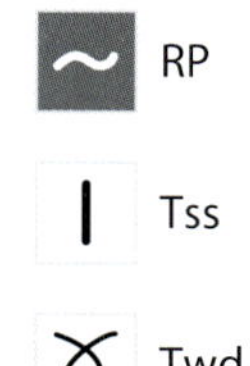

Stitch Key

459 TWD & TKS VERTICAL STRIPE

Worked over a multiple of 2 stitches.

Round 1 FP: With MC, [Twd, Tks] rep.

Round 1 RP: With CC, Std RP.

Repeat Round 1.

Reverse

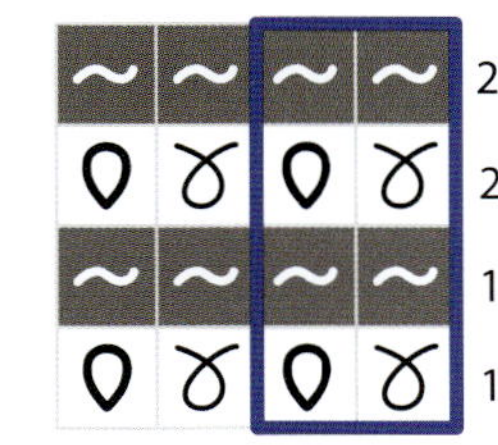

Stitch Key

460 TWD & TPS VERTICAL STRIPE

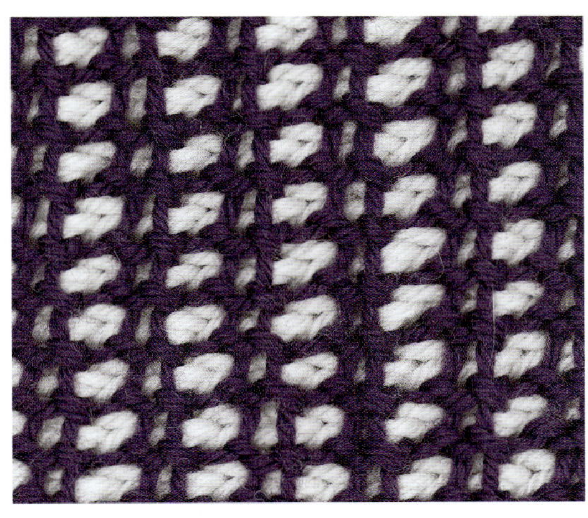

Worked over a multiple of 2 stitches.

Round 1 FP: With MC, [Twd, Tps] rep.

Round 1 RP: With CC, Std RP.

Repeat Round 1.

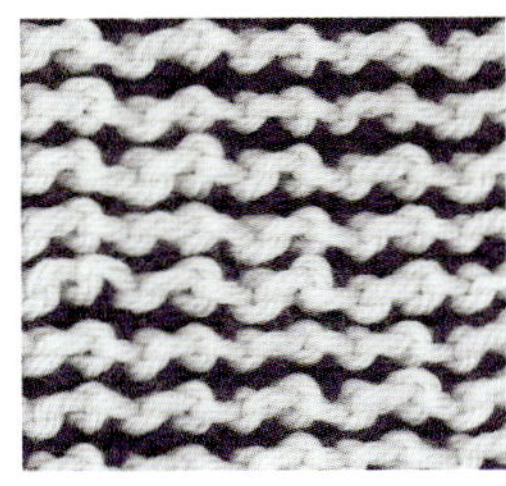

Reverse

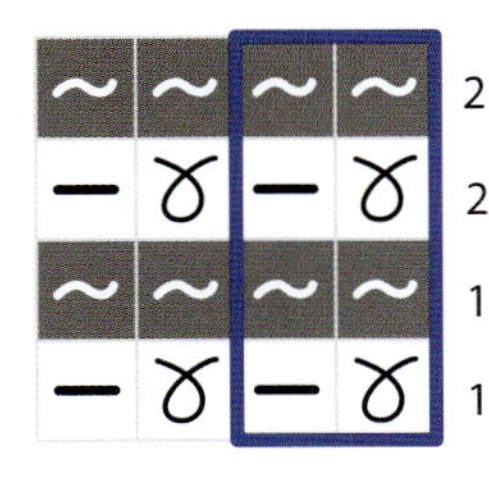

Stitch Key

461 TWD & TRS VERTICAL STRIPE

Worked over a multiple of 2 stitches.
Round 1 FP: With MC, [Twd, Trs] rep.
Round 1 RP: With CC, Std RP.
Repeat Round 1.

Reverse

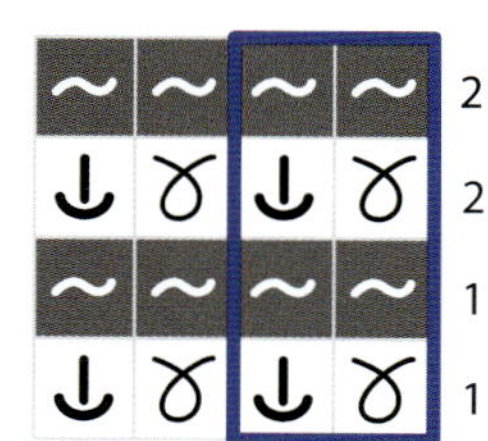

Stitch Key

462 TKS & TTOP VERTICAL STRIPE

Worked over a multiple of 2 stitches.
Round 1 FP: With MC, [Tks, Ttop] rep.
Round 1 RP: With CC, Std RP.
Repeat Round 1.

Reverse

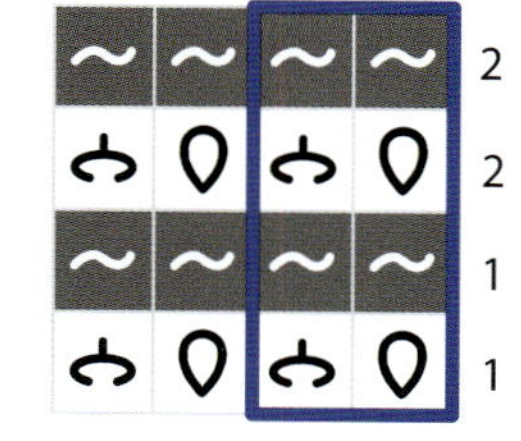

Stitch Key

463 TSS & TBSS VERTICAL STRIPE

Worked over a multiple of 2 stitches.

Round 1 FP: With MC, [Tss, Tbss] rep.

Round 1 RP: With CC, Std RP.

Repeat Round 1.

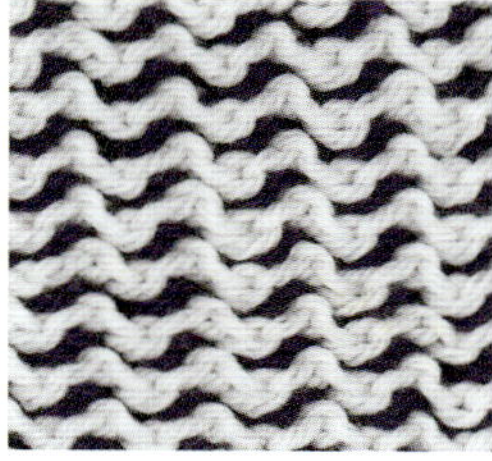

Reverse

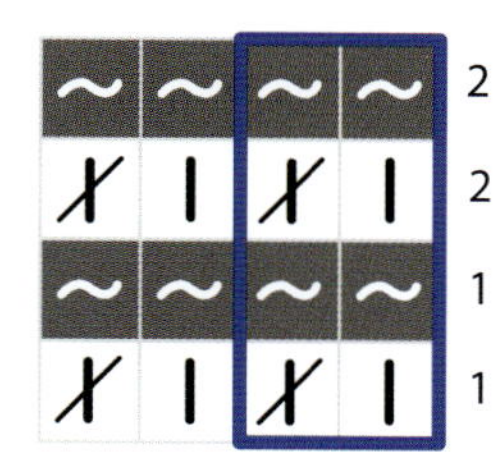

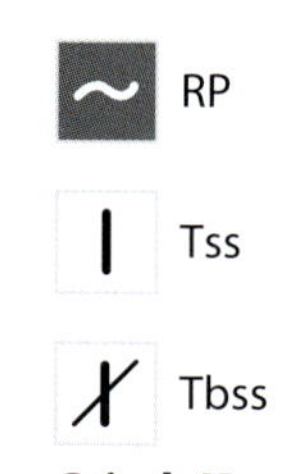

Stitch Key

464 TKS & TRS HORIZONTAL STRIPE

Worked over any number of stitches and 2 rounds.

Round 1 FP: With MC, Tks.

Round 1 RP: With CC, Std RP.

Round 2 FP: With MC, Trs.

Round 2 RP: With CC, Std RP.

Repeat Rounds 1 and 2.

Reverse

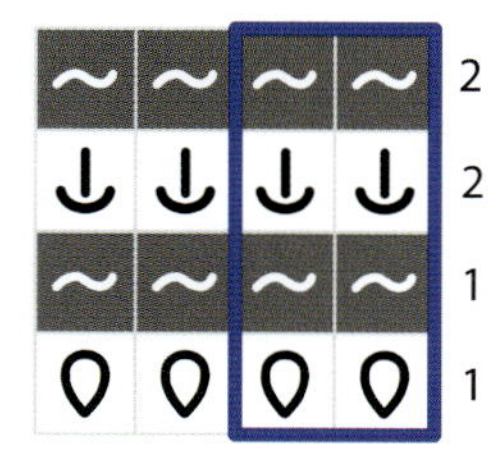

Stitch Key

465 TSS & TRS HORIZONTAL STRIPE

Worked over any number of stitches and 2 rounds.

Round 1 FP: With MC, Tss.

Round 1 RP: With CC, Std RP.

Round 2 FP: With MC, Trs.

Round 2 RP: With CC, Std RP.

Repeat Rounds 1 and 2.

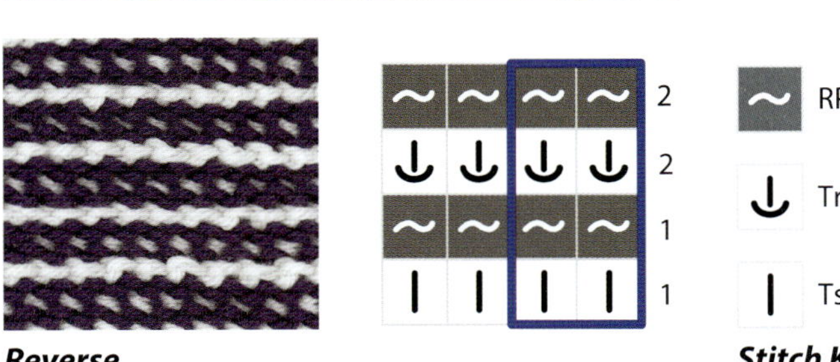

Reverse

RP

Trs

Tss

Stitch Key

466 TSS & TKS HORIZONTAL STRIPE

Worked over any number of stitches and 2 rounds.

Round 1 FP: With MC, Tss.

Round 1 RP: With CC, Std RP.

Round 2 FP: With MC, Tks.

Round 2 RP: With CC, Std RP.

Repeat Rounds 1 and 2.

Reverse

RP

Tss

Tks

Stitch Key

467 TSS & TPS HORIZONTAL STRIPE

Worked over any number of stitches and 2 rounds.
Round 1 FP: With MC, Tss.
Round 1 RP: With CC, Std RP.
Round 2 FP: With MC, Tps.
Round 2 RP: With CC, Std RP.
Repeat Rounds 1 and 2.

Reverse

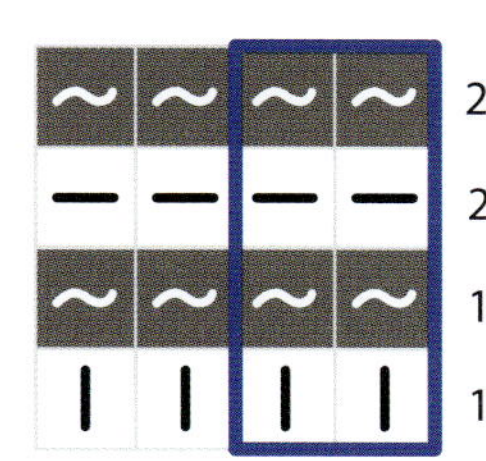

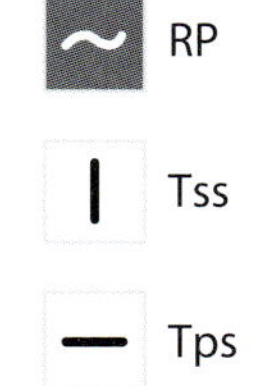

Stitch Key

468 TSS & PTRS HORIZONTAL STRIPE

Worked over any number of stitches and 2 rounds.
Round 1 FP: With MC, Tss.
Round 1 RP: With CC, Std RP.
Round 2 FP: With MC, Ptrs.
Round 2 RP: With CC, Std RP.
Repeat Rounds 1 and 2.

Reverse

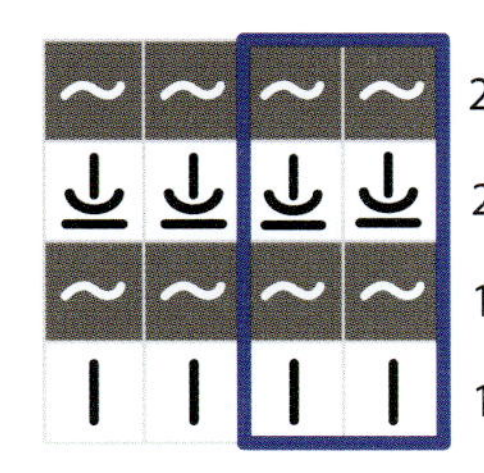

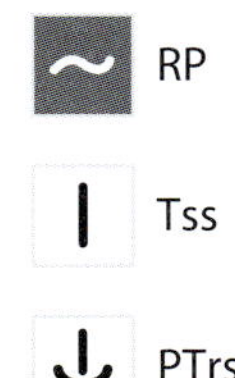

Stitch Key

469 TSS & TWD HORIZONTAL STRIPE

Worked over any number of stitches and 2 rounds.
Round 1 FP: With MC, Tss.
Round 1 RP: With CC, Std RP.
Round 2 FP: With MC, Twd.
Round 2 RP: With CC, Std RP.
Repeat Rounds 1 and 2.

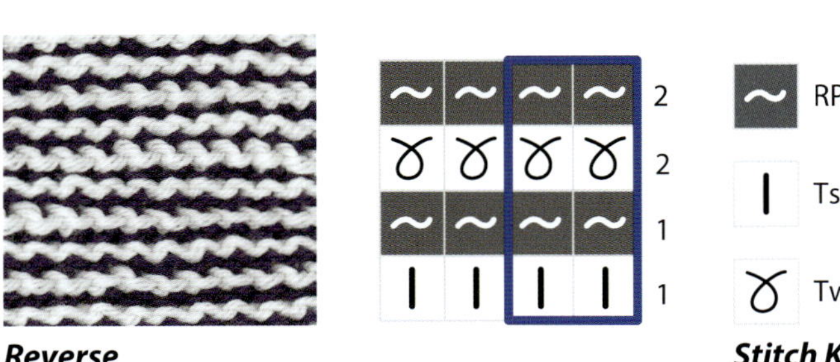

Reverse

Stitch Key

470 TRS & TWD HORIZONTAL STRIPE

Worked over any number of stitches and 2 rounds.
Round 1 FP: With MC, Trs.
Round 1 RP: With CC, Std RP.
Round 2 FP: With MC, Twd.
Round 2 RP: With CC, Std RP.
Repeat Rounds 1 and 2.

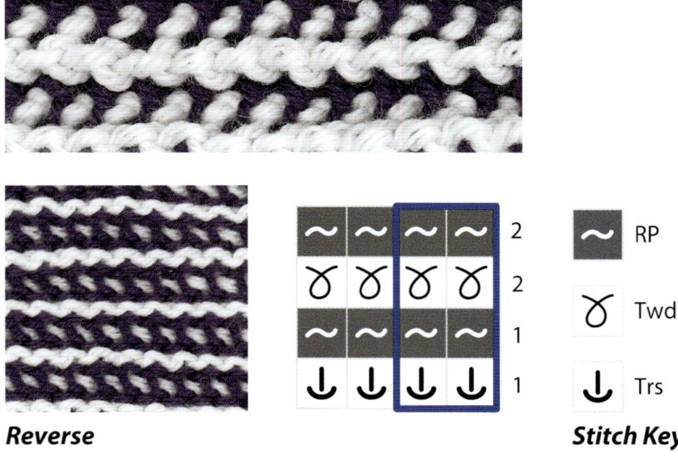

Reverse

Stitch Key

471 PTRS & TPS HORIZONTAL STRIPE

Worked over any number of stitches and 2 rounds.

Round 1 FP: With MC, Ptrs.

Round 1 RP: With CC, Std RP.

Round 2 FP: With MC, Tps.

Round 2 RP: With CC, Std RP.

Repeat Rounds 1 and 2.

Reverse

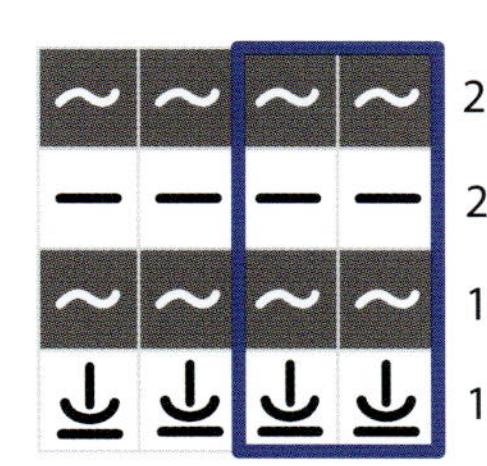

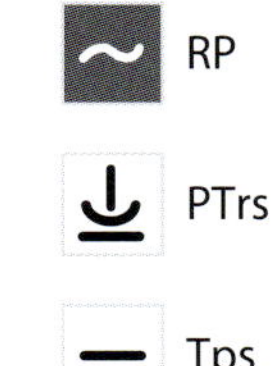

Stitch Key

472 TSS & TPS HONEYCOMB

Worked over a multiple of 2 stitches and 2 rounds.

Round 1 FP: With MC, [Tss, Tps] rep.

Round 1 RP: With CC, Std RP.

Round 2 FP: With MC, [Tps, Tss] rep.

Round 2 RP: With CC, Std RP.

Repeat Rounds 1 and 2.

Reverse

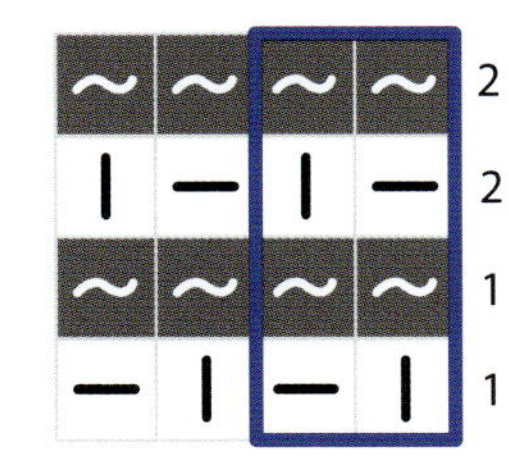

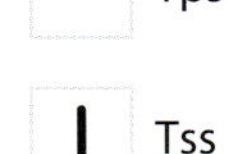

Stitch Key

473 TSS & TRS HONEYCOMB

Worked over a multiple of 2 stitches and 2 rounds.
Round 1 FP: With MC, [Tss, Trs] rep.
Round 1 RP: With CC, Std RP.
Round 2 FP: With MC, [Trs, Tss] rep.
Round 2 RP: With CC, Std RP.
Repeat Rounds 1 and 2.

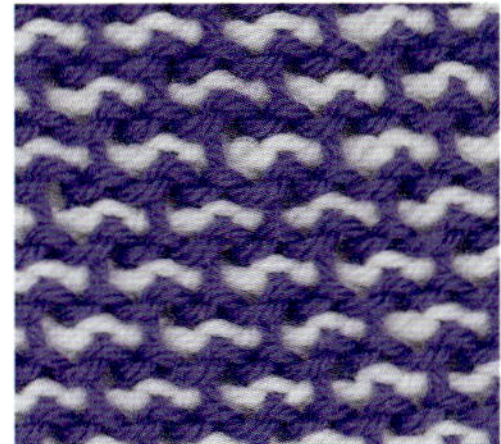

Reverse

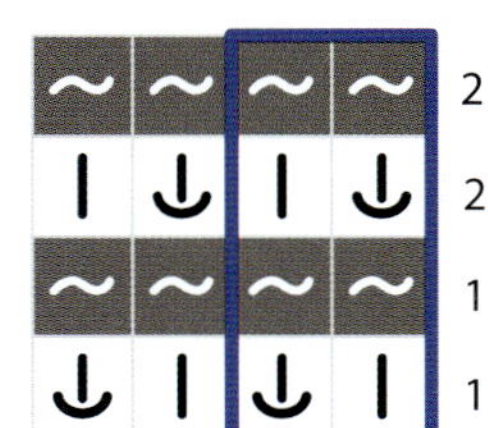

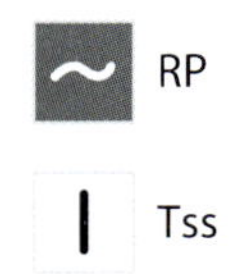

RP

Tss

Trs

Stitch Key

474 TSS & TKS HONEYCOMB

Worked over a multiple of 2 stitches and 2 rounds.
Round 1 FP: With MC, [Tss, Tks] rep.
Round 1 RP: With CC, Std RP.
Round 2 FP: With MC, [Tks, Tss] rep.
Round 2 RP: With CC, Std RP.
Repeat Rounds 1 and 2.

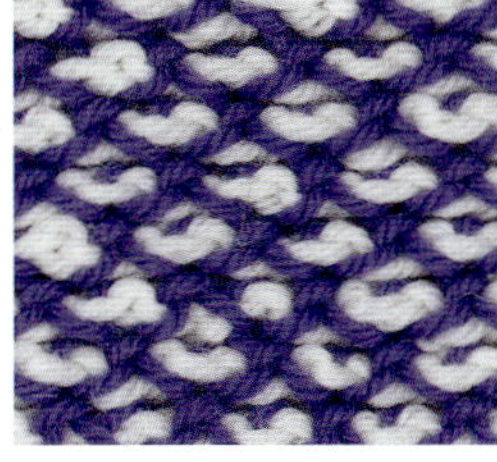

Reverse

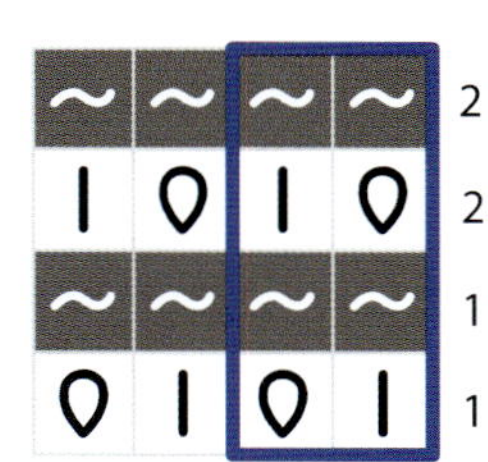

RP

Tss

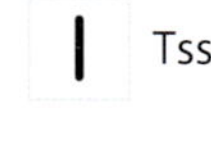

Tks

Stitch Key

475 TRS & TPS HONEYCOMB

Worked over a multiple of 2 stitches and 2 rounds.

Round 1 FP: With MC, [Trs, Tps] rep.

Round 1 RP: With CC, Std RP.

Round 2 FP: With MC, [Tps, Trs] rep.

Round 2 RP: With CC, Std RP.

Repeat Rounds 1 and 2.

Reverse

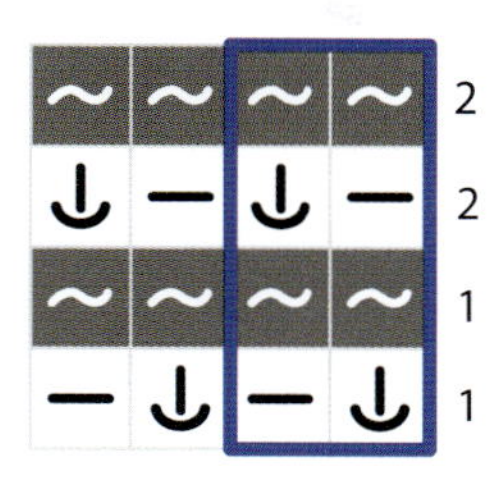

Stitch Key

476 TKS & TPS HONEYCOMB

Worked over a multiple of 2 stitches and 2 rounds.

Round 1 FP: With MC, [Tks, Tps] rep.

Round 1 RP: With CC, Std RP.

Round 2 FP: With MC, [Tps, Tks] rep.

Round 2 RP: With CC, Std RP.

Repeat Rounds 1 and 2.

Reverse

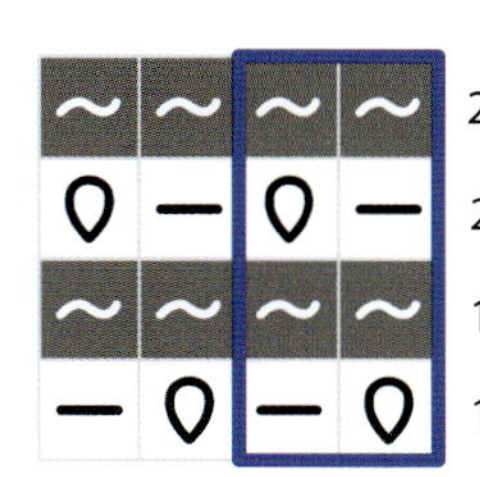

Stitch Key

477 TKS & TRS HONEYCOMB

Worked over a multiple of 2 stitches and 2 rounds.

Round 1 FP: With MC, [Tks, Trs] rep.

Round 1 RP: With CC, Std RP.

Round 2 FP: With MC, [Trs, Tks] rep.

Round 2 RP: With CC, Std RP.

Repeat Rounds 1 and 2.

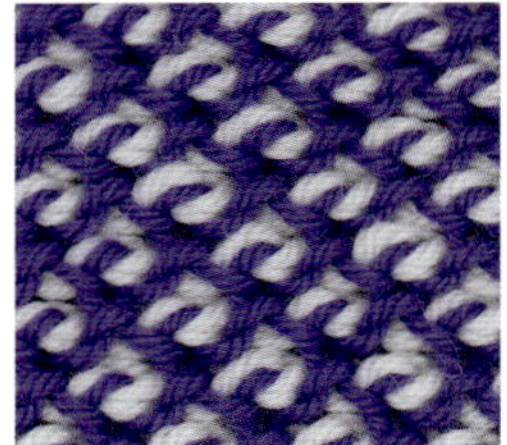

Reverse

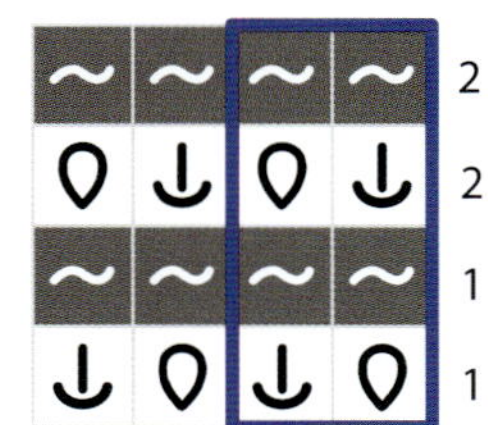

Stitch Key

478 TSS & TWD HONEYCOMB

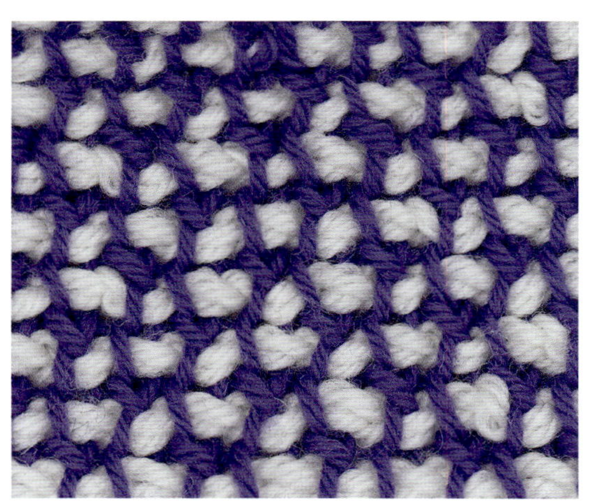

Worked over a multiple of 2 stitches and 2 rounds.

Round 1 FP: With MC, [Tss, Twd] rep.

Round 1 RP: With CC, Std RP.

Round 2 FP: With MC, [Twd, Tss] rep.

Round 2 RP: With CC, Std RP.

Repeat Rounds 1 and 2.

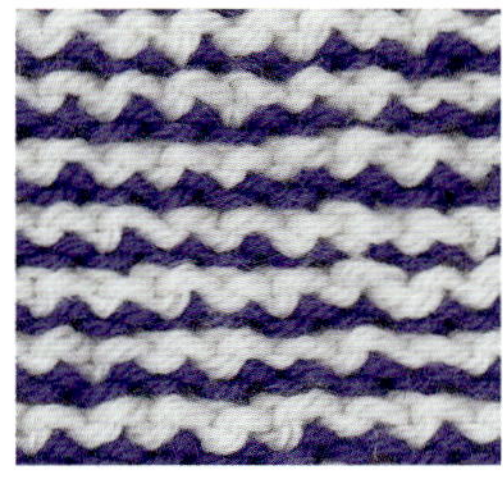

Reverse

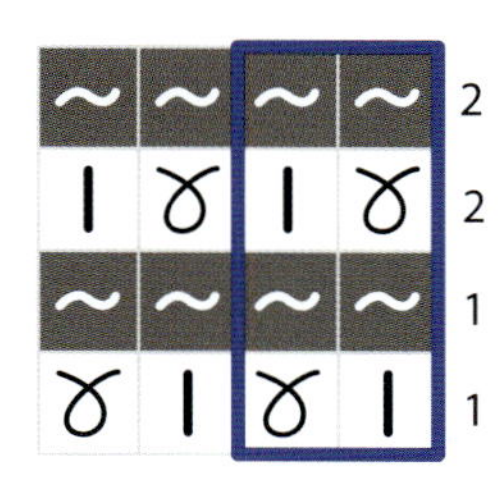

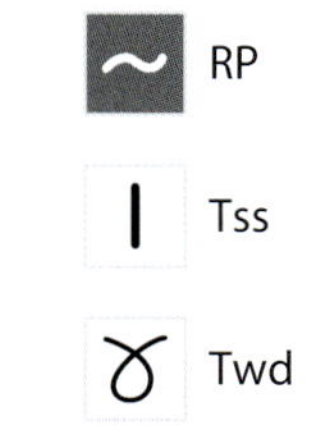

Stitch Key

479 TKS & TWD HONEYCOMB

Worked over a multiple of 2 stitches and 2 rounds.
Round 1 FP: With MC, [Tks, Twd] rep.
Round 1 RP: With CC, Std RP.
Round 2 FP: With MC, [Twd, Tks] rep.
Round 2 RP: With CC, Std RP.
Repeat Rounds 1 and 2.

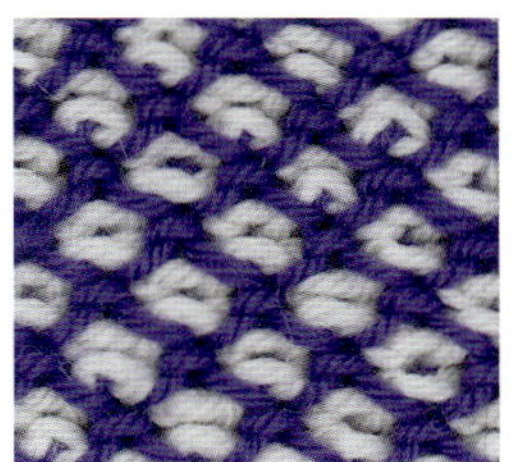

Reverse

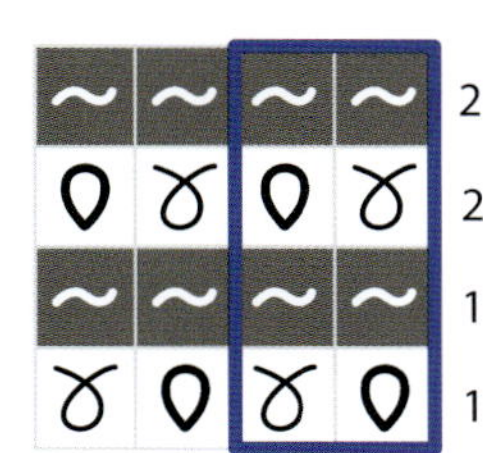

RP

Twd

Tks

Stitch Key

480 TPS & TWD HONEYCOMB

Worked over a multiple of 2 stitches and 2 rounds.
Round 1 FP: With MC, [Tps, Twd] rep.
Round 1 RP: With CC, Std RP.
Round 2 FP: With MC, [Twd, Tps] rep.
Round 2 RP: With CC, Std RP.
Repeat Rounds 1 and 2.

Reverse

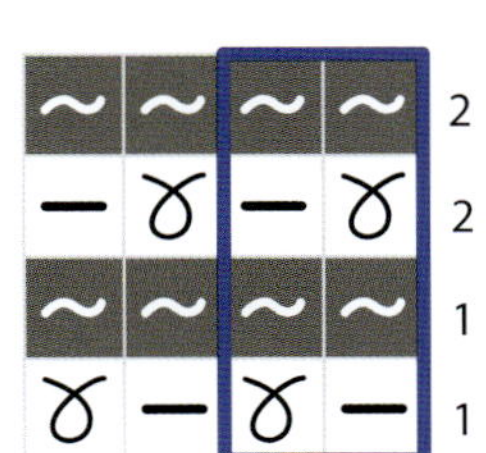

RP

Twd

Tps

Stitch Key

481 TRS & TWD HONEYCOMB

Worked over a multiple of 2 stitches and 2 rounds.
Round 1 FP: With MC, [Trs, Twd] rep.
Round 1 RP: With CC, Std RP.
Round 2 FP: With MC, [Twd, Trs] rep.
Round 2 RP: With CC, Std RP.
Repeat Rounds 1 and 2.

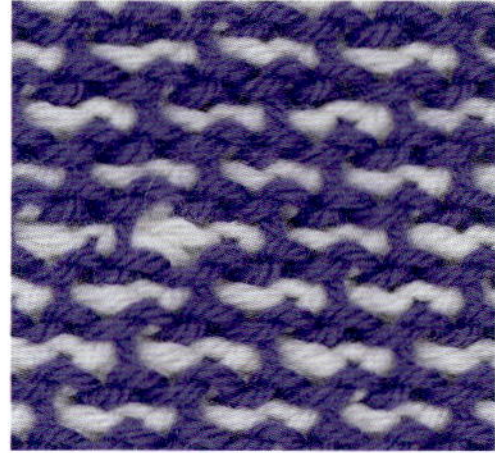

Reverse

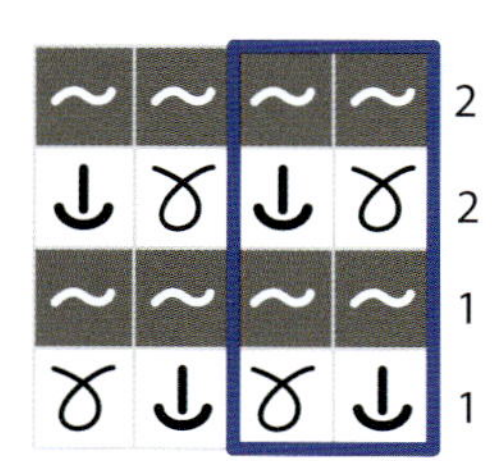

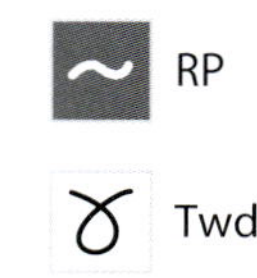

Stitch Key

482 TKS & PTRS HONEYCOMB

Worked over a multiple of 2 stitches and 2 rounds.
Round 1 FP: With MC, [Tks, Ptrs] rep.
Round 1 RP: With CC, Std RP.
Round 2 FP: With MC, [Ptrs, Tks] rep.
Round 2 RP: With CC, Std RP.
Repeat Rounds 1 and 2.

Reverse

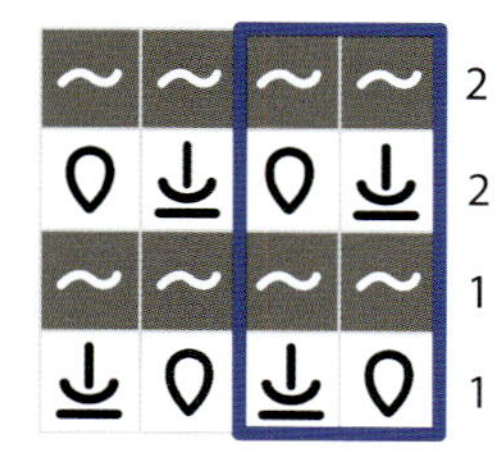

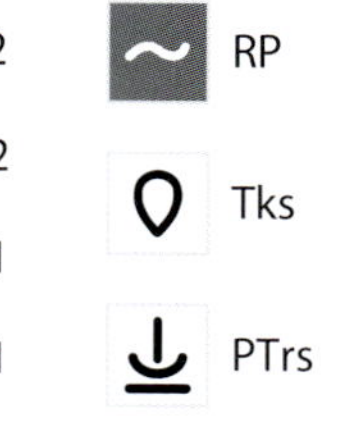

Stitch Key

483 TKS & TWTKS HONEYCOMB

Worked over a multiple of 2 stitches and 2 rounds.

Round 1 FP: With MC, [Tks, TwTks] rep.

Round 1 RP: With CC, Std RP.

Round 2 FP: With MC, [TwTks, Tks] rep.

Round 2 RP: With CC, Std RP.

Repeat Rounds 1 and 2.

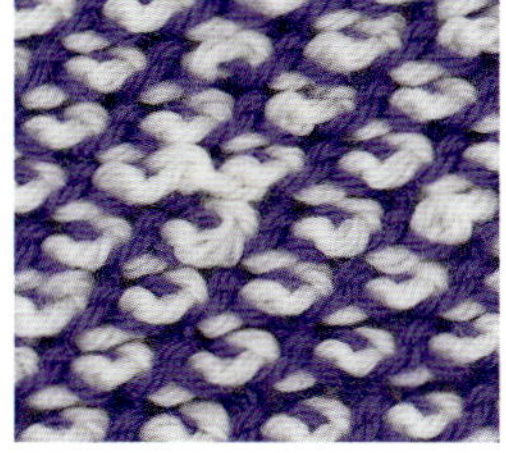

Reverse

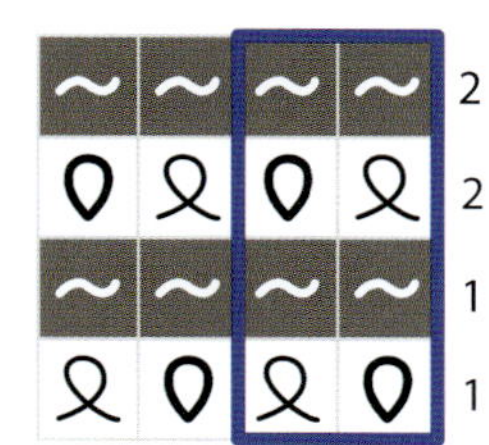

 RP

 Tks

 TwTks

Stitch Key

484 TSS & TTOP HONEYCOMB

Worked over a multiple of 2 stitches and 2 rounds.

Round 1 FP: With MC, [Tss, Ttop] rep.

Round 1 RP: With CC, Std RP.

Round 2 FP: With MC, [Ttop, Tss] rep.

Round 2 RP: With CC, Std RP.

Repeat Rounds 1 and 2.

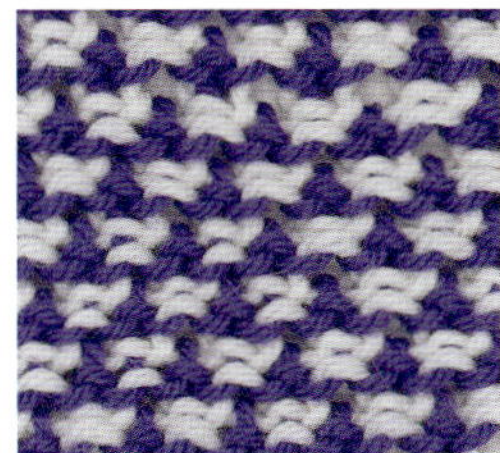

Reverse

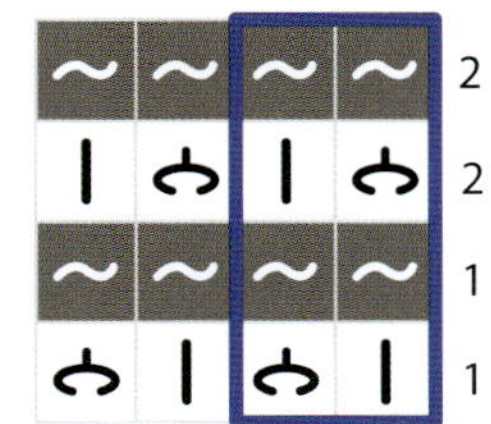

 RP

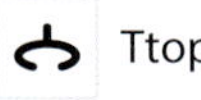 Ttop

Tss

Stitch Key

485 TFS & TTOP HONEYCOMB

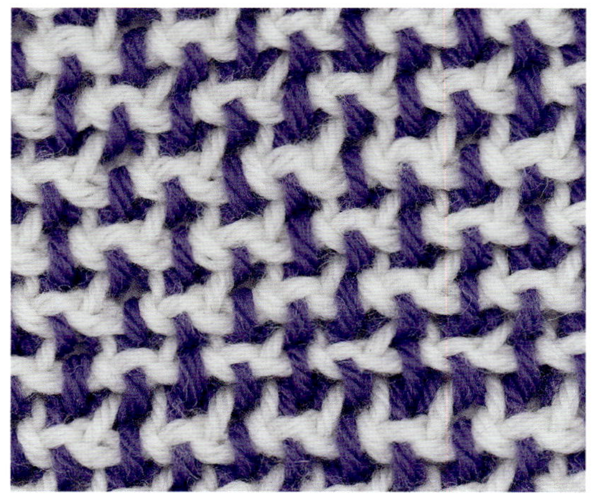

Worked over a multiple of 2 stitches and 2 rounds.

Round 1 FP: With MC, [Tfs, Ttop] rep.

Round 1 RP: With CC, Std RP.

Round 2 FP: With MC, [Ttop, Tfs] rep.

Round 2 RP: With CC, Std RP.

Repeat Rounds 1 and 2.

Reverse

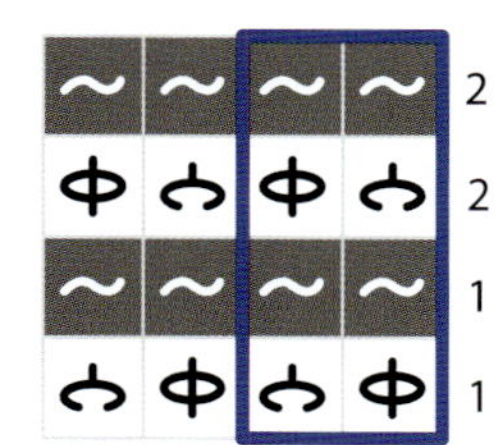

Stitch Key

486 TPS & TTOP HONEYCOMB

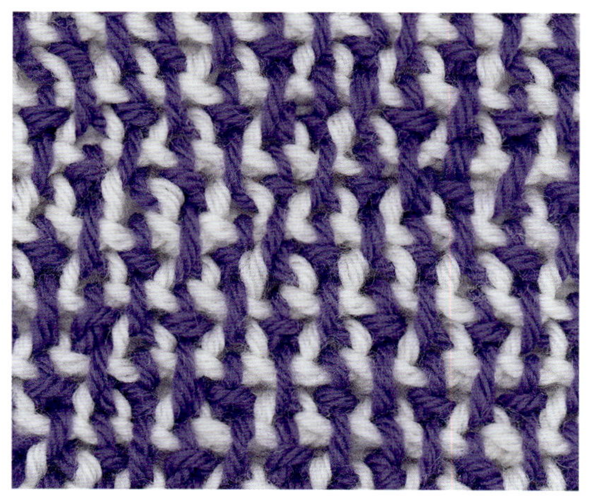

Worked over a multiple of 2 stitches and 2 rounds.

Round 1 FP: With MC, [Tps, Ttop] rep.

Round 1 RP: With CC, Std RP.

Round 2 FP: With MC, [Ttop, Tps] rep.

Round 2 RP: With CC, Std RP.

Repeat Rounds 1 and 2.

Reverse

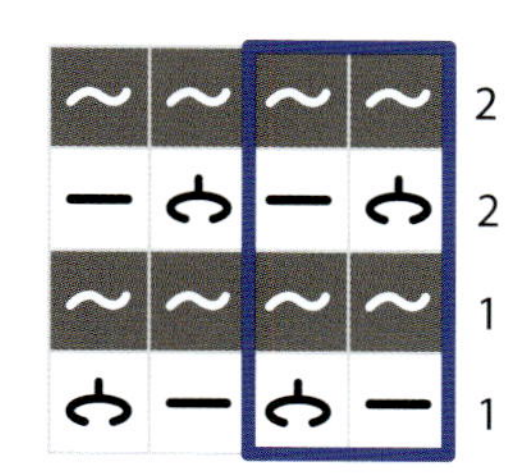

Stitch Key

487 TKS & TTOP HONEYCOMB

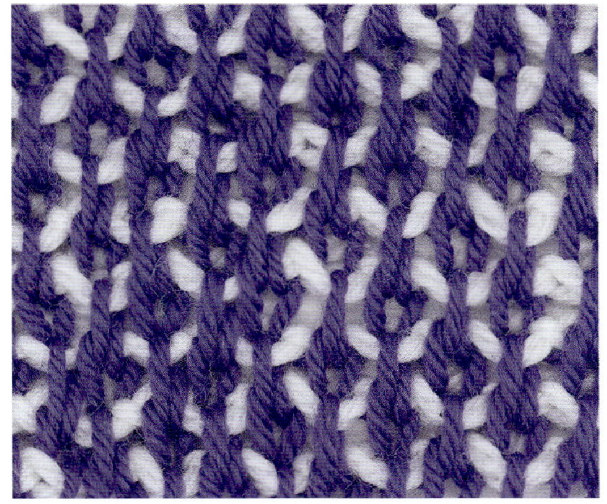

Worked over a multiple of 2 stitches and 2 rounds.

Round 1 FP: With MC, [Tks, Ttop] rep.

Round 1 RP: With CC, Std RP.

Round 2 FP: With MC, [Ttop, Tks] rep.

Round 2 RP: With CC, Std RP.

Repeat Rounds 1 and 2.

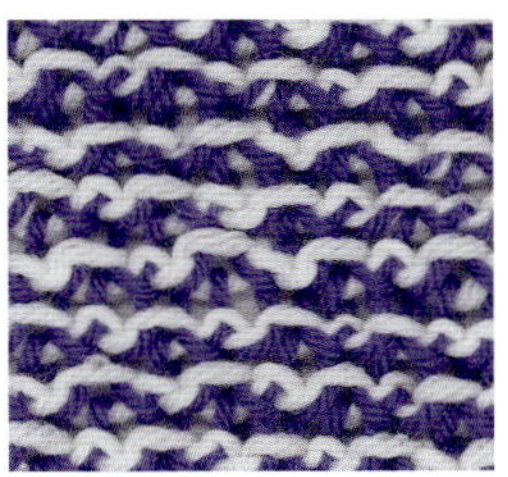

Reverse

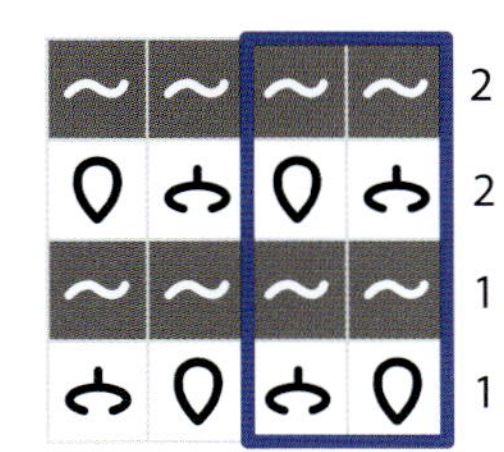

RP

Ttop

Tks

Stitch Key

488 TSS & TWUP VERTICAL STRIPE

Worked over a multiple of 2 stitches.

Round 1 FP: With MC, [Twup, Tss] rep.

Round 1 RP: With CC, Std RP.

Repeat Round 1.

Reverse

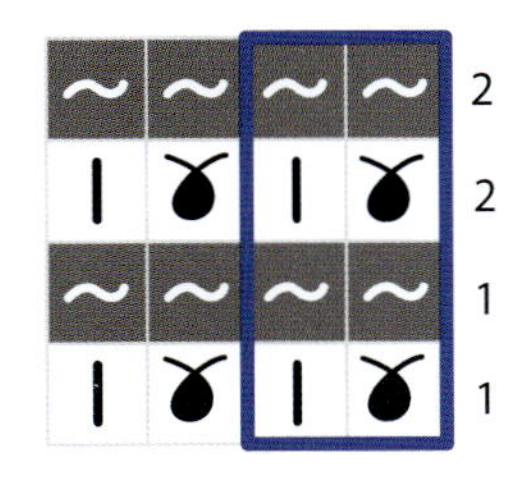

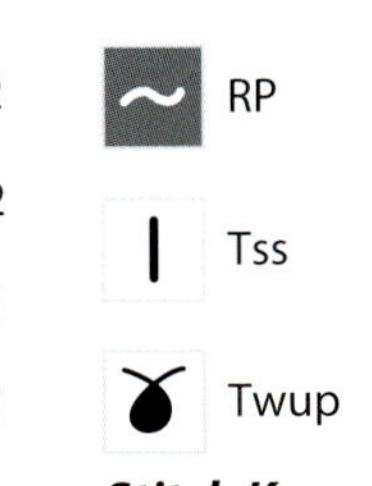

Stitch Key

489 TSS & TWUP HONEYCOMB

Worked over a multiple of 2 stitches and 2 rounds.
Round 1 FP: With MC, [Twup, Tss] rep.
Round 1 RP: With CC, Std RP.
Round 2 FP: With MC, [Tss, Twup] rep.
Round 2 RP: With CC, Std RP.
Repeat Rounds 1 and 2.

Reverse

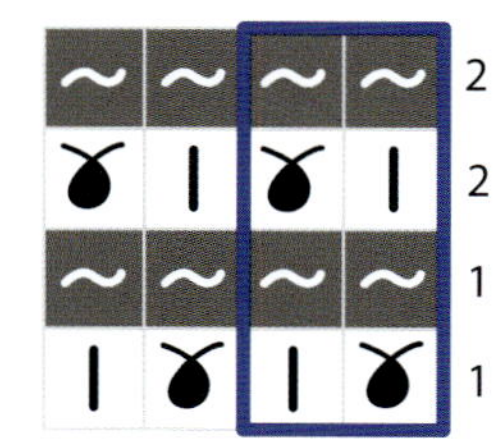

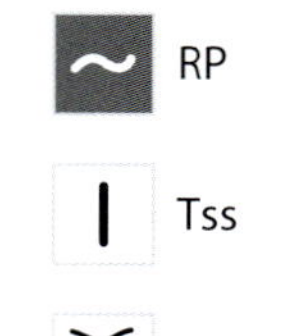

Stitch Key

490 TSS & TSLST HONEYCOMB

Worked over a multiple of 2 stitches and 2 rounds.
Round 1 FP: With MC, [Tss, Tslst] rep.
Round 1 RP: With CC, Std RP.
Round 2 FP: With MC, [Tslst, Tss] rep.
Round 2 RP: With CC, Std RP.
Repeat Rounds 1 and 2.

Reverse

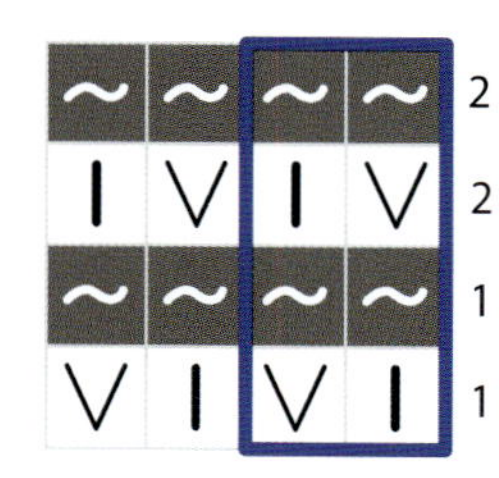

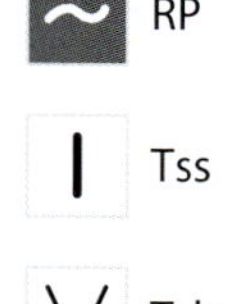

Stitch Key

491 TSS & PTSLST HONEYCOMB

Worked over a multiple of 2 stitches and 2 rounds.

Round 1 FP: With MC, [Tss, PTslst] rep.

Round 1 RP: With CC, Std RP.

Round 2 FP: With MC, [PTslst, Tss] rep.

Round 2 RP: With CC, Std RP.

Repeat Rounds 1 and 2.

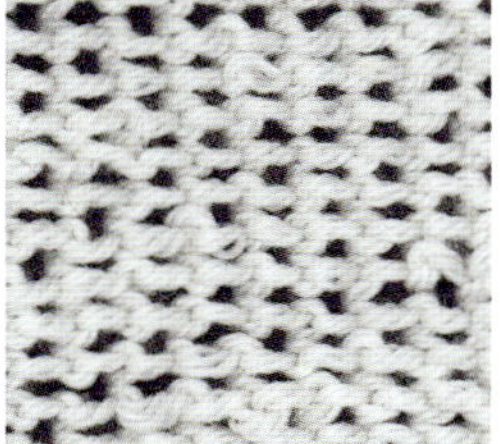

Reverse

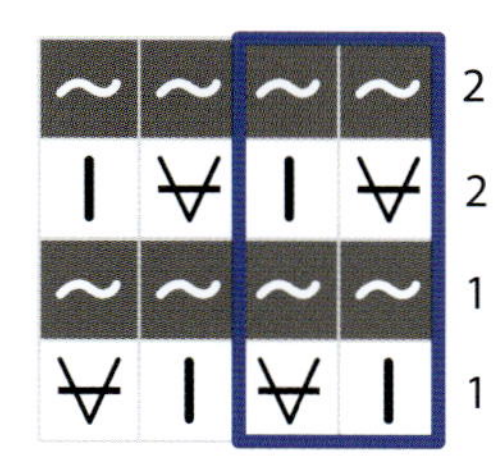

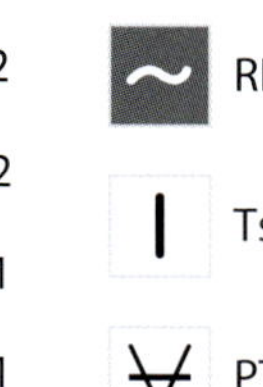

Stitch Key

492 CROSS STITCH

Worked over a multiple of 2 stitches.

Round 1 FP: With MC, Tx rep.

Round 1 RP: With CC, Std RP.

Repeat Round 1.

Reverse

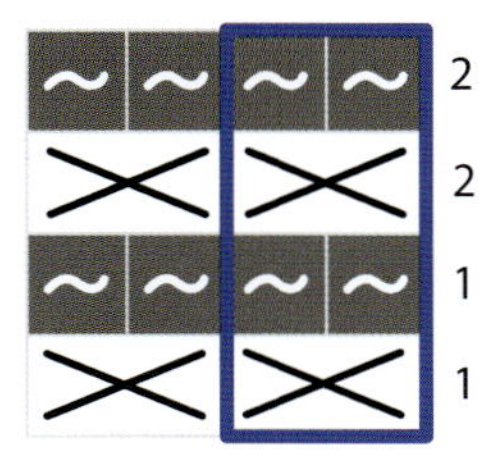

Stitch Key

493 CROSS STITCH STAGGERED

Worked over a multiple of 2 + 2 stitches and 2 rounds.

Round 1 FP: With MC, Tx rep.

Round 1 RP: With CC, Std RP.

Round 2 FP: With MC, Tss, Tx rep until 1 st rem, Tss.

Round 2 RP: With CC, Std RP.

Repeat Rounds 1 and 2.

Reverse

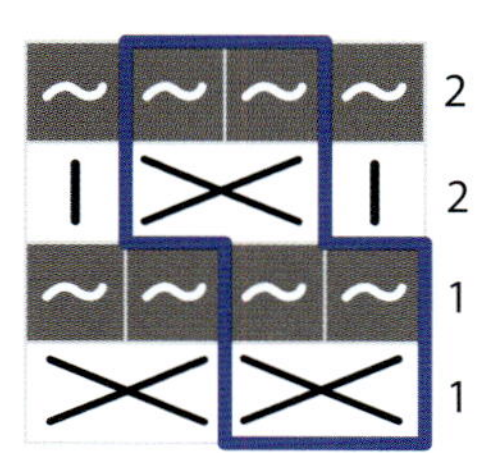

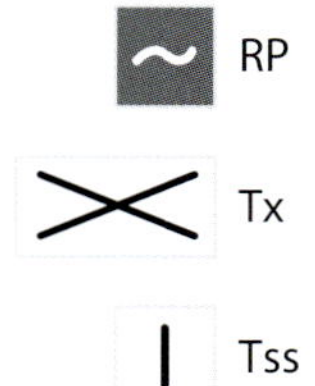

Stitch Key

494 LATTICE STITCH

Worked over a multiple of 2 stitches.

Uses L-St (Stitch 185, page 103).

Round 1 FP: With MC, L-St rep.

Round 1 RP: With CC, Std RP.

Repeat Round 1.

Reverse

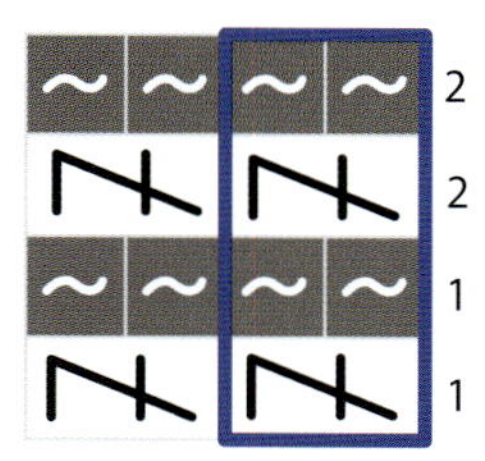

Stitch Key

495 LATTICE STITCH STAGGERED

Worked over a multiple of 2 + 2 stitches and 2 rounds.
Uses L-St (Stitch 185, page 103).
Round 1 FP: With MC, L-St rep.
Round 1 RP: With CC, Std RP.
Round 2 FP: With MC, Tss, L-St rep until 1 st rem, Tss.
Round 2 RP: With CC, Std RP.
Repeat Rounds 1 and 2.

Reverse

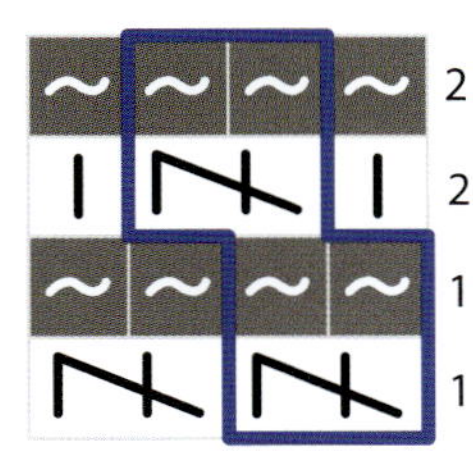

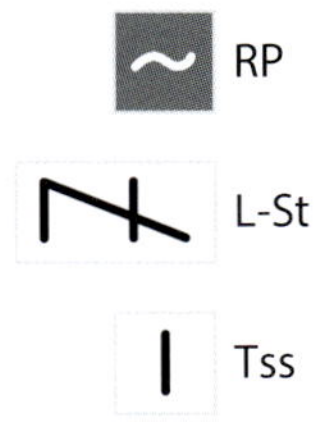

Stitch Key

496 BAMBOO 2-STITCH ALIGNED

Worked over a multiple of 2 stitches.
Uses B-St2 (Stitch 189, page 105).
Round 1 FP: With MC, B-St2 rep.
Round 1 RP: With CC, Std RP.
Repeat Round 1.

Reverse

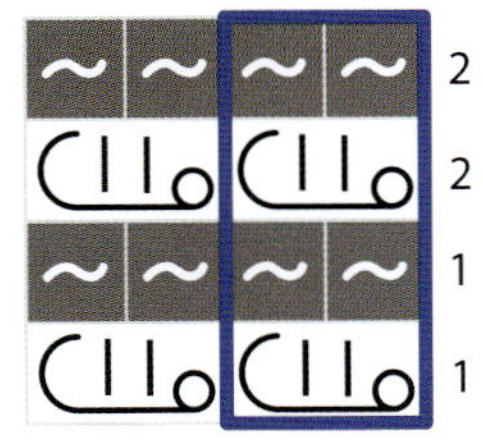

Stitch Key

497 BAMBOO 2-STITCH OFFSET

Worked over a multiple of 2 + 2 stitches and 2 rounds.
Uses B-St2 (Stitch 189, page 105).
Round 1 FP: With MC, B-St2 rep.
Round 1 RP: With CC, Std RP.
Round 2 FP: With MC, Tss, B-St2 rep until 1 st rem, Tss.
Round 2 RP: With CC, Std RP.
Repeat Rounds 1 and 2.

Reverse

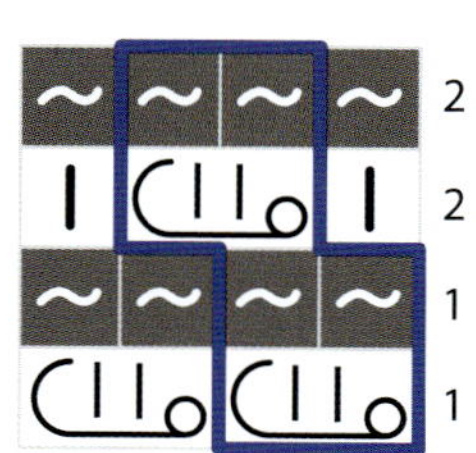

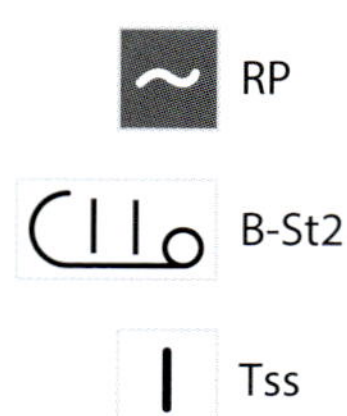

Stitch Key

498 BAMBOO 3-STITCH ALIGNED

Worked over a multiple of 3 stitches.
Uses B-St3 (Stitch 190, page 106).
Round 1 FP: With MC, B-St3 rep.
Round 1 RP: With CC, Std RP.
Repeat Round 1.

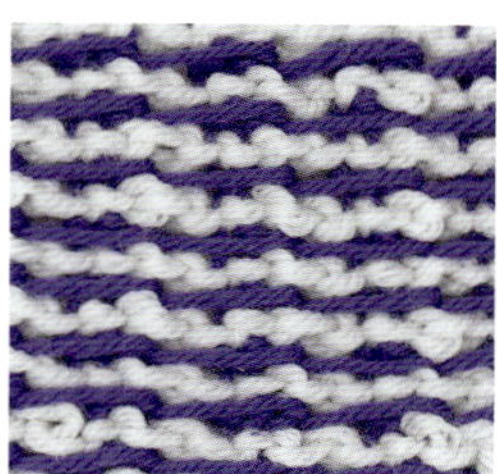

Reverse

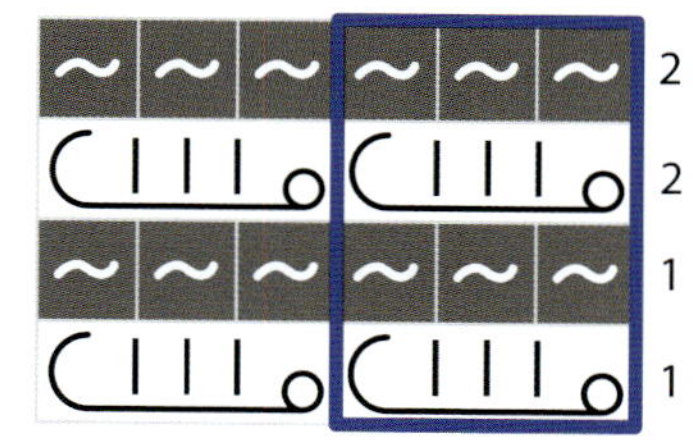

Stitch Key

499 BAMBOO 3-STITCH OFFSET

Worked over a multiple of 4 stitches and 2 rounds.
Uses B-St3 (Stitch 190, page 106).
Round 1 FP: With MC, [B-St3, Tss] rep.
Round 1 RP: With CC, Std RP.
Round 2 FP: With MC, Tss 2, [B-St3, Tss] rep until 2 st rem, Tss 2.
Round 2 RP: With CC, Std RP.
Repeat Rounds 1 and 2.

Reverse

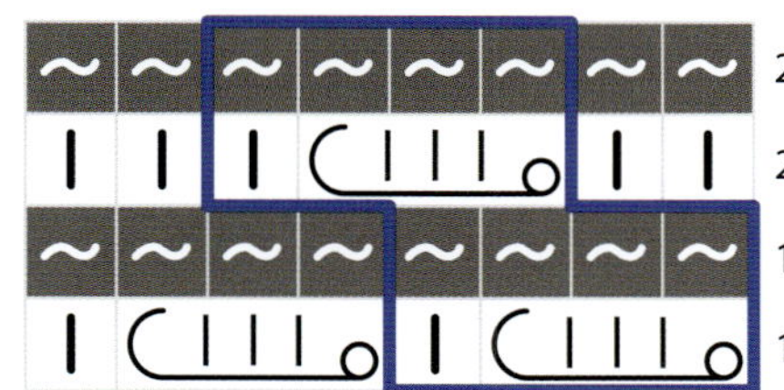

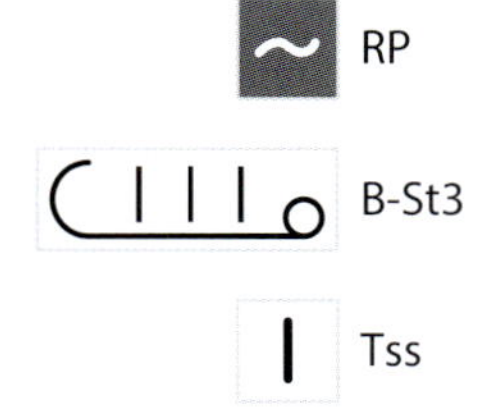

Stitch Key

500 FPTC IN THE ROUND

Worked over any number of stitches.
Round 1 FP: With MC, Fptc.
Round 1 RP: With CC, Std RP.
Repeat Round 1.

Reverse

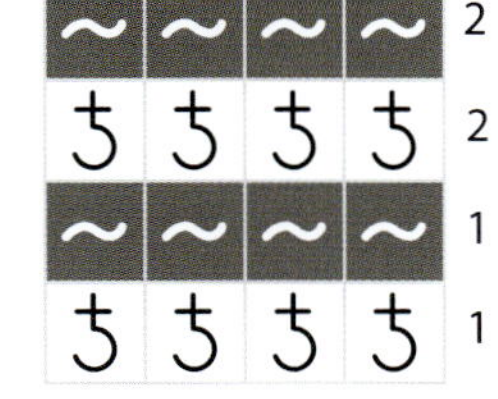

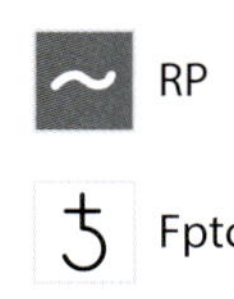

Stitch Key

501 BPTC IN THE ROUND

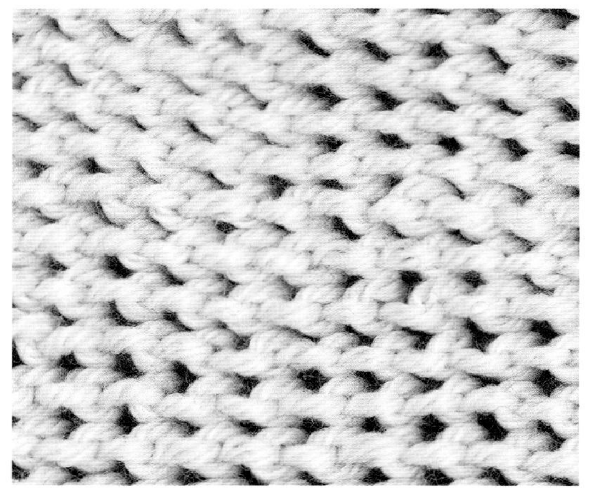

Worked over any number of stitches.

Round 1 FP: With MC, Bptc.

Round 1 RP: With CC, Std RP.

Repeat Round 1.

Reverse

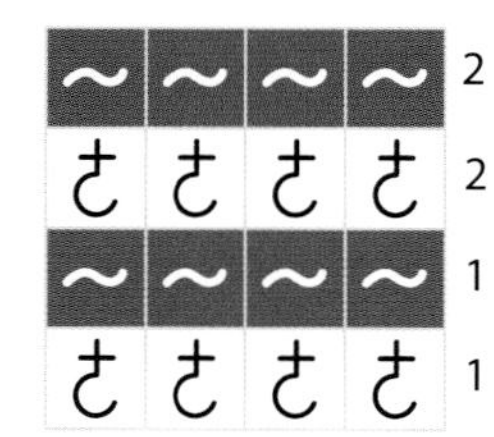

Stitch Key

STITCHES AND ABBREVIATIONS INDEX

Use this index to find the stitch number and tutorial for stitches used in this book.

Stitch Abbreviation	Name	Stitch Number
2/1Bk	2/1 Back Cable with Tks	332
2/1Bt	2/1 Back Cable with Tss	338
2/1Fk	2/1 Front Cable with Tks	331
2/1Ft	2/1 Front Cable with Tss	337
2/2Bk	2/2 Back Cable with Tks	334
2/2Bt	2/2 Back Cable with Tss	340
2/2Fk	2/2 Front Cable with Tks	333
2/2Ft	2/2 Front Cable with Tss	339
3/3Bk	3/3 Back Cable with Tks	336
3/3Bt	3/3 Back Cable with Tss	342
3/3Fk	3/3 Front Cable with Tks	335
3/3Ft	3/3 Front Cable with Tss	341
Bptc	Back Post Tunisian Stitch	66
BptcDc	Back Post Double Crochet	68
BptcTc	Back Post Treble Crochet	69
ch	Chain	
ExBptc	Extended Back Post Tunisian Stitch	67
ExFptc	Extended Front Post Tunisian Stitch	61
ExPFptc	Extended Purled Front Post Tunisian Stitch	65
ExTe	Extended Edge Stitch	4
ExTfs	Extended Tunisian Full Stitch	45
ExTks	Extended Tunisian Knit Stitch	15
ExTps	Extended Tunisian Purl Stitch	35
ExTrs	Extended Tunisian Reverse Stitch	26
ExTss	Extended Tunisian Simple Stitch	2
Fptc	Front Post Tunisian Stitch	60
FptcDc	Front Post Double Crochet	62
FptcTc	Front Post Treble Crochet	63
PBptc	Purled Back Post Tunisian Crochet	70
PFptc	Purled Front Post Tunisian Stitch	64

Stitch Abbreviation	Name	Stitch Number
PTbs	Purled Tunisian Bottom Bar Stitch	58
Ptfs	Purled Tunisian Full Stitch	50
PTks	Purled Tunisian Knit Stitch	20
PTmks	Purled Modified Tunisian Knit Stitch	23
Ptrs	Purled Tunisian Reverse Stitch	31
PTslst	Purled Tunisian Slip Stitch	72
Pttop	Purled Tunisian Top Stitch	52
PTts	Purled Tunisian Top Bar Stitch	55
PTwTks	Purled Twisted Tunisian Knit Stitch	24
RTbs	Reverse Tunisian Bottom Bar Stitch	59
RTfs	Reverse Tunisian Full Stitch	49
RTks	Reverse Tunisian Knit Stitch	19
Rttop	Reverse Tunisian Top Stitch	53
RTts	Reverse Tunisian Top Bar Stitch	56
slst	Slip Stitch	
Tbps	Back Bar Tunisian Purl Stitch	40
Tbpsu	Back Bar Tunisian Purl Stitch with Yarn Under	41
Tbs	Tunisian Bottom Bar Stitch	57
Tbss	Tunisian Back Bar Simple Stitch	8
Tdc	Tunisian Double Crochet	9
Te	Tunisian Edge Stitch	3
Tfdc	Tunisian Full Double Crochet	47
Tfrs	Tunisian Reverse Front Bar Stitch	30
Tfs	Tunisian Full Stitch	44
Tftc	Tunisian Full Treble Crochet	48
Tkdc	Tunisian Knit Double Crochet	21
Tks	Tunisian Knit Stitch	14
Tks2Tog	Tks 2 stitches together	74
Tktc	Tunisian Knit Treble Crochet	22
Tmfs	Modified Tunisian Full Stitch	46
Tmks	Modified Tunisian Knit Stitch	16
Tmps	Modified Tunisian Purl Stitch	36
Tmrs	Modified Tunisian Reverse Stitch	27
Tmss	Modified Tunisian Simple Stitch	5
Tpdc	Tunisian Purl Double Crochet	42
Tps	Tunisian Purl Stitch	34
Tps2Tog	Tps 2 stitches together	76

Stitch Abbreviation	Name	Stitch Number
Tpsu	Tunisian Purl Stitch with Yarn Under	37
Tptc	Tunisian Purl Treble Crochet	43
Trdc	Tunisian Reverse Double Crochet	32
Trs	Tunisian Reverse Stitch	25
Trs2Tog	Trs 2 Stitches Together	75
Trtc	Tunisian Reverse Treble Crochet	33
Tslst	Tunisian Slip Stitch	71
Tss	Tunisian Simple Stitch	1
Tss2Tog	Tss 2 stitches together	73
TssBkH	Tunisian Simple Stitch with Back Horizontal Bar	12
TssBtH	Tunisian Simple Stitch with Bottom Horizontal Bar	11
Ttc	Tunisian Treble Crochet	10
Ttop	Tunisian Top Stitch	51
Tts	Tunisian Top Bar Stitch	54
TwbTks	Twisted Back Bar Tunisian Knit Stitch	18
Twd	Twisted Down Tunisian Simple Stitch	7
TwdTrs	Twisted Down Tunisian Reverse Stitch	29
TwTbss	Twisted Tunisian Back Bar Simple Stitch	13
TwTks	Twisted Tunisian Knit Stitch	17
TwTps	Twisted Tunisian Purl Stitch	38
Twup	Twisted Up Tunisian Simple Stitch	6
TwupTps	Twisted Up Tunisian Purl Stitch	39
TwupTrs	Twisted Up Tunisian Reverse Stitch	28
Tx	Tunisian Cross Stitch	180
yo	yarn over	
yu	yarn under	

Other Abbreviations	Meaning	
CC	contrasting color yarn	
FP	forward pass	
MC	main color yarn	
rem	remain(s)	
rep	repeat	
RP	return pass	
st sp	stitch space	

REFERENCES

Grabowski, Angela. *Encyclopedia of Tunisian Crochet*. Abilene, TX: LoneStar Abilene Publishing, 2004.

Guzman, Kim. *Tunisian Crochet Stitch Guide.* Berne, IN: Annie's Attic, 2013.

Ohrenstein, Dora. *The New Tunisian Crochet*. Loveland, CO: Interweave, 2012.

Silverman, Sharon Hernes. *Tunisian Crochet*. Mechanicsburg, PA: Stackpole Books, 2009.

ACKNOWLEDGMENTS

I want to thank my husband, Stefan, for being so patient when I said I wanted to write a second book. You kept me sane and took up way more than your share of chores while I was working on this project.

Thank you to Sharon Carter of Dragon Hill Studio for always being a helpful idea sounding board as well as helping me word things clearly.

Thank you to Britt (KnotBadBritt) for being the most amazingly supportive crochet BFF. Designing comes with amazing highs as well as brutal lows. Thank you for being on this crazy rollercoaster with me.

Thank you to Tom and Linda Diak of DyakCraft for making my favorite Tunisian crochet hooks. Quality tools really can truly elevate the maker's experience. The metal and laminated wood hooks in this book were handmade by Tom.